101 Harley-Davidson Twin Cam
Performance Projects

Chris Maida with Mark Zimmerman
Photography by Jeff Hackett

First published in 2005 by Motorbooks International, an imprint of MBI Publishing Company, Galtier Plaza, Suite 200, 380 Jackson Street, St. Paul, MN 55101-3885 USA

Motorbooks International titles are also available at discounts in bulk quantity for industrial or sales-promotional use. For details write to Special Sales Manager at Motorbooks International Wholesalers & Distributors, Galtier Plaza, Suite 200, 380 Jackson Street, St. Paul, MN 55101-3885 USA.

ISBN 0-7603-1639-2

Edited by Peter Schletty
Designed by LeAnn Kuhlmann

Printed in China

CONTENTS

CONTENTS

PREFACE AND ACKNOWLEDGMENTS

Many thanks for taking the time to read this. Most people, including myself, skip this part. The exception is when I'm curious about what the authors are trying to accomplish, so I'll be sure to do that by the end of this paragraph. Another reason why I'll read this type of page is when there's a reoccurring element in the book that I want more info about. In *101 Projects For Twin Cams*, that would be the Information Boxes that you'll find in every project. What we are trying to accomplish is to simply provide you with what you need to modify your Harley-Davidson Twin Cam motorcycle the way you want without making costly and aggravating mistakes.

Each project comes complete with an Information Box, which gives you, in a concise form, what you need in the form of time, money, skill, parts, and tools to do that project. The time and money values are often given in ranges, since there are a number of things—like what manufacturer's parts you use—that can affect how much a job will cost in cash and hours.

As for the skill levels, a Level One rating means anyone who knows what end of a tool to use should be able to do that project. Level Two means you should be familiar with tools and machinery. A Three rating indicates that you should be comfortable doing Level One and Two projects, as well as working on complex assemblies. Level Four projects require very special tools and the training to use them properly. These projects are for mechanics that have been successfully spinning wrenches for a number of years and are ready for a more complex job.

The parts and tools listings tell you what you'll need to do that particular job. You'll notice that the tool and part lists for some engine projects are very specific, while others are more general. This is because the engine projects cover specific installations on a Twin Cam engine, and since the A (rubber-mount) and B (counterbalanced) engines are almost identical, I'm able to tell you exactly what you'll need. In contrast, chassis and some engine projects cover a wider range of options, so the parts and tools lists are more general. For example, a tool list may just say, "Basic hand tools." A look into the first section, Work and Tools, will list what this encompasses.

The aim of some projects are to educate the reader about systems and theory rather than give a step-by-step install. Some projects are engine related and have instructions as well as a series of installation photos, just like the tech stories I write for *American Iron Magazine* as its editor.

Each Information Box also has Tips, which are bits of information that will hopefully make the job go a little easier. There are also Performance Gain and Complimentary Modification listings. The first tells you what you'll gain by doing that particular project, whether it's horsepower or "bling" factor. The second gives you some advice, as in what project we suggest you can also do when bolting up the project at hand.

Finally, it's time to thanks the people that helped make this all happen. First on the list is my buddy Mark Fabrizi, the owner and head wrench of Marquee Customs & Classics. Most of the engine install sequences were shot at Mark's shop, with him doing the installation. Readers of *American Iron Magazine* should recognize his big hands, as they've seen them often in *AIM* tech stories. Our thanks also go to the crew at Harley-Davidson of Danbury, Connecticut, for their help, as well as Fred's Auto Machine Shop. We also extend a huge thanks to the many manufacturers who participated in the installations, which, of course, made them and this book possible.

Mark Zimmerman would specifically like to thank Al and Carl Lucchino, Bob Carey, Liam Gleason, Rod Pink, and last but certainly not least, his good friend and racing buddy, Dan Voldstad.

—Chris Maida

SECTION ONE

Work and Tools

PREP 1

The Work Area

Let's be perfectly honest. One of the neatest things about owning a Harley-Davidson (H-D) motorcycle is that they are so inviting to work on. By the same token, owning one is also justification for putting together some sort of storage/work area where you can while away the off-season hours by working on your Harley.

Work areas can be as plain or as fancy as you'd like them to be. Personally, I spend a lot of time in my shop, so I want it to be as comfortable as possible. My garage is more than just a place where I go to work on motorcycles. It's a therapeutic hobby shop, a secure storage facility, and a safe haven where I can shut out the cares of the world for a few hours, if need be. It is by design that my garage door locks from the inside.

As they say in real estate, location is everything. First consider the placement of the work area: For most of us, the choice will boil down to using an outbuilding (such as a garden shed), a portion of the family garage, or the basement.

Basements

By and large, I don't recommend working on fuel-run machines or storing any type of motor vehicle in a basement. Some basements are damp and cramped, and neither characteristic is conducive to a happy work environment. But more importantly, basements tend to house water heaters and furnaces with pilot lights, both of which tend to come on at unpredictable times, usually just after you've spilled half a gallon of gasoline on the floor. The equation here is simple: Gasoline *plus* Flame from oil burner *equals* Large Fire and no more house.

There is also the problem of fumes. Lots of motorcycle maintenance jobs require the use of aerosol solvents or lubricants, many of which are flammable or toxic and have no place in your home, particularly if you share it with children or animals. Filling the house with eau de Carb Clean is just bad form, and obviously, running an engine in an enclosed basement is unacceptable in any situation.

Finally, unless you have lower-level access, getting bikes into and out of most basements is always problematic. You can imagine how much fun wrestling that new Ultra Glide down your cellar steps would be.

If you have no real choice and you can make the basement a relatively safe place to work then by all means go for it, but be sure there is at least one good-sized ABC (all fires) fire extinguisher close at hand and you have plenty of ventilation. And, please, try to stay as far away as possible from the water heater and furnace.

Garden Sheds

Lately I've seen some very nice shops built out of garden sheds, although I've also seen some for which I'd use the term loosely. These stand-alone buildings can generally be purchased pretty reasonably and work quite nicely as one-man shops.

The big advantage here is that you build a dedicated shop that suits your needs without, in most cases, sharing it with the family grocery-getter. Of course you may not want to spend the money on a separate shed when you've got a perfectly good garage. If you opt for a shed-type building, make certain it's installed over a solid foundation, preferably one of poured concrete. Also give some thought to the shed's location: You'll need access to electricity. Some thought must also be given to the terrain access to the shed location.

One of the guys I ride with located his shed "way out back somewhere." Just getting the bike on the road means riding over a few hundred yards of wet grass, mud, or snow, depending on the season. Last time I saw him he was looking for a paving contractor.

Building a Shop

For one reason or another, most of us will end up working in the family garage, which is just fine and dandy. But before you lay the first wrench on your bike let's take a quick look around. What do you see? A black hole catchall for everything from the kids' toys to the wife's old dishes or an organized workspace?

Over the years I've seen home shops that were little more than a dirt floor surrounded by four walls and a roof and I've seen some that would put a NASA clean room to shame. I'd like to say that the work turned out was independent of the condition of the shop. (I'd *like* to say that, but I really can't.) In my experience, guys that take pride in their shops take pride in their work.

That being said, the first step is to give the joint a thorough cleaning. If climate conditions warrant it, the place should be insulated and installed with some form of heat. The type of heating is up to you, but I'd argue against a wood stove simply because of the fire hazard. Good lighting is a prime requisite; double-bulb fluorescent light fixtures

When you work on bikes for a living, shelf space is always at a premium. This is one way to handle it.

can be purchased very reasonably, and a few hung in the right places will make finding that widget you dropped a whole lot easier. Besides, you'll look silly holding a flashlight in your mouth while you re-jet the carburetor.

Along with good lighting, why not splash a little color on the walls? Better yet, hang a few sheets of pegboard. You can even purchase pre-painted pegboard in a semi-gloss white.

Once the place is clean and bright you can start to fill it up with all sorts of necessities. First and foremost is a good solid workbench. These can be bought fully assembled in a variety of shapes and sizes with everything from drawers and electrical outlets to backlighting and built-in stereos. Or, if you like playing with wood, a very serviceable workbench can be knocked together out of 2 x 4s and plywood in an afternoon. I'd also invest in some shelving; again this can be purchased or built out of lumber. Either way, make sure the workbench is sturdy enough to withstand some fairly strenuous use. The shelving should be capable of handling loads of at least two hundred pounds or better.

Most shops never seem to have enough electrical outlets; now is the time to add a few. Tripping over an extension cord while carrying a freshly painted part will no doubt ruin almost anyone's day.

Once the basic shop is laid out, feel free to embellish. A radio is always pleasant and a refrigerator is almost a requirement. A phone is also handy, especially one that can be switched off or unplugged. A shop stool will give you someplace to rest, and they come in very handy when you're doing some bench work. I also keep a few of those inexpensive camp chairs lying around. They're just the thing to have when friends come calling.

I'm also keen on decorating the walls with posters, calendars, or anything else that will brighten up the old cave. I'm especially fond of posters with poker-playing dogs.

While I'll discuss outfitting the shop in the Tools section, there are two items no shop can afford to be without. The first is a fully charged ABC fire extinguisher. The second is a comprehensive first aid kit. Both of these can prevent "uh-oh" incidents from turning into full-fledged disasters.

A last note on shops: Motorcycles are very intriguing devices, especially to small children, as are tools and most sharp, shiny objects. The consequences of mixing small, tender fingers with rotating chunks of steel are something everyone can live without. Anytime you leave the shop, particularly when sharp or moving parts of your motorcycle are exposed, you should lock the door.

PREP 2
Work Practices

As my Dad used to say, "There's the right way, the wrong way, and my way." When we're talking about work practices, we're really talking about how you work in general, rather than how you actually turn a bolt or remove a wrist pin. Your shop manual will provide you with specific procedures for dealing with most of the specific mechanical procedures and problems that you'll run into. What it won't impart are those hard-learned lessons that only come with a graduate course in the school of hard knocks. The following lessons are what I'd call my way of doing things. Follow them if you want. If you don't think the lessons provide valid observations, then by all means do it your way.

Cleanliness is indeed next to godliness. Dirty shops aren't much fun to work in, and neither are they very efficient places. A dirty shop makes it more likely that debris will find its way into an open engine. A dirty shop makes it hard to find what you need. And a dirty shop, particularly one with a dirty and slippery floor with parts strewn across a workbench, makes it that much easier to slip and get hurt or damage some expensive part. A shop should be straightened up a bit after every task, or at least at the end of the day. If the job is exceptionally long, take a few minutes every so often to clean up and organize your tools.

Along those same lines, some thought should be given to the storage of drained oil, used brake fluid, and the like. Most auto supply shops carry sealed drain pans. These can be had for less than twenty bucks and hold about 5 gallons of waste oil. You can change your bike's oil several times over and still have room left for a brake fluid flush. These containers are basically spill-proof when the caps are on, allowing convenient transport to your local recycling center.

Safety in the shop shouldn't need discussing, but it's an issue that few ever think about. Obviously open flames and gasoline don't mix. That means that any and every open flame needs to be extinguished if there is even the slightest chance of spilling gasoline or anything else flammable. And, yes, that does mean you should put out your

Nice, neat and professional. Using the pegboard to store the easily damaged sheet metal is a nice touch. It keeps the expensive pieces out of harm's way.

A photo is worth a thousand words. This is a shop that I'd trust to work on my bike.

cigarettes and shut off your space heater or wood stove anytime there is even the remotest chance of anything flammable being sparked.

Trash tends to accumulate fairly quickly in any shop, from old pizza boxes to oily rags to empty aerosol cans. A steel trash can with a lid will hold it all and if anything combustible gets mixed up with a spark or cigar butt, it'll just smolder until it runs out of oxygen rather than burst into flame.

A Dozen Practical Tips That You Ought to Know
Tip Number 1
Never assemble something partway, intending to "get back to it in a little while." Either complete the task at hand, or leave it in such a way as to make it perfectly obvious that the job isn't done.

Here's what usually happens: You're replacing some component or other. For the sake of example we'll use adjustable pushrods. All the pushrods are in place, but you've only adjusted three when your buddy sticks his head in the door and invites you out for a plate of wings and a few cold ones. Frankly, cold ones (at least the ones I'm familiar with) have no place in the shop until all the work is done, but you're all big boys and girls so I'll expect you to act with some restraint. Four hours later, or maybe the next day, you get back to the bike. Only you forget that

one pushrod still needs adjusting. Of course after you start the bike you'll be reminded big time.

So here's the solution: You can leave yourself a note, you can finish the job before you go out, or you can leave the part sitting on the bench. When I was a dealership mechanic, I used to see things like this happen all the time. Guys would come back from lunch and forget that they hadn't torqued that last bolt or bent over the lock tab on the clutch nut and then assemble the whole plot before remembering, which meant doing it over—for free. Or they would just let it go, which usually meant that they weren't long on the job.

Tip Number 2
Don't be afraid to ask a friend for help. Lots of us are embarrassed to admit that we can't do everything by ourselves. Trust me, it's a lot less embarrassing to ask a buddy for help when you're wrestling the front end off your Electra Glide than it is to have the tank refinished because the bike tipped over.

Tip Number 3
Always make sure the bike really is secure before you and your buddy wrestle the front end off of it. There is nothing worse than seeing your new Deuce do a Titanic onto the garage floor.

Tip Number 4

Take a moment to cover up painted parts with rags, towels, or what have you, before you start to unbolt the adjacent parts. One slip of the wrench, one dropped bolt, and "ding"—no more pristine paint.

Tip Number 5

Always make sure that the replacement part is the correct one for your bike before you strip off the old one. True, sometimes there are screw-ups. But there is nothing worse than pulling your clutch apart on a Saturday night before a big ride and then finding out the replacement clutch plates are the wrong ones and the shop closed ten minutes ago.

Tip Number 6

By the above logic, always make sure you have all the parts you need, and enough time to go get the ones you forgot and get the bike back together in time for the big ride.

Tip Number 7

Motorcycles are made up of lots of small parts, the kinds that get lost really easily. It's a lot easier to keep track of those small parts if you use some method of organizing them. Try storing them in plastic sandwich bags, cupcake baking tins, or re-sealable plastic containers.

Tip Number 8

Case bolts, being of several different lengths, are easy to mix up. Rather than tossing them in a pile, try drawing an outline of the case on a chunk of cardboard. As you remove the bolts from the case, push them through an appropriate hole in your cardboard. When it's time to assemble the case you'll know where each bolt belongs.

Tip Number 9

Opinions differ on this subject, but unless the service manual tells you differently I recommend using a light lubricant on every threaded fitting on the motorcycle, including the axles and the spark plugs. Use anti-seize compound on the spark plugs. Other threaded fasteners should be given a light coat of either anti-seize or white lithium grease. Axles should get a very light coat of white lithium or bearing grease.

Tip Number 10

Gasket sealers should be applied very, very lightly. All it normally takes to seal a joint is a wet sheen. Whatever squeezes out of the joint on the outside has squeezed into the interior of the engine. Big balls of silicone sealer floating around in the oil passages won't do anyone any good.

Tip Number 11

Thread-locking compounds subscribe to the above theory. When Loctite says a drop, they mean one drop.

Tip Number 12

Always bear in mind that working on your bike should be fun. When the fun turns to frustration, put down the tools and take a break.

PREP 3
Tools

Every Harley-Davidson owner worth his salt should own and understand the use of basic mechanic's hand tools. But that doesn't mean you need to spend thousands of dollars on shiny new hardware. I'll be the first to admit that I'm a "tool junkie." I buy and use lots of tools and I'm always on the lookout for something new and innovative; in most cases the manufacturers never fail to disappoint me. You, on the other hand, may not be so inclined. If that's the case, feel free to buy just what you need to work on your bike. For instance, if you're only able to do the most basic maintenance, than all you really need are a few common hand tools. Besides, you can always buy individual tools on an "as needed" basis.

Part of the fun of owning an H-D is the ability to adapt it to the owners' needs. These needs may be nothing more than a quick handlebar adjustment or the installation of some easily installed accessory, or they may involve extensive engine or suspension modifications. Your motorcycle also will require periodic, routine maintenance. While your local dealer will be only too happy to perform the maintenance (and charge you accordingly), most or all of it can be performed by the owner who simply has the interest, this book, a few common hand tools, and a spare hour or two.

As everyone knows, breakdowns usually rear their ugly heads at inconvenient times. A modestly equipped home workshop can change that broken clutch cable or flat tire from a ride-stopping disaster into something like a minor inconvenience. In all cases though, you'll need a few basic hand tools to get the job done.

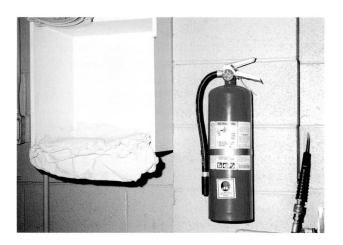

Safety first. If you're going to work on your bike at home, make certain there's a fire extinguisher close by. Make sure it's ABC rated (all fires) and make sure it's kept charged.

You May Already Be a Tool Junkie.

By nature, quite a few riders are mechanically inclined or, at the very least, have an interest in mechanics. Most of us that are bent that way tend to accumulate tools, and chances are good that the majority of riders already have at least a smattering of the tools needed to perform casual maintenance tasks.

Quality Doesn't Cost—It Saves.

Quality tools can be moderately priced or very expensive; inexpensive tools probably are of poor quality. Stay away from cheaply priced, bargain-basement tools. They don't fit fasteners very well, and tend to round off fastener edges, making them difficult to remove. Cheap tools (in the vernacular, "no-name tools") usually feel awkward in your hand and they seem to break at inopportune times, generally allowing your knuckles to crash into something solid or sharp, most often both. It's much easier to stay away from no-name tools than it will be to repair the damage to your bike or body caused when one slips or breaks.

A good tool, in and of itself, is a beautiful thing and the pride of ownership that accompanies buying a good tool is akin to that of owning a motorcycle. Good tools are a pleasure to work with. They fit the fastener well, preventing damage, and they are aesthetically pleasing, which I find is conducive to good work. Bear in mind that a quality tool is a lifetime investment; I've had my socket set since my dad bought it for me when I was thirteen. Thirty-five years later I'm still using it. In fact, I'm still using tools that I inherited from my wife's grandfather, many of which were purchased in the 1920s and '30s.

Expense Versus Practicality

Professional mechanics buy a lot of their tools from franchised tool vendors that come right to the shop with a garish truck chock full of chrome-plated iron. Ninety-nine percent of these tools are purchased on the installment plan, which, if nothing else, ensures that the tool man will be returning to the shop on a weekly basis. Mechanics pay a premium price for these tools because the tools are top-of-the-line quality, the vendor is extending credit, and the vendor is conveniently showing up at the work place.

If money is no object, then seek out the local Snap-on, MAC, or Matco tool truck and spend away. If you plan on buying everything you need at one fell swoop—something I don't recommend—you can probably get them to drive to your house for a private viewing, sort of like your own little chrome-plated fashion show.

When I was a mere stripling, just starting out in the business, I was on a first-name basis with the local Snap-on dealer. I think I pretty much put his kid through medical school. Now I'm a little (not much, just a little) wiser. Although I'm still on a first-name basis with the local Snap-on guy, I now buy most of my common tools through Sears (Craftsman tools), the local home improvement

chains (Home Depot carries the Husky line), or the neighborhood hardware store.

Other reasonably priced tools, SK Tools, Blackhawk, and Proto to name three, are available through hardware outlets, industrial supply houses, and auto parts jobbers. All are excellent tools and carry lifetime full-replacement guarantees.

My recommendation is this: If tool status is your thing, buy Snap-on (or any other of the truck-vendor brand), which, quite honestly, are presumably the best tools in the world from a standpoint of comfort, durability, and appearance. But, and I say this with 35 years of twisting wrenches behind me, a Craftsman tool (or any other high-quality tool) is just as functional, just as durable, just as comfortable in your hand and costs maybe 50 to 75 percent less.

Having said all of that, let me qualify something. In my experience, there are times when only a Snap-on socket or screwdriver will remove a frozen fastener without ruining your day. Snap-on uses, and has patented, something they call "flank drive." Without going into detail, I will only say that it does work. While it is certainly possible to remove any kind of rusty hardware with a variety of tools, a flank-drive tool will do it without screwing up the fastener and in a manner that lets you reuse it.

Quality

Any name-brand tool is a good one. If the manufacturer offers a lifetime guarantee you can be confident that the tool is decent. Every so often you may run into a brand you're not familiar with. Look for the words "Forged" or "Drop Forged" stamped on the tool; they may or may not be there. If they aren't, it doesn't necessarily mean it's a bad tool. But if they are there, it is an indication that the tool is of good quality.

This fellow takes a lot of pride in his work and it shows. To a gearhead this is tool box nirvana.

WORK AND TOOLS

Amassing Tools

There are as many ways to build a tool collection as there are tools. Don't think for a moment that you'll need to go out and spend a ton of money. You'd be amazed at how few tools you'll really need, especially if you're only planning to perform routine maintenance and the occasional small repair. You'll also be absolutely astounded at how quickly your tool collection will grow if you give it half a chance. Here are my recommendations (all learned through hard experience) to the first-time tool buyer.

• Don't be tempted to buy one of those giant all-inclusive sets of tools. They include a lot of stuff you don't need and are often missing a few crucial items. If you are tempted to buy one, look for a set designed for trade school students or apprentice mechanics.

• At the risk of repeating myself, good tools are something you buy once. With any kind of care, a good tool will last a lifetime.

• Buy the right tool for the right job; if you plan on using a hammer to break loose that stubborn case (a perfectly acceptable procedure, by the way), make sure you purchase a plastic mallet, not a 3-pound drilling hammer.

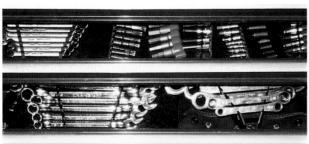

A fool for a tool? Perhaps. But I like to think of it as being well prepared.

What Will I Need?

Everyday motorcycle maintenance and repair generally revolves around inspecting, removing, and reinstalling various parts of the motorcycle. Those parts are held on to the motorcycle with a variety of common nuts, bolts, and screws. In other words, threaded fasteners. Common sense tells you that they need to be turned. Your initial tool purchase should revolve around turning tools, wrenches, sockets, and screwdrivers.

In addition to a set of common hand tools, the avid Harley owner/mechanic will require a few special tools. How many depends on how involved you plan to become with the mechanical end of motorcycling.

Tool Storage

Once you've started to put together a decent tool kit you'll need someplace to store it. Tool storage is obviously a matter of choice but, obviously, the better organized the tools are, the easier they'll be to find. Some guys like to hang everything on a pegboard. Pegboards are a great way to keep tools neatly arranged, and nothing looks better than a neat, well-ordered workshop with a board full of tools. The practical advantage is that everything is within reach and it's easy to see if any tool has gone missing. The not-so-practical side of hanging everything on the wall is that it forces you to work in one place. The other problem is that your tools are exposed for the world, and inconsiderate borrowers to see and use, with the distinct possibility that said borrower will forget to return them.

The practical solution is a dedicated toolbox. Good solid toolboxes range from small carry boxes available for around ten bucks, right up to giant rolling cabinets, which can cost many thousands of dollars, and which include amenities like clothes closets and stereos. I'd recommend that you start with a good solid-steel toolbox with a locking top. If you opt for a rolling model, be prepared to spend a minimum few hundred dollars, although some very nice homeowner models can be purchased for less than $200.

The following tools should cover just about any maintenance or emergency repair situation you're likely to come across. Since we're only dealing with H-D motorcycles here, the preponderance of tools are going to be fractional. However, there are some instances when metric tools will be required; these may be purchased as needed. Likewise, there will be situations when special tools are necessary.

Basic Hand Tools

Socket set, 1/2-inch drive (7/16 to 1 1/4 inch)
Socket set, 3/8-inch drive (1/4 to 3/4 inch)
Socket set, 1/4-inch drive (3/16 to 9/16 inch)
Allen wrench set (fractional)
12-inch adjustable wrench
Screwdriver set (#1, #2, #3 Phillips and common slotted
blades from 1/8 to 3/8).

14

Spark plug socket (11/16)
Common pliers
Needle-nose pliers
Diagonal cutting pliers
Locking pliers (Vise Grip, medium size #7)
16-ounce hammer
Plastic-faced hammer (16 ounce)
Impact driver
Feeler gauges
Spark plug gauge
Tire gauge
Battery hydrometer
Wire crimping tool
Test light
Hacksaw and blades
Gasket scraper
16-inch pry bar or small crowbar
Small flashlight

Note that there are a lot of tools not listed; for instance, files, extendable magnets, flare-nut wrenches, tap and die sets, volt-ohm meters, and other semi-specialized tools. I figure if you need a file or whatever for a particular job, you'll be smart enough to go get what you need.

Motorcycle-Specific and Special Tools

Special tools fall into two broad categories. First are those geared toward general, albeit motorcycle-specific, tasks. For example, tire irons, chain breakers, and fork-oil-level indicators fall into this category. Second are the tools designed specifically for working on a particular motorcycle or engine. These tools are things like crankshaft rotor pullers, flywheel alignment jigs, and clutch hub pullers. Normally, by the time you've reached this stage of the game you're moving into the more sophisticated areas of repair. These tools should always be purchased as needed. Chances are that most of us won't need flywheel alignment jigs too often.

Dedicated or special tools are generally available through your local motorcycle shop, or from specialist aftermarket companies. As a side note, some of the more esoteric tools may only be available from the factory. You'll usually pay through the nose for them but, in theory, you won't be buying a whole lot of them and you won't be buying them very often.

Motorcycle-Specific Tools—General Use:

Plastic rim protectors
Two tire irons
Fork level tool
Spoke wrench
Adjustable hook spanner (a perfect tool for adjusting steering head bearings and shock absorber preload).

Kind of a small list, isn't it? Don't worry, it'll grow. Just wait until you start rebuilding your friends' engines.

Dedicated Harley-Davidson Tools:

Without knowing exactly how involved you plan to become, it's impossible to say what you'll need. Frankly, I wouldn't go out and stock up on anything expensive unless I knew for sure I was going to need it. My advice is when you order parts for a particular job, also buy any special tools you'll need. Trust me; make sure you have the tools in hand *before* you start the job. Trying to replace something like the cam bearings without using the correct tool is an exercise in futility. Special tools are available from Kent-Moore and Jim's to name just two sources, and can also be purchased through your local H-D dealership.

Shop Equipment

You didn't think I was done yet, did you? While you can certainly accomplish most maintenance and repair chores with the basic tools I've listed above, your life will be much easier if you invest in some miscellaneous shop tools. There's no need to go off the deep end here. Chances are slim that you'll need a lathe for instance. But some, like a bike lift, really are in the must-have category:

A nice sturdy vise, preferably one with 4-inch or larger jaws.
A bike lift. This can be an air or electrically powered professional-style lift or a hydraulically operated bike jack. Since most of you probably don't have the need for a full-size lift, I'd recommend starting with a bike jack; these are generally available for somewhere right around $100, and can be purchased at any Sears store, auto supply shops, and via mail order.
A compressor is always handy; generally compressors suitable for home use are rated at between two and five horsepower.
A small solvent tank or parts washer is incredibly useful. These can be found at auto parts stores for $100 or less.
Pressure washers will hose away more gunk in five minutes than you can wash off with a bucket and hose in an hour. Find one at Home Depot or another "big-box" hardware store.
Along with your compressor you might want to pick up an assortment of air tools. In fact, some stores include an assortment of tools as an incentive to buy the compressor. If you only purchase one air tool, make it a 1/2-inch impact gun.
If you have the skill to use it, or are willing to learn, a small gas welding outfit is hard to beat. With one of these you can cut, braze, and weld, as well as heat up stubborn parts.
A soldering iron is a must-have. I'd recommend a nice 300-watt Weller.
Of course, a propane torch has lots of uses in every shop. I use mine to light my favorite cheap cigar.

Expendable Items

By expendables I mean shop supplies that are going to be used up: aerosol sprays, rags, welding gases, oil, grease, rags, and, every once in a while, your patience. I'll leave you with a list of what I normally stock and suggest that it's the minimum you'll need to keep from running out to the store every hour or so.

Single-edge razor blades. Handy for slicing and dicing.

You can't have too many shop rags; use 'em and lose 'em.

Paper towels. Plain or fancy, heavy-duty or cheap generic, you'll use them by the yard.

Waterless hand cleaner. Unless you like to hear your significant other yelling about grease on the doorknobs.

Sandpaper in various grades. I always seem to run out of what I need at the most inopportune times.

Scotch Brite. See sandpaper, above.

Various grades of grease and oil. You'll accumulate these a lot faster than you can imagine. We'll discuss these in the appropriate chapters.

Loctite. Even Twin Cams vibrate.

Mechanic's and safety wire for tying and binding.

Various penetrating, lubricating, and assembly oils such as WD-40, CRC, Belray 6 in 1, STP, etc., and so on, not to mention anti-seize compounds.

Polishes and waxes. See grease and oils, above.

Brake, carb, and electrical aerosol solvent.

Skin cream. Believe me, working on machinery will give you chapped hands that hurt like nobody's business. A little hand cream will keep cracks and bleeding to a minimum.

There you have it, a baker's dozen of the most common expendable items. Of course, you'll add plenty of others as you go. Both patience and cash are coming to mind almost immediately!

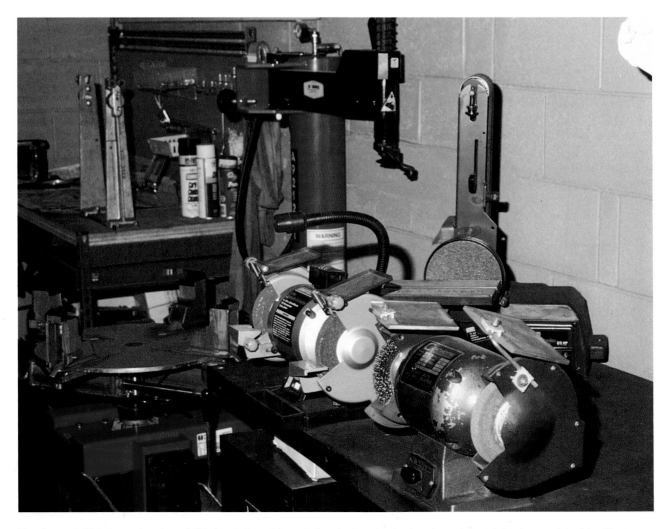

There's no substitute for good equipment. Grinders, belt sanders, and wire wheels make shaping, sharpening, and cleaning go a lot quicker. The pneumatic tire changer is a must-have for the professional.

Simple Maintenance

VINs and Engine Case Numbers

SIMPLE MAINTENANCE

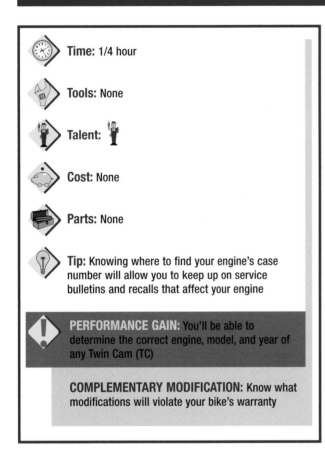

Time: 1/4 hour

Tools: None

Talent: 👨

Cost: None

Parts: None

Tip: Knowing where to find your engine's case number will allow you to keep up on service bulletins and recalls that affect your engine

PERFORMANCE GAIN: You'll be able to determine the correct engine, model, and year of any Twin Cam (TC)

COMPLEMENTARY MODIFICATION: Know what modifications will violate your bike's warranty

Back in the day, during the pre-AMF era (before 1970) of Harley-Davidson, life was a lot simpler and so were the designations that the Motor Company used to identify its engines and bikes. Back then, there were no frame Vehicle Identification Numbers (VINs). These bikes are identified by a simple (relatively speaking) engine number, comprised of about eight or nine numbers and letters. For example, a 1962 Duo-Glide—a Panhead-powered bagger—would have an engine number such as 62FLH2984. The first two numbers are the year of the bike, while the letters identify the type of engine and bike. FL marks the model as a Duo-Glide, and the H means the bike is equipped with a higher compression engine. The last four numbers are sequential production numbers.

But that's not the case with any of the Twin Cam models. Modern Harleys have a 17-digit VIN—you need to know the code to understand it. This was done to bring H-D's VINs in line with the manufacturer VINs of every type of motorcycle, automobile, truck, and off-road equipment around the world. This also was to make it harder for thieves to renumber (tattoo) stolen bikes.

This 17-digit VIN is stamped on the right side of the frame's steering head and repeated on the Federal Certification Label, which is the metallic label on the frame's right downtube, just in front of the front exhaust pipe. Understanding the 17-digit VIN requires the accompanying code key and three charts, which give the letters designating the different models, engines, and model years.

Using the code key and charts, let's see how this system works when applied to a 2004 Road Glide. Our sample bike would have the following frame VIN code: 1HD1FSW134Y600080. Using the code key, the frame's 17-digit VIN would break down like this:

1 = USA country code
HD = Harley-Davidson
1 = 901-cc or larger motorcycle
FSW = FLTRI with rubber-mounted, EFI (electronic fuel injection) Twin Cam 88 engine
1 = Regular introduction date
3 = Harley-Davidson manufacturer's code
4 = 2004 model year
Y = York assembly plant
600080 = Production number

A shortened version of the frame VIN number is on the upper left engine case, just under where the two cylinders meet. This is where the old-style engine VIN used to be back in the pre-AMF days. The engine number has 10 digits, as well as stars stamped before and after the VIN to mark the beginning and end of the number. The stars are there to also make it harder for thieves to change the number illegally. This engine number contains the model and year identifiers, which use the same letter designators as the frame VIN, and the production numbers. And though the

The bike's 17-digit VIN is stamped on the right side of the frame's steering head. On a Road King, it may be under the wiring harness.

engine VIN does not have all that the frame does, the numbers used should be exactly the same on both the frame and engine.

Using our 2004 Road Glide as an example, here's how to read its FSW4600080 engine number:

FSW = FLTRI with rubber-mounted, EFI Twin Cam 88 engine

4 = 2004 model year

600080 = Production number

The Year Letter Code chart tells what letter or number designator is used for each model year in the VIN code key. The fourth digit in the engine VIN and the tenth in the frame VIN will have one of these letters or numbers. The letters I, O, Q, U, and Z are not used in the letter code. And, as you can see, the code switches over to numbers in 2001, and then back to letters in 2010.

The Model Letter Code chart shows the model letter codes for most Twin Cam models, which are found in the first, second, and third digit positions in the engine VIN, and the fifth, sixth, and seventh positions in the frame VIN. The first two letters in the code are the model identifier while the third letter distinguishes the engine type and displacement. Using our Road Glide as an example, FS is the model identifier, while W indicates the engine's type and displacement as a rubber-mounted, EFI Twin Cam 88. A rubber-mounted, carb-equipped, Twin Cam 88 has a V as the third letter. The Engine Letter Code chart shows what the other engine letter identifiers are.

There's another important number on your engine that you should know about and it's called the case number, though some mechanics call it the engine's production number. The case number contains the date the engine was manufactured and the order in which the engine came off the assembly line. It can be found on a Twin Cam's right crankcase, just forward of the cam cover and below the oil

filter mount. And though you don't need to know how to decipher it, it's important to know where to find it, so you can give it to your local H-D dealership to find out if there are any recalls or service bulletins that affect your engine.

Now that you have all this coding information at your fingertips, you'll be able to look at any Twin Cam's VIN and tell what model and year it is, as well as what engine it has. You'll also never be able look at a bowl of alphabet soup the same way again.

The case number, which contains the date the engine was manufactured and the order in which the engine came off the assembly line, can be found on the right crankcase, just forward of the cam cover and below the oil filter mount.

Engine Letter Code

B	Counter-balanced 88-inch EFI
C	Rubber-mounted 95-inch EFI
D	Counter-balanced 95-inch EFI
E	Rubber-mounted 103-inch EFI
V	Rubber-mounted 88-inch Carb
W	Rubber-mounted 88-inch EFI
Y	Counter-balanced 88-inch Carb

The engine number has 10 digits and contains the model and year identifiers, which use the same letter designators as the frame VIN, and the production numbers. Stars mark the beginning and end of the number.

Year Code Chart

Model Year	Letter/Number Code
1999	X
2000	Y
2001	1
2002	2
2003	3
2004	4
2005	5
2006	6
2007	7
2008	8
2009	9
2010	A
2011	B

The 17-digit VIN is repeated on the Federal Certification Label, which is the metallic label on the frame's right downtube, just ahead of the front exhaust pipe.

The VIN Code Key

Position	Position in VIN Classification
1	Country code (1 for USA)
2, 3	Manufacturer (HD for Harley-Davidson)
4	Type of motorcycle (1 for heavy weight, which is 901-cc and larger)
5,6,7	Model letter code (model, engine type, and displacement)
8	Introduction type (1 for regular introduction date, 2 for mid-year introduction date, 3 for California model, and 4 for Anniversary models)
9	VIN Check Digit (any number from 0 to 9, or the letter X)
10	Model year (a letter or number)
11	Assembly plant (Y for York, K for Kansas City)
12-17	Sequential production number

Model Letter Codes

Dyna Models	Letter Code	
FXD	GH	
FXDI	GM (2004)	
FXDX	GJ	
FXDXI	GR (2004)	
FXDL	GD	
FXDLI	GN (2004)	
FXDW	G	GE
FXDW	GI	GP (2004)
FXDS	GG	
FXDXT	GL	

Touring Models	Letter Code
FLTR	FP
FLTRI	FS
FLHRCI	FR
FLHR	FD
FLHRI	FB
FLHTCU	FC
FLHTCUI	FC
FLHTCUI Shrine	FL
FLHTCUI w/SC	FG
FLHTC	DJ
FLHTC Shrine	DG
FLHTCI	FF
FLHTCI Shrine	FK
FLHT	DD
FLHTI	FU
FLHRS	FX
FLHRSI	FY

Softail Models	Letter Code
FXST	BH
FXSTI	BV (2002–04)
FXSTS	BL
FXSTSI	BZ (2001–04)
FXSTB	BT (2000–04)
FXSTBI	JA (2001–04)
FXSTD	S (2000–04)
FXSTDI	JB (2001–04)
FLSTC	BJ
FLSTCI	BW (2001–04)
FLSTS	BR
FLSTSI	BY (2001–03)
FLSTF	BM
FLSTFI	BX (2001–04)

Performing the 10,000-Mile Service

 Time: 5–8 hours

 Tools: Just about everything you own, plus a torque wrench, grease gun, funnels, and a jack

 Talent:

 Cost: Around $100

 Tip: Keep an accurate logbook of all maintenance procedures, when you did them, and how much they cost.

 PERFORMANCE GAIN: All-around better performance as a result of regular maintenance.

COMPLEMENTARY MODIFICATION: Now is the time to rectify any of those annoying little things the factory likes to do

I'm a firm believer in the old adage that an ounce of prevention is worth a pound of cure. A decent preventative maintenance program can keep roadside repairs to a bare minimum as well as keep your bike alive and well for many long years. The first question is what constitutes preventative maintenance and the second, I suppose, is how often it should be done.

Preventative maintenance is essentially a routine inspection, adjustment, and lubrication of the various bits and pieces that make up your motorcycle. By inspecting, adjusting, and, if need be, replacing these items on a regular basis you can prevent them from failing unexpectedly, which at best is inconvenient and at worst can leave you stranded, injured, or dead.

Preventative maintenance is generally prefaced with the word *routine*, which as we all know is defined as "regular or timely." In most cases, manufacturers specify either a time frame or mileage for performing routine preventative maintenance. Harley-Davidson likes to see its motorcycles serviced at regular mileage intervals. The services are broken down into three broad categories: minor (performed every 2,500 miles), major (performed every 5,000 miles), and the big daddy of services, the 10,000-mile, or chassis, service.

The minor service is essentially an oil change and inspection, the type of thing you can do in an hour on a Saturday morning. Major service includes changing all of the engine and transmission fluids, adjusting several things, and replacing a few items. A major service will eat up the better part of a morning and then some, particularly if you need to make anything more than minor repairs.

The chassis service is the big kahuna of services. During the 10,000-mile service, everything from the steering head bearings to the wheel bearings should be inspected, adjusted, lubricated, replaced, or polished. Well, okay, maybe not polished but you get the picture. I'd venture to say that if you religiously perform the 10K service, your motorcycle should last damn near forever. The problem is that, to be effective, routine service needs to be performed in a timely fashion. For some riders, reaching 10,000 miles may take a lifetime. In which case, many vital service points may go untouched. If that were the case, I'd definitely recommend shortening the intervals between chassis services. In fact, I'd say that a chassis service should be performed once a year, whether or not the bike actually accrues the mileage.

This brings up another point, namely what do you do if you rack up high yearly mileage, say 30 or 40K per year? Obviously you'll need to service the bike more often. But if it were my bike this is how I'd do it:

Once a year, I'd give the bike a complete stem-to-stern chassis service. Since I live in an area of the country with a fairly harsh winter I'd plan on doing it when the bike is going to be off the road anyway. As a side issue, many dealers offer winter service specials, which you can use to your advantage. I'd service the bike according to schedule after the riding season starts. But I wouldn't do it all at once. For example, when the bike needs a rear tire, I not only replace the tire, I service and inspect the wheel bearings, rear brake, and rear suspension as well. When I change the engine oil, I also change the tranny oil. If the brake pads need changing, perhaps it's time to change the brake fluid as well. In essence what I—and hopefully you—do is to "over-service" the bike. That way I never need to tie up the bike for any length of time during the prime riding season. Clearly you won't be servicing all of the motorcycle all of the time. But you will be hitting the high points and, frankly, the rest of the stuff can wait for the giant, once-a-year 10K chassis service.

As for what you should be servicing, start by following the owners'/service manual's suggested schedule. As you become more familiar with your bike and its particular requirements, you'll find that there may be some items that need more frequent attention, and some that can be looked at a little less often. If you've installed some accessory or other that needs routine maintenance, for example forward controls which may need some periodic lubrication and adjustment, you'll need to add them to the list of "to do" items.

By the way, taken as a whole, the chassis service may seem to eat up more time wrenching than you'd rather devote to one sitting, especially when you could be out riding. But taken as individual jobs, the majority of the jobs take less than an hour to perform, at least according to the Harley-Davidson flat rate manual. In fact, the factory time for a complete chassis service on a stock dresser is only 5 1/2 hours. My point is that if time is really a deciding factor, there's no reason why you can't spread the service over one, two, or even three days or weekends if you really need to.

Logbooks

In the tips section I mentioned keeping some sort of maintenance logbook. Using a logbook serves several purposes. For starters, it helps eliminate a lot of guesswork. Frankly, I have a lot of trouble remembering when I replaced the last tire or serviced the air cleaner. The logbook is a convenient way of keeping track. A logbook also helps you keep track of mechanical anomalies, so you can determine if any maintenance trends are developing, and correct them before you have a serious problem or be prepared to deal with them on a routine basis. Logbooks are also a great sales aid should you decide to sell your bike. A well-documented service history, detailing the service performed, any parts installed and the total cost, goes a long way toward answering questions a potential buyer has regarding the quality of care the bike received while you owned it.

Service Procedures—10,000-Mile Service
(Use this guide in conjunction with the shop manual)

Basic Service—Lubricate/Change/Service
Change engine oil
Service air filter/replace
Clean tappet screen
Change primary fluid
Change transmission oil
Lubricate levers
Lubricate pedals
Lubricate cables
Lubricate any hinges and locks
Check brake fluid level, change as required
Clean fuel tank filter, replace or clean inline filters
Check tires for wear, adjust pressure
Lubricate steering head bearings
Change fork oil

Chassis Items
Check brake pads; replace as necessary
Check brake lines and calipers
Check spokes
Check wheel bearings; replace as required
Check and adjust steering head bearings; replace as needed
Inspect and adjust suspension, inspect air lines
Wrench-check all fasteners; torque as indicated
Torque all engine mounts
Adjust drive belt
Check wheel alignment

Electrical System
Service battery
Inspect electrical system, seal connections with dielectric grease; repair any worn or chaffed wiring
Lubricate switches with lubricant such as WD-40

Engine Checks
Replace spark plugs
Check timing
Check and adjust engine idle

Authorized HD dealerships should use and present you with a checklist along with an itemized bill. You can get the same checklist from your owner's manual, without the bill.

Lubricating Cables

 Time: About 15 minutes per cable

 Tools: Open-ended wrenches, sized to fit the cable adjusters

 Talent:

 Cost: Under $15

 Tip: The more you lube your cables; the less often you'll need to replace them.

 PERFORMANCE GAIN: Smooth cables work better, are less likely to break, and don't strain your wrists

COMPLEMENTARY MODIFICATION: Upgrade to stainless-steel cables

There is nothing worse to operate than a motorcycle with dry, binding, kinked, or fraying cables. Nothing worse, except maybe a motorcycle with a busted cable. The thing is, there's absolutely no excuse for having less-than-perfect cables on your bike. Cable maintenance is a snap, and well within the ability of even the rankest novice to perform.

Cable Theory

Back in the dark ages of motorcycling, the clutch and throttle were operated by either a system of bell cranks and levers or by a length of piano wire running through a steel outer cover. As you can imagine, both of these methods left something to be desired when it came to smooth predicable operation. With the invention of the multi-strand wire control cable, things were much improved, which is why the "Bowden" cable is still in use today.

Initially, the Bowden cable was little more than a few dozen thin steel wires twisted into a spiral. The cable was inserted into a flexible, spring steel sheath to protect it and act as a guide. A cloth, or later a rubberized plastic outer cover, was used to keep the elements out of the cable innards but retain some lubricating oil. Barrels or eyes were soldered or crimped onto both ends of the cable to

provide attaching points for the control levers. Today the basic control cable remains largely the same, although modern materials and assembly methods have made them far more durable than their predecessors. Presently, some high-tech cables use Teflon-coated inner liners to smooth their operation, or perhaps have stainless-steel or Kevlar outer sheaths. But by and large they still work in exactly the same fashion and require the same minimal maintenance, little more in fact, than the occasional shot of oil, some periodic adjustment, and a dab of grease or anti-seize.

The question is why do so many riders neglect their cables? Part of the problem is that a cable deteriorates so slowly that many of us don't realize there's a problem until the darn thing goes "ping" and leaves us stranded.

Doing It

Your Harley-Davidson has only two cables that need attention; actually three, since most of you have throttles with two cables, but I'm sure you figured that part out by yourself.

The clutch cable is the harder working of the three, so let's start there. Begin by backing off completely the inline adjuster. Then remove the eyelet from the clutch lever;

I prefer using some sort of pressure lubricating device to oil my cables but this method will also work. It just takes a lot longer. Allow the lubricant to fully penetrate the cable. Wait until it dribbles out the other end before stopping.

(this step isn't strictly necessary, but I recommend it). Install a cable pressure-lubricating tool (I like the Motion Pro tool #08-0182 and their lubricant 15-0001) onto the cable end and fill the sucker with lube. As an alternative you can just spray lube into the cable itself, but that method isn't nearly as effective. You'll probably find that you'll need to lubricate the cable halves above the adjuster and below the adjuster separately. Once both sides of the cable are well oiled, fill the eyelet with white grease or anti-seize compound. This will prevent the eyelet from binding in the lever and breaking the cable at crimp. With the cable back in the lever, apply a dab of anti-seize to the cable adjuster threads and readjust to the factory recommended specifications, or a reasonable facsimile thereof. That wasn't so bad, was it? And now you don't need Godzilla-like strength just to operate the clutch.

Throttle cables are even easier to lube. Back off the throttle cable adjusters. Pull the cable out of the adjuster as far as it will go and install the cable-lubricating tool. Lube the bejesus out of each cable. Readjust the throttle free play to the recommended settings. Ride off into the sunset. As a side issue, any time the throttle drum is removed from the handlebar, the area of the bar under the drum should be coated with white grease and the cable nipples that fit into the drum should also be greased.

Alternatives and Inspection

Normally, Harley cables are pretty straightforward and anything from dedicated cable lubricant to WD-40 can be used to safely lubricate them. However, if the cables have been replaced with aftermarket cables, they might be Teflon-lined. Teflon-lined cables shouldn't require any lubrication and, in fact, some lubricants may make them gummy. If you suspect that the cables are Teflon-lined, use a product like Tri-Flow (aerosol Teflon) to lubricate them. Tri-Flow works fine on standard cables and won't hurt a Teflon-lined one.

Anytime you're adjusting or greasing the control cable, take an extra minute or two to look for obvious and not-so-obvious signs of damage. Tears or abrasions in the outer cover should be temporarily repaired with a wrap of electric tape, until the cable can be replaced. A kinked or bent cable is also a prime candidate for replacement and, of course, any frays in the inner cable (you'll see them most often at the lever end) mean the cable is past its sell-by date.

Bear in mind that smooth, easy-to-operate cables make the bike easier to ride and don't wear you out. If it's he-man muscles you want, go to the gym. Pulling a rusty, crusty, clutch cable or twisting a bound-up throttle is just the wrong way to pump it up.

Changing the Engine Oil and Filter

 Time: 30 minutes

 Tools: Oil filter wrench, drain pan, 3/8-inch drive ratchet and 4-inch extension, 5/8-inch socket

 Talent:

 Cost: Under $50

 Parts: Oil filter, four quarts of 20W-50 oil

 Tip: Wear gloves, as engine oil isn't the best thing to let soak into your skin.

 PERFORMANCE GAIN: An engine that will last a lot longer than one that doesn't get regular oil and filter changes

COMPLEMENTARY MODIFICATION: Proper servicing of the transmission and primary fluids

All who own and operate a motorcycle should understand the need for this basic service procedure, performed at the intervals called for by the H-D Motor Company. The lubricating oil that is circulated throughout the engine by the oil pump is what allows all the engine's moving parts to keep moving. Without a thin barrier of oil between the moving parts of the engine, the whole assembly would quickly come to a grinding halt.

But keeping things slippery is not the only function of engine oil. Modern lubricants also fill the role of cleaner and trash remover, in the sense that good engine oil also cleans the inside of the engine. In fact, carbon deposits and other unwanted debris become suspended in the oil as it circulates through the engine, with the larger particles (relatively speaking) getting caught in the oil filter. The engine oils of the pre-AMF days didn't have this capability, which is why engines built up sludge deposits over time. However, when a modern engine has sludge inside, it's due to the use of lousy oil or infrequent oil and filter changes. By the way, the filter in an Evo catches particles 30 microns and larger, while a TC 88's filter will scrub out particles as small as 10 microns. However, you shouldn't run a TC 88 filter on an

Evo. An Evo oil pump is not as strong as a Twin Cam's. That means the 10-micron filter element may restrict oil flow, which will open the filter's bypass valve.

Engine oil also acts as a cooling agent. As oil circulates throughout the engine it carries away heat. Hopefully, the bike is also equipped with a good oil cooler which helps the oil cool the engine. (See Project 63.)

The fourth job of quality oil is to help keep the engine leak-free. This may sound strange since oil is what you see leaking out when a seal or gasket is not up to the task. Actually, oil helps the seals, gaskets, and piston rings keep oil and the various gases inside the engine in their proper places. In fact, a rubber seal can't keep oil inside the engine without a film of oil to help it.

As for the debate about whether to use mineral (fossil) or synthetic oil in a Harley-Davidson, the introduction of the Motor Company's own synthetic oil (SYN3), which can be used in the engine, transmission, and primary, opens up synthetic oil use to those who will not use a product unless it is given H-D's blessing. Personally, I

Use a 5/8-inch socket and ratchet to remove the drain plug under the oil tank on a Softail.

think this is a great turn of events since owners can now have peace of mind no matter if they want to use synthetic or fossil oil.

Now that you know why it's important to keep the slippery stuff fresh and flowing, here's how to change it and the filter: After you've brought the engine up to operating temperature, put a drain pan under the bike. Then use a 5/8-inch socket to remove the drain plug that's at the end of the drain hose, yet solid mounted onto the frame, under the oil tank on Softails. For Dynas, you also use a 5/8-inch socket to remove the engine oil drain plug under the transmission, ditto for Touring models. Once all the old oil has drained out, and with it the particles suspended in the oil, reinstall the drain plug after first checking the O-ring. (Torque the plug on Dynas and touring models to 14–21 foot-pounds.) Then add 3 1/2 quarts of the proper grade oil. (Note: Oil level is checked with a hot engine.)

Place the drain pan under the oil filter. Remove the oil filter with a filter wrench. (By the way, H-D makes a good one and it's part number HD-42311. You'll also need a 3/8-inch drive ratchet and 4-inch extension.) Once the filter comes off the engine, clean up the spilled oil and the sealing surface on the engine case. Then put a little fresh oil onto the new filter's rubber gasket. Now screw the new filter onto the engine's filter stud with your hand until the gasket just touches the engine case. Then screw the filter another half or three-quarter turn. Just use your hand, not the filter wrench. (By the way, you can also use a K&N filter, which has a 17-mm nut on the end for easy installation and removal. No filter wrench is needed for removal.)

When you start the engine, check around the drain plug and oil filter for leaks. Also check via the idiot light or the oil gauge that the oil pressure comes up as it should, as the case may be.

Dynas and Touring models have the drain plug under the transmission. Use a 5/8-inch socket and ratchet here, too.

Remove the old oil filter with a suitable filter wrench. An automotive one may damage the sensor in the front left side of the case.

Put a little fresh oil onto the new filter's rubber gasket before screwing it onto the engine's filter stud.

Changing Transmission and Primary Oil

 Time: 30 minutes

 Tools: T40 Torx driver, T27 Torx driver, drain pan, 3/8-inch Allen wrench, 5/8-inch socket, 6-inch extension, and a ratchet

 Talent:

 Cost: Under $25

 Parts: 20–24 ounces of tranny oil, 32 ounces of primary oil

 Tip: Wear gloves, as oil isn't the best thing to let soak into your skin.

PERFORMANCE GAIN: The transmission and primary's components will last a lot longer than units that don't get regular oil changes

COMPLEMENTARY MODIFICATION: Before you refill the primary chain case, check the primary chain (Project 9) and adjust or replace as needed

Most bike owners know how important it is to change the engine's oil and filter regularly. However, many of them neglect to do the same for their primary system and transmission. The service manual calls out specific change intervals for both, which should be adhered to as religiously as engine oil and filter changes. To service the primary system, use a T40 Torx driver to remove the magnetic drain plug at the bottom of the primary chain case and let the old fluid drain into a suitable container. If there are lots of metal slivers on the magnetic drain plug, check the primary components for excessive wear or damage. Some slivers, however, are normal. After cleaning the drain plug, reinstall it into the primary cover. Then remove the five T27 Torx bolts on the derby cover and the four bolts on the chain inspection cover. Put both covers and all hardware aside for now.

With the bike upright and level, fill the chain case with the proper grade of fresh oil (I used Spectro oil for both the primary and tranny) until it reaches the bottom edge of the diaphragm spring. Or you can go 2 3/4 inches down from the center of the clutch adjuster screw. Either way, the primary's capacity is stated to be 32 ounces. Once

filled, wipe (and inspect) the derby cover's quad ring and its groove clean. Then reinstall the cover and quad ring onto the outer primary cover and torque the Allen bolts to 7–9 foot-pounds in a crosswise pattern. Do the same for the inspection cover.

On the rubber-mount models, the tranny's magnetic drain plug is on the right side of the oil pan and it's removed with a 5/8-inch socket. On Softails, the drain plug is above and between the two rear shocks. Let all the old fluid drain into a suitable pan. Then remove the oil filler plug with a 3/8-inch Allen wrench and check the O-rings for nicks, etc.; also check the O-rings on the drain plug. Clean the drain plug and replace the O-rings if necessary. If there are lots of metal slivers on the magnetic drain plug, check the transmission components for excessive wear or damage. When all the oil has drained out, reinstall the drain plug and torque it to 14–21 foot-pounds. Then fill the transmission with 20–24 ounces of the proper grade of oil, or until the oil level is at the full mark on the filler cap's dip stick. Be sure the bike is upright and level and the filler cap is resting on the threads when you check the level. Then reinstall the filler plug to 25–75 inch-pounds.

Servicing these two vital, oil-dependent components of your Harley-Davidson at the proper intervals (every 5,000 miles for both the primary and tranny, after the first 1,000-mile change) and keeping a periodic eye on the fluid levels will keep them working flawlessly for many thousands of happy miles.

Use a T40 Torx driver to remove the magnetic drain plug at the bottom of the primary chaincase and let the old fluid drain into a suitable container. Then reinstall the plug. (Sometimes the plug is underneath the cover.)

After removing the derby and inspection covers with a T27 Torx driver, with the bike upright and level, fill the chaincase with fresh oil until it reaches the bottom edge of the diaphragm spring.

On the rubber-mount models, the tranny's magnetic drain plug is on the right side of the oil pan and it's removed with a 5/8-inch socket. Once the old oil is out, reinstall the drain plug and torque it to 14-21 ft-lbs.

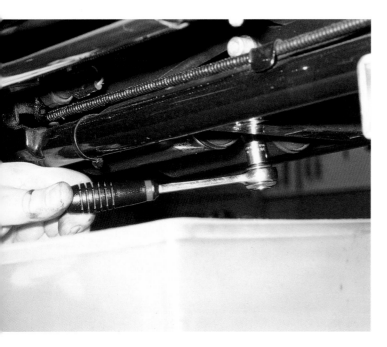

On Softails, the drain plug is above and between the two rear shocks. Use a 5/8-inch socket to remove it. Let all the old oil drain into a suitable pan. Then reinstall the drain plug and torque it to 14-21 ft-lbs.

Remove the oil filler plug with a 3/8-inch Allen wrench and fill the tranny until the oil level is at the full mark on the filler cap's dipstick. The bike must be upright and level, with the filler cap resting on the threads.

Servicing the Air Cleaner

 Time: Under 30 minutes

 Tools: 5/16-inch Allen wrench, T27 Torx driver

 Talent:

 Cost: $20–100

 Parts: Air cleaner element

 Tip: Be sure to wipe out the air cleaner housing and cover with a clean rag before installing the new element.

 PERFORMANCE GAIN: Smoother idle and better fuel mileage

COMPLEMENTARY MODIFICATION: Don't just change the element; swap out that stock air cleaner box for one that flows more freely

Start by removing the air cleaner cover bolt, which is done with a 5/16-inch Allen wrench. After noting that the outer cover and rubber gasket fit inside the backing plate, pull the cover off.

Remove the three T27 Torx bolts and cover bracket and set them aside.

Remove the old filter element, noting that there are two soft rubber hoses that protrude into the back of the element. Pull them out of the element, but leave the other ends attached to the backing plate. Replace the gasket if needed.

Is your engine idling a little rough? Has the bike's fuel mileage been dropping? When this happens most people immediately think that the carb's jetting (or the EFI's fuel maps) need to be readjusted. And, in a way, they're right, but the fix isn't fiddling with the idle mixture settings. The problem is that the air filter element is clogged, which is hindering airflow into the engine and making the fuel/air mixture too rich.

Thankfully, the fix is a lot easier than futzing with the fuel settings, as the accompanying photos show. Just swap out the dirty element for a new one, which will run about $20 or so. Or, better yet, upgrade to a K&N filter element that flows more freely. These elements can be washed when they get dirty, which means no more running to get parts. One purchase, which will run you about $80 or so, does the deed for many future changes. In fact, the H-D service manual calls for the air cleaner element to be checked and serviced as needed—which will vary depending on where the bike is ridden—every 2,500 miles.

After wiping out the backing plate and outer cover, install the hoses into the new filter element. Reinstall the element and cover bracket. Reinstall the outer cover and torque the cover bolt to 3–5 ft-lbs., a tad tighter than snug.

Choosing, Reading, and Replacing Spark Plugs

SIMPLE MAINTENANCE

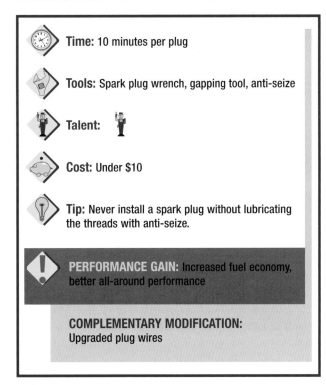

Time: 10 minutes per plug

Tools: Spark plug wrench, gapping tool, anti-seize

Talent:

Cost: Under $10

Tip: Never install a spark plug without lubricating the threads with anti-seize.

PERFORMANCE GAIN: Increased fuel economy, better all-around performance

COMPLEMENTARY MODIFICATION:
Upgraded plug wires

Spark plugs are pretty simple items. Basically little more than a hunk of wire surrounded by porcelain, jammed into a threaded body, and screwed into the cylinder head. Doesn't sound like too much, does it? Yet try running your engine without them!

The other side of the coin is that installing the wrong one, particularly one of the wrong heat range, can create some serious engine problems, not the least of which may be a holed piston.

Under normal circumstances, choosing the correct spark plug for your bike is relatively straightforward. If the engine is bone stock you simply consult the factory service manual, or your owner's manual, and install the recommended spark plug. Of course, if the bike has been modified, the factory recommendations may no longer apply. The question is, how do you know which plug is the right one for your bike, given the literally hundreds of available choices, particularly if it's been modified? If you know a little something about spark plugs, the job is fairly easy.

Plug Basics

Essentially, spark plugs do three things. First, they convey electrical energy from the ignition system into the combustion chamber where that energy can set the combustion process into motion. Secondly, they convey some of the residual heat from the combustion into the engine's cooling system. In the case of Harley-Davidson motorcycles, this means transferring the heat into the cylinder head where it can be whisked away by the breeze. Last, but by no means least, the spark plug is our window into the combustion chamber. By carefully observing the firing end of the spark plug you can determine the health of the air/fuel mix, and get a pretty good idea as to the overall health of the engine.

Heat Range

This is one of the more confusing things associated with spark plugs. Some guys, including those who should know better, will tell you that a hot plug "burns hotter," implying that the spark from a "hot plug" is somehow hotter or more powerful than a cold plug. Wrong. A spark plug's heat range refers only to its ability to transfer heat out of the combustion chamber. A cold plug transfers a lot of heat out of the combustion chamber quickly. A hot plug transfers less heat and takes a longer time to do it. Hot plugs are used in mildly tuned, low-speed engines. Because their tip temperatures stay high they burn off carbon deposits that are associated with slow running. Cold plugs are used in high-speed and hard-application circumstances such as racing or high-speed, long- distance touring.

Selecting the correct heat range for your engine is crucial. The working end of the plug operates at between 750 and 1,750 degrees Fahrenheit, the crucial part of the equation being the word "between." The optimum operating temperature for a plug is right around 1,100 to 1,200 degrees F, or just slightly below the optimum combustion chamber temperature of 1,400 degrees F.

The internal design of the spark plug determines its heat range. Heat flow through the plug is controlled by the plug's insulator nose length. The insulator nose length is the distance from the plug's firing tip to where the porcelain bonds to the metal shell of the plug.

The shorter the nose length, the cooler the plug. Why? Because the heat has a shorter path to follow before it dissipates into the surrounding cylinder head.

It doesn't matter what type of engine the spark plug is installed in. If the engine burns gasoline (LP and other alternative fuel engines have their own requirements) the spark plug tip temperature must remain between 600 degrees F and 1,750 degrees F.

Below 650 degrees, the spark plug insulator will not stay hot enough to burn off the by-products of combustion, namely carbon. Eventually these deposits will build up and the spark, rather than jump the gap between the tip and ground electrode, will take the path of least resistance, flowing through the carbon track to ground, creating a fouled plug. The result may be a misfire or it may result in a "no start" condition; it depends how badly fouled the plug is.

What happens when plug tip temperatures get too high? That's when it really gets ugly. Above 1,750 degrees the plug tip starts to overheat, and soon the ceramic around the center electrode begins to blister. The next step is an incandescent and molten tip. After that comes pre-ignition and detonation. Eventually, severe engine damage results.

Between identical plug types, the difference from one heat range to the next is on the order of about 50 to 80 degrees F. Projected tip plugs normally increase the firing end temperature by 50 to 65 degrees F. As you may surmise, simply changing heat ranges up or down may cure or at least alleviate certain problems.

For example, if you anticipate a summer's trip through the desert, two up, fully loaded, and towing a trailer on your Ultra Glide, you might want to install a slightly colder plug. Conversely, if you plan on riding your Softail to work through the winter you may want to install a slightly hotter plug.

So how do you know which plug is right for your bike? At the risk of overstating the obvious, if the plug doesn't foul at low speed and doesn't exhibit any signs of overheating at other speeds, the plug is essentially the correct one for your application.

Diagnosis: Picking the Right Plug

The spark plug is our "window" into the combustion chamber. An experienced rider or tuner can determine or at least make an educated guess into what's happening inside the cylinder by examining the spark plug insulator and tip. As you might imagine, reading the plug and translating the results into a course of action can take years of practice to develop. While most spark plug catalogs have some sort of color chart describing the most common problems and their effect on the spark plug, the photos generally indicate a worst-case scenario; chances are that your plugs won't be so dramatic. That being the case, I'd always recommend showing your plugs to an experienced tuner if there are any questions.

Reading the Tip

Rich mixtures: Obviously the air/fuel ratio has a great effect on engine performance and spark plug life. If the mix is too rich you lose power, the plug tip temperature drops and possibly fouls; the engine runs "fat"; the plug tip will look black and may be covered with carbon, or even worse, unburned fuel; the plug will foul easily.

Lean mixtures: If the mix is lean, the cylinder temperature and plug tip temperature soar. Pre-ignition and detonation become real possibilities, and the end result is major engine damage. The plug tip will have a bleached look to it. The electrodes themselves may be eroded or show signs of physical damage (serious electrode damage or erosion is usually indicative of too hot a plug, rather than a lean mixture).

Modifications and Their Effect on Spark Plugs

High compression: It won't matter if you mill the head, swap cams, or add a turbo. If the compression goes up, you'll need a colder plug, higher-octane fuel, and properly adjusted ignition timing and carburetion. Again, as heat goes up and the engine is used harder, you'll need a colder plug.

Ignition timing: Feel like advancing that timing for a little more giddy up? Advancing the timing ten degrees raises the plug tip temperature by 70 to 100 degrees C. Dependent on the appearance of the plug tip, a colder plug may be required.

Like to tour long distance, maybe while pulling a trailer? Be aware that the firing end temperature is proportional to load and engine speed. If your trip includes lots of highway pounding during the summer, while toting a heavy load, you may want to drop down a heat range.

Tips and Materials

Often overlooked in the search for the right plug is the tip design and the materials used to construct the spark plug. The standard plug is normally referred to as an "L-gap" or standard-type plug. In this design, the ground or side electrode extends across the center electrode. These work fine in most stock applications.

"J-gap" plugs have a side electrode that extends only to the center of the center electrode. Because the center electrode is more fully exposed, J-gap plugs are somewhat more resistant to fouling than a conventional spark plug. This also requires less voltage to fire at high rpm. This makes them a good candidate for a mildly breathed-on engine.

"V-groove" plugs have a 90-degree groove milled in the center electrode. These plugs take less voltage to fire and the sparks occur nearer the edge of the electrode. V-groove plugs generally improve start-up characteristics, help the bike idle better, and improve fuel economy.

From left: a moderately used plug—this one is certainly still useable; a low mileage plug—note that the coloring process has just started to take place; and a brand new plug.

Materials

Typically, a standard spark plug's center electrode is made of some sort of nickel/copper alloy. These plugs work well enough but there are alternatives. Currently, platinum-tipped plugs are very popular. Thin wire platinum center electrodes greatly increase spark plug life. In some automotive applications, platinum plugs last upward of 100,000 miles. They are expensive but provide superior performance over lots of miles.

"Racing plugs" usually have electrodes made of precious metals, usually gold/palladium or platinum. These plugs stand up well to abuse, require less voltage to fire, and are very resistant to fouling. In most cases they are extremely expensive, but when ultimate performance is your goal, what's money?

You Want What?

Once you've examined your plug and decided that a different heat range is in order you'll need to consult either the shop manual or the spark plug manufacturers' catalog to determine what plug will best suit your needs, or at least provide a starting point for further experiments. Rather than cross-reference the H-D plug with one from another manufacturer, I'd recommend you look up the plug manufacturer's recommendation and start with that. The cross-references rarely translate into exact heat matches, making it easy to get sidetracked. On the same issue be aware that not all spark plug numbering systems follow the pattern. For example Champion plugs get colder as the numbers get lower, i.e., a #6 plug is colder than a #8. However, NGK plugs are just the opposite; a #6 plug is hotter than a #8. By the same token, some manufacturers try to cover a given heat range with one plug, while another may list several in varying temperatures to cover the same spread. As I said, given the choice, use the spark plug manufacturer's recommendation any time you need to use a plug other than the one recommended by Harley.

Plug Installation

It's safe to say that most plugs are improperly installed right from the get-go. Here's the right way to install one:

Before removing the old plug, thoroughly clean the surrounding area to prevent dirt from entering either the combustion chamber or lodging in the threads. If you have to, use a soda straw, and blow the crap away with lung pressure. I like to flush the area with brake cleaner or WD-40. Set the gap on the new plug by bending the side electrode only.

Make sure you set or check the gap; most pre-gapped plugs aren't. Furthermore, use only a wire gauge to set the gap. Flat feeler gauges aren't accurate enough. If you plan on increasing or decreasing the gap to take advantage of some trick ignition or special circumstance, never vary from the original spec by more than .008. This will ensure that the electrodes remain parallel to each other.

I shouldn't have to mention it, but never use the porcelain insulator as a fulcrum point to adjust the gap. Not unless you need another bad plug.

The next is a controversial point. I use anti-seize compound on my plugs. Some will tell you it insulates the plug from the head preventing heat transfer. I don't buy that. In fact, I'd argue that it enhances it. It also prevents stripped threads. If you choose to use it, and I do recommend you do so, apply it sparingly.

When installing the plug it should always be tightened to the recommended torque specifications. An under-torqued plug can allow combustion gas leakage. Under-torqued plugs don't transfer heat effectively either. On the other hand, over-torquing can warp a plug's internal seals causing similar problems.

Proper torque for a spark plug inserted into an aluminum head is 18–21.5 foot-pounds for a 14-mm plug, and 10.8–14.5 for a 12-mm plug. If you have no torque wrench, run the plug in until the gasket seats and then give the plug an additional half to two-thirds turn.

Finally, unless there is some dire emergency, never install a cold plug in a hot engine. The differing rates of expansion could cause the plug to seize in the head, creating installation problems on the spot or removal problems down the road.

Plug Chops

The plug chop used to be the accepted method of reading a plug. You'd get the bike up to speed, usually flat out in third or fourth gear, whip in the clutch, and simultaneously kill the engine. With the clutch in you'd coast to the side of the road or racetrack, remove the plug, and give it a good look. You'd then jet the engine or change plugs accordingly. Nowadays, things are a bit different.

In the first place, gasoline formulations have changed and they take longer to color a plug. In some cases, it might be 300–500 miles before you see any real color. In the second place, the cops take a very dim view these days of guys making banzai power runs on local side streets and highways.

My suggestion is to do much of your tuning work on a dyno. If that's not possible, and we all know it isn't always, you have two alternatives. The first, of course, is the traditional plug chop. The second is to simply ride the bike and check the plugs at a given interval. Initially at 100 miles, if the plugs look good, run them another hundred or two and recheck them. If they look good you're all set. If not, make your changes and repeat.

Obviously, the color will be affected by idling, around town riding, and so forth. But overall you'll be able to get a pretty good idea of how the engine is working.

Inspecting and Adjusting the Rear-Drive Belt

 Time: 15 minutes

 Tools: Harley-Davidson belt tensioning gauge (H-D #35381) or the equivalent

 Talent: –

 Cost: Free

 Tip: Routine inspection of the belt prevents those sudden "Uh-oh, why ain't she moving?" moments.

 PERFORMANCE GAIN: A little regular adjustment and the removal of any debris can significantly increase belt life

COMPLEMENTARY MODIFICATION: Clearance issues between the belt and its guard can shorten the belt's life. Now is the time to make sure the guard is properly spaced

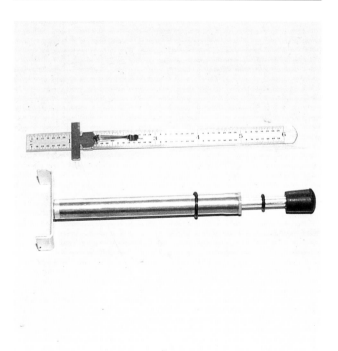

The factory tool and a 6-inch ruler are the handiest way to measure belt tension.

Fitting a rear-drive belt was one of the Motor Company's better ideas. Drive belts are clean, quiet, and require just about zero maintenance. The operative phrase here being "just about." Properly maintained, a drive belt can last almost indefinitely (normal life span is 70,000 to 90,000 miles). However, an over-tightened belt may destroy itself and damage other components in short order. By the same token, belts do tend to pick up bits of road debris. Fortunately, if the debris is removed in a timely manner the belt is more often than not left undamaged.

The first order of business is to inspect your belt on a routine basis. The factory calls for a belt inspection at the initial 1,000-mile service and at 2,500-mile intervals thereafter. Of course, if it were my belt, I'd give it at least a cursory glance a little more often than that; for example, whenever I washed the bike or adjusted the tire pressure.

Initially, the inner surface of the belt has a thin coating of lubricant applied to it. This will burnish its way into the belt during the break-in period, so its absence after a few hundred or so miles is no cause for concern.

Absent physical damage, your drive belt needs to be checked only for correct tension and physical wear. Here's the deal: A belt that is too loose is, well, it's too loose. I've honestly never heard of one coming off, especially with all of the guards in place, and I doubt that you could get one so loose that it would slip, although I suppose that one could if they really tried. The reality is that most of the damage happens because someone inadvertently over-tightens the belt. Overly tight belts lead to all types of unpleasantness. They can overload the countershaft and cause a leak at the pulley seal. They wear faster than normal, and in a worst-case scenario they might even strip the splines on the pulley.

The question is how tight is too tight as opposed to being just tight enough? Harley-Davidson recommends having the rider sit on the bike while applying ten pounds of pressure to the midsection of the belt, via their belt tension gauge (part #HD-35381), and then measuring the deflection, which should be between 5/16 and 3/8 of an inch.

As you can imagine, this can be a little awkward when working alone. But it can certainly be done. If you don't have the correct tool there are alternatives. The first is to use a fisherman's scale; these are sold in tackle shops for about five bucks and work just fine. The second method is to grasp the belt where it exits the primary case, about halfway between the primary and the swing arm. Give the belt a twist while observing it; if you can twist the bugger a full 90, degrees it's too loose. If it won't twist past 30 degrees, it's too tight. The magic number? You guessed it, if the belt can be twisted to somewhere around 45 degrees, it's just right.

Wear is the other bugaboo. Normally, belt wear is monitored by observing where the belt sits in relation to the pulleys on which it's riding. A new belt rides high on its pulley, and as it wears it tends to drop down. The closer to the center of the pulley the belt rides, the more it's been worn. Unfortunately, even a new drive belt rides fairly well down in its pulleys. However, if you observe a new Harley drive belt you'll see that it doesn't quite touch the valley between the pulley teeth. However, as it wears it moves closer to them. When the belt is shot it'll be fully bottomed out. At that point, replace the belt or you'll soon be walking.

Finally, watch the edges of the belt. Cracks or wrinkles will appear on the belt teeth as the belt ages. These run parallel to the belt pull. When the cracks span the width of the belt tooth and/or run from the top of the tooth to the bottom, the belt is kaput. Replace it now or you'll be walking.

With the correct tension applied to the belt via the scale, measure the deflection on the ruler. If it's between 5/16 and 3/8 of an inch you're good to go.

Checking and Adjusting the Primary Chain

 Time: Under 30 minutes

 Tools: 3/16-inch Allen wrench, 9/16-inch socket, gasket removing tool

 Talent:

 Cost: Under $10

 Parts: Inspection cover gasket

 Tip: Check the chain's adjustment whenever you change the primary fluid, which should be done every 5,000 miles.

 PERFORMANCE GAIN: Smooth power transfer from the engine to the clutch/transmission group

COMPLEMENTARY MODIFICATION: Check and, if needed, adjust the rear belt

SIMPLE MAINTENANCE

Many people blow off checking the chain simply because it usually doesn't need any adjustment. Unfortunately, they drop into the habit of not checking it for so long that the chain goes way out of adjustment and starts to affect the ride quality of the bike. The chain should be checked every time you change the fluid.

For example, do you have excessive vibration, more than you had a few thousand miles ago? It may be due to a badly worn, tight, and/or dry primary chain. Does the engine seem to buck forward and back when you're trying to cruise at a steady speed? The primary chain is probably way too loose, which could also cause a racket on the left side of the bike as the chain slaps against the inside of the primary covers.

Checking the chain's tension is as easy as adjusting it, if you should find that it's too loose or tight. Once all the old primary fluid is drained out of the primary system, remove the inspection cover using a 3/16-inch Allen wrench, noting where the two long and two short bolts go. Discard the gasket under the cover and clean off the inspection and outer primary covers. Now take a look at the primary chain. Is it well oiled? If it's dry or even brown in appearance, you may have been running the primary with not enough or no oil in the system, which could have damaged the chain as well as the clutch. If the chain's links

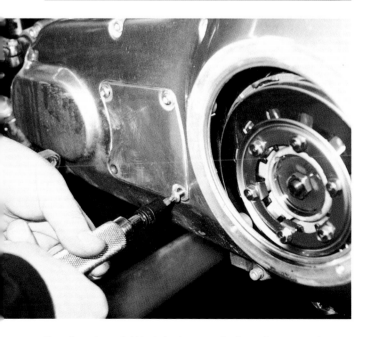

Once the primary fluid is drained, remove the inspection cover using a 3/16-inch Allen wrench, noting where the two long and two short bolts go. Discard the gasket.

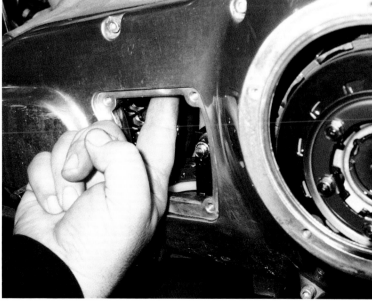

Check the primary chain's adjustment by lifting up on the upper run of the chain. When the engine is cold, the upward movement—not the total movement—of the chain should be 5/8–7/8 inch.

do not pivot smoothly on their pivot shafts when you lift up on it to check its adjustment, the chain has been run too dry and must be replaced.

Check the chain's adjustment by lifting up on the upper run of the chain, which is right inside the cover. When the engine is cold, which is the best time to check chain tension, the upward movement—not the total movement—of the chain should be 5/8–7/8 inch. If the engine is hot, the upward movement should be 3/8–5/8 inch. If the chain is tighter, or looser, than the required amount, loosen the 9/16-inch adjusting nut a few turns, just enough to be able to move the adjusting shoe assembly, and move the shoe to get the required free play in the chain. Lightly tighten the nut.

However, before you make an adjustment you must first find the tightest section of chain. Do this by shifting the transmission into second gear and rolling the bike forward to move the chain on the sprockets. Then check this section of chain the same way you checked the last one. Do this until you have checked all of the chain. When you find the tightest section adjust it so it has the required amount of free play (it's okay if some sections are looser, but the tightest section must be within limits). Tighten the adjusting shoe's nut to 21–29 foot-pounds. (By the way, if you can't move the adjusting shoe up far enough to tighten the chain so that it's within spec at the tightest part, it's time to replace the chain.) You can now reinstall the inspection cover with a new gasket and torque the cover bolts to 84–108 inch-pounds. After you shift the tranny back into neutral, refill the primary with oil, as per Project 5.

If the chain needs adjustment, loosen the adjusting shoe's 9/16-inch nut a few turns and move the shoe up to tighten the chain or down to loosen it to get the required free play. Then tighten the shoe's nut to 21–29 ft-lbs.

Replacing Brake Pads

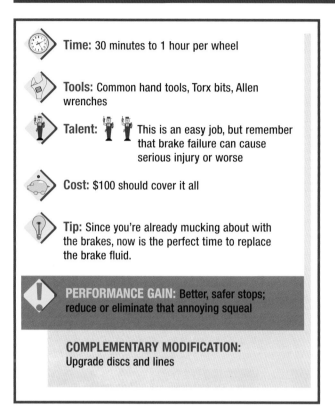

Time: 30 minutes to 1 hour per wheel

Tools: Common hand tools, Torx bits, Allen wrenches

Talent: This is an easy job, but remember that brake failure can cause serious injury or worse

Cost: $100 should cover it all

Tip: Since you're already mucking about with the brakes, now is the perfect time to replace the brake fluid.

PERFORMANCE GAIN: Better, safer stops; reduce or eliminate that annoying squeal

COMPLEMENTARY MODIFICATION:
Upgrade discs and lines

Over the years, Harley-Davidson brakes have run the gamut from poor, to less poor, to acceptable. Currently, the brakes are firmly in the "not too bad, but not great" category. In general, the brakes fitted to the Twin Cam series bikes are capable of stopping a stock bike from a reasonable speed in a reasonable amount of time and distance. The key word being "reasonable." Once the bike has been hot-rodded to any extent, new brakes are pretty much required. Since brake system upgrades are detailed elsewhere in this book, we'll only touch here on the pads themselves.

Brake Magic
Brake pads are brake pads right? Not exactly. Brake pads differ greatly in friction material as well as in the method used to attach the material to the brake backing plate.

Essentially there are two types of brake pads. The first is the sintered pad. Sintered pads are often referred to as metallic pads because they contain a fair amount of copper alloy or metal. Combining a mix of finely ground raw materials, typically graphite and copper alloy among other things, under great heat, creates sintered pads. The resulting material is then bonded under heat and pressure to the backing plate. Sintered pads stop very well under all conditions,

especially when wet, but accelerate disc wear and may create some excess noise. Since metallic pads create and transfer more heat into the caliper, some are constructed with an insulating design or clip-on insulators to protect the caliper and hydraulics.

Organic pads are those that are created from a mix of resins and fibers. In other words, glue and string! At one time asbestos was the fiber of choice, but these days Kevlar has replaced it. Some organic pads have bits of metal embedded in them; these are the so-called semi-metallic pads. As a rule, organic pads are softer, and therefore easier on the discs. They are also quieter. On the downside, they don't stop as well as the metallic pads, particularly when they are wet. They also wear faster, can fade when hot, and may require special break-in techniques to avoid becoming work-hardened or "glazed."

As an aside, there are some pads that contain high concentrations of ceramic material. These "stones" are highly resistant to heat, and are mainly used in race applications although some ceramic material may be found in over-the-counter brake pads intended for everyday use.

As you probably realized, each pad has its own stopping characteristics; some work better in the rain, some need to be smoking hot before they'll grip. Some improve the feel of the brakes; some tend to be overly sensitive. The question is always which is the right pad for your application, and without burning through the literally hundreds of available choices how do you know when you've found it?

You Want What?
Picking a new brake pad is what the English call a "suck it and see" experience. If you opt for the stock pads, or aftermarket ones with an identical (if there is such a thing) compound, you'll at least know what you are getting; a pad with a consistent, if somewhat wooden feel that works well enough under most circumstances. The problem is that there is a proliferation of pads, all with varying compounds out there and unless you try each one you really won't know how they feel or if you'll like them.

The first thing is to honestly assess your braking requirements. Realistically you need to consider—and be honest here—just how hard you really want or need to stop, and remember that tire adhesion is the limiting factor in all cases. If you're riding a stock bike with hard as granite tires on it, a set of really grippy pads could easily overpower the tires. Are you just hopping around town, which puts little strain on the brake components, or are you planning a month-long tour through the Rocky Mountains, two-up with everything including the kitchen sink? Do you ride in the rain a lot? Do you want the ultimate in stopping power, even if it means chewing through a few sets of pads and rotors, or would you rather sacrifice a bit of "whoa" if it means saving some dough?

Bear in mind that if you opt for a pad that stops on a dime and returns eight cents change you may find that you are replacing the pads and quite possibly the rotors at inconvenient and expensive intervals. Conversely, some pads sacrifice feel and stopping ability for long life. If you're not too hard on the brakes, great, these pads will last a lifetime. But if you need to stop the bike right NOW, hard pads may not get the job done. Remember you only need to come up an inch, or less short, on the brakes to hit whatever it was that pulled out in front of you.

So How Do You Know What Pads to Buy?

Well that's the million-dollar question isn't it? Obviously if you're happy with the way the stock pads work and feel than you can simply trot on down to the local H-D dealership and pick up a new set. But that's not really the answer you're looking for, is it? Most, in fact all, reputable brake pad manufacturers have some sort of catalog listing that describes the basic characteristics, including performance, wear, and suitability of application. Most of these catalogs are available over the Internet as well, so start your research there.

Typically, you'll find a photo or drawing of a brake pad with a brief description of how the pad works and any other information the manufacturer feels is worth mentioning. You can then compare, say, a Dunlop Pad to an EBC or SBS pad and make an informed decision. Don't be afraid to seek information from the counter guys or mechanics down at the local shop, as well as other riders. The shop guys in particular should have a good feel for what works and what doesn't and should be able to at least steer you away from a pad that is wrong for your application.

Without putting too fine a point on it, your brakes may well be the only thing that stands between you and disaster—choose them wisely based on your needs, not the size of your wallet.

A General Guide to Pads

Stock: Available from any H-D dealer. Adequate performance, long-lasting, and easy on the rotors. Less-than-stellar feel.

Vesrah: Decent, inexpensive, aftermarket replacement pad; long-wearing, not much improvement in feel over stock. Basically wears and performs like a stock pad.

EBC: Very good pads, very easy on the rotors and very grippy. EBC can be a little touchy when hot, but unless you're planning on road racing your Softail, that shouldn't be a problem.

Ferodo: The Lord of the Pads. These are available in a bewildering array of compounds so some research is in order. If you're building a hot rod, these are the pads to use. Unfortunately, the sacrifice may be high rotor wear, depending on the pad compound.

SBS: Another good all-around pad; works better than stock with few, if any, downsides.

Installation Tips

Your service manual will fill in any of the blank spots when it comes time to replace your brake pads. In short, replacing the pads is a simple and straightforward job although the consequences of doing it wrong can be dire. But there maybe a trick or two the manual doesn't point out.

Foremost, make sure that everything is scrupulously clean before you reassemble it. If you need to, wire brush all the hardware; and of course, give the appropriate threaded pieces a light coat of anti-seize. The manual will point out any other areas that require lubrication.

Secondly, it's easier to change the pads if you do them one at a time. Remove the first pad, open the caliper bleed screw* and use a screwdriver or small pry bar to lever the piston back into the caliper. Be gentle as you're prying against the disc, and use a rag around the sharp end of the tool to prevent scratching the disc. Once the first pad has been swapped you can do the second in the same manner. After the new pads are in place, as after any brake work, pump the brake until it feels good and solid and top off the brake fluid. Make the first few stops gentle ones, particularly if the new pads require a "break in" period.

(*Don't forget, brake fluid will be forced out when you retract the caliper piston so be prepared to contain the brake fluid.)

Choosing the correct pad for your riding style, tires, etc., is crucial for rider safety. Since most Twin Cams receive some sort of modification or enhancement, it makes sense that the brakes receive similar attention.

Before reassembling the brakes, make sure the equipment is clean and free of debris.

Adjusting the Clutch

 Time: Under 1 hour

 Tools: 1/2-inch, 9/16-inch, and 11/16-inch wrenches, T27 Torx driver, 7/32-inch Allen wrench, 11/16-inch socket and ratchet

  Talent:

 Cost: None

 Parts: None

 Tip: If you have the required amount of free play at the clutch handle, no problem getting the tranny into neutral when stopped, and the clutch doesn't slip, leave the adjustment alone.

 PERFORMANCE GAIN: Proper clutch operation and no loss of power due to a slipping clutch

COMPLEMENTARY MODIFICATION: Now's a good time to also check the primary chain's adjustment

The service manual calls for the clutch to be adjusted every 5,000 miles after the initial 1,000-mile service, which is the same time you should be changing the engine oil and filter, as well as the tranny and primary system oil, and a few other little service items.

Few things make it a hassle to ride like struggling to get the tranny in neutral, fighting to keep the bike from creeping forward when stopped in gear, or getting a left forearm pump from working a stiff clutch in traffic. A clutch in need of adjustment will also have way too much slop in the clutch lever, which makes it hard to start out from a stop, especially on a hill, making you look like you just borrowed the bike for the day from your buddy. Avoid all these nasty little annoyances by doing minor servicing

on the bike when it's raining out, so when the sun does shine you're ready to roll. I shouldn't have to say this, but if it's working fine, leave it the heck alone.

Here's how to do the deed when it's called for: The bike should be at ambient temperature and in an upright and level attitude. (Don't do a clutch adjustment with a hot engine and tranny, as it changes the settings.) Move the clutch cable boot out of the way and loosen the cable adjuster with a 1/2-inch and 9/16-inch wrench, so the cable has plenty of slack in it. Remove the derby cover using a T27 Torx driver and set the cover, hardware, and quad seal aside. Using a 11/16-inch wrench or socket, loosen the clutch adjuster screw's locknut and screw the clutch adjuster screw in (clockwise) with a 7/32-inch Allen wrench—to take up all the free play between the clutch pushrods—until it lightly seats against the pushrods. Then back the screw out one half to one full turn. While keeping the adjuster screw from turning, tighten the locknut to 6–10 foot-pounds, so the adjustment can't change.

Move the cable boot out of the way and loosen the cable adjuster with a 1/2-inch and 9/16-inch wrench, so the cable has plenty of slack.

After you've removed the derby cover, loosen the clutch adjuster screw's locknut with an 11/16-inch wrench or socket and adjust the clutch adjuster screw with a 7/32-inch Allen wrench as per the accompanying text.

At the handlebars, squeeze the clutch lever at least three times to properly set the ball and ramp release mechanism in the transmission's right side cover. Move the cable adjuster until almost all the slack at the clutch lever has been taken up. Then pull the cable ferrule away from the lever bracket to measure the cable's free play. Adjust the cable so the ferrule can be pulled only 1/16 inch to 1/8 inch away from the lever bracket. Then tighten the cable adjuster's locknut and slip the cable boot back into place. After you wipe all the oil from the quad seal, the cover, and the seal's groove in the outer primary cover, reinstall the derby cover using the stock hardware and torque the bolts to 7–9 foot-pounds in a crisscross pattern.

After squeezing the clutch lever at least three times, adjust the cable so its ferrule can be pulled away from the lever bracket 1/16 to 1/8 inch.

Tighten the cable adjuster's locknut and slip the cable boot back into place.

SECTION THREE

Intake and Exhaust

PROJECT 12

Installing a Screamin' Eagle Air Cleaner

 Time: 1 hour

 Tools: Needle-nose pliers, T30 drive, blue Loctite, 1/2-inch wrench/socket, 3/4-inch wrench/socket, 5/32-inch and 5/16-inch Allens, and torque wrenches in foot-pounds and inch-pounds

 Talent:

 Cost: $150

 Parts: SE air cleaner kit

 Tip: You must re-jet the carb, or remap the EFI system if so equipped after installing this kit or a too-lean engine condition will exist, resulting in possible engine damage.

 PERFORMANCE GAIN: 2–3 horsepower

COMPLEMENTARY MODIFICATION: A freer-flowing exhaust system, so check out Project 22

Assemble a flat washer onto the banjo bolt, followed by the mounting bracket, another washer, the chrome breather bushing, and then another flat washer. Do both banjos this way.

With 88 cubic inches on tap, you'd think a stock H-D engine would put out more than 62 horsepower. And though you're right to assume that, there's a government agency called the EPA that forces the Motor Company to muzzle its motors to conform to ever-stricter government emission restrictions. Unfortunately, these restrictions result in your 88-inch motor putting out the power that a properly breathing 60-incher does. Thankfully, the fixes, though costly, are doable, which is the reason for this section of the book.

The way to get more power from your favorite H-D is to let the sucker breathe, and one of the easiest and quickest ways to do that is to chuck the stock air cleaner, which is very restrictive, and bolt up a freer-breathing version. There are many of these on the market and all are designed to do the same thing and allow more air to get into the engine. That being the case, I decided to go with the Motor Company on this one and show you how to install a new air cleaner using a Screamin' Eagle air cleaner. I installed kit

#29440-99B, which fits 2000 and later Softails, and 1999 and later Dynas and Touring models equipped with the stock CV, an SE CV, or SE flatslide carb, as well as 2002 and later EFI units. (Kit #29441-99A fits 1999–2001 EFI bikes and goes on in a very similar way.)

This install is very straightforward and easy to do, as long as you take your time. Our starting point has the stock air cleaner and breather assembly completely removed from the carb/EFI unit and heads. (Be sure to save the air cleaner cover and cover bolt, as you'll be reusing them.)

Start the assembly by slipping a flat washer onto the banjo bolt, followed by the mounting bracket. Then slip on another washer, then the chrome breather bushing, followed by another flat washer. Then do the same for the other banjo bolt on the other side of the mounting bracket. After putting a little blue Loctite on the threads of both bolts, attach the whole assembly to the heads by threading in the banjo bolts, but don't tighten them yet. Just leave them snug for now. Position the left and right breather bushings so the fittings are at about the ten and two o'clock positions, respectively, facing each other.

After slipping both rubber hoses through the holes made for them in the backing plate, position the backing plate onto the face of the carb/EFI unit and align the hoses and fittings. Then slip the hoses over their fittings with a needle-nose pliers. Do not tear the hoses.

Slip the supplied gasket between the backing plate and carb/EFI unit, taking care to line up the holes in the gasket with the backing plate mounting holes and air hole. Then loosely bolt up the backing plate to the mounting bracket using a T30 drive on the two top flathead screws, with a little blue Loctite on their threads. Then thread the three studs, with a little blue Loctite on their threads, into the face of the carb/EFI unit. First tighten the two flathead screws to 55–60 in-lb with a T30 drive. Then check that the backing plate sits flush with the mounting bracket and carb face. If there's a gap, change the washers on the banjo bolts, so that the backing plate sits flush. Then tighten the three studs, using a 1/2-inch socket, to 55–60 in-lb. The banjo bolts are then tightened to 10–12 ft-lb with a 3/4-inch wrench/socket. (Make sure the hoses are not kinked, or the engine will not vent properly into the air cleaner assembly.)

You can now install the filter element using the three supplied buttonhead screws using a 5/32-inch Allen. Put a little blue Loctite on their threads. Then reinstall the stock air cleaner cover and cover bolt using a 5/16-inch Allen. (You may want to put a thick washer on the inside of the cover, if you see that there's a gap between the cover and the filter element.) Finish the install by removing the protective backing from the adhesive on the inside of the new Screamin' Eagle cover insert and attach the insert to the stock cover.

Loosely bolt up the backplate to the mounting bracket using a T30 drive on the two top flathead screws. Then thread the three studs into the face of the carb/EFI unit. First tighten the screws to 55–60 in-lb with a T30. After checking that the backplate sits flush with the bracket and carb, tighten the studs with a 1/2-inch socket to 55–60 in-lb.

Attach this assembly to the heads, but just leave the banjos snug for now. Position the right and left breather bushings, so the fittings are at the 10 and 2 o'clock positions, respectively.

The banjo bolts are then tightened to 10–12 ft-lbs with a 3/4-inch wrench/socket. Make sure the hoses are not kinked, or the engine will not vent properly into the air cleaner assembly.

After slipping both rubber hoses through their holes in the backplate, position the backplate onto the carb. Then slip the hoses over their fittings with a needlenose pliers.

You can now install the filter element using the three supplied buttonhead screws using a 5/32-inch Allen. Then reinstall the stock air cleaner cover and cover bolt using a 5/16-inch Allen.

Installing an S&S Air Cleaner

 Time: 30 minutes

 Tools: Flat-bladed screwdriver, Philips screwdriver, pliers, hose cutters, 1/4-inch Allen wrench, 3/4-inch wrench

 Talent:

 Cost: $90–190

 Parts: S&S Cycle air cleaner kit for your model carb/bike

 Tip: Be sure to re-jet the carb after installing this kit if you're swapping out a stock air cleaner.

PERFORMANCE GAIN: About two horsepower over the stock air cleaner

COMPLEMENTARY MODIFICATION: Install a performance exhaust system

The S&S Cycle teardrop design is the most recognized air cleaner in the world and it's been an S&S trademark for decades. In fact, some owners have one on their bike even though they don't have an S&S carb lurking underneath. First introduced in the 1970s, the teardrop combines classic good looks and great performance. This air cleaner features an air horn style, radius airway on the backing plate, and an internal air directional cone on the inside of the dimpled cover, which combine to provide improved airflow into the carb.

The accompanying photos show some of the major steps needed to install this air cleaner onto a Super E or G carburetor. (Project 16 shows you how to install an S&S Super E or G carb, while Project 18 shows how to install a performance intake manifold.) However, the teardrop is available for many different style carbs, like H-D's Keihin CV, as well as a variety of older carbs, such as the Tillotson, Bendix, and butterfly Keihin. Be sure to specify what carb and year/model engine/bike you plan to use it on, as S&S has kits for many different applications.

The starting point for this installation is the back of the backing plate. Start by pushing the two black plugs into the holes in the plate. The next step, if your air cleaner/carb is so equipped, is the carb enrichener actuator mechanism. The parts are assembled in this order: The wave washer goes onto the stud first, followed by the steel washer and then the clear plastic washer. The lever can now go on with the screw. Another plastic washer can then go on, followed by the brass washer, smooth side out, and the last screw. Before proceeding, make sure the enrichener lever moves smoothly. If it doesn't, find out what you did wrong.

Next up are the two breather assemblies. Here's the order of assembly: The head bolt first gets a flat black plastic washer, followed by the banjo bolt, and another plastic washer. Bolt the two breather assemblies you just made to the heads using a 3/4-inch wrench and position the banjo bolts so that they face each other. Place the backing plate against the face of the carb and see if the backing plate fully contacts both the face of the carb and the breather assemblies in the head. If they don't, use the shims in the kit to make it so.

Once the breathers are properly shimmed, screw the backing plate onto the face of the carb, with the new gasket in place and engaging the enrichener. (Note: The backing plate screws have a locking compound and a lock washer on them, so they will not loosen up and be ingested by the engine.) Then install the breather hose with the supplied clamps, so it attaches to both banjo fittings and the fitting on the back of the backing plate. (You will have to cut it to fit.) The two breather bolts can now go into the breather assemblies with a little Loctite on the threads. The air cleaner element can then go in, followed by the chrome teardrop cover with the three supplied screws.

Installing the carb enrichener starts with the wave washer going onto the stud, followed by the steel washer, and then the clear plastic washer. The lever can now be fastened with a screw.

The other plastic washer then goes on, followed by the brass washer, smooth side out. Another screw holds it all together. Before proceeding, make sure the enrichener lever moves smoothly.

Each breather assembly gets a flat black plastic washer, followed by the banjo bolt, and then another plastic washer. Install them into the heads using a 3/4-inch wrench. (Shim the breather assemblies as needed.)

Install the backing plate onto the face of the carb, with the new gasket in place and engaging the enrichener. Then install the hose, with the supplied clamps, and cut to fit.

The two breather bolts can now go onto the breather tubes, with a little Loctite on the threads, using a 1/4-inch Allen wrench.

The air cleaner element can now go on, followed by the chrome teardrop cover with the three supplied Philipshead screws.

Rejetting the Stock CV Carb

 Time: 1–6 hours

 Tools: Phillips screwdriver, wide flat-bladed screwdriver, short and narrow flat-bladed screwdriver, 5/16-inch wrench, drill and 1/16-inch bit, sheet-metal screw

 Talent:

 Cost: $40–90

 Parts: Tuner's kit with assorted CV carb main and slow jets

 Tip: Make only one change at a time and keep notes on what you've changed including the results

 PERFORMANCE GAIN: Eliminating poor engine performance due to too lean or too rich carb settings, with improved mileage, throttle response, and power output

COMPLEMENTARY MODIFICATION: Install a freer-flowing air cleaner, as per Projects 12 or 13, or exhaust, as per Project 22, if you haven't already

Though some mechanics try to make dialing in the stock Keihin CV carb sound very complicated, it's really not hard to do, if you know what to change and how to change it. By that, I mean you need to know what jet needs to be changed and which way you need to go with it: richer or leaner. As for how long the job will take and how much better the engine will run, that depends on how far the jetting is out when you start. It could take an hour, or the better part of a day.

If you've got a stock engine and you just swapped out the exhaust pipes and air cleaner for a set of freer-flowing ones—an excellent decision, by the way—you may be done in an hour or two by just going up a size or two on the main and slow jets. The jet's size is the number that's stamped right onto the jet. The larger the number, the bigger the jet, and the richer the fuel/air mixture will be. For example, in many cases you'll end up with a 190 or 195 main and a 48 or 50 slow jet when you have swapped out

the exhaust pipes and air cleaner for a freer-flowing set, because the stock jetting will now be too lean in most cases. (In fact, the stock slow jet will definitely be wrong, so you should start your testing with a 48 in the carb.) A lean condition can cause detonation/pinging problems, with the result being holes in the pistons and burnt valves.

When making jetting adjustments, always first get the engine at normal operating temperature before doing any testing. When you go to make a jet change, always work to the rich side first, until the jetting is too rich. Then lean the jetting out a step at a time until the engine is too lean by one jet. Then just go one richer. You'll know you've got it right when the engine responds correctly. This is safer than going lean first and possibly making the engine too lean, causing detonation and possible engine damage.

The first setting to adjust is the idle mixture circuit. Unfortunately, the idle mixture screw is sealed under an aluminum plug to prevent an owner from changing it. (You can thank the EPA for that.) If you want to remove the aluminum plug, you'll have to remove the carb from the engine. Then carefully drill a small hole in the plug, but don't go deep. After you thread a small screw into the hole you just drilled, pull out the screw—complete with plug—with a pliers. Our buddy Dr. Dyno does it a different way, with the carb still on the bike: Use a long 1/8-inch drill bit to make a hole in the right rear side of the tower that the plug is in, about 1/8 inch above the plug. You then use the blunt end of the drill to pry down on the plug and pop it out of the carb.

Now that you have access to the idle mixture screw, turn the screw all the way in until it gently bottoms out. Then turn it two and a half turns out from the fully closed (bottomed) position. You can now reinstall the carb onto the engine and start the bike. Once the engine is up to normal operating temperature, adjust the idle speed so the engine idles at 1,000 rpm. Using a short, narrow, flat-bladed screwdriver, slowly turn the idle mixture screw out until the idle drops. Then slowly turn the screw back in until the idle again drops, counting the number of quarter-turns as you go. Now turn the screw back out so it's at the halfway point between the two settings where the idle dropped, which is the midpoint between the too rich and too lean settings. (By the way, adjusting the idle mixture is the way you get rid of those annoying pops through the carb when the engine is at idle, or just off idle.)

Then readjust the idle speed, so it is again at 1,000 rpm. After you have installed the correct slow and main jets, which I'll discuss next, you should readjust this setting. In fact, you need to readjust the idle mixture and speed after every slow or main jet change. (Tip: If your engine is acting like it's too lean, swap out the main and slow jets for the next larger ones now, while you have the carb off to remove the idle mixture plug.)

Once the idle mixture is set, it's time to adjust the slow (also called the intermediate) jet, which controls the fuel/air mixture from slightly off idle to three-quarter throttle. The best way to adjust the slow jet is with the accelerator pump disconnected from the throttle wheel. This is because the accelerator pump, which pumps extra fuel into the carb when you open the throttle, can give false readings during test rides. However, when making jetting adjustments for a cruising bike, you can get by with the pump still connected if you always turn the throttle slowing during your slow jet test runs, so the effect of the accelerator pump is minimized.

When the slow jet is correct, the engine will pull strong and smooth all through the rpm range when you roll on the throttle slowly. (A stumble may be due to opening the throttle too quickly, if the accelerator pump is disconnected.) You'll know the slow jet is too small (lean) if the engine pops through the carb when you try to accelerate, pings and knocks at low rpm, has poor acceleration, surges when you're trying to hold a steady speed, or the exhaust pops excessively during deceleration. An engine that seems to take a lot longer to warm up (needs the choke on) than other Twin Cams is probably jetted too lean. If the slow jet is too large (rich), the engine will accelerate sluggishly, hesitate, or backfire through the exhaust. Also, if the throttle response is crisp when the engine's cold, but gets worse after the engine is at operating temp, the slow jet needle may be one size too rich.

When adjusting the slow jet, you may prefer a carb that is slightly on the rich side of the correct range. A *slightly* over-rich condition lets a Harley accelerate better at low rpm and low throttle settings. It will also help prevent engine ping/detonation on very hot days, as a lean-running, overheated engine will ping easier than an over-heated, richer-running one. However, you will lose some fuel economy if you run it a tad on the rich side.

The main jet, which controls the last quarter turn of the throttle, is always adjusted last. Since testing is done at full throttle, find an open stretch of road where you don't have to worry about traffic turning in front of you, or, head out to a drag strip. Better yet, use a dyno; Project 42 tells you how. Contrary to popular thought, the main jet changes will not be drastic for most engine modifications. As stated earlier, bolting up a freer-flowing air cleaner and exhaust will probably require going up one or two main jet sizes.

When running your full throttle tests, if the engine spits through the carb or dies, the main jet is too lean, while hesitation, sluggish acceleration, or backfiring through the exhaust means the main jet is too rich.

Once you think you have the slow and main jets dialed in, it's time to take a long test ride. The color of the inside of the exhaust pipes is a good indicator of jetting. Dark gray is okay, though a black pipe means the jetting is too rich. The spark plugs are also good indicators of a rich condition. Take a nice long ride at a steady speed with a fresh set of spark plugs, so the plugs can color evenly. Take it easy with the throttle, so the accelerator pump does not give you a false reading. If the plugs have black, sooty deposits on the electrodes, this is a sure sign of a too-rich

Remove the float bowl using a Phillips head screwdriver on the four bowl screws.

Replace the main jet using a flat-bladed screwdriver. Be sure to hold the brass tube it's in with a 5/16-inch wrench.

The slow jet is in the hole next to the main jet, which is removed with its emulsion tube in this photo. You'll need a narrow flat-bladed screwdriver to get to it. The idle mixture screw is alongside the float bowl (arrow), under a plug, on the outside of the carb.

After checking that the float bowl O-ring is in good shape, reinstall the float bowl using a Phillips head screwdriver.

condition. For more information on how to read plugs, as well as the proper way to get a true plug reading after you've made a jetting change, read Project 7: Choosing, Reading, and Replacing Spark Plugs. Once you know you have the slow and main jets correct, reattach the accelerator pump if you disconnected it earlier.

As for how to do the actual step-by-step process of changing the main and slow jets, you don't have to remove the carb from the engine, although I have done so to make it easier for you to see what I'm doing. Start by closing the fuel tank's petcock and running the engine to use up the fuel in the float bowl. Once the engine runs out of fuel, unscrew the four Phillips-head screws that hold on the float bowl. (There may be a little gas left in the bowl.) Then slip the accelerator boot off the float bowl housing and remove the float bowl from the carb body.

To change the main jet, unscrew the jet from the emulsion tube with a flat-bladed screwdriver. Be sure to hold the emulsion tube with a 5/16-inch wrench, so it

doesn't turn. Once the old jet is out, install the new one in the same way. Do not jam the jet into the emulsion tube. Tightening it a tad over snug is fine, like the one you just took out. As for the slow jet, you'll find it in the hole next to the main jet. You'll need a narrow flat-bladed screwdriver to change it.

Before you reinstall the float bowl, check the condition of the bowl's O-ring. If it's in good shape, reinstall the bowl. If it's in questionable condition, buy a new one. (Tip: Put a few *tiny* spots of Loctite QuickTite super glue gel into the groove to hold the new O-ring in place as you reinstall the bowl.) Now reinstall the float bowl, with the accelerator pump rod in its hole, using the four OEM Phillips-head screws. Slip the accelerator boot back over the float bowl housing with your finger. After you open the petcock and check for fuel leaks, start the engine and let it get up to operating temperature. Then readjust the idle mixture and speed. You can then take the bike out for a test ride to see if the jet change you made was correct, or if you need to make another.

PROJECT 15

Installing a Dynojet Thunderslide Kit

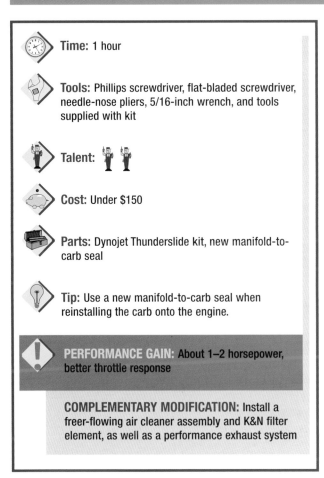

Time: 1 hour

Tools: Phillips screwdriver, flat-bladed screwdriver, needle-nose pliers, 5/16-inch wrench, and tools supplied with kit

Talent: 🥜🥜

Cost: Under $150

Parts: Dynojet Thunderslide kit, new manifold-to-carb seal

Tip: Use a new manifold-to-carb seal when reinstalling the carb onto the engine.

PERFORMANCE GAIN: About 1–2 horsepower, better throttle response

COMPLEMENTARY MODIFICATION: Install a freer-flowing air cleaner assembly and K&N filter element, as well as a performance exhaust system

There are many reputable companies around that will modify a stock CV carb, so it can properly meet the demands of a worked engine, whether it's a stock displacement Twin Cam or one that has been punched out to 95 inches. However, there's also a do-it-yourself carb upgrade kit for stock or mildly modified engines that will reap you a little horsepower, as well as quicker throttle response. The kit is called the Thunderslide and Dynojet, the same company that makes the dynos used to check an engine's horsepower and torque, makes it. This kit is simple to install and comes with all the parts you need to do the job, including any special tools.

The carb must be removed from the engine to install the kit. Start disassembling the carb by backing off the idle speed screw (count the turns), so the throttle assembly is no longer under spring pressure, which will make it easier to remove. Four Phillips-head screws are all that hold the carb's top cover on. (Note that one screw also holds the throttle assembly and has a metal collar. Don't lose this collar.) Once the cover's off, pull out the top spring, which

is not attached to anything in the carb. You can now remove the diaphragm and slide assembly, which has the needle and needle retainer inside it. Drop the needle retainer, which is also called a spider, out from the bore of the slider. Then remove the needle from the slide.

Flip the carb over and remove the float bowl by unscrewing the four Phillips-head screws. Slip the accelerator boot off the float bowl housing and remove the float bowl from the carb body. Loosen the main jet in the emulsion tube with a flat-bladed screwdriver and remove the stock emulsion tube with a 5/16-inch wrench. Install the new Thunderslide emulsion tube using the flat-bladed screwdriver, followed by the new main jet and slow jet, as per the kit's instructions.

Before you reinstall the float bowl, remove the plug that covers the idle mixture screw using the 5/32-inch drill bit and screw supplied in the Dynojet kit. Then turn the idle mixture screw in until it *lightly* bottoms out. Then back it out three and a half turns. Now reinstall the float bowl using the four OEM Phillips-head screws. Slip the accelerator boot back over the float bowl housing with your finger.

Back at the other end of the carb, remove the diaphragm from the stock slide by just pulling it off and over the lip on the slide. This is best done when the diaphragm is dry. (Note: If you put even a tiny hole in the diaphragm, get a new one. The carb will not work right if any air can leak through the diaphragm.) Snap the large Dynojet slide retainer onto the new black plastic Dynojet slide, with the radial grooves facing up. Center the stock diaphragm onto the new slide retainer and snap the other new retainer, with the radial grooves facing down, onto the slide. The diaphragm should curl up when you are done.

Install the E-clip onto the Dynojet needle's #4 groove, counting from the top, using needle-nose pliers. The needle spacer goes onto the top of the needle, with the beveled end facing up into the needle retainer (spider). Drop the Dynojet needle and needle spacer/needle retainer assembly into the slide. Position the retainer so its feet do not cover the holes in the slide. Now drop the diaphragm/slide assembly into the carb body. Position the needle so it slides into its hole in the bottom of the carb's throat. You can now drop in the slide spring that comes with the Dynojet kit. (Don't reuse the stock spring.) Reinstall the top cover using three of the stock Phillips-head screws. Then reinstall the throttle assembly using the metal sleeve and the last top screw.

Put the idle speed screw back where it was when you started (remember counting the turns?) and readjust as needed once you finish reassembling the bike and fire off the engine.

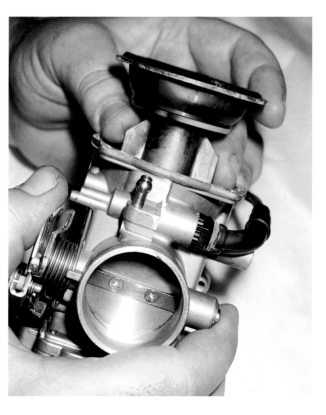

After removing the four Philips screws and top cover, gently pull the diaphragm and slide assembly, which has the needle and needle retainer inside it, from the carb body.

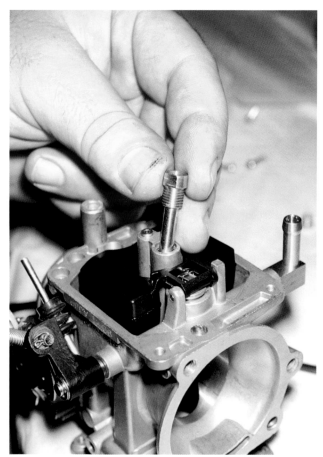

Remove the four Philips screws and float bowl. Remove the stock main jet and emulsion tube with a 5/16-inch wrench. Then install the new Dynojet emulsion tube.

Install the new main and slow jets, as per the Dynojet instructions using a flat-bladed screwdriver.

Snap the large Dynojet retainer onto the Dynojet slide, with the grooves facing up. After centering the stock diaphragm onto the new slide retainer, snap on the other new retainer, with the grooves facing down.

After you remove the plug that covers the idle mixture screw (using the drill bit and screw supplied in the kit), turn the mixture screw in until it *lightly* bottoms out. Then back it out 3-1/2 turns.

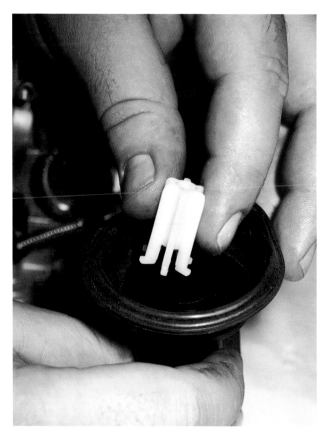

After dropping the Dynojet needle into the slide, position the needle spacer/needle retainer assembly in the slide so its feet do not cover the slide's holes. Then install the slide assembly into the carb body.

PROJECT 16

Installing an S&S Super E/G Carburetor

 Time: 30 minutes

 Tools: Flat-bladed screwdriver, ball-end 5/16-inch Allen wrench, two 3/8-inch open end wrenches

 Talent:

 Cost: $250

 Parts: S&S Super carb kit for Twin Cam

 Tip: Be sure to jet the carb to match your engine's present configuration.

 PERFORMANCE GAIN: About 4–6 horsepower, depending on the engine's other performance upgrades

COMPLEMENTARY MODIFICATION: Works best when part of a combination of performance upgrades, like high performance air cleaner, manifold, and exhaust system

The Super E and G, like all S&S carbs, are butterfly types, which means there's a plate in the throat of the carb—controlled by the throttle cables—that regulates airflow through the carb and into the engine. These carbs have fully adjustable idle speed and idle mixture settings, as well as changeable intermediate (off-idle response and low- to midrange) and main (midrange to high-speed) jets. These jets allow a tuner to properly adjust all fuel settings to suit the engine's particular needs. Both carbs also have an adjustable accelerator pump, which provides great throttle response at any rpm.

For easier starts, both the E and G come with an enrichment device instead of a choke. This leaves the bore of the carb unobstructed for better airflow characteristics. To activate the enrichment device, simply lift up on the enrichment lever that's connected to the S&S air cleaner's backing plate (see Project 13).

The E and G's throttle wheel and cable bracket accept stock H-D 1981 and later Big Twin two-cable throttle

If you're going to use the stock throttle cables, you must install the S&S-supplied special cable holder, which is held on by one screw, onto the carb.

First offered in late 1990, S&S Super E and G Shorty carburetors were developed specifically for use on Big Twins and Sportsters and are now the most widely used carbs in the world. The Super E and G are called Shorty carbs because the installed length is the same as a stock carb's, unlike the longer Super B and D. This allows for greater legroom and a more comfortable riding position.

The Super E and G are identical, except for throat and venturi sizes, and have an E or G stamped into the throttle side of the carb. The Super E has a 1 7/8-inch (47.6-mm) throat (measured at the butterfly) and a 1 9/16-inch (39.6-mm) venturi. The E is recommended for any displacement Big Twin or Sportster engine, with or without performance upgrades. The Super G has a 2 1/16-inch (52.3-mm) throat and a 1 3/4-inch (44.5 mm) venturi. The G should only be used on engines 88 cubic inches or larger, with high performance upgrades such as ported heads, hot cams, and a performance air cleaner, intake manifold, and exhaust system.

setups, so the E and G (with an S&S manifold) can be bolted to your stock H-D without cable changes. However, be sure to state that you are using the carb on a Twin Cam. This way, S&S can supply the correct cable holder with your carb.

The Super E or G can be bought separately, or as part of a complete kit, which consists of a matching manifold, spacer block, teardrop air cleaner, and all needed hardware, hoses, extra jets, etc.

Installation

To install a Super E or G onto your engine, turn the fuel petcock off. Then completely remove the stock air cleaner, carb, and intake manifold. After installing a new S&S manifold, as per Project 17, install the carb by first slipping the two S&S-supplied Allen bolts into the manifold from the left side. If you're going to use the stock carb cables, you then need to install the S&S-supplied special cable holder, which is held on by one screw, onto the carb.

The next part on is the spacer block, which goes on with its O-ring facing the manifold. The carb, which also has an O-ring on it to seal it to the spacer block, can now get bolted to the manifold using a ball-end 5/16-inch Allen wrench.

Install the drain hose onto the fitting on the lower right side of the carb. Route the hose to the front of the engine in a way that will prevent it from getting burned by the hot exhaust pipes while still allowing fuel to drop harmlessly to the ground if the float bowl overfills. Then attach the stock cables to the S&S cable holder and throttle wheel, which is on the left side of the Super E or G. Now adjust the throttle cables as per the H-D service manual. Be sure to check that the throttle snaps fully closed free and clean once you're done adjusting the cables. Attaching the S&S-supplied fuel line with the black heat shield finishes the carb install. After turning on the petcock and checking for fuel leaks, install the air cleaner. You're then ready to dial-in the carb's jetting, as per the carb's supplied instructions. Be sure to also check out the accompanying Tuning Tips sidebar.

The carb can now get bolted to the manifold. The carb also has an O-ring on it to seal it to the spacer block. Tighten the carb bolts using a ball-end 5/16-inch Allen wrench.

After installing the S&S manifold, as per Project 17, slip the two S&S Allen bolts into the manifold. Then position the spacer block, with its O-ring facing the manifold, onto the bolts.

Tuning Tips

Though tuning instructions are included with every Super E and G, here are a few helpful tips to help you dial in your carb.

Always tune a carb when the engine is at normal operating temperature.

Always go richer until the jetting is too rich; then lean the jetting until the engine responds correctly. Going to the lean side first may make the engine very lean, causing detonation/knock problems and possible engine damage.

Always start a tuning session by adjusting the idle mixture and then the idle speed (1,000-1,100 rpm). Putting the idle mixture screw at one and one-half turns out from gently seated is a good starting point.

Where the idle mixture screw ends up once you're done dialing it in can give you a clue as to whether the intermediate jet, the next jet you need to adjust, is too rich or too lean. If the idle mixture screw is turned out more than one and three-quarters turns, the intermediate jet is too small (lean). However, if the idle mixture screw is less than one turn out, the intermediate jet is too large (rich).

Always readjust the idle mixture screw and then the idle speed every time you make an intermediate or main jet change.

All intermediate jet tests should be done with the accelerator pump turned all the way down (off) because the accelerator pump can give you false indications during your test runs. You can turn the pump off by turning the accelerator pump's adjusting screw all the way in (clockwise) until it touches the pump's arm. Be sure to count the exact number of turns, so you can put it back to the same spot when you're done with your jetting adjustments.

When the intermediate jet is correct, and the accelerator pump is off, the engine will accelerate smoothly when you roll on the throttle. If the intermediate jet is too small (lean), the engine will spit through the carb. If it's too large (rich), it will backfire through the exhaust, accelerate sluggishly, or hesitate. A slightly lean intermediate jet will give the best gas mileage, while a slightly rich one will give the best acceleration. Once the intermediate jet is dialed in correctly, you can put the accelerator pump back to its original setting.

Always adjust the main jet last. Testing is done at full throttle, so pick an open stretch of road or a drag strip where you've got lots of room to play. If the engine cuts out or spits through the carb, the main jet is too lean, so go up two jets. If the engine hesitates, backfires through the exhaust, or accelerates sluggishly, the jetting is too rich. Drop it down two jets. Then readjust the idle mixture and speed, and test again.

The fuel line, drain hose, and stock cables can now be attached to the carb. Then open the petcock and check for fuel leaks.

PROJECT 17

Installing a Performance Intake Manifold

 Time: 1–2 hours

 Tools: 1/4-inch Allen wrench

 Talent:

 Cost: Under $100

 Parts: Intake manifold, intake manifold seals, carb-to-manifold seal

 Tip: An aftermarket performance carb usually comes with its own performance manifold, so check before you buy one.

 PERFORMANCE GAIN: 1–2 horsepower

COMPLEMENTARY MODIFICATION: If you're having the heads ported, send the manifold with the heads, so it can be matched to the new intake ports

Your engine's intake manifold is much more than just something to which the carb is bolted. It's really an extension of each head's intake port and as such, should smoothly blend the exit end of the carb to the opening of each head's intake port. In fact, when you install onto your engine a performance carb with a larger bore, a matching performance manifold should also be installed as part of the upgrade for a number of reasons. First, a matching manifold will not have ridges or steps at the transition points from carb to manifold to head. Second, in most cases, the volume of the stock manifold is not large enough to make full use of the larger carb you just bolted up. Third, most performance manifolds have gentler radiuses on the inside corners than the stock manifold for better airflow characteristics. In fact, these three reasons are why the stock manifold would probably hinder that new carb you just bolted on, not help it.

In fact, if you're having the heads ported, send the manifold along with the heads and have it flowed and ported to match the new intake ports. This way, you'll have a smooth transition from the manifold to the newly redesigned intake ports for maximum airflow. After all, the name of the game in the intake system is laminar flow and anything that can cause turbulence there should be rectified as much as possible.

Thankfully, most performance carbs come with a matching manifold, so here's how to install one, using an

After threading the two 1/4-inch Allen bolts on the left side of the heads in a couple of turns, push the S&S manifold into place on the head, so the flanges engage the bolts and the seals fit snugly into the intake ports.

S&S unit as our model. With the stock air cleaner, carb, and manifold removed from the engine, start the installation by swapping the stock MAP sensor over to the new manifold using the stock hardware. Then swap over the stock mounting flanges from the old manifold to the new S&S one, and be sure to install new seals. (The front flange is marked with an F, while the rear has an R. Don't mix them up.)

To connect the new manifold to the heads, thread the two bolts on the left side of the heads in a couple of turns. Push the manifold into place on the heads, so the flanges engage the bolts and the seals fit snugly into the intake ports. Then install the other two bolts onto the right side of the heads. Now, stick your finger into the manifold and make sure it meets both intake ports cleanly, with no ridge or step. Then tighten all four bolts to 8–12 foot-pounds with a 1/4-inch Allen wrench. As for that black cap on the fitting on the right side of the S&S manifold, it's for a VOES hose. You're not using a VOES on a Twin Cam, so leave the cap where it is, or you'll have a very unwanted air leak.

This S&S manifold seals to an S&S carb via an O-ring on the carburetor. However, a Screamin' Eagle manifold needs a carb-to-manifold seal installed before the carb can go onto the manifold. Be sure to check the instruction sheet for your carb/manifold setup to find out where the carb-to-manifold seal goes on your installation.

Then install the other two bolts. After making sure the manifold joins with both intake ports cleanly, with no ridge or step on the inside, tighten all four bolts to 8–12 ft-lbs.

The S&S manifold is now ready for the carb. By the way, the black cap on the fitting to the right is for a VOES hose, which you're not using, so leave it alone.

Replacing the OEM Vacuum-Operated Petcock

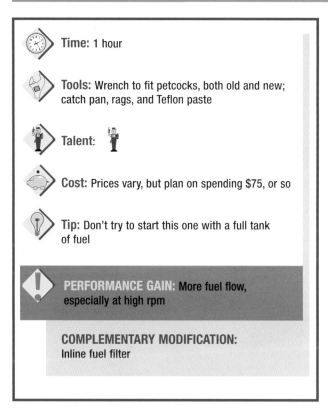

Time: 1 hour

Tools: Wrench to fit petcocks, both old and new; catch pan, rags, and Teflon paste

Talent:

Cost: Prices vary, but plan on spending $75, or so

Tip: Don't try to start this one with a full tank of fuel

PERFORMANCE GAIN: More fuel flow, especially at high rpm

COMPLEMENTARY MODIFICATION: Inline fuel filter

Like many manufacturers, Harley-Davidson uses a vacuum-operated petcock to control fuel delivery on their carbureted models. Vacuum petcocks work on demand, meaning you'll never need to turn them on or off (although the factory does recommend using them much like a manual petcock, which to my mind defeats their purpose). By and large, vacuum-operated petcocks are a good thing. Since fuel won't flow unless vacuum is applied to the petcock diaphragm the chances are remote of walking into the garage some morning only to see your Twin Cam floating in a sea of gasoline because you forgot to shut the petcock off the night before. On the downside, the stock vacuum-operated petcocks don't flow enough fuel, especially at high rpm, to satisfy the needs of many modified engines.

There are three reasons to consider replacing the OEM petcock with a manual one. First of course would be a failure of the OEM. Admittedly, few of them fail, but if for some reason yours does and the bike is past warranty, a manual petcock is a reasonable alternative. Second, fuel flow; if you plan on building a hot rod, especially one with a big-inch motor, you're going to need all the fuel you can get. Many aftermarket petcocks double or even triple the flow rate of the stocker. Last but never least is appearance;

let's be honest, the stock petcock is a utilitarian hunk of gray pot-metal. The aftermarket ones are by and large nicely made and shiny as all get out. Whose bike couldn't use just a bit more eye candy?

Replacing the petcock is as straightforward as you'd expect it to be. Start by running the fuel down as low as practical. Drain the remainder of the fuel into an approved container, and no, an empty bucket isn't an approved container. You can drain the fuel by either applying a bit of vacuum to the valve with a pump or, by unscrewing the valve partway and letting it drain into your catch can. As you'd expect, the smoking lamp should always be out when working around fuel.

Once the dripping has concluded, remove the valve from the tank and compare it to your chosen replacement. The fuel delivery pipe should face the same way and the threads should be identical to the threads on the valve you've just removed, although some aftermarket items may use a different thread and adapter nut to make it all work. Apply a dab of Teflon paste or a wrap of Teflon tape if you're a traditionalist to the threads of the petcock and tank. Run the union nut onto the petcock and then install the new petcock to the tank. Hand tighten it, and then snug it up with a wrench. You don't have to apply a ton of pressure here, just enough to keep the thing from leaking. Remember to cap off the vacuum port; you can find a rubber cap intended for that purpose at any auto parts store.

After draining the fuel, remove the stock petcock.

Reconnect your fuel line and you're good to go. Don't forget that from now on you'll have to turn the petcock on when you start the bike and turn it off anytime it sits for more than a few minutes. Just as you did in the days before vacuum-operated petcocks, which kind of brings us full circle, doesn't it?

In comparison to the old valve, make sure the fuel delivery pipe faces the same direction and that the threads line up correctly. Add a dab of Teflon paste or tape to the new threads before installation.

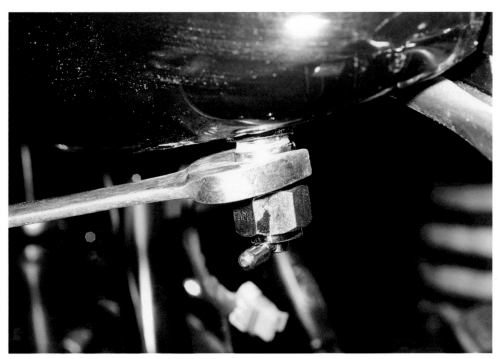

The new petcock should be snug and tight. Reconnect the fuel line, cap off the vacuum port, and you're done. Just remember to shut it off after riding.

Understanding the Twin Cam EFI System

 Time: None

 Tools: None

 Talent:

 Cost: None

 Parts: None

 Tip: If you plan on building a custom Twin Cam, you must use a wire harness that takes into consideration the TC 88 engine management system.

 PERFORMANCE GAIN: You should know how the engine's EFI system works if you plan on making high-performance modifications

COMPLEMENTARY MODIFICATION:
Using performance parts that are not included in an H-D Stage I or II kit will require additional ECM calibration; see Projects 20 and 21 for more information

Though all present Twin Cam 88 and 88B models are equipped with the single-throat Delphi electronic fuel injection system, pre-2002 rubber-mounted TC 88 models were fitted with the dual-throat Magneti Marelli EFI. These two systems are similar in most respects, with some of the sensors and the style of induction module being the main differences. To help you understand how these two EFI systems work, we'll first discuss both types of induction modules, which is the part in an EFI-equipped bike that takes the place of a carburetor, and then cover the different sensors.

The induction module, or throttle body, is the device that controls the flow of outside air into the combustion chamber and mixes this air with fuel. This unit occupies the location behind the air cleaner where normally the carburetor and intake manifold would be. The single-throat, two-piece Delphi unit, which consists of a throttle body and intake manifold, is similar to a carb in that the intake manifold bolts to the heads and the throttle body bolts to

the intake manifold. The dual-throat Magneti Marelli unit also bolts to both cylinder heads, just like an intake manifold on a carbureted bike, but this module is one piece with no separate throttle body or intake manifold.

Both types of induction modules regulate the amount of air that enters the combustion chambers the same way a carburetor does, with throttle (butterfly) plates actuated by the throttle cables. However, instead of having a float bowl and jet/needle metering system to control the delivery of fuel into the incoming airstream, both modules have two injectors that spray fuel into the intake tract. These fuel injectors are mounted after the butterfly plates (or *butterflies*) and before the module bolts to the cylinder heads. And although the butterflies control airflow through the induction module, a device called the Electronic Control Module (ECM) controls the amount of fuel that gets delivered to the engine. The ECM on an EFI-equipped engine also controls the engine's ignition timing, which is when the spark plugs fire to ignite the fuel/air mixture in the engine's combustion chambers.

The ECM is a solid state, sealed unit that is mounted under the bike's seat, or one of the side panels, depending on the model. It's the ECM that opens the fuel injectors, which are electrically operated solenoid switches. The fraction of a second (actually, milliseconds) that an injector is opened so it can spray the appropriate amount of fuel into the intake system, is called the injector's *pulse width*. The fuel supplied to the injectors comes from a fuel pump, via a fuel regulator, at a specific pressure—43.5 psi for the Magneti Marelli system and 55–62 psi for the Delphi. This fuel pump is located inside the fuel tank.

The ECM is loaded with reference tables (like an old multiplication table, only much more intricate), called maps, that tell it how long to open the injectors for a specific set of conditions. For example, if the engine is at operating temperature, spinning at 3,500 rpm, at 3,000 feet above sea level, on an 80-degree-F day, with the throttle opened 50 percent, the ECM will reference the tables of data that are stored in its memory (at the factory) and find out what pulse width to use for this specific set of conditions. And if the throttle is closed to quarter throttle, or any of the other conditions change, so do the tables that the ECM references, which changes the injector's pulse width. This self-adjusting sequence happens in nanoseconds. The ECM constantly readjusts the amount of fuel injected into the intake system based on the information sent to it by an array of electronic sensors located at various places around the engine and chassis.

EFI Sensors

BAS: bank angle sensor
BARO: barometric pressure sensor
CMP: camshaft position sensor
CKP: crank position sensor
ET: engine temperature sensor
IAT: intake air temperature sensor
MAP: manifold absolute pressure sensor
TP: throttle position sensor
TSM: turn signal module
TSSM: turn signal security module
VSS: vehicle speed sensor

As mentioned earlier, most of the sensors used by the Magneti Marelli and Delphi systems are the same, but there are some differences. The Magneti Marelli system uses three primary sensors. These are the crank position sensor (CKP), throttle position sensor (TP), and camshaft position sensor (CMP). The secondary sensors, which are used to fine-tune the system, are the engine temperature sensor (ET), intake air temperature sensor (IAT), and barometric pressure sensor (BARO).

This is the dual-throat Magneti-Marelli module that's used on all pre-2002 rubber-mounted engines. The two red plastic devices on the top right of the module are the fuel injectors.

Note the TP throttle position sensor (A), the MAP manifold pressure sensor (B), and the IAT Intake Air Temperature sensor (C) on this single-throat, Delphi induction module.

As for the Delphi system, it uses only the CKP and manifold absolute pressure sensor (MAP) as its primary sources of information. The IAT, engine temperature (ET), and TP sensors are secondary sensors. These secondary information gatherers help the ECM finely adjust the amount of fuel delivered, just as the secondary sensors do for the Magneti Marelli unit. The Delphi system also uses a Vehicle Speed Sensor (VSS) that tells the ECM whether the bike is moving or not, which helps the ECM set the engine's idle speed.

Let's go over the sensors, starting with the Magneti Marelli system's three primary sensors since it was first used on Twin Cams, then we'll do the same for the Delphi. The CKP sensor is located on the front left side of the engine's crankcase. This magnetic sensor, which generates an AC signal that it sends to the ECM, reads the 30 teeth that are cut into the engine's left flywheel. There are also two teeth missing from the flywheels, which act as a reference point for top dead center (TDC). The CKP sensor determines engine speed rpm and the position of the flywheels for the ECM.

The TP sensor, which is mounted on the left side of the throttle body if looking at the right side of the engine, measures if the rider has opened or closed the throttle, how fast he has done it, and how much.

The CMP sensor, which is only found on the Magneti Marelli system, is mounted on the cam cover, under the ignition cover. The CMP sensor tells the ECM the engine's phase by sensing when the Quantum Hall Effect ridge—which is the raised section that goes halfway around the face of the rear camshaft sprocket—is passing by it.

As for the Delphi system, one of its two primary sensors is the CKP sensor used by the Magneti Marelli unit. However, the Delphi relies on a MAP sensor for its other primary sensor instead of using the TP sensor and the CMP as on the Magneti Marelli system. The MAP sensor, which is located on the top of the intake manifold, measures the pressure inside the manifold.

The camshaft position sensor (CMP) is only found on the Magneti-Marelli system. It lives on the cam cover, under the ignition cover. The CMP senses when the ridge on the rear camshaft sprocket passes by it.

The Magneti Marelli unit's secondary sensor is the ET sensor, which (you guessed it) measures engine temperature. The ET is located in a well that's machined into the front cylinder head, near where the induction module/intake manifold attaches. The ECM uses the ET's information during the engine warm-up to set the idle speed. The engine's temperature is also used to determine how much fuel the injectors will deliver at different throttle settings and conditions.

The IAT sensor is mounted on the left side of the throttle body, near the throttle position (TP) sensor. The IAT measures the temperature of the air entering the intake system. The ECM uses this info, as well as data from the BARO sensor, to determine air density, which changes with altitude and weather conditions. This helps the ECM set the injectors' pulse width during cold start and warming up periods.

The BARO sensor, which is mounted right next to the ECM, helps the ECM compensate for altitude changes by monitoring ambient atmospheric pressure.

On the Delphi, the ET sensor and IAT sensor are also used as secondary sensors. The TP sensor, however, is a secondary input on the Delphi, not a primary sensor like on the Magneti Marelli system.

And though it is not used to compute fuel delivery to the engine, there is another sensor in a Twin Cam's ECM engine management system: the bank angle sensor (BAS). The BAS is located under the left side cover on Magneti Marelli–style bikes, and is part of either the Turn Signal Module (TSM) or Turn Signal Security Module (TSSM), which is an optional, factory-installed unit, on Delphi bikes. If the motorcycle is tilted more than 45 degrees on Delphi bikes or 55 degrees on Magneti Marelli machines, which is what occurs when the bike falls over, the bank angle sensor trips and kills the engine by shutting down the engine's ignition system. To reset the bank angle sensor, simply lift the bike back up and turn off the ignition for at least 10 seconds. Then turn the ignition back on and fire off the engine.

To help control the amount of heat that the engine puts out on a hot day, all 2002 and later EFI bikes also have a three-part engine temperature control strategy. This system senses the rear cylinder head's temperature and if it hits 338 degrees when the bike is in motion, this system will lower the engine's operating temperature by enriching the fuel mixture. When the bike is stopped and idling, or is rolling along at a very slow speed for a long time, this system modifies fuel delivery when the engine temperatures reach 356 degrees. If the engine's temperature goes above 374 degrees, engine idle speed is dropped by 100 rpm. (Actually, the ECM starts making tiny idle speed adjustments once the engine hits 320 degrees.)

The engine management system also has an Ion Sensing system, which detects detonation or a misfire in either cylinder. If trouble is detected for two or three spark plug firings, the system retards the ignition timing as needed to stop the problem.

Both of these systems work well—though the Delphi works much better than the Magneti Marelli—as long as you stay with the stock components. If you change anything that will affect the engine, like a freer-flowing air cleaner or exhaust system, hotter cams, etc., the stock fuel maps contained in the ECM will not be correct for the new engine configuration. The engine will run too lean, which can cause major engine damage. Once engine modifications have been made, the EFI system must be recalibrated to handle the changes in the engine's fuel requirements.

If you are installing an H-D Stage I or Stage II package, and use only the supplied parts, the ECM recalibration kit for that particular Stage kit should properly adjust fuel delivery to prevent the engine from running too lean and causing engine damage. However, if you use parts other than those supplied in these kits, you will have to use either an H-D Screamin' Eagle EFI Race Tuner or an aftermarket EFI tuning module to properly dial-in the engine's fuel requirements (see Projects 20 and 21). Also, many large displacement engine companies, like S&S or Zipper's, also offer tunable EFI systems with their engines. These engines and EFI modules bolt right into the stock H-D chassis and can be tuned to cover a wide range of engine fuel requirements.

The crank position sensor (CKP) is located on the front left side of the engine's crankcase. This sensor reads the teeth cut into the engine's left flywheel to determine engine rpm and flywheel position.

The engine temperature sensor (ET) is located in a well that's machined into the front cylinder head, near where the induction module/intake manifold attaches to the engine.

Installing a Screamin' Eagle EFI Race Tuner

 Time: 1–2 hours, in most cases

 Tools: A computer (a laptop is best) using either a Windows 95/98/2000/ME or NT 4.0 operating system, equipped with a serial or USB port, and a CD drive, with a minimum of 32 Mg of RAM and 10 Mg of available hard drive space

 Talent:

 Cost: $460

 Parts: Screamin' Eagle EFI Race Tuner System

 Tip: As you modify tuning files, also make a log that chronicles what files you've modified and why

 PERFORMANCE GAIN: Anywhere from 1 to 10 horsepower, depending on how well the bike was previously tuned

COMPLEMENTARY MODIFICATION: Any performance-orientated engine modification you feel like making

In Project 21, Installing and Adjusting the Power Commander IIIr, I explain why an owner must reset (tune) the fuel and air mixture on their bike's EFI system after performance modifications have been made to the engine. These performance upgrades include changes made to the exhaust or intake system, installing performance camshafts, compression and/or displacement increases, or any other engine component modifications that will affect the fuel/air mixture requirements of the engine. Failure to do so will probably result in an engine that's running too lean. (If many changes are made, the engine may not run at all.) An excessively lean engine will allow a detonation/engine knock condition to exist, which will cause engine component damage if not corrected.

And though a Dynojet Power Commander IIIr (PC IIIr) is fully able to adjust H-D's EFI system so the engine will operate correctly—if a balanced package of performance components is used—some people prefer to have only

Harley-Davidson parts on their bikes. To that end, H-D now offers its own fully adjustable, EFI tuning setup, the Screamin' Eagle EFI Race Tuner System, for owners of Delphi-equipped bikes. Prior to this kit, the only options Harley offered were its Stage I and II recalibration chips, which didn't always do the trick, even when only the specified SE parts were used in the engine's performance upgrade.

One great feature of the Screamin' Eagle Tuner System is that the only change made to the bike, other than the performance parts you've bolted up, is the recalibration of the stock EFI module, also called the ECM. There are no other modules or parts that must be permanently bolted to the bike to adjust the EFI settings. The stock EFI system uses the same parts it came with. The only change is to the ECM's internal information. This SE tuning system can be used to make both fuel and ignition timing adjustments, just like the many aftermarket systems presently available. However, this SE system can also act as an engine data acquisition tool that a racer can use to make specific adjustments to several different tuning tables/maps inside the ECM.

The Screamin' Eagle EFI Race Tuner System comes with a CD containing the Basic and Advanced Tuning Mode programs, a Data Mode program, and whatever Screamin' Eagle EFI calibrations are available for Delphi-equipped bikes when you buy the kit. The kit also comes with a User's Manual, computer interface module, a special cable to connect the computer module to the data connector on the bike, and a nine-pin, male-to-female serial port to connect the computer interface to your computer.

Uploading the New Maps

Once you've modified the stock fuel and/or ignition-timing tables/maps as you want using a computer and the Race Tuner software, downloading them into the stock ECM is an easy procedure. Simply have the bike's ignition turned off. Then plug the SE EFI Race Tuner's four-pin data cable into the four-pin data connector—which is the same one the dealership uses to hook up a Scanalizer to check the bike's systems—and tighten the two thumbscrews. Now plug the nine-pin end of the Tuner's data cable, which is the female one, into the supplied interface module and tighten those thumbscrews. The kit comes with a nine-pin serial cable, too. Plug this cable's male end into the interface module and, again, tighten the thumbscrews. Plugging the nine-pin serial cable's female end into your computer's serial port and tightening the thumbscrews finishes the hook-up. With the Race Tuner program

INTAKE AND EXHAUST

running on the computer and ready to upload the new tables/maps, you can now turn on the bike's ignition. (Do not start the engine.) After waiting at least 10 seconds for the ECM's programming lockout interval to elapse, click on the Program ECM box to start the process of reprogramming the bike's ECM. This takes a minute or two to do, so be sure not to interrupt this process or the ECM will get reprogrammed with unusable data. Result: Your engine won't start. Once the reprogramming process is done, turn the bike's ignition off, and disconnect the cables and interface module. After waiting at least 10 seconds, you can start the bike and see if the new tables/maps you just loaded into the ECM make the engine run the way you want.

Two Tuning Modes

The Screamin' Eagle EFI Race Tuner System has two different tuning modes. The first and easiest is the Basic Tuning Mode, which is for simple tuning tasks. If you've never tuned an EFI system before, this is the mode you should use. Basic gives you two tuning tables. The first is the Main Fuel Table, which allows you to adjust the ECM's air/fuel ratio (AFR as the Tuner's manual calls it), for the front and rear cylinders at the same time. The other is the Main Spark Table, which is used to adjust the ignition system's spark advance for both the front and rear cylinders. The tuner can also adjust other ECM settings, like engine displacement, fuel injector rate, turn the knock sensor off, and set the engine's rpm limit. (Note: When resetting the

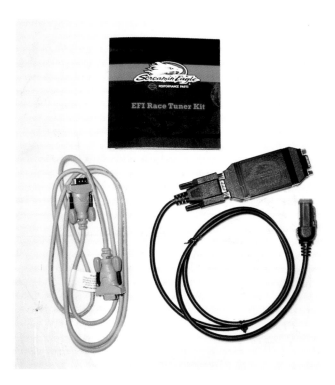

Here's what comes in the Screamin' Eagle EFI Race Tuner System: The software CD, a User's Manual, computer interface module, a module-to-bike cable, and a nine-pin module-to-computer cable.

ignition's rev limiter, don't set it higher than 6,200 rpm if you're still using the stock valve springs, or if you have a Twin Cam B engine, even if you installed a performance valve spring kit.)

The Advanced Tuning Mode, which is the other tuning option, is for experienced tuners only. This one allows you to access nine of the ECM's tables and settings. The first is the air/fuel ratio, which is used to simultaneously adjust the ECM's AFR target value for both the front and rear cylinders. The second and third tables are for the volumetric efficiency (VE) values for the front and rear cylinders, respectively. These two allow you to individually adjust the fuel/air mixture for each cylinder. If you increase the value of a VE cell it tells the ECM that more air is entering that cylinder's combustion chamber (either front or rear, depending on what tables you are altering) at the rpm and throttle position for that cell. If the ECM is told that more air is present, it figures this in and increases the amount of fuel to achieve the AFR value required for that cell, which enriches the fuel mixture for that throttle position and rpm. This is just the thing to get rid of a too-lean condition, such as popping through the intake, at a specific rpm. The reverse is also true, so if you need to get rid of a blubbering problem due to a too-rich mixture condition just reduce the required VE cell values to make the ECM think there's less air, so it leans out the mixture at those settings.

The fourth and fifth tables allow you to readjust the spark advance timing settings for the front and rear cylinders, respectively. You can even mess with the Warmup Enrichment settings, which are used to adjust the amount of extra fuel the ECM sends to the engine while it's warming up, as well as the Cranking Fuel tables that adjust the amount of extra fuel needed to start the engine.

The last two of the nine tables you can adjust are the Idle RPM (speed), which sets the speed at which the engine idles during warmup or when at operating temperature, and the IAC Warmup Steps. This one is for adjusting the IAC settings, which assists the idle control as the engine is warming up.

Because the Advanced Mode gives the tuner lots of flexibility regarding the range of adjustment for the tables/maps, the SE Racer Tuner System has preset tuning limits in the software to keep you from making setting changes that may damage the engine. The tuner can see what cells have been blocked out when checking the Look-up tables. The green colored cells indicate that the settings cannot be adjusted lower, while red colored cells indicate that the setting cannot be adjusted higher.

Three Tuning Options

H-D has divided its tuning guide into three different environment sections and gives you solid information on how to use the Race Tuner system to dial in your engine. They are EFI tuning with basic tuning mode by feel on closed-course track; EFI tuning with advanced tuning mode and data mode on closed-course track; and EFI tuning with advanced tuning mode, a chassis dynamometer and an AFR meter. This allows you to pick the format you want and just follow the guidelines listed in that section. You don't have to jump around the book, cobbling together instructions to get the job done.

Each tuning section contains the information you'll need listed under headings that are questions such as How would I adjust the AFR? or How would I adjust spark timing? Each section also tells you how to test the engine's performance two different ways, both of which need to be checked. The first is how the engine performs with the throttle held at a steady setting under a light load and cruising in first, third, and fifth gears at various engine rpm settings. The other is how it performs at full throttle under a heavy load doing roll-on acceleration runs in second, third, or fourth gear. Each of these runs is started at 2,000 rpm and brought up to the engine's redline.

As you can see, the Screamin' Eagle EFI Race Tuner System is very thorough and, once you start using it, you'll

also see it's well designed. However, the Advanced Mode is pretty involved, especially if you start messing with everything. Just remember to save old tables on the laptop with notes on what it is, and then make new ones. This way, if the changes you made to the tables on a new file make the engine run like garbage, the old file is still saved on the computer, so you can just load it back in and start anew.

Once the software is loaded onto your computer, you can alter the ECM's tables and then download them into your bike's existing ECM. There's no need to change the ECM or add another electronic device to it.

After connecting together the data cable, interface module, and serial cable to your computer's serial port, plug the data cable into the bike's four-pin data connector, which is the same one used for a Scanalizer.

PROJECT 21

Installing and Adjusting the Power Commander IIIr

 Time: Under 1 hour

 Tools: 3/16-inch Allen, flat-bladed screwdriver, wire cutters, 3/8-inch socket, needle-nose pliers, 5/32-inch Allen, heat gun

 Talent:

 Cost: $350

 Parts: Power Commander IIIr, Velcro

 Tip: The PC IIIr can be used on stock bikes, as well as those with performance modifications, to correct fuel mixture–related problems.

 PERFORMANCE GAIN: Anywhere from 1 to 10 horsepower, depending on how well the bike was previously tuned

COMPLEMENTARY MODIFICATION: Any performance-orientated engine modification you feel like making

B ack when all Harleys were equipped with a carburetor, making performance changes to the engine involved proper part installation and re-jetting the carb, so the fuel/air mixture was at the proper ratios to accommodate the new engine components. Usually, the only tools needed to rejet a carb are a screwdriver, some jets, and an open stretch of road. That all changed when H-D started putting EFI systems onto its bikes.

As great as EFI is, it can be a monster to get right, at least, that's the way it was in the early days of H-D fuelie machines. Many times, the engines were factory set way too lean, which caused detonation problems, as well as lousy acceleration, popping back through the air cleaner, and other nastiness. However, that all changed once the aftermarket companies started getting the hang of the EFI game. Now there are a few very adjustable modules on the market that you can plug into the bike's existing harness, which will enable you to adjust the fuel maps for your machine easier and better than you could ever do with a screwdriver and a handful of carb jets.

The one we're going to install is the newest version of the most popular fully adjustable module, as well as the one that's been on the market the longest: Dynojet's Power Commander IIIr. The PC IIIr is a fuel injection—and ignition timing adjustment—module that plugs into the stock wiring harness without any changes to the harness. That means simply removing the PC IIIr returns the bike to its stock configuration. The PC IIIr can be ordered already programmed for your engine's performance package, which makes it a plug-in-and-ride installation. However, the PC IIIr also comes complete with software and a cable link, so you can change the maps using a Windows 95/98/ME/2000/XP computer. You can also upload alternate maps or download maps from Dynojet's Web site. This feature allows you to always reprogram the PC IIIr to fit whatever performance modifications you decide to make in the future. If you have a very special application or a problem child that just won't respond to anything you try, Dynojet also has Approved Power Commander Tuning Centers, which are listed on Dynojet's Web site, located throughout the country.

The PC IIIr also allows you to fine-tune the low-, mid-, or high-rpm range to get rid of any minor glitch that might surface. There are three faceplate buttons that allow you to move the fuel curve richer or leaner as needed in each separate range. The Fine-Tuning sidebar explains how to do this.

I'm going to show you how to install a PC IIIr on a Softail, which is more involved than doing it on a Dyna or Touring model. Start by removing the seat, and disconnecting

After removing the battery and disconnecting the harness plug for the taillight, unbolt the module from the bike using a 3/16-inch Allen. Then unplug and remove the module.

and removing the battery from the bike (do the negative cable first). After disconnecting the harness plug for the taillight, which is on the right side of the bike, unbolt the module from the bike using a 3/16-inch Allen. Then unplug and remove the module.

Once you remove the top to the fuse box, cut all the wire ties—not the wires!—on the harnesses under the fuse box. After removing two screws for the fuse box with a 3/8-inch socket, pull the ECM tray's holding plug out with a needle-nose pliers. Remove the tray from the rear fender.

Push in the single tab located under each fuse box, so you can slide each fuse box down to its lowest position on its mounting bracket. Install the new ECM tray into the rear fender and push the holding plug into place. Then reinstall

the fuse box bracket—use buttonhead bolts for extra clearance if you have a custom seat—using a 5/32-inch Allen. Now reinstall the battery into its box and reattach the positive cable, but don't attach the negative cable at this time.

Push the fuse box top cover onto the fuse box. Note the height of the cover, which cannot be higher than the bracket of the fuse box or it will interfere with the Power Commander unit. Install the PC IIIr harness onto the stock ECM unit, and then bolt the ECM into the new ECM tray with the stock bolts using a 3/16-inch Allen.

After connecting the other end of the PC IIIr harness to the stock harness, push the stock harness down into the left side of the chassis, so the connectors can sit on the left side of the frame. After reconnecting the taillight harness, use

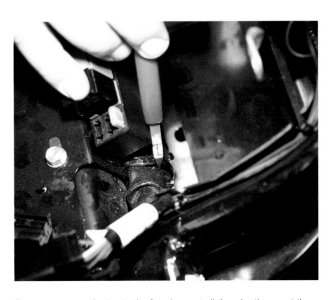

Once you remove the top to the fuse box, cut all the wire ties—not the wires!—on the harnesses under the fuse box.

Then push in the single tab located under each fuse box, so you can slide each fuse box down to its lowest position on its mounting bracket. Install the new ECM tray into the rear fender.

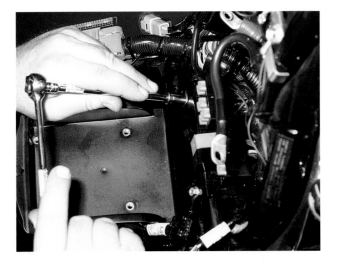

After removing the two screws for the fuse box with a 3/8-inch socket, pull the ECM tray's holding plug with a needlenose pliers. Then remove the tray from the rear fender.

Then reinstall the fuse box bracket and push the fuse box top cover onto the fuse box. Note the height of the cover, which cannot be higher than the battery or the fuse box's bracket.

fastening tape such as Velcro to attach the connector and PC IIIr so they lie flat on the frame. This will keep the seat from rubbing on them (the stock seat has more clearance than a custom seat). If needed, carefully use a heat gun to soften the harness wiring a little, so you can get the harness down into the frame and get the connectors to lie flat. Then attach the battery's negative cable. You're now ready to fire off the engine and fine-tune the PC IIIr, if needed.

Install the PC III harness onto the stock ECM unit and harness, then bolt the ECM into the new ECM tray. Velcro the connector and PC IIIr so they lay flat on the frame.

Fine-Tuning

The PC IIIr's three faceplate buttons allow you to adjust the fuel curve richer or leaner as needed to get rid of a minor performance glitch. However, don't try to use this feature to fix a problem caused by having the wrong map installed in the PC IIIr. It can only be used to fine-tune the correct map.

First put the PC IIIr in button programming (BP) mode by turning the bike on while pressing all three buttons at the same time. With PC IIIr in BP mode, pressing the Low, Mid, or High button will select that rpm range. The rpm LED will indicate what range is selected.

Once an rpm range is chosen, the Rich/Lean indicator will display how the fine-tuning mode is affecting that range's fuel delivery. If the two LEDs in the middle of the scale are lit, which is the neutral, or zero, position, the fine-tuning mode is not affecting the amount of fuel being delivered for that rpm range. Each LED light on the scale represents a two-percent increase or decrease, depending on whether it is moved toward the rich or lean side of the scale.

To make an adjustment, tap the button to richen the selected rpm range. Changes are indicated by the lit LED moving toward the rich side of the scale. To lean out the mixture, hold the button down. This will make the lit LED move toward the lean end. Note: If you don't do anything with the buttons for 10–20 seconds, the PC IIIr will go out of programming mode.

Once you have the rpm ranges adjusted the way you want, leave the bike on, without touching the buttons, for about 30 seconds. This tells the PC IIIr to save the settings you have made and go out of button programming mode. When this happens the lit LED will drop to the lowest position on the scale. Verify that the PC IIIr is out of programming mode by opening and closing the throttle, which should make the lit LED move up and down the scale. Do not turn the ignition switch off before the Power Commander goes out of programming mode or the changes you made will not be saved.

The smart way is to make adjustments one LED at a time and then take a test ride to see if the problem has been corrected. After all, it's so easy to make an adjustment that if the first one was not enough, you can just stop on the road, make another change, and test it out until the problem is fixed. The PC IIIr is properly adjusted when there are no problems like surging, overheating, blubbering, pinging, flat spots, etc. This means the engine's fuel settings are about 90 percent optimized, which is dialed in for street applications. Going to 100 percent optimization is an extreme that should be sought by racers and dyno shootout competitors only.

Installing a Performance Exhaust System

 Time: 2–3 hours

 Tools: 9/16-inch socket, 7/16-inch deep socket, 1/2-inch socket, 6-inch extension and ratchet, torque wrench, exhaust clamp pliers, blue Loctite, and 1/4-inch Allen

 Talent:

 Cost: $130–1,200

 Parts: New exhaust gaskets for heads, new performance exhaust system, heat shields if not a double-walled pipe system

 Tip: Check carb jetting or EFI calibration to see if engine is running too lean after exhaust installation.

 PERFORMANCE GAIN: 2–8 horsepower, as well as an increase in torque, depending on system used and engine's other performance upgrades

COMPLEMENTARY MODIFICATION: Install a high-flow air cleaner kit for better performance

To be blunt about it, no other single component can make or break an engine's power output like the exhaust system. You can have everything else on the bike perfectly matched—cams, intake system, compression ratio, headwork, and ignition—but if the pipes are a rotten match to the other components, the engine just won't put out the kind of power of which it's capable. The wrong pipes can kill low-end power, give you flat spots in the mid-range, or flatten out the horsepower curve up top. Many a tuner has changed every jet possible in their carb trying to get a flat spot out of the power curve, when all along it was a lousy set of pipes.

When selecting an exhaust, be sure to first check what the system is designed to do. Sometimes, a performance pipe is made to produce high horsepower in a specific rpm range or develop low-end torque at the expense of top-end power. For instance, drag pipes are just that, pipes for drag racing. These pipes usually make the most horsepower at

the upper end of the rpm curve, where a racer needs it. However, low-end power usually suffers and that's where most street riders spend 90 percent of their time. Those seeking a deep rumbling exhaust note should use a tuned system, like a Thunderheader or Bassani system, to get plenty of what they crave, as well as great performance. On the other end of the noise spectrum, those looking to get good low- and mid-range power with a quieter exhaust note can run a set of performance mufflers like Screamin' Eagle slip-ons, which offer both of these benefits. The trick is to match the pipe to the engine's combination of performance parts and power band.

Though there are many factors that a good performance exhaust must address to be effective, we'll just cover a couple of the more common terms: backpressure and scavenging. Backpressure is resistance to the flow of exhaust gases in an exhaust system. The best-known causes of backpressure are baffles and other restrictions placed in a pipe to reduce noise. However, the diameter of the header pipe, the length of the pipe, and other factors also affect backpressure. All engines need some level of backpressure to perform well over all the engine's rpm ranges; the trick is having the right amount for that engine's particular combination of cams, headwork, etc. Scavenging is when the exiting exhaust gases help to draw exhaust fumes out of the cylinder, as well as draw in the next fresh fuel/air mixture charge into the cylinder.

There are several different systems presently on the market and all fit into the following two main categories: a

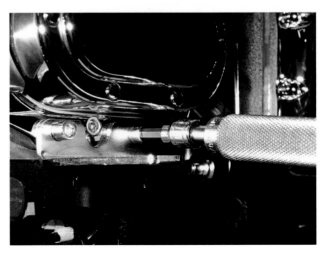

After installing the stock clamps onto the new header pipes using exhaust clamp pliers, bolt the transmission mount for the front pipe to the tranny using a 1/4-inch Allen.

two-into-two system, or a two-into-one. We'll cover the two-into-two systems first, starting with straight pipes, which are pipes that have no internal baffling or restrictions whatsoever. Drag pipes fall into this category, as well as several stepped pipe systems. (Stepped header pipes are used on some systems to help with scavenging.)

The next style is true-dual mufflered systems, which have a separate exhaust pipe for each cylinder. These systems can have both pipes on the same side of the bike, or, as seen on many baggers, one on each side. A variation on the dual-muffler type is a dual system that has a crossover pipe, which is a small pipe that connects the two main exhaust pipes. This is the style of system that H-D installs at the factory. The stock pipes, as everyone knows, have very restrictive mufflers, which increase backpressure and reduce scavenging. To counteract these two negatives, H-D uses a crossover pipe, which reduces the restriction caused by the mufflers by equalizing the exhaust pressure between the pipes.

That brings us to the tuned two-into-one system, which is the most commonly used performance exhaust. The two-into-one system has both header pipes—the ones that come from each head—connected to a single large volume collector/muffler. These systems are great for making low-end torque and a solid midrange. This style exhaust comes in two flavors, fixed and adjustable. The fixed systems include the Thunderheader, Bassani, and Vanes & Hines Pro-Pipe. Systems like these are tuned when manufactured for a wide variety of setups and work very well when installed on a modified and/or large displacement engine. Adjustable systems, like the SuperTrapp and White Brothers E-series systems, have discs that the tuner can add or remove from the end of the collector, which allows him to adjust the exhaust to match the engine's requirements.

All of these systems, except for the straight pipes, have internal baffling or restrictions to help control sound. The systems that use mufflers can have them as a separate part, which can be removed from the header pipes, or with the muffler one-piece with its header pipe. The better systems also use these internal restrictions, as well as pipe shape and length, to improve backpressure and scavenging characteristics, which result in better engine performance.

The key to making more power with a mufflered system is to use mufflers with a large internal volume. Case in point: Stock bagger mufflers have a larger volume than those found on Dyna models, which is why a stock bagger always makes more horsepower and torque than a stock Dyna, even though the engines are exactly the same.

To show you how to install a set of two-into-one pipes, we're going to bolt up a set of Bassani jet-coated pipes to a 2003 Road King Classic. Our starting point has the stock pipes removed, as well as the saddlebags and right floorboards, front and rear. The first step is to swap the stock exhaust clamps over to the new Bassani header pipes using exhaust clamp pliers. Then bolt the Bassani-supplied transmission mount for the front pipe to the

After putting new gaskets into both exhaust ports, bolt the header pipes to the heads using a 1/2-inch socket and the stock hardware. Leave all the nuts slightly loose for now.

Slip the Bassani P-clamp over the front pipe and put both its tabs on top of the tranny clamp you installed earlier.

tranny using a 1/4-inch Allen. After putting new Bassani-supplied gaskets into both exhaust ports, bolt the front header pipe to the head using a 1/2-inch socket and the stock hardware. Leave the nuts slightly loose for now. Now bolt up the rear pipe, again using the 1/2-inch socket on the stock hardware and leaving the nuts slightly loose.

Slip the Bassani P-clamp over the front pipe and put both its tabs on top of the tranny clamp you installed earlier. After slipping the two muffler clamps onto both ports of the muffler, slip the muffler over both header pipes. Leave the clamps loose. Using the stock hardware—with a little blue Loctite on the threads—and clamp bracket, loosely bolt up the muffler to the saddlebag bracket using a 1/2-inch socket. Then slip the bolt, with a flat washer above and below the clamp, into the P-clamp. Install the nut, with blue Loctite on its threads, onto the bolt using a 9/16-inch socket, but leave it loose for now.

With all the parts installed and loosely connected to each other, it's time to tighten up the system. This must be done from the head back, or you'll preload the system. Preloading results in cracked brackets or worse down the road. Start by tightening up the front and rear header clamp nuts by walking them all down together with a 1/2-inch socket until they are torqued to spec. Next, tighten down the P-clamp's hardware. You can now tighten down both muffler clamps using a 7/16-inch deep socket. The last one to be tightened is the rear muffler clamp. Do not force a part into alignment. If needed, shim the clamp so that it aligns without being forced. For example, I needed to use a couple of extra spacers to close the gap due to an uneven saddlebag bracket.

After slipping the two muffler clamps onto both ports of the muffler, slip the muffler over both header pipes. Leave the clamps loose.

Using the stock hardware and clamp bracket, loosely bolt up the muffler to the saddlebag bracket using a 1/2-inch socket. (Put a little blue Loctite on the bolt threads.)

Exhaust Care Tips

To cure the chrome or coating on pipes, run the engine at idle for about 30 seconds to a minute. Then shut the engine down and then let the pipes cool to room temperature. Do this three or four times.

Improper jetting, whether too rich or too lean, will discolor chrome pipes. However, all pipes will discolor by the cylinder heads due to the high heat. Optional heat shields are the best fix for this, or running a pipe with a double wall.

Remove oil with rubbing alcohol and shine pipes with glass cleaner. Do this before starting the engine and heating up the exhaust system, which will bake the oil onto the pipe.

Then slip the bolt, with a flat washer above and below the clamp, into the P-clamp. Loosely install the nut, with blue Loctite on its threads, onto the bolt using a 9/16-inch socket.

With all the parts installed and loosely connected to each other, tighten up the system, starting with the heads and working back to the rear muffler clamp. Here's the finished job!

SECTION FOUR

Suspension and Chassis

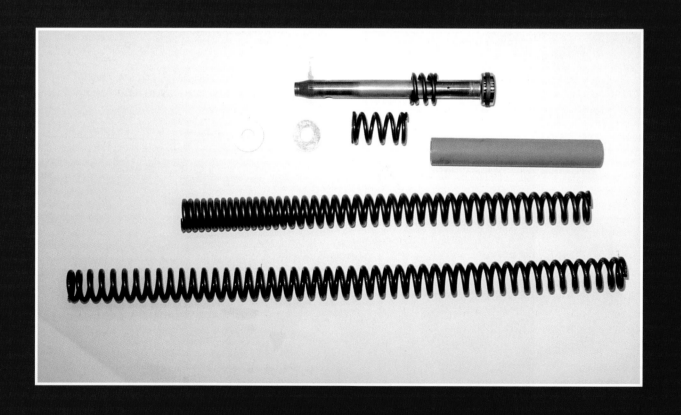

How to Fix Clunking Forks

Time: 15 minutes to 1 hour

Tools: Common hand tools, drain pan

Talent:

Cost: A few bucks worth of fork oil

Parts: New drain screw washers

Tip: Now is the time to upgrade the front suspension.

PERFORMANCE GAIN: Not only do you lose that annoying clunk, you'll also improve handling

COMPLEMENTARY MODIFICATION:
Suspension upgrades

With your bike on the stand, rock the forks and check for movement. A loose steering head might be the culprit. Or perhaps, more likely, you're getting insufficient damping and a fork oil change is in order.

There you are just tooling along enjoying the day when your wheels encounter a bit of jounce and "clunk"–there go your front forks. That sucks, it's annoying and downright unseemly. Fortunately the fix is easy and straightforward. But first we'll need to do a bit of investigating.

Fork clunks usually come in two varieties. The first is caused by loose steering head bearings, the second by wimpy front fork damping.

If you suspect that the steering head bearings are loose, as evidenced by clunks when coming to a stop or some front-end banging when you whack your front wheel over an obstacle; the first check is to simply come to a complete stop, hold on the front brake, and try to rock the bike back and forth. If the steering head bearings are loose, you'll either feel some motion in the fork or hear a distinct clunk as the bike rocks to and fro. It may help to have an assistant hold their hand on the top fork clamp; if they report some movement, the steering head bearings are likely loose and should be adjusted. If you want some additional confirmation, place the bike on a work stand that raises the front wheel clear of the pavement. What's that? Your lift raises both wheels clear? That's not a problem. With the front end clear of the pavement grasp the fork close to the axle. With the bike secured on the stand, hold the fork in the straight-ahead position, and try to move it back and forth, in line with the frame. If movement is detected, the steering head bearings are loose. Check your service manual for the correct adjustment procedure.

In the event that your steering head bearings are not loose—and chances are pretty good that they aren't—the next most likely culprit of clunk is insufficient front fork damping. The fork oil is responsible for damping out unwanted suspension movement. The amount and viscosity of the oil also determines how fast, and in very broad strokes, how far the suspension will compress.

If the fork oil is too light, or there isn't enough of it, the front fork may over compress or bottom during the compression stroke or top out during the rebound stoke. Either way you'll end up with an annoying clunk. By increasing the viscosity of the oil you slow down its rate of compression and rebound. This alone should be enough to prevent bottoming and topping. For added insurance, though, or if clunking is still an issue after changing the fork oil, adding an additional ounce of oil (over and above what the factory recommends) should solve the problem once and for all.

Bear in mind that air is infinitely compressible. Normally there is some volume of air trapped inside the fork tube. When this trapped air is compressed it acts as a spring but, as they say, "Wait, there's more." Not only does air act as a spring, it acts as a progressive spring. During the initial inches of fork travel the air barely affects the action. However, as the fork moves further and the air becomes more compressed, its springing qualities become accentuated. In short, the more you compress the air, the greater it resists compressing. By adding fork oil you reduce the volume of trapped air. Since the volume is reduced, the air compresses more quickly and the effect of the compressed air is greater. In reality you have changed the "spring rate" slightly. So by changing the fork oil height, and hence the amount of available free air space we can custom tailor the fork action to suit our individual requirements. Changing the amount of the oil does not change the damping rate; only a change in viscosity can do that. But it will make the overall "spring rate" somewhat stiffer; I'd start by adding one extra ounce and see how it feels.

Changing the Fork Oil

Here's where it gets down and dirty. Obviously, if you're performing some fork upgrades that require a total disassembly of the front end or something close to it, changing the fork oil is part and parcel of the job. But what if you

only want to change the oil and nothing else? Well, you could change the fork oil the old-fashioned way, which entails propping the bike up, removing a bunch of tin work—at least on the dressers—and the fork tube caps and everything else, then pouring the oil back into the forks via a funnel.

Or you could do it by using the method a lot of pro wrench's use.

1. Prop the bike up so that the forks are unloaded.

2. Remove the fork drain bolt and allow the fork oil to run out; this can take some time. To speed up the process, find or make yourself an adapter that will screw into the drain holes. You can make one out of an old pen cap or tip, or make something up using the appropriate threaded fitting. Plug your adapter into a Mityvac or the equivalent-style vacuum pump and suck the old oil right out of there.

3. To fill the forks you can use either a vacuum pump set to pressure or an old-fashioned squirt can and length of tubing. Hold your finger over the hole to prevent the fresh oil from dripping out when you install the drain bolt, but don't be overly concerned if a drop or two does ooze out. Don't forget to add that extra ounce of fork oil, either!

In all honesty, most of the Big Twins that I've ridden have felt somewhat under damped, since the stock oil recommendation is generally either ATF or five-weight oil and because these are heavy bikes, that's understandable. My recommendation is to swap the stock stuff for either ten- or fifteen-weight or something like Screamin' Eagle's heavy-weight oil. Heavier oil will better dampen the suspension movement, eliminating the wallows, and a bit of extra oil should remove any clunks while providing a little extra springing. All in all, this is a cheap and effective method for tweaking the suspension.

Installing a Cartridge Fork Emulator

 Time: 4–5 hours depending on skill level and model

 Tools: Common hand tools, torque wrench, caliper, 3/8-inch electric drill, or drill press, 5/16-inch bit, and an optional impact gun

 Talent:

 Cost: $150–200

 Parts: Race Tech Gold Valve Cartridge Emulator kit

 Tip: The heavy touring bikes have as much to gain with this modification as the sport models.

 PERFORMANCE GAIN: Better and more predictable handling

COMPLEMENTARY MODIFICATION: Upgrade the rear suspension, add better brakes and tires

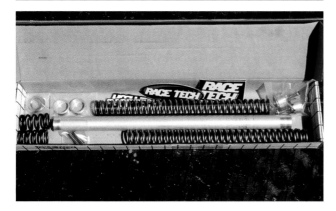

The Race Tech kit contains everything you'll need except fork oil.

As delivered, the Twin Cam Harleys don't handle too badly. They don't handle particularly well, but they're far from the lumbering beasts they used to be. The major fault with them is that the suspension internals are, at best, somewhat primitive, particularly the front fork, which is at least a generation behind most current designs. The problem with the Big Twin fork is that all damping is controlled by drilled orifices located in a fixed rod, rather than by valves. During the compression stroke of the suspension, oil is forced through the compression damping holes. On rebound, the oil returns via the rebound holes. Since the size of the holes is predetermined, the damping rates never change. It is true that changing the viscosity of the fork oil will affect both the compression and rebound damping rate. But in general, simply going to heavier or lighter oil

You may find it easier to remove the dampening rod bolt with the fork still in the triple clamp, particularly if you're doing the job sans air tools. Tip: If you slide the fork down in the clamp, and then snug up the pinch bolt, you'll be able to remove the top nut with out wrestling the fork tube all over the place.

does little to help overall performance. This type of fork is called a damping rod fork and has been used since the early 1930s.

The real solution is to install a more sophisticated damping system. One that reacts to the size of the bump and the speed at which it's struck. The way to do this is through the use of multiple valves located within the suspension unit. This is exactly what a state-of-the-art cartridge fork does; it is so called because suspension activity is controlled by an inner "cartridge" where the suspension valves are located. While there are several methods of achieving the same end, fundamentally all work in the same way.

For the sake of example let's look at the most popular method of cartridge fork valves, the coning washer. As I said about the stock H-D fork, damping, both compression and rebound, is controlled by a series of drilled holes. As the fork compresses, oil is forced through the holes. If you use a heavy oil, the fork compresses slowly and vice versa with a lighter oil. During the rebound phase the oil returns through another set of holes, and responds to changes in oil viscosity in exactly the same way. As you may guess, the ratio of hole size and oil viscosity compared to the size of the bump is critical. Unfortunately such a system can only be made to work well over a very narrow range.

In a coning or bending washer system a piston (or sometimes two, one for compression and one for rebound) is located in the fork tube. The piston has a ring of holes drilled in it. A thin, strong, and very flexible primary washer covers these holes. The washer has other washers, spacers, or springs positioned over it, all of which are used to modify the primary washer's stiffness. When the fork compresses slowly the oil forces the primary washer to lift slightly, allowing the oil to flow through the holes. However, if a really large hit occurs, the primary washer

moves further off its seat allowing more oil to flow. Hence, damping is proportional to the speed at which the fork compresses. The same system is employed on the rebound side of the fork, because the rate at which the primary washers bend or lift is almost infinitely adjustable and the suspension action can be easily tailored to work almost perfectly over very wide parameters. Obviously, this is a very simple explanation of a complex subject but essentially, that's modern suspension in a nutshell.

The problem is how do you adapt that technology to our Big Twin. Well, you could go out and buy a trick fork, adapt it to fit and tune it to work. That's pretty expensive and somewhat complex. Or you could install a Race Tech Gold Valve Cartridge Emulator, which is what I recommend, so called because the Gold Valve lets your standard damping rod fork emulate the performance of a cartridge fork—a much cheaper and easier alternative. And one that will work as well under 99% of the circumstances a street rider will ever encounter.

The Gold Valve is essentially a damping piston that drops into the standard H-D fork between the damping rod and the spring. A flat washer is located above the holes in the piston and controlled by an adjustable spring. Due to its design, the Gold Valve is only used to control compression damping. Oil viscosity is used to alter rebound characteristics. Once the rebound damping is set, the compression rate is adjusted via the Gold Valve.

Installing a Gold Valve is a straightforward procedure; however, the forks will have to be dismantled, and the original damping rod removed. The factory drilled compression holes will need to be opened up and a few new ones installed. This will ensure that all of the fork oil passes through the Gold Valve without being restricted by the OEM undersized orifices.

Because the fork is going to be apart, this is the perfect time to replace any leaking fork seals, worn-out bushings, or chewed-up fork tubes. It's also the time to install new fork springs; ones that are correctly calibrated for your weight and riding style. These can be purchased through Race Tech, Progressive, Works Performance, or any place else that strikes your fancy. It is also the time to upgrade the brakes, particularly since the suspension modifications will keep the old gal from nose-diving under heavy braking.

Proper reassembly of the front fork and brakes will be critical to your continued good health and well-being.

I also will remind you that suspension modification is very much like any other tuning process. If you follow to the letter the instructions that come with the Race Tech kit the bike will handle much better than it ever has. But due to individual circumstances some fine-tuning may be required. If that turns out to be the case, work slowly and methodically. Make one change at a time and take notes. The Race Tech Gold Valve is completely tuneable; in the end you should have a bike that handles in exactly the way you want.

The instructions will show you where to open up the damping bolt.

SUSPENSION AND CHASSIS

Step 1: Support the bike so the front end can be removed.

Step 2: Remove front wheel and fender as per the H-D manual for your bike.

Step 3: If you don't have an air tool, use a 6-mm Allen wrench to remove the bolt from the lower leg before you loosen the fork tube in the triple tree.

Step 4: Loosen the lower triple tree bolt with a 5/8-inch wrench and then slide the fork tube down about 4 inches; retighten the bolt. Loosen the spring retaining nut; loosen the triple tree bolt again and slide the fork leg out of the trees.

Step 5: Remove the spring retaining nut. Note: The nut is under pressure from the fork spring, so watch out for it when you remove the nut. Remove the spring. If you are going to replace the fork seals, check your service manual. However, if you are not going replace them, invert the fork tube and allow the damping rod and spring to drop out.

Step 6: Locate the damping holes. These are the large holes found at the bottom damping rod (Race Tech instructions detail this).

Step 7: Locate the original stock hole. At 7/16 inch above and below the center of stock hole mark two spots at 90 degrees from original hole. Drill a 5/16-inch hole in the damping rod at each position; you'll drill four holes in each rod altogether. You need six holes in each rod to allow enough oil flow. If the original hole is less than 5/16 inch, open it up as well. (Do not touch the rebound holes.) See the Race Tech diagram for the exact hole size and location.

Step 8: Install the proper topping spring on the damper rod and then drop the rod into the lower leg. After checking the emulator preload, drop it into the lower leg so it sits on top of the damper rod, followed by the Race Tech fork spring. The spring sits directly on the emulator. (NOTE: Race Tech has its own procedure for setting preload. They recommend backing off the nut and then tightening it by some number of turns, usually four. Since their method is somewhat subjective I've found that it helps to measure the height of the nut to ensure that the preload on both valves is as equal as possible. I use a caliper to make sure both emulators are set equally.)

Step 9: Check spring preload length per instructions; cut the preload spacer to achieve the correct amount of sag, about 1 1/4 inches works well. (The spacer will end up being about 5 inches long).

Step 10: Then drop in a washer, the spacer you cut, and then another washer.

Step 11: Reinstall the fork leg about halfway up the tree. Snug the lower tree bolt and reinstall the top nut. Loosen the lower tree bolt again and then position the leg so the flat on the top nut faces out toward the tree cover bolt and slip it up into the top tree. Tighten the lower tree bolt again.

Step 12: I then pour 12 ounces of Spectro Type E oil into each leg, and bleed the legs accordingly. As an alternative, the fork oil level height can be adjusted before the forks are installed per Race Tech instructions.

You can use a hand held drill, but a small drill press makes life a lot easier.

Lowering Front Forks

Time: 2–3 hours

Tools: Ratio Rite or other measuring device, funnel, drain pan, common hand tools, an air or electric impact gun (optional, but very handy), fork oil, rags, brake cleaner and/or solvent, a means of supporting the bike off ground

 Talent: This isn't real NASA stuff, but it sucks if the front fork falls off

Cost: You can do this one for virtually nothing or you can buy a specific lowering kit; they run about $100 or so.

Parts: Cheap guys can get away with a length of aluminum pipe. The sky's-the-limit types can buy the lowering kit of their choice from White Brothers or Progressive. Also, pick up some new drain screw gaskets and a set of damper rod bolt washers, as well as a quart of fork oil.

Tip: Lowering just one end of the bike creates frame geometry issues; both ends of the bike should be modified in concert. Lowering the bike will have a detrimental affect on the ground clearance; if you're already dragging the hard parts through the turns lowering the bike any further may prove detrimental to your health.

 PERFORMANCE GAIN: Sorry, this one is all about style

COMPLEMENTARY MODIFICATION: Upgrade fork springs; install Race Tech Gold Valve, lower rear end

How low can you go? I'm not a big fan of lowered—"slammed" in the vernacular—bikes. In most cases, Harleys already have ground clearance issues and dropping them down beyond the stock ride height only serves to exacerbate the problem. At the same time lowering the bike always means reducing suspension travel. Go very much lower than stock and essentially you'll end up with a rigid-framed bike that rides like a buckboard. But fashion being what it is, I don't suppose the trend is going to reverse itself anytime soon.

Before you undertake any lowering projects it's important to realize just what you want to accomplish and also how the changes will affect the overall frame geometry. If you lower only the front fork the rake and trail will be reduced. The bike will turn somewhat quicker, and may become twitchy or jittery at speed. More weight will be placed on the front tire, which may overload it during hard braking or spirited cornering.

Conversely, if you lower only the rear of the bike the overall effect is to increase the rake and trail. This results in slower steering, a reluctance to turn, and a heavier feel at the handlebar.

In both instances, ground clearance is reduced.

My suggestion is to always lower both ends of the bike by an equal amount so that something very close to the factory geometry is maintained. To that end, the companion chapters to this one are Projects 29 and 30, lowering a Softail rear end and lowering a Twin shock rear end, respectively. My strong recommendation is that you perform the appropriate rear-end modification at the same time as you modify the front end.

Actually lowering a standard, damping rod front end is as simple as rearranging some of the internal parts.

The Fast and Dirty (and Cheap) Method

Over the years, I've modified hundreds of race-bike front ends using the el-cheapo method and have never had one go wrong. The big advantage to my way of doing it is that it's a cheap and easy way to experiment with the bike's ride height.

Since you'll need to remove the fork tubes, you'll need to lift the bike at least high enough to remove the front wheel. When the wheel is removed, the bike may have a tendency to tip backward so make certain it's well supported and tied down. Nothing ruins your day like watching your pride and joy do a barrel roll onto the garage floor.

Per your service manual's instructions, remove the front wheel, fender, and brakes. Drain the fork oil. Loosen one fork tube in its clamp and slide it down a few inches. Retighten the lower clamp and break the fork tube's cap bolt loose; but don't remove it from the fork tube just yet. Loosen up the lower clamp bolt and remove the fork tube.

Now comes the tricky part: *Don't use the air tools on the cap bolt,* use your standard hand tools, and be careful, there is usually a fair amount of spring preload on the bolt. As you get to the last few threads the bolt will have a tendency to fly out of the tube. If your head is in the way,

A specific lowering kit removes all the guess work.

Included in the kit are shorter damping rods, a length of PVC tubing to make preload spacers and a shorter spring. The longer, stock spring is shown at the bottom.

and that bolt gets away from you it's going to smart. Besides, most people look pretty silly with a bolt stuck in their forehead.

Once the bolt is out of the way you can remove any preload spacers, followed by the spring. Have a catch basin handy; the spring and all of the other parts will be drenched in slippery fork oil.

Here's where you get to use air or electric impact tools. Invert the fork leg; if possible place the open end of the fork tube in the catch basin to avoid making a big mess. Insert an 8-mm Allen socket into the damper rod-retaining bolt located at the bottom of the lower leg. With any luck the bolt should spin right out. You can now remove the lower leg from the fork tube; once the lower leg is removed you can tip the fork tube upside down and the damper rod should fall right out.

If the bolt doesn't spin out or you don't have any air tools the procedure is slightly different.

If the damper rod spins when you hit the retaining bolt with the air gun you can try jamming the rod with a broom handle, or length of pipe or what have you. If you're real nice to the local H-D shop, they may even let you borrow the correct holding tool. In fact, and this is a real heresy, many import shops have the correct tool because the H-D fork is made in the land of the rising sun and the damper rod is one common to lots of imported bikes. If worse comes to worst and you simply can't get the bolt out or the head strips, use a 5/16 drill bit to remove the head of the bolt. Just pick away at the bolt head until it is just about gone, then tap it dead center with a punch. The head should separate from the shaft, and you can then remove the damping rod from the fork tube; at that point you'll be pleasantly surprised to find that what's left of the bolt should unscrew with nothing more than light finger pressure.

But here's another trick that works well. If you don't have access to air tools try unscrewing the damper rod bolt while the forks are still completely assembled. Once the front axle is removed, the bolts are accessible. With the fork caps still tight, the fork springs maintain plenty of pressure on the damper rod; nine times out of ten it's

enough to prevent the rod from turning when you remove the screw. So here's the drill: remove the wheel, fender, brakes, etc. Loosen up the damper rod retaining bolt by at least a few turns, then follow the procedure I've outlined for removing the fork cap bolts, etc. Once the fork is out of the bike and the spring removed proceed to remove the damper rod bolt.

Shortening the Fork (El-Cheapo Method)

To shorten the fork all you really need to do is install a spacer between the damper rod and the fork tube. This causes the damper rod to ride higher up in the fork tube. Since the lower leg location is controlled by the damper rod position, the fork is now shortened, accordingly. Making up spacers is pretty simple. Almost anything that fits is acceptable. I've used old valve springs, pieces of aluminum cut to fit, steel tubing, and in a pinch, stacks of washers. My recommendation is to cut a spacer from a piece of round aluminum stock, preferably on a lathe so that it's nice and square. Most machine shops can whip something out for around twenty bucks. I would start with a 1-inch spacer, assembled with the original bottoming spring and see how the bike rides and handles before lowering it any further. The advantage to using this method is twofold: it's cheap, and you can add spacers until you get the exact ride height.

Off-the-Shelf Kits

The biggest advantage to using an off-the shelf lowering kit is that everything is figured out; guesswork is eliminated. The kits typically include all the spacers, new springs, and complete detailed instructions. Most kits even supply a piece of PVC pipe that can be cut to length for use as preload spacers.

The preliminary work required to install a kit is identical to that described above. Fundamentally, installing a kit differs only in detail from making and installing your own spacers. As a rule of thumb the kits are somewhat more complete as well. For example, the White Brothers

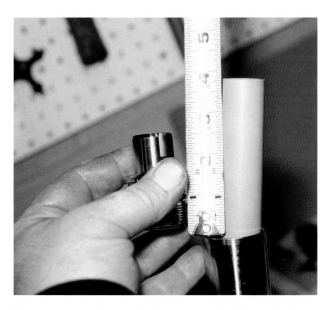

Measure your preload space. In this case, we've elected to make the spacer flush with the top of the fork tube.

kit includes spacers, new fork springs, new topping springs, and all of the ancillary hardware needed to lower the front end. The kit can be assembled using different combinations of springs and spacers to provide either a 1 1/4-inch drop or a 2-inch drop.

Preload and Oil Levels

When reassembling the new lowered fork you'll have to adjust the spring preload. Because the suspension travel is reduced, you also may want to install stiffer springs; these are usually supplied with the lowering kits, but are of course available separately.

Setting preload is a generic procedure. With the bike suspended so the forks are fully extended, install the fork springs. Install the flat washer on top of the spring, either the OEM or one supplied with the kit. Measure the distance from the washer to the top of the fork tube. Next measure the portion of the fork cap bolt that threads into the fork tube, i.e., from the thread to the shoulder. Subtract the second measurement from the first. Add one inch—one inch being the standard starting point as far as preload goes. The hot tip in preload spacers is a hunk of PVC pipe. Most of the aftermarket lowering kits will include an appropriately sized section of pipe. Trim the pipe to length with a hacksaw, making sure that the ends are filed or sanded square.

Because the forks are now shorter, the fork tube volume is reduced. This means that the fork oil level will need to be adjusted to suit. If you install the OEM-specified volume of oil, the forks may become too stiff because the air trapped in a fork tube acts like a spring. If you reduce the amount of free space inside of the tube, the air compresses faster, and it becomes much harder to compress.

Aftermarket kits will usually list a recommended fill height or amount, as well as a suggested viscosity. If you

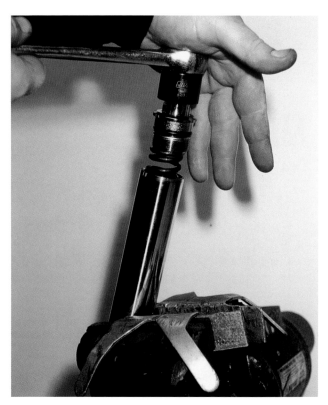

If you have trouble compressing the spring and reinstalling the cap at the same time, use the ratchet and socket to install them as a unit. Be careful threading the nut in, if you cross-thread it using that half-inch ratchet, you'll have a devil of a time repairing the damage.

opt to forgo using a kit, and are uncertain as to how much oil to pour back in, I'd suggest you start with the stock weight and amount. If the action feels too harsh you can reduce the oil level by an ounce at a time until you achieve the results you like. If the action is too soft, I'd increase the viscosity level by one grade and give 'er a ride. With some experimentation you'll eventually end up with the right combination for your riding style.

Race Tech Kit

As detailed in Project 24, the Race Tech Gold Valve Cartridge Emulator is most definitely the hot setup when it comes to improving the action of damper-rod front forks. Race Tech also offers the Gold Valve Emulator as part of their lowering kit. While it's not my job to shill for any manufacturer, the Gold Valve does work wonders for the suspension and I heartily recommend installing one.

Final Notes

Setting up a suspension can be time consuming, simply because there are so many variables. When a suspension is modified, as we've done with this project, the number of variables increases. Sometimes it takes quite a bit of experimenting to get it perfect. But, stick with it; in the end it will be worthwhile.

Installing New Fork Springs

 Time: 1–2 hours

 Tools: Common hand tools, rags, white grease or anti-seize lubricant

 Talent:

 Cost: Prices vary; figure on at least $60

 Parts: Fork springs

 Tip: Make certain the forks are fully extended when you remove and replace the fork caps to minimize the effects of spring tension on the caps.

 PERFORMANCE GAIN: Decent springs will eliminate that "mush-a-matic" sensation. The bike will handle better, respond quicker to steering inputs, and feel more confident through the turns

COMPLEMENTARY MODIFICATION: Any suspension upgrades, and any suspension service; i.e., now is the right time to change the fork oil

Replacing the fork springs may seem like a real no-brainer, and in a sense that's true. The actual nuts and bolts of replacing the springs are extremely straightforward for most of the bikes in the H-D lineup. Even the bikes where spring replacement is complicated by fairings and sheet metal aren't all that difficult to work on.

Where spring replacement does get a little complicated is in two areas: spring selection and preload/sag adjustment. Selection is greatly simplified if you know a little about springs.

There are four common types of springs. Front fork springs normally come in two basic varieties: Straight wound and progressive. Springs are commonly listed by "weight" which means the amount of weight needed to compress them. For example, a common straight-wound spring is described as a 100-pound spring, meaning it takes one hundred pounds to compress the spring one inch, 200 pounds to move the spring two inches and so

on until the spring is completely compressed or "coil bound." Therefore, the effect of weight on a straight-wound spring is cumulative rather than progressive. Straight-wound springs are easy to identify; all of the coils are evenly spaced.

Somewhat better are progressive springs. Progressive springs are designed to become progressively stiffer as they are compressed. A common rating in a progressive spring is 60–90, meaning it only takes 60 pounds to move the spring the first inch. As the spring compresses the rate increases taking on additional weight to move it the next inch, usually around 75 pounds for the spring in our example, and 90 more pounds to move it an additional inch. These weights are approximate because each manufacturer winds his springs a little differently but if you do the math you'll see that it takes 225 pounds to move the progressive spring through three inches of travel, and only 135 pounds to move it the first two inches.

Essentially, progressive springs soak up small bumps easily providing a comfortable ride, but when a large hit is felt the spring becomes progressively stiffer to help maintain control. In general, progressive springs are preferable because they are more versatile, combining a comfortable ride with the ability to soak up large impacts. They are also more expensive to fabricate which is why many manufacturers still use straight-wound springs. You'll be able to identify progressive springs because the coils will be wound closer together at one end than at the other.

Selecting Fork Springs

The easiest way to select a fork spring is to consult the manufacturer catalog and pick a spring that's rated for your weight and the type of riding you do. In general, most aftermarket suppliers will only offer one, or maybe three choices of springs. Each spring will have a brief description of its characteristics and a recommended application. The recommendations are usually based on the weight of the bike and rider, rather than the way the bike is ridden. If you like your meals super-sized, look in the heavy-duty spring column. In my experience, about 99 percent of the time the catalog recommendations are just about spot-on. The people that design and build aftermarket suspension parts do a lot of experimenting and know what works and what doesn't.

Swapping Springs

There is only one way to change fork springs. Basically you'll need to remove the old springs and insert new ones.

A procedure that we've touched on several times already. So I'm only going to hit the high points here. Start by positioning the bike so that the front wheel is clear of the ground; this will relieve the most of the spring preload making it far easier to remove the spring caps. Depending on the year and model of your bike, remove what you need to in order to access the fork springs. On some models this may entail removing the fork legs from the bike. If this is your case, you'll find it easier to loosen the fork caps if you slide the leg about halfway through the lower clamp. Retighten the lower clamp, and break the cap loose, then remove the leg from the bike.

Once the leg is off the bike, carefully remove the fork cap and lift out the old spring. If you impart a slight twisting motion to the spring as you remove it, most of the residual fork oil that clings to the spring will remain in the tube.

Install the new spring per the manufacturer's instructions; a straight-wound spring is simply placed into the fork tube, progressive springs are installed with the close-wound coils positioned at the top of the tube. Some kits will include new preload spacers or at least the raw material needed to make them as noted above. Again, follow the manufacture's instructions regarding preload spacer length and installation procedures.

Assuming you're not going ahead with any other work, the next step is to reassemble the fork, reinstall the fork tube, and replace any of the bits and pieces you removed, and repeat the procedure on the other fork tube. But—there's always a "but" isn't there?—while simply upgrading the fork springs is generally a good thing and will certainly help your hog's handling, taking it one step further and setting up the bike's "sag" will mean the difference between a good handling bike and one that handles great. See Project 29.

A straight spring (top) and a progressive spring (bottom).

Swapping the Shock on a Springer

Time: Maximum, 1 hour

Tools: Common hand tools, motorcycle lift, or a jack and a block of 2x8

Talent:

Cost: Cut the best deal you can on a shock, but figure on spending around $150

Tip: Place an old towel on the front fender to prevent dropped tools or parts from scratching the paint.

PERFORMANCE GAIN: The front end will lose that mushy feel

COMPLEMENTARY MODIFICATION: This one stands alone, although if you have the time, money, and inclination, now is also the time to upgrade the rear suspension

The Springer fork gets more than its fair share of abuse, particularly from members of the sport-bike crowd. But in many ways, the joke's on them. While the Springer fork may look somewhat, uh, dated, or even downright archaic, it is actually a very good front-end design with several notable advantages over the telescopic design.

For starters, the fork is extremely rigid and resists both side loads and bending stresses better than the majority of currently used telescopic forks. In addition, the geometry of the Springer provides a built-in anti-dive characteristic under braking. Finally, since damping is independent of the fork construction, the Springer is somewhat easier to maintain than its oil-filled counterpart.

Damping, or more accurately the lack of it, has always been the downfall of the Springer forks. Originally the design used a large friction damper located on the side of the fork. Turning a hand screw created more or less friction between sliding elements of the fork. The tighter the damper, the bigger a bump it took to get the fork moving, and the slower it moved. As you can imagine, this wasn't the best solution. The problem was, and still is, that friction dampers need a big hit to overcome initial stiction.

Once they start to move though, very little damping occurs. In essence, they provide too much damping at low speed and not nearly enough at high speed.

When H-D reintroduced the Springer fork they realized that friction damping, which had been at best, a marginally successful solution in the 1930s just wasn't going to cut it in the 1990s. They did the predictable thing of course, and replaced the old friction damper with a small hydraulic damper or shock absorber. The only problem was that they used a damper with all the structural integrity of your average screen door closer.

After a few miles the stock shock gives up the ghost and the bike starts to wallow around like a foundering tanker in a hurricane. The solution is as simple as it gets.

Swapping a springer front shock is about as easy as it gets. The shock is located, directly under the headlight.

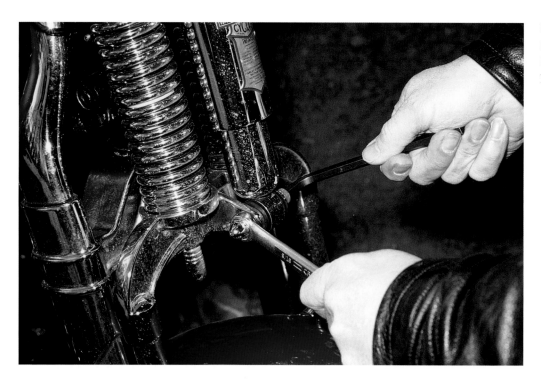

Replacing it is a simple matter of unbolting it, and replacing it with something you like better.

Begin by jacking up the front end of the bike until the weight has been removed from the front end. Make certain that the bike is secure. A pair of helping hands may come in handy if you do not have a way to secure the bike while it's jacked up.

Cover the front fender with heavy toweling, rags, plastic bubble wrap or whatever to prevent paint damage—not to mention mental anguish—should you drop a tool or hunk of hardware during the removal and installation process.

Remove the lower shock bolt. If the bolt doesn't come out freely, resist the temptation to give it a shot with your trusty mallet. Chances are the shot will drive the bolt out harder than you'd planned, shooting it across the floor or into something that would be better off for not having a bolt shot into it. A better solution would be to raise or lower the jack slightly to remove any preload that's holding the bolt under tension.

Once the lower bolt has been removed, remove the upper bolt. Chances are that the bolts are in good shape, but inspect them anyway. If there are any signs of damage, replace them with new OEM bolts or ones of corresponding grade.

Read the manufacturer's instructions before installing the new shock, even if you're an experienced wrench. If for no other reason, do it to humor me.

Installation is really just a reversal of the removal procedure. Apply a very light coat of anti-seize or white lithium grease to the bolts before reinstalling them and don't forget to use a little Loctite on the nuts. As in the removal, if the bolts don't slip through, use the jack to adjust the height of the bike.

Adjusting Front and Rear Preload (Sag)

 Time: Up to 2 hours

 Tools: Common hand tools, hacksaw, tape measure, note pad and pencil, and a pair (or three) of helping hands

 Talent:

 Cost: Scrounge up a foot-long section of PVC pipe and you won't have to pay a penny

 Tip: Sag settings are generally overlooked when it comes to setting up Harley-Davidson motorcycles, yet sag is one of the key factors in bike handling.

 PERFORMANCE GAIN: Better handling and a more comfortable ride

COMPLEMENTARY MODIFICATION: Any other suspension work may as well be done now

Basics

When you're adjusting the suspension preload, what you're really adjusting is the ride height of the motorcycle or what the racers call "sag." Many riders intuitively think that by adjusting the spring preload they are stiffening the spring. They aren't, the only way to stiffen the spring is to install a stiffer spring. Preload simply determines the ride height of the bike, and how much of the available suspension travel there is for you to use. The suspension feels stiffer because increasing preload exerts some tension on the spring causing it to compress slightly; it takes a bit more pressure to move it any further. Before I get into the nuts and bolts of preload, let's define some terms and the concepts they represent.

Ride Height: The height at which your motorcycle sits; it's measured at the front and rear. The ride height determines how much of the suspension is available to soak up the bumps and how much is used just sitting on the bike. The regular procedure is to measure the ride height at the front and rear axles. Measure from the axle to some point directly, or as close to directly above it, as possible. Don't forget to write down the numbers.

Sag: The difference in height, measured as suspension travel, between a bike with its suspension fully topped out, and with the suspension loaded with the weight of a rider and fuel. Sag is independently set at the front fork and the rear shock using either built-in adjusters or preload spacers.

Spring Preload: The force exerted by the springs when the suspension is fully extended. The spring preload adjustment determines how much sag you have and in most cases, ride height.

The hardest part of this operation is determining how much sag you need. The rule of thumb is that the sag should be equal to one fourth to one third of the suspension travel. Don't become confused though, that doesn't mean you should add the front and rear travel together. Sag is always independently adjusted at the front and rear. To properly adjust the sag you must know how much total travel the suspension has to start with. You can find that by looking it up in the service manual or by removing the springs from the suspension and actually measuring how much travel is available.

Once you know how much suspension travel is available the rest is pretty straightforward. For the sake of example we'll say the rear sag of a particular bike is four inches. Since we're making this easy on ourselves that means you want one fourth of that, or one inch as sag setting. Then adjust the rear preload so that the difference in ride height between unloaded and fully loaded is one inch. Once the rear has been adjusted repeat the same procedure at the front. Simple, isn't it?

Adjusting Sag

The first dimension to measure is the suspension height at full suspension extension. Place the bike on a stand or lift so that both wheels clear the ground. Measure from the center of the rear axle to some convenient point on the frame. Make your measurements in as straight a line as possible. Record the measurement. Do the same on the front axle, measuring from the front axle to the lower triple clamp. If you have an FX-style front end you can cheat a little; simply fasten a tie wrap snugly to the fork leg and slide it down until it rests against the lower leg. Next ease the bike down onto its wheels, then grab a buddy or two. With the bike sitting on its wheels, sit on it wearing your normal riding gear. Have your buddy or buddies hold the bike in the upright position. If you normally carry a passenger have them sit on the bike as well, and if you normally tote everything including the kitchen sink around, make sure the bags are full. Have a third friend

85

(you're not running out of friends yet are you?) take a measurement at exactly the same position at the rear of the bike as your initial measurement and write it down. On FL's take a measurement at the front axle; if you have an FX front end just jack the bike back up and measure the distance from the tie wrap to the lower leg. Subtract the second number from the first; the remainder is the sag. If it's less than what you want—which honestly is somewhat unlikely—you'll need to remove preload; if it's greater, you'll have to add preload.

Making the Adjustment

Rear preload adjustments are easy. Depending on the shock absorbers you're using, adjustment will be either via a ramped collar or in the case of Softails a threaded adjuster. In my experience most twin-shock Harley's are going to come up betwixt and between when it comes to setting the rear sag. You'll turn the adjusting collars one ramp and find that you've either reduced sag more than you want to, or you haven't been able to reduce it enough, so you give the collar another twist, which now removes more of the sag than you'd like. At this point you can install new shocks and springs, or—and this is what I'd do—take the bike for a ride and see how she feels. Softails with their adjustable collars will provide a bit more in the way of adjustability and you should be able to get the sag exactly where you want it.

In the front, things are a bit more complicated because you'll normally need to make up a spacer to preload the front fork springs, the exception being the Dyna Sport, which uses sport bike–style preload adjusters. The procedure used to measure the front sag is identical to that used at the rear. To adjust the preload you'll need to make up some PVC or aluminum spacers. Take pains to get the ends of the tubing as square as possible when you cut it. Thin washers should be used between the spring and the spacer; under no circumstances should the spacer rest directly against the spring. You may need to do some experimenting until you get the sag just right. One trick is to use stacks of washers to increase preload; keep adding washers a few at a time until you get the desired results. You can then cut your tubing to the correct length on the first try.

As with all suspension adjustments setting the correct sag will take a bit of trial and error. There are a lot of variables involved here and not many hard-and-fast rules. It's really a try-it-and-see process. Don't be afraid to experiment; the end result will be well worth it.

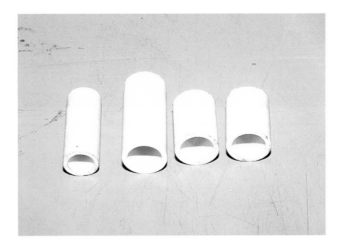

The easiest way to adjust front fork sag is to make a couple of spacers out of the correct diameter PVC pipe. After making your calculations per the text, install the preload spacer, and test ride the bike. Experiment with both longer and shorter spacers until you achieve the correct preload or sag.

Remember, adjusting the shock collar does not alter the spring's "weight," simply the ride height (sag).

Lowering the Rear of a Softail and Installing New Rear Shocks

 Time: 1 hour

 Tools: Floor jack, 3/4-inch wrench, 11/16-inch wrench, pliers

 Talent:

 Cost: $400–$800

 Parts: Alternative shocks

 Tip: Lowering a bike is serious business; handling is affected, as is ground clearance; make sure you fully understand what you are trying to accomplish.

 PERFORMANCE GAIN: Well, it looks good. If you're vertically challenged, lowering the bike will make it easier to plant your feet at stops. Better shocks equals more comfortable ride, and improved handling

COMPLEMENTARY MODIFICATION: Lowering the front fork, installing emulator valve

Swapping out the rear shocks on the Softail models can be considered a two-fer; if you're happy with the stock ride height you might want to consider upgrading the rear boingers simply to improve the ride and handling or to replace a worn-out set of stockers. Alternatively, you may want to lower the bike for a different look. Because the procedures are nearly identical, we'll cover both at the same time.

Worn-out rear shocks are a fact of life. As mileage accrues, internal parts wear, and the oil starts to break down. The end result is a bike that wallows through the turns, bottoms out over the slightest bumps, and rides like a buckboard. At that point it's time to swap them for something better. By the same token, you may simply want to lower your bike a bit for that custom look. Both ends are accomplished by the same means. Replacing the rear shocks is a piece of cake; a job that even a rank novice should be able to perform without any drama.

There are a couple of things that will make swapping the shocks somewhat easier. First, it might be wise to enlist the aid of a friend, particularly if you're new to this kind of work. Softails are fairly heavy and you'll be jacking the rear of the bike clear off the ground. A second pair of hands will prove extremely helpful. If your buddy hesitates, an offer of pizza and suds will usually do the trick. Second, you'll find that the rear securing bolts are really, really tight, and they're in an awkward spot. Because of the cramped quarters you won't be able to get a regular socket on the bolts. You may be able to use a "crow's-foot" wrench and breaker bar. Snap-on does make a box wrench adapter, part #SRES 24, that will work with a breaker bar to loosen the bolts. The adapter should make life considerably easier.

Since the owner of our project bike was happy with the ride height, but less so with the handling in general, he elected to do a straight swap. If he had wanted to lower the bike the procedure would have been the same, although I would have selected a pair of shocks that gave him the ride height that he wanted. Bear in mind that if I had changed the ride height, the overall geometry of the motorcycle would have been affected. Lowering the rear of the bike had the same effect as increasing the rake. Therefore, the bike would have handled a bit slower, and felt slightly heavy steering. My point here is that if you do decide to lower the bike, you're going to get something more than a new look. Make certain that you fully understand the implications of lowering, or for that matter raising, your motorcycle's suspension, before you do so.

The first step is to secure the bike onto a suitable lift. Not everyone has a motorcycle lift in their garage. If you don't, you'll need to come up with some way of securing the bike while the wheels are off the ground. Trust me, a plastic milk crate won't do the job. There are some very

First, place the jack, which is needed to raise the rear wheel off the ground, onto the frame support as shown.

good, inexpensive motorcycle jacks available through some of the large discount stores. Many auto parts stores also carry reasonably priced jacks. Here's a trick, though: you can do this job on the floor if you use a small jack to lift the rear end of the bike; you'll need a helper or two to steady the bike and help you change the shocks, but what are friends for?

Remove the two stock rear shock bolts using a 3/4-inch wrench. You'll need an 11/16-inch wrench for the front two bolts, which are easier to get to. (If the bolts are stiff, you'll need a 3/4-inch crows-foot and breaker bar to loosen the two rear bolts.)

Here's what the new chrome Progressive Suspension shocks look like compared to the stock units.

Remove the E-clip, nut, and chrome cap with bushing from the new shock. Leave the other chrome cap with bushing on the shock stud.

Angle the shock so you can install the front stud into the frame hole. Then reinstall the chrome cap with bushing, nut, and E-clip onto the stud. Leave the nut loose for now and adjust it later as per instructions.

After you put a little anti-seize on the shoulder part of the bolt, slip it into the shock and then thread it into the swingarm. Use the jack to lift or drop the rear of the bike so the bolt is properly lined up.

Adjust the ride height using the supplied tool

Adjusting the Shocks

It will be somewhat easier to adjust the suspension preload before the shocks are installed on the motorcycle. Follow the manufacturer's instructions. To set the preload on the Progressive Shocks, loosen the locknut and then use the supplied tool to adjust the preload.

I've found that it's easier to loosen the bolts while the motorcycle still has both wheels firmly planted on the ground. Begin by loosening the front nut(s) followed by the rear bolts. Do not try to remove any of the bolts or the shocks at this point.

Next, jack up the bike so the rear wheel is slightly off the ground. If needed, have a buddy steady the bike. You don't want to jack the bike so high that the weight of the wheel and swing arm preloads the suspension. If you are

using a jack that holds the bike some distance off the floor, place a small hydraulic or screw jack beneath the rear wheel.

Support the wheel so the shocks are free to move. You can do this most easily by using the jack to support the rear wheel.

Remove one shock. You may have to fiddle with the jack to remove preload.

Slip the eyebolt end of the new shock into place; coat the shaft of the bolt with anti-seize; and install the opposite end of the shock. Again, the jack may have to be adjusted to line up everything properly. Repeat for the opposite side.

Apply Loctite and tighten the rear bolts, followed by the front ones. Torque all hardware and make any adjustments to the manufacturer's specifications. Install the supplied E-clips after everything is tightened.

Lowering a Twin Shock Rear End

Time: 1–2 hours

Tools: Appropriate sockets, open-end wrenches, torque wrench, Loctite, white grease or anti-seize compound, lift or small floor jack

Talent:

Cost: $175 and up

Tip: Use a jack to support the bike while you swap the shocks to save time and tempers.

PERFORMANCE GAIN: Shortening the rear allows vertically challenged riders to reach the pavement. Don't forget, you're losing ground clearance, which may cause solid parts to drag if you ride aggressively

COMPLEMENTARY MODIFICATION: Lowering the front fork, putting lifts in your boots

There are two ways to lower the rear end of your Twin shock rear end. The preferable way is by bolting on a shorter pair of rear dampers. The alternative is to use a set of lowering blocks.

The one advantage to using lowering blocks is their cost. If the budget is a big issue, lowering blocks are one way to go. The problem I have with them is that they change the angle of the shock, which affects the spring rate, in effect softening it up to some degree. This can affect handling, how much is debatable, but if you install the blocks and decide later that the bike doesn't handle the way you'd like it to, you're back to square one, and you're out the price of the blocks.

The second issue is that installing the blocks may complicate the installation of saddlebags, no small thing if you're on a Dresser.

Be that as it may, lowering blocks is one way to go should you choose them, and thousands of them are in use with no apparent ill effects.

Installing Shorter Shocks

Changing the height of the rear of the bike has some overall chassis geometry ramifications that should be considered. Dropping the rear one inch has roughly the same effect as raking the chassis one degree. That may not seem like much but it's enough to change the way the bike feels and responds. There are two other factors that need to be considered as well. First is the obvious, namely that ground clearance is going to be reduced, something you may want to keep in mind the first time you feel like pitching the bike into a hard corner. Second, when purchasing the new shorter shocks, be aware of the possibility that on the Dyna models the belt guard may whack the fender when the shock is fully compressed. If that seems likely, trial-fit one shock without the spring installed and move the swing arm from full extension to full compression. Make any adjustments to the belt guard and recheck the fit before installing the other shock and the springs.

Begin the installation by supporting the bike on a work stand or jack. Position the bike so that the rear wheel is unloaded. Remove the rear axle. The wheel can stay where it is, the belt can stay on the pulley. Unbolt one shock, run a piece of wire or stout cord from the upper shock mount to the lower. The cord is just to prevent the swing arm from crashing down when the other shock is removed; there is no need to get too fancy here. Remove the other shock. Following the shock manufacturer's instructions, install necessary spacers, bushings, or shims to fit the shock to your bike. If you suspect there may be clearance issues mount one shock, preferably without the spring, and stroke the swing arm from full extension to full compression, making sure that nothing binds.

Installation

Mount first one shock and then the other. Hand tighten the mounting hardware. When viewed from the rear the shocks should be in line. If one end of the shock appears to be inclined more toward the centerline of the bike than the other the shock will tend to bind. Use washers to shim the shock until it is perfectly straight. Make sure no part of the shock or spring hits any portion of the frame or an accessory. Put a drop of Loctite on the shock bolts and torque them to factory specifications; clean and lightly grease the rear axle before installation; and torque the rear axle nut to the recommended specification. Ride off into the new—and somewhat lower—sunset.

SUSPENSION AND CHASSIS

Lowering a twin shock rear is no more difficult than unbolting the old stuff, and installing the new shorter shock.

PROJECT 31

Servicing Rubber Engine Transmission Mounts

 Time: 2 hours and 30 minutes to 3 hours and 30 minutes

 Tools: 1/2-inch, 9/16-inch, and 5/8-inch wrenches with matching sockets (don't forget the ratchet and extension), torque wrench, jack, motorcycle stand, lubricant such as WD-40

 Talent:

 Cost: $200 (approximately)

 Tip: Inspect the mounts often, like every 5,000 miles and replace as required to avoid headaches.

 PERFORMANCE GAIN: If you wanted a paint shaker you should have bought a Sportster; replacing worn mounts will put the glide back in your stride

COMPLEMENTARY MODIFICATION: Now may be the time to replace the swingarm bushings, especially if the bike has high miles

There are only two ways to keep engine vibration from reaching the rider. One is to build a smoother engine; the other is to engineer some sort of system that will prevent the vibration that does exist from reaching the rider. Harley has done both.

On the FLT, FXR, and Dyna models Harley has isolated the engine and transmission from the chassis by interposing rubber mounts. They didn't originate this system; a British motorcycle called the Sunbeam used rubber motor mounts back in the 1950s, as did Norton in later years. However, Harley's system seems to work the best. Designing a rubber engine-mounting system takes more than a trip down to the rubber store to pick up some rubber billet. If the rubber is too hard, too much vibration may be passed on to the rider, too soft and the mounts destroy themselves in short order.

How do you know when the mounts are worn out? The first clue is usually an increase in the amount of engine vibration transmitted to the rider. If the situation is allowed to deteriorate, the rubber mount may separate. If

that happens you'll hear or feel a banging, especially during rapid on-off throttle transitions.

The Dynas use a slightly different mounting system. One that's been known to break if the lower mount gets whacked by the edge of a pothole. The first clue here is a noticeable increase in vibration levels shortly after you've encountered one of the aforementioned obstacles.

Routine inspection and periodic replacement of the mounts should forestall any real problems. On FX and FL models, the front mount is easy to see and inspect; if it looks torn or damaged, it is; replace it ASAP. The pivot mounts are a bit trickier. The quick and dirty inspection goes like this: Remove the chrome inspection cap from the swingarm pivot; the pivot bolt should be roughly centered in the swingarm pivot. If the bolt appears to be biased toward the top of the hole, the mounts are shot.

When it comes to replacing the mounts, your shop manual will provide the blow-by-blow details, as well as the variations between models, but here are the high points.

To replace the pivot mounts, position the jack under the engine/transmission. Use the jack to remove any pre-load from the suspension. Remove the end caps, which should allow the mounts to drop out—occasionally in several chunks. Install the new mounts, and torque to the prescribed specifications. Replacing the mounts one at a time is an exercise in futility. Always replace the pivot mounts as pairs and always replace the front engine mount in conjunction with the pivots.

The service life of the mounts varies from bike to bike. I've heard of many bikes that racked up 50,000 to 60,000 miles before the mounts needed changing and just as many that were lucky to make 10,000. If nothing else, it makes a good case for inspecting them on a regular basis.

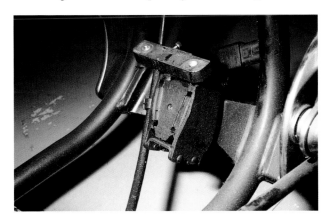

Replacing worn engine mounts is a sure way to improve comfort and reduce vibration-induced wear on your bike.

SUSPENSION AND CHASSIS

91

Installing Rear Air Shocks

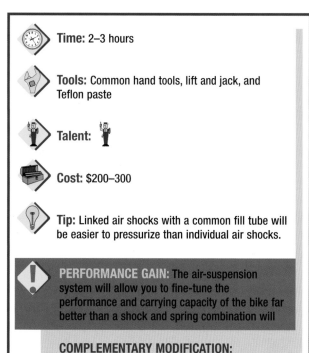

Time: 2–3 hours

Tools: Common hand tools, lift and jack, and Teflon paste

Talent: 👨‍🔧

Cost: $200–300

Tip: Linked air shocks with a common fill tube will be easier to pressurize than individual air shocks.

PERFORMANCE GAIN: The air-suspension system will allow you to fine-tune the performance and carrying capacity of the bike far better than a shock and spring combination will

COMPLEMENTARY MODIFICATION:
Fork upgrades

SUSPENSION AND CHASSIS

We've been over this before but it bears repeating. Many riders intuitively believe that by cranking up the suspension preload, the spring is somehow made stiffer. It isn't. Cranking up the spring preload only changes the bike's ride height. The only way to stiffen the spring is by physically installing a stiffer spring.

This can create some problems for riders that pay close attention to the way their bikes handle. For instance, suppose that during the week you use your bike primarily to ride to work, but on the weekend you like to load up the significant other, some camping gear, and take off for parts unknown. Or maybe you're one of those who tools around at a moderate pace most of the time but likes to go for the occasional Sunday afternoon charge down racer road. In both cases, the suspension requirements vary greatly from the first instance to the second.

Obviously, you could just crank up the suspension preload to accommodate the increased weight of the passenger and luggage or your hard-charging riding style. Maybe it would work, maybe it wouldn't, it would really depend on how much suspension travel you use riding solo and how much wallow you're willing to accept. Or, you could install a slightly stiffer spring; it's a bit of a headache and an option that certainly doesn't appeal to me.

What you really need is some sort of spring that can be easily adjusted to accommodate a wide range of loads and road conditions. The solution is what's commonly known as an air shock, or more correctly, an air-assisted shock absorber.

Air shocks replace the conventional spring with an internal air bladder, although most shocks retain some sort of vestigial spring that prevents the shock from collapsing in the event of a broken air line or other catastrophic failure. In common practice both shocks are linked together through a common fill tube. This allows the shocks to be pressurized together, which eliminates any imbalances that might be caused by leakage or inaccurate filling.

A small on-board compressor pressurizes the most sophisticated air shock systems. These are really the way to go because the ride height can be adjusted on the fly. Less sophisticated designs are filled through a conventional Schrader valve mounted at some convenient point. Due to the small volume of air involved, a small hand pump is easier to use than a typical gas station or shop air compressor. Likewise, many of the pumps sold specifically for suspension work have a bleed screw incorporated in them making accurate adjustment of the air pressure somewhat easier.

The air shock provides an advantage over the conventional spring because air is infinitely compressible. And when air is compressed it offers a naturally progressive

The heart of the system, and the part that makes this set up so convenient to use is the on board compressor.

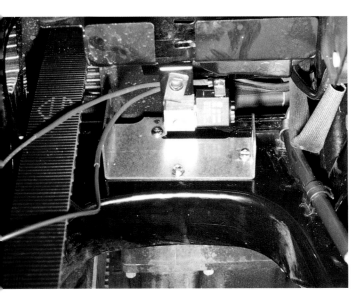

Watch that belt! It'll saw through those lines in a heartbeat.

Once everything is buttoned up, you'll barely know it's there-until you need it!

The air gauge lets you keep track of everything from the cockpit.

resistance to further compression. Simply put, that means that the harder you try to compress the air, the more it resists being compressed. In other words, it offers true raising rate suspension action.

The other advantage is that the ride height of the bike can be adjusted simply by adding enough air—within the manufacturer's recommended limits of course—to overcome the weight of the added luggage or passenger. For those of you with a sporting bend, the "spring rate" can be varied according to the type of riding you plan on doing simply by adjusting the pressure.

Overall the air shock is a worthwhile addition for any rider whose riding circumstances vary greatly from one trip to another. On the downside, air shocks do have some issues. Some riders just don't like to be bothered adjusting the air pressure on a routine basis. Some air shocks also tend to lose air pressure a bit quicker than they should, although often a leaky shock can be traced to a sloppy installation, particularly in sealing the air lines. Finally, some riders just don't want the added complication. On the upside, the installation is simple and straightforward, the disadvantages are few, and few shock absorbers offer the overall versatility and ease of adjustment.

SECTION FIVE

Tires, Wheels, and Brakes

Balancing Wheels

Time: Figure at least 30 minutes apiece to remove the wheels and another 30 minutes to balance each one

Tools: Work stand to lift the bike, common hand tools, wheel balance stand (which can be easily built at home)

 Talent: If you can get the wheels off, you can balance them

Cost: At the cheapest a few bucks, if you send the wheels to a dealer for balancing it could run $50–75

Tip: Balance the wheel every time a new tire is mounted.

 PERFORMANCE GAIN: Longer tire life, better handling

COMPLEMENTARY MODIFICATION: New tires; inspect and service wheel bearings

Wheel balance is one of those dirty, unglamorous jobs that's not much fun to do. Sort of like washing the dishes. The problem is that an unbalanced wheel will wear out the tires faster and cause handling problems. Out-of-balance wheels also increase vibration levels, which can damage other components.

Essentially there are two forms of balancing: static, and dynamic. Static balancing, as the name implies, essentially means that when the wheel is placed in any position it stays there. The theory is that if the wheel is in balance at 0 miles per hour, then it should be reasonably close at 60 or 80 miles per hour. While on the face of it this may seem unlikely, the truth of the matter is that static balancing, when done properly, is extremely accurate. I've seen race bikes approach 200 miles per hour on statically balanced tires with nary a shimmer.

Dynamically balancing, or spin balancing a tire involves spinning the tire up to about 45 miles per hour or more and taking a reading. Specialized equipment is required to spin balance a wheel and it ain't cheap. I'd have

to say that purchasing a spin balancer for home shop use isn't really very practical.

Spin balancing is quite accurate and it takes a lot less time to perform than a static balance job. But for most of us it means taking the wheels off the bike and down to the local shop. And it means leaving the wheels there for a day or two, until someone can get to them. If you choose to have your wheels dynamically balanced all you need do is remove them, trot them down to your friendly neighborhood motorcycle shop and pick them up when they're done. Not much challenge in that is there?

Obviously, the biggest advantage static balancing has is that it can be done in your home workshop.

Stick-on weights are required for solid wheels . . .

. . . and mags.

95

Theory

The theory of wheel balancing is simple. Wheels have heavy and light spots. Since you can't remove weight from the heavy spots, you add weight to the low spots; when the high and low spots are equal the wheel is in balance and will rotate smoothly.

Nuts and Bolts

As you can appreciate, a wheel can only be static balanced when there is absolutely no drag on it. If you plan on leaving the wheel(s) on the bike while you balance them, this means you'll have to remove the brake calipers, drive belt, and anything else that can cause drag. I'd recommend leaving the axle nut loose so as to not preload the wheel bearings as well. A better solution may be to build a small wooden upright stand capable of holding the wheel and axle assembly so that it's free to rotate, or purchasing a dedicated wheel stand.

If you're mounting a new tire make certain that the dash of paint on the tire indicating the tire's light spot is positioned at the valve stem. Now is also the perfect time to inspect, repack, and re-shim the wheel bearings as required. Before you begin, be certain to remove any old balance weights.

If the wheel is mounted in the fork or swingarm, make certain it is 100 percent free to rotate on its own. Give the tire a slight push and wait for it to stop spinning. In theory, the heaviest portion of the tire will come to rest at the bottom. Mark the spot with a crayon and give it another spin. If the same spot comes to rest at the bottom you've found the heavy spot. If the tire comes to rest in a different spot altogether, it's in balance. Double check by rotating the wheel to different positions. If it remains at rest no matter where you place it, the tire is in balance.

Chances are about 50/50 that a brand-new tire properly mounted will be in balance. If it isn't you'll need to add a bit of weight to the light spot, which as I'm sure you've figured out will be directly opposite the heavy spot.

Wheel weights come in all shapes and sizes. There are stick-on weights with adhesive backing and ones that clip onto the edge of the rim. For spoke wheels there are weights that are made to slip over the spoke. Ideally, the weight should be as close to the center of the rim as possible. For that reason I recommend stick-on weights for solid wheels, and the slip over style for spoked rims. If you have spoked wheels and you're on a tight budget you can wrap lengths of solder around the spokes.

Once you've determined that some weight is necessary you'll need to experiment a bit. If the wheel is slightly out of balance, start with a 1/4-ounce weight. Tape it to the rim with masking or duct tape and check the wheel balance again. Repeat the process until the wheel balances before affixing the weight permanently. Try to split the weight evenly. For example if you need to add a 1-ounce weight, place two 1/2-ounce weights on either side of the rim.

If the wheel seems to take an extraordinary amount of weight before it will balance, break the tire down and rotate it 180 degrees on the rim to relocate the heavy spot. Run through the balance procedure again; chances are you'll use less weight.

Statically balancing a wheel demands concentration and patience, and it's hardly as much fun as installing a hot cam, for instance. But trust me, in the end, it's just as important.

Weights that slide over the spokes are used on wire wheels, although a twist of solder will work in a pinch.

The ultimate in wheel balancing is the high speed, computerized dynamic wheel balancer. This is a shop-only item, but whatever they charge you is worth it.

TIRES, WHEELS, AND BRAKES

96

Building and Maintaining Wire Wheels

 Time: 30 minutes (maintenance) to 6 hours (building and truing a new wheel)

 Tools: Spoke wrench (preferably a spoke torque wrench), truing stand, dial indicator or wheel run-out indicator, tools to remove and install wheels

 Talent: – You'll need a ton of patience to build a wire wheel

 Cost: A custom wheel and spoke set could run you up to $1,000 or more per wheel

 Tip: Before starting make absolutely certain that your proposed tire and rim combination is going to fit your frame and fork.

 PERFORMANCE GAIN: Lighter wheels improve handling and acceleration

COMPLEMENTARY MODIFICATION: The obvious one is a tire upgrade; however, now is also the time to upgrade the brakes. You may also need to upgrade the driveline, particularly if a wide rear tire is being installed

Frankly speaking, I can't stand truing wheels, let alone building them. It can be done, but it's a frustrating job. When I need a wire wheel laced up, I call a professional wheel builder, ship him the hub and measurements, and let him have at it. But some souls find wheel work incredibly satisfying, and who am I to argue?

Wheel Maintenance

Since servicing the wheel bearings comes at the end of this section, for the time being we're only going to consider wheel maintenance as it applies to the spokes and their interaction between the hub and rim.

Wire wheels should receive at least a cursory examination at every minor service. There is no need to go overboard here, but the rims should be checked for dents around their periphery and cracks around the spoke holes. The spokes themselves need to be checked for tension and adjusted if they are loose.

The time-honored method of checking a spoke is to give a light tap with a small wrench or screwdriver. A snug spoke will give off a nice musical "ping"—a loose one will sound flat. There's no need to worry about all of them giving off a C-sharp, or E-flat; just a nice tight ring will do. Alternatively, you can place a spoke wrench or better yet a spoke torque wrench on each spoke nipple and give it a slight tug.

If the spokes are found to be a bit loose they'll need to be tightened in a set pattern to avoid yanking the wheel out of true.

Start by locating the spoke closest to the tire valve stem. Give the spoke a 1/4 turn, or using a spoke torque wrench, tighten it to the correct torque. Skip the next two spokes and tighten the fourth the same way. Proceed around the wheel, tightening every fourth spoke until you come back to the valve stem. At the stem, move forward one spoke, and repeat the process. Keep the cycle going until all of the spokes have been tightened. Recheck the spoke tension; if it's still off, repeat the process, never tightening the nipple more than a quarter of a turn until all the spokes are tight. At least 99 percent of the time routine maintenance will be all you'll ever need to perform to keep your wire wheels in good shape; the other 1 percent of the time the wheel will need to be trued.

Truing a wheel is more involved than simply tightening the spokes. By truing I mean ensuring that the rim runs straight, with neither side-to-side runout, called either axial run out or wobble, nor up-and-down runout, called radial runout or hop. In the main axial, run out is easier to cure but also more likely to occur. Although rims can be trued with the tire mounted and the wheel positioned in the frame or fork, I don't believe in doing it that way. My preference is to remove the wheel from the bike, remove the tire and tube from the wheel, and use a truing stand. Because the procedures are essentially the same for truing a freshly laced wheel or one that's just out of true, I'll cover the wheel-building procedure.

Wheel Assembly

The start of the wheel lacing process is pretty simple. Unless you're simply replacing damaged components with new ones, you'll need to determine what hub you want to use, what rim you want to lace it to and what size and spoke pattern you plan to use. These aren't decisions that should be made lightly and I strongly urge you to seek the advice of a qualified wheel builder before embarking on this aspect of modification, especially if this is your first foray as a wheelwright. In addition to the above you'll also need to know how much offset, if any, the rim has in regards to the hub. The easiest way to determine this is to measure the existing rim and sketch out the spoke pattern. Measure the edge of the rim from both sides of the hub, noting which side is the pulley side and which is the brake side. Of course, if you're lacing up a wider rim, those dimensions will need to adjusted accordingly. The spoke pattern or "cross" is determined by how many spokes intersect or cross each other on their way from the hub to the rim; the norm is a cross-three or cross-four pattern.

Available spokes come in a variety of shapes, sizes, and styles. Depending on the style of hub you use, the spokes may alternate by length or by whether they are positioned to the inside of the hub or the outside. Use your drawing, the factory service manual, or the spoke/hub manufacturer's specific recommendations regarding the spoke pattern.

After the spokes are in the hub, place the rim over the hub and then fan the spokes out. Notice that the rim's dimples all face a different direction. For the sake of argument we'll assume your hub uses inner and outer spokes. Locate an outer spoke that lines up with a dimple, put a dab of grease under the head of the nipple and run it onto the spoke a few turns. Proceed to the next outer spoke and repeat.

Once all the outer spokes have been connected on one side, repeat the process using the inner spokes. Flip the rim over and repeat for the other side. If the threaded end of the spoke protrudes through the rim too far, try moving it one hole in another direction. To avoid damage to the rim install a nipple as soon as its spoke is in place. Once all of the spokes and nipples are in place thread them down finger tight.

An alternative method is to just install the inside spokes into the hub. Lace them into position on the rim and then install the outside spokes. Either way works equally well.

Harley-Davidson manuals recommend using an initial set of spokes to true the wheel and then tightening the remaining spokes in a prescribed pattern. I've never used their method but have been told that it works quite well. If you're simply replacing stock parts with new factory stuff I'd recommend you use the factory-prescribed method of building and truing the wheel.

Truing the Wheel

Place the freshly completed wheel in your truing stand, or if you'd prefer, you can set it back in the swingarm or front fork. Chances are it'll revolve like a drunk's merry-go-round. The first step is to adjust for offset. If things went favorably, your rim offset should be pretty close. If the rim is too far to the left, tighten only the spokes on the right and vice-versa.

You shouldn't have to screw the nipples down very far to move the rim. If you find them bottoming out, something's wrong. Possibly the spokes are too tight or the spokes are in the wrong holes.

Frankly, truing wheels, let alone building one of these 80-spoke wonders, would drive me right up the wall. They sure look good though!

Once offset has been adjusted we'll have to adjust radial (up-and-down) runout. Mount a pointer to the bottom of your stand, or to a handy spot on the bike. Find the high and low spot of the rim. At the low spot tighten the spokes at the top and loosen the ones at the bottom. You'll probably need to do this a few times until the wheel is true. When your rim is true to about 1/8 inch or less, stop.

Most rims are bent around a mandrel and then welded at the joint. You may find that the wheel "kicks" or "jumps" at the spot where the rim itself has been welded. There's not much you can do about it. Many rims exhibit this behavior; it's nothing to worry about.

Lateral (side-to-side) runout and spoke tension are adjusted at the same time. Move the pointer to the side of the rim; if the rim pulls to the right adjust the spokes on the left. Repeat until the rim runs true, within 1/32 inch or so. By now the spokes should all have at least equal tension on them. Test them by tapping each with a screwdriver. A snug spoke should have a nice "ping" to it, a loose one a dull "clack."

Initially, each spoke should only be run down finger tight. Once truing commences the spoke should only be tightened one quarter of a turn at a time. When the wheel runs true and the spokes are snug, STOP! Over torquing a spoke will pull the wheel out of true and make the spoke more likely to break.

Once the wheel is true, seat the nipples in the rim by giving them a tap with a hammer and brass punch. Recheck your handiwork and then carefully grind or file off any spokes that are out of the nipple to prevent them from grinding through the inner tube. Finally, give the tire well a few wraps of duct tape.

The right way to true a wheel: A true pro, my buddy Dan uses a dial indicator and truing stand to get this wheel perfect.

Mounting the tires can be tricky, particularly if the rim is painted or alloy. Plastic rim protectors are available from most motorcycle shops and should be used to prevent unnecessary damage. I also use a plastic bucket to support the wheel while mounting the tire, although you may find that having the local dealer mount your tires is less aggravating.

Once the bike has a few miles on it—say 500 or so—you can re-torque the spokes by giving each one a tug with a spoke wrench. Don't worry if any are loose. This is normal, as the spokes tend to loosen slightly while they fully seat. Tighten them a quarter turn at a time until they are all snug again.

Spoke Tools

What do you use to turn those pesky spoke nipples? You can use a small adjustable wrench. Of course they are awkward and tend to round off the nipples. A better tool is a dedicated spoke wrench. Spoke wrenches are available in a multitude of shapes and sizes. Some incorporate several sizes in one wrench. Others are cut to fit a particular size.

If you're in the market for a high-tech spoke wrench, there is even a spoke torque wrench available with interchangeable heads made by Fasst Company (562/601-8119). It's a little pricey at over $100 but it will definitely ensure that all the spokes are correctly torqued.

Servicing the Brakes—Changing the Brake Fluid

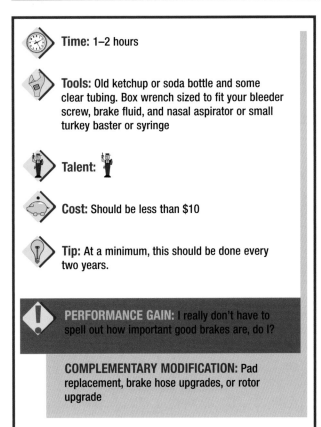

Time: 1–2 hours

Tools: Old ketchup or soda bottle and some clear tubing. Box wrench sized to fit your bleeder screw, brake fluid, and nasal aspirator or small turkey baster or syringe

Talent:

Cost: Should be less than $10

Tip: At a minimum, this should be done every two years.

PERFORMANCE GAIN: I really don't have to spell out how important good brakes are, do I?

COMPLEMENTARY MODIFICATION: Pad replacement, brake hose upgrades, or rotor upgrade

TIRES, WHEELS, AND BRAKES

Since we've already dealt with brake pad replacement and we're going to address some brake-system upgrades further along, it's time to take a quick look at what's possibly the most neglected aspect of brake system maintenance: the brake fluid.

Brake fluid, like motor oil, needs to be changed on a routine basis, preferably every two years. The problem is that most brake fluid is hydroscopic, meaning it has an affinity for water, and will absorb moisture out of the atmosphere. Given enough time, this means that the boiling point of the brake fluid drops to the point where brake fade becomes a genuine possibility.

To their credit, Harley-Davidson has sidestepped that particular issue by engineering their current brake systems to work with DOT 5 brake fluid. DOT 5 is a silicone-based brake fluid and is non-hydroscopic and non-corrosive. Using DOT 5 did present the Motor Company with some slight problems, but in the main their system works very well, so long as it is properly maintained. Although DOT 5 doesn't absorb water from the atmosphere the way that DOT 3 and 4 do, it does decay over time, primarily because moisture finds its way into the system through

condensation and power washers, and of course some dirt contamination is inevitable. Hence the need for the occasional fluid change. Bear in mind though that DOT 5 is not interchangeable with any of the other brake fluids. Before doing any brake fluid work, make absolutely certain that you have the proper brake fluid for your motorcycle and brake system. If you've bought the bike used and there is even the remotest possibility that the previous owner installed aftermarket components that use DOT 3 or 4, stop and find out exactly what kind of fluid is in the system before proceeding.

Changing the Fluid

After determining proper brake fluid, drain the entire brake system, refill it, and bleed it exactly as you would when replacing one of the brake system components. As you might guess, this can be a time-consuming and messy procedure. Since you're only going to change the brake fluid itself, here is a much simpler method and one that's just as effective.

Fasten a hose to the bleeder screw, just as you would if you were preparing to bleed the brakes. Run the other end of the hose into your ketchup or soda bottle to catch the old brake fluid.

Place a small amount of fresh brake fluid in the bottle—just enough to cover the end of the hose. This will prevent air from being drawn into the system should you inadvertently forget to close the bleed nipple when you release the brake lever. There are several methods you can use to change the fluid; all work equally well. The simplest method is to open the bleeder screw and pump the brake lever, which will force the old brake fluid through the system and out the open bleeder screw. Keep your eye on the master cylinder and refill it as soon as the level drops to the add mark. The advantage is that this method is quick, and damn-near foolproof. However, you should bleed the brakes in standard fashion when you're done, just to make certain no air was drawn into the system during the exchange process. On the downside it uses quite a bit of brake fluid and it pumps lots of old dirty brake fluid and the attendant crud, through the hoses and caliper. For those reasons it's not my favorite method. Another method involves a bit of extra work. Use the aspirator, syringe, or turkey baster to evacuate the old juice from the master cylinder. With a clean rag, wipe up any sludge lying at the base of the reservoir. Fill the master cylinder with fresh, clean fluid, pump the lever a time or three and then hold it to the bar, or floorboard, footpeg, or whatever. Loosen the brake bleeder and watch the dirty fluid issue forth. Close the bleeder screw and repeat the process, keeping a close eye on the fluid level. It'd suck if you drew air into the system through the master cylinder and had to start all over again. Keep at it until only clear, clean fluid comes out. The advantages with this method should be self-evident; no contaminants are drawn into the brake system and the chance that air will enter the system is nil.

I'd recommend the first method if you change the fluid on a regular basis; use the second method if you don't change the fluid on a regular basis or if the fluid is particularly grimy. Repeat every two years.

Lastly, even though DOT 5 brake fluid is non-corrosive it's never a good idea to splash the stuff around. Protect your eyes at all times and toss a cover over painted parts. Dispose of the old stuff responsibly, which doesn't mean pouring it down the nearest storm drain.

The time-honored way to bleed brakes is to have a buddy pump them up while you catch the fluid in a suitable container. Don't forget to hold the lever down when you open the bleed screw.

The most efficient way to bleed brakes, particularly if you're working alone, is via a vacuum pump. These can be purchased at any auto parts store for under 50 bucks. The line wrench will prevent damage to soft brake line fittings.

Installing Braided Brake Lines

Time: 23 hours

Tools: Wrenches needed to remove brake lines; container of fresh DOT 5 brake fluid; catch can for used fluid; small piece of fuel line or rubber hose that fits securely over the caliper's bleed nipple; aerosol brake wash; and an optional Mityvac or other type of vacuum brake bleeding pump

Talent: This is a simple job; however, the results of doing it wrong could be devastating. Before undertaking this project you should feel entirely comfortable working on the brake system.

Cost: Brake line kits start at $50 and head upward

Tip: Replace all brake hose washers with new ones.

PERFORMANCE GAIN: Firmer brake feel, better stopping

COMPLEMENTARY MODIFICATION: Since the brake fluid will be drained from the system, now is the perfect time to install those trick calipers or billet master cylinders

When disc brakes first became popular for motorcycle use the master cylinders were connected to the calipers via spongy, flex-prone rubber hoses. It wasn't long before performance-minded riders found out that the stainless-steel jacketed, plastic brake lines used in the aircraft industry and on race cars not only worked better but gave the bike a tricked-out look, as well.

At first, everyone bought the fittings, cut the hose, usually along with their fingers in the process, and made up their own lines. Currently, just about any length, style, and color of stainless-steel brake line is available over the counter, which greatly simplifies the conversion process.

Actually, there are two types of hose available: The first is the straightforward stainless-steel stuff that most of us have seen at one time or another. Normally, the stainless is left in its bright state or anodized to another color. The second type replaces the stainless-steel mesh with a Kevlar cover. Both work equally well. The Kevlar is less obtrusive, and won't saw through your paint the way a stainless-steel hose will. But of course the stainless has that high-tech look and is shiny to boot. As the saying goes, "You pay your money, and you make your choices."

Installing the Lines

Begin the installation by draining out all of the old brake fluid. Ideally you should connect a vacuum pump to the caliper bleeder screw and evacuate the system by vacuum; don't forget to do both calipers if you're working on a dual-disc front end. As an alternative you can simply pump the system down by using the brake lever.

Once the old fluid is out of the system, remove the old brake hose from the master cylinder, junction block (if there is one), and the caliper(s). Even though Harley specifies DOT 5 brake fluid, which is non-corrosive, it's still not a good idea to slather the stuff all over; be sure to wipe up any spills as they occur. After the hose has been removed it might be prudent to flush out the master cylinder with some brake wash and a few ounces of clean fluid. Compare the length of the stock hose to its replacement. If the lengths aren't identical, or at the very least nearly so, make sure you have the right hose for your application before proceeding.

Install the new hose on the bike. Make certain that the hose has a natural lay to it; if it appears to be twisted or stressed try removing the caliper end and letting the hose

Once the system has been drained, the old lines can be removed and the new ones installed. Position the lines where you want them and tighten the bolt.

unwind itself before bolting it back in place. My feeling is that new sealing washers are dirt-cheap insurance against leaks, not to mention sudden and untimely brake failure. For that reason I recommend you always replace the old washers with new as a matter of course. If you feel you'd rather save a few bucks and risk your life, by all means, be my guest.

Before refilling the master cylinder make absolutely certain that the hose is properly routed and protected from chaffing damage. Likewise, make sure that anything that would be damaged by the hose's steel sheath—such as the paint on your front fender—is also protected. I've seen steel lines saw through an aluminum fork leg, so if there is direct contact between the hose and anything else, you'll need to separate the two. A piece of clear plastic hose can be used as an insulator between the hose and whatever it's contacting, if need be.

When you're satisfied with the installation and routing of the hose, double check the banjo bolts, making sure that they are tight, and then refill the master cylinder with fresh DOT 5 brake fluid.

Bleeding the Brakes

Brake bleeding is a skill every budding mechanic needs to develop, particularly since this section and Project 39, Upgrading the Brake Calipers, involve some major brake surgery. In the main, bleeding is a simple if somewhat tedious and occasionally messy task.

First let's take a very quick look at some basic physics. Fluid is essentially incompressible, meaning that it transmits energy well; in fact it works much like a solid in that respect. On the other hand, air, or more accurately gas, is infinitely compressible, meaning it stores energy, and does not transmit it as well as a fluid. Since the brake system is completely drained, and fresh fluid installed, air has entered the system and become mixed with the new fluid, or worse, trapped in bubble form in some portion of the brake system. Because air is trapped in the system the

Carefully route the cable, and secure it to the caliper.

brake lever either won't have any effect at all, or will have a spongy feel to it. This is because the trapped air will absorb the energy you are trying to transmit through the brake fluid when you pull the brake lever. Rather than move the pistons in the caliper, our energy will be absorbed in compressing the air trapped in the brake line.

To rid the system of trapped air you need to bleed it. Bleeding is nothing more than removing or "bleeding" any trapped air from the brake system. Every mechanic I ever met has his own preferred method of bleeding brakes. Some like to do it manually, some use a vacuum bleeder, some like to "back bleed" the system.

I'll start with the simplest method and work up the ladder.

Manual Bleeding

This is the most common and easiest method of bleeding a brake system, and unfortunately, the most time consuming. If you've never done it before or it's a long reach from your brake lever or pedal to the caliper bleeder screw, you want to enlist the aid of a friend. By the way, the procedure for bleeding the front and rear brakes is identical.

Remove the rubber dust shield from your brake calipers bleeder screw.

Attach a piece of hose to the bleeder screw. You may want to crack the screw loose with a box end wrench before attaching the hose; you can even leave the wrench on the screw to make it a bit more convenient.

Place the open end of the hose into your catch can and pour a few ounces of brake fluid into the can, just enough to cover the open end of the hose. The fluid will prevent air from being drawn into the system should you forget to tighten the screw as you pump the brakes. The fluid will also act as a visual aid to determine if air bubbles are being forced out of the system.

Since the system is empty, fill the master cylinder to full line, placing a rag over the top of the cylinder to prevent splashing. Open the bleeder screw at least one full turn. Pump the lever until fluid runs out the screw. (Keep an eye on the master cylinder and refill it as soon as the level drops to the add mark.)

Once fluid drips from the bleeder screw, close it. Pump the brake lever until some resistance is felt, or until you've pumped it about 20 times.

With the lever held against the handlebar (or the stop if it's a rear brake pedal) loosen the bleeder screw. Fluid should spurt out, although it may be more of a dribble at first. Hold the lever down while you loosen the screw; don't let it up until the bleed screw is tight again. Watch the end of the hose if possible; you should initially see some air bubbles coming out.

Repeat the process until the lever is good and firm, or no air bubbles appear in the brake fluid.

As I mentioned, this method can be slow and tedious; I've spent up to an hour bleeding brakes this way so don't be alarmed if it seems to take forever.

Alternatives

If the system just won't bleed you may need to "back bleed" it. This involves forcing brake fluid into the brake line from the bleeder screw end. This requires a special syringe normally sold in auto parts stores. The syringe should come with directions; however, the short and nasty of it is that you fill the back bleeder with brake fluid and attach it to the open bleed nipple via a short piece of hose. Pushing the plunger forces the fluid, under pressure, into the brake caliper and through the brake line into the master cylinder. By forcing the fluid into the system under pressure, the air bubbles are pushed upward toward the master cylinder where they evaporate into the air. You can then bleed the system in the normal fashion, just to be certain there is no residual air trapped anywhere.

Vacuum Bleeders

Vacuum bleeders come in two forms; the manual type, which is configured like a small hand pump, and the more expensive air-driven models. Both work in the same fashion. First the master cylinder is filled. The pump incorporates a good-sized, sealed reservoir. The pump is connected to the bleeder screw, which is then cracked open. The pump pulls a vacuum in the system; you regulate the vacuum by either a hand lever or squeeze handle. The vacuum draws fluid through the system, depositing it along with any trapped air into the reservoir. To ensure that no air can find its way back into the system, you should close the bleeder screw while the pump is still drawing a vacuum. These things really do the job. But they do move a lot of fluid so you really need to keep an eye on the master cylinder to avoid sucking it dry.

A Word to the Wise

Since we've performed some open-brake surgery, check and double check your work at each stage of the game. Once you're satisfied that the job has been done right with no loose ends left undone, check everything once more. Make your first test ride a slow one, and then recheck the system for leaks. You may also find that after a few rides the brakes require bleeding again. This happens a lot when you've manually bled the brakes and didn't quite get all of the trapped air out of the system. As the brakes are used, the air will migrate out of its hiding place, generally finding it's way into the caliper, where you can get rid of it. Occasionally it'll work the other way too; a brake may feel a little soft initially but as the bike is ridden the air will work its way to the master cylinder and evaporate on its own. In any event, as with all things of this nature, work slowly and patiently; of all the jobs you may do on your Harley, not many have the dire consequences of a bad brake job.

Use a piece of fuel line, or preferably a section of clear plastic hose, to connect the bleed screw to the catch can.

Upgrading Your Brake Discs

 Time: 1 hour per wheel

 Tools: Jack, wheel removal tools, appropriate sockets needed to remove the rotor bolts; Loctite, cardboard or rubber cushion to lay the wheel on

 Talent:

 Cost: $100–200 (or more) per rotor depending on size and style

 Tip: Rotor bolts may seize to the hub, making removal difficult; a heat gun or impact wrench can save time and temper.

 PERFORMANCE GAIN: If you want to go, you have to slow; better rotors make stopping a lot easier

COMPLEMENTARY MODIFICATION: Better rotors + better calipers + stainless brake lines = awesome stopping and a custom look

There are only two ways to increase your stopping power. You can give the brakes more leverage or you can increase their gripping power. Since Projects 37 and 39 have to do with grip, let's talk a little about leverage.

Prior to the advent of the Twin Cam lineup, the OEM disc brakes installed by the Motor Company have varied between slightly better than the drum brakes they replaced (debatable), and not horrible. With the introduction of the four-piston caliper and 11 1/2-inch rotor as used on the Twin Cam–series bikes the brakes became decent although not outstanding. Which is kind of a shame because while they aren't exactly a weak point, they certainly don't distinguish themselves the way the rest of the bike does.

As you might guess, increasing the diameter of the brake rotor will increase stopping ability simply because a larger rotor offers more mechanical advantage than a smaller one. That being the case, the obvious choice in increasing the "whoa" is to opt for bigger rotors than the standard-equipment, factory-fitted, 11 1/2-inch discs.

What you may fail to realize is that larger rotors are also more fade resistant because their large surface area cools better. So the bottom line is more stopping ability and less chance of fade. Who says you can't have your cake and eat it too? The state of the art in Twin Cam–rotor diameter, at least at the time of this writing, seems to be holding steady at around 13 inches. Trust me, fitting a pair of 13-inch rotors and the appropriate calipers to the front of any Twin Cam ought to have the bike stopping on a dime and returning eight cents change. Which lets me neatly segue into another point that needs making.

If you decide that larger rotors are the way to go—and in most cases they really are—don't forget that you'll need to position the calipers to fit. If the game plan is to replace the calipers along with the rotors this shouldn't be much of an issue; however, if budgetary considerations force you to use the OEM calipers, make sure that either an adapter bracket is available or that one can be fabricated. By the same token, if you're buying calipers now and plan on upgrading the rotors down the road make sure that your new, tricked-out calipers can be used with whatever rotors you're planning to buy.

Fixed Versus Floating Rotors

Fixed or solid rotors have gone the way of the dodo. Fixed rotors are rotors that mount solidly to the wheel hub (or less frequently to the rotor carrier, which is then solidly mounted to the hub). Floating rotors consist of two components. An inner carrier that bolts solidly to the hub and an outer disc. Rivets or "buttons" join the two sections. The buttons have some play in them, which allows the disc to float on the hub, hence the name.

As a rotor heats up it wants to expand. In fact because the heating is never uniform, it wants to expand at different rates. The outer edge, which does the brunt of the work, heats up first and gets hottest, while the inner circumference stays relatively cool. Using a fixed rotor design, the rotor can't expand outward because it's bolted solidly to the hub so it does the next best thing, it deforms into a cone shape. Cones don't work nearly as well as discs when it comes to stopping heavy, fast motorcycles. When the disc is allowed to float freely on the carrier, it has room to expand outward when it gets hot, rather than warp. Solid rotors work but floating rotors work better. Every Twin Cam comes from the factory with solid rotors. The Motor Company adds a small wrinkle by machining expansion slots in their rotors, which does diminish the coning effect, although it doesn't eliminate it entirely. The Screamin' Eagle catalog lists floating rotors as a direct

Floating rotors incorporate buttons between the rotor hub and the rotor itself. This allows the rotor to expand without warping.

Use a locking compound on the securing bolts and securely tighten them to factory recommended specifications. I'd strongly recommend using a torque wrench.

replacement for the stock uniform expansion discs. These are a worthwhile upgrade and may be all you need, particularly if you just want a bit of an edge over the stock binders, so a wade through the catalog might be wise before going aftermarket.

Replacing the Rotors

Here's the drill: You'll need to raise the bike high enough to remove the wheel. Pull the wheel and lay it, disc side up of course, on a hunk of cardboard, rubber mat, or old carpet, to protect the rim. Using an impact driver or air gun, remove the bolts holding the rotor to the hub. If they prove stubborn, use a hot air dryer or bottle torch to warm up the bolts. With the old disc out of the way, install the new rotor, preferably using new hardware. If you reuse the old hardware first clean it, and use a drop of blue Loctite to prevent it from loosening. Torque the bolts to the recommended specification using a cross pattern. Install the

Front to Back

After riding any number of Twin Cams, I can honestly say that the last thing the rear wheels of any of them need are better brakes. All of the Twin Cam models can easily lock the rear wheel. For that reason my advice is to upgrade only the front brakes. That being said, if you're like me you'll want everything to match, at least appearance wise. My recommendation is to spec the fronts in the appropriate oversize and get the matching rear in the stock size.

new caliper bracket if one is required and reinstall the wheel tightening all of the fasteners to the factory recommended settings. Pump up the brake and spin the wheel to ensure that everything went back together the way it was supposed to before lowering the bike back to the floor.

Upgrading Calipers

 Time: 1–2 hours

 Tools: These vary according to caliper design, but figure on a few Allen wrenches, some Torx bits, a wrench to fit the bleeder screw, and some common box wrenches (1/2-inch, 9/16-inch and perhaps a 5/8-inch). It'll also be handy to have a Mityvac or other bleeding pump on hand. You'll also need a catch can, brake fluid, and new sealing washers

 Talent:

 Cost: New calipers can get pretty costly; figure anywhere from $200 to over $1,000, depending on how nuts you want to get

 Tip: Really think this one through; while more brake is always better than less, you can spend a ton of money on race-quality brakes that on a street bike are just so much eye-candy.

 PERFORMANCE GAIN: Stoppies are us; it's real nice to have lots of braking force

COMPLEMENTARY MODIFICATION: Stainless-steel lines, new rotors

Having ridden my fair share of Twin Cam Harleys I'd have to say that by and large the stock brakes aren't bad. The flip side of that is that while they are a vast improvement on what came before, they aren't great either, particularly when the mill's been breathed on.

There are several ways to increase stopping power; you can, in order of ease, increase the efficiency of the brakes by switching to a pad material with a higher co-efficiency of friction. You can decrease the amount of energy lost by flexing lines by installing stainless-steel lines; you can install larger-diameter rotors to increase the overall brake "leverage," although chances are you'll need to install new calipers to match. You can double up the brakes on single-disc front ends, which obviously doubles your stopping power, and takes a huge bite out of your wallet, as well. Or you can do the most practical thing and

install upgraded calipers, to replace the standard, but not outstanding, four piston jobs. Since we've covered most of the other bases let's talk about installing new calipers, but first let's take a look at the theory behind them.

Theory

Why do multiple piston calipers work better than single or dual piston calipers? The simple answer is size, but perhaps not in the meaning you might think.

Early disc-brake calipers generally had one or, at most, two large pistons squeezing the pads against the rotor. As the performance envelope increased, the size of the brakes grew. Pretty soon the pad track, the area of the rotor covered by the brake pad, got to be fairly wide. This created a problem in that the outer diameter (OD) of the rotor grew out of proportion to the inner diameter (ID). Since the rotor OD got hot from brake friction, while the ID of the rotor stayed substantially cooler, the rotors began to warp. The solution, pioneered in 1982 by Brembo, was to reduce the size of the caliper piston while adding more pistons. Brembo's 4-piston caliper had two small pistons per side. This created a long, thin caliper, with a corresponding reduction in pad width compared to the 2-piston caliper. With the reduced rotor width, the heat differential between the rotor ID and OD was reduced. "Floating" the rotor as discussed in the previous section, also helped eliminate the problem and rotor warping ceased to be the problem it had been.

By 1990 6-piston calipers were available, which allowed the use of very narrow rotors and still provided braking power that was unheard of just a generation or two before, even on factory-built Grand Prix bikes.

Differential Bore Calipers

As the calipers got longer and more powerful it created another problem. Friction causes heat, and as the brakes became more powerful they created more heat. This heat vaporizes any surface debris on the rotor and pads, plus a portion of the pad material itself. The vapor that is trapped between the pad and rotor tries to force the pads back into the caliper. Picture a long, thin, 6-piston caliper, gripping a rotor under hard braking. As the leading edge of the rotor gets squeezed by the first piston, it gets hot, and it then rotates a few millimeters where it encounters a second piston, which adds a little more heat. Finally it encounters the third piston, which adds even more heat. The rotor edge then leaves the caliper and takes its turn in the cool air before repeating the process. As you might imagine, this can lead to uneven pressures at caliper bores,

If eye candy is all you need, consider polishing up the stock caliper.

which means both uneven braking force, as well as uneven wear at the pad. For this reason, it's not unusual to find that the first piston in a 6-piston caliper or even in some 4-piston calipers is relatively small, while the next in line grow proportionally larger.

Front Upgrades

If you want to stop harder you've either got to increase the size of the rotor or the clamping force you apply to it. Because the focus of this section is clamping force, we'll only consider the caliper. Riders replace the calipers for one of two reasons (three, if you count those that just plain wear out). The first is appearance; the second is to minimize those *OH MY GAWD, SHE AIN'T GONNA STOP!* If it's eye candy you're after there are any number of direct replacement options. Whether the bike will stop any harder depends on variables like caliper piston-size, the rotors you use, and so on. For maximum "whoa" power, the 6-piston calipers are hard to beat, in particular, the differential bore versions. Besides, they look tricked out, so it also takes care of the first part of the equation. Most aftermarket calipers are direct bolt-on replacements, although some may require a special bracket or adapter. Follow the manufacturer's and the

service manual's explicit instructions when mounting the new calipers, and always use new sealing washers on the hose connections. Although the new caliper(s) can certainly be installed without draining the brake fluid, I'd recommend that you take this opportunity to drain and refill the brake system as detailed in Project 36 and/or 37. I'd also suggest that now is the perfect time to install new, stainless-steel brake lines as well, or at least new rubber OEM hoses, if yours show signs of old age. New calipers are available from a variety of manufacturers. Performance Machine is probably the best known, with companies like Wilwood, and GMA not far behind. With a bit of thought and some help from the aftermarket you'll be able to build a brake system that lets your hog stop on a dime and return nine cents change.

Rear Upgrades

In my experience this is sort of a moot point because all of the Twin Cams that I've ridden have had rear brakes that were entirely capable of locking the rear wheel anytime you wanted them to. For that reason I'd suggest that if you want to upgrade the rear caliper for cosmetic reasons go right ahead, but if it's increased stopping power you need–invest all your budgeted brake bucks at the front.

Changing Wheels (Rear-Wheel H-D Kit)

Time: About 3 hours, not counting changing the tire

Tools: Floor jack, breaker bar, 15/16-inch socket, 1/2-, and 7/16-inch wrench, 3/8-inch 12-point wrench

Talent: 👤 – 👤👤 A novice can do this, if he is careful, but remember part of the job involves fitting a new caliper and bleeding it. If you don't feel comfortable working on the brake system find someone who is!

Cost: $500

Parts: The kit contains everything you'll need

Tip: I recommend enlisting the aid of a buddy to help with the heavy lifting. If you're new to this you may be better off having the local shop swap the tire for you.

PERFORMANCE GAIN: Bigger is better

COMPLEMENTARY MODIFICATION: Now is the time to install those custom pulleys, high-tech calipers, or that sticky rear tire

start with shifting the entire driveline to the right 1/4 inch or more and end up with installing a custom frame. Those projects are outside the scope of this book and frankly, they shouldn't be taken lightly.

Fortunately Harley-Davidson offers a kit that allows you to fit a 150-series tire to a stock rim. You also get to keep the stock belt, which makes the whole undertaking a lot easier. The kit includes spacers, a new brake caliper, and all the hardware needed to complete the installation.

From a practical standpoint, the 150 is the widest tire that should be mounted to a stock rim. If you decide to try and shoe-horn something larger on there, you're courting disaster; the stock rim cannot adequately support a larger section tire. It may go on, and you may be able to make it all fit in the swing arm, but there is always the chance that the inadequately supported tire could be forced off the rim during hard cornering or when carrying a heavy load.

All that having been said, installation of the kit is as straightforward as it gets. Follow the instructions to the letter, particularly when it comes to installing and bleeding the new caliper. An extra pair of hands will also be helpful; there is some heavy and awkward lifting involved. Since you've already got the wheel off, now is also the perfect time to inspect and service the wheel bearings, and to install that custom pulley you've been lusting after.

Our starting point has the bike up on a floor jack and the rear wheel removed and the tire changed to the new 150-series. The drive belt guards are all removed, too.

Bigger is always better, right? Well, maybe, is my personal opinion but millions of H-D riders have opted for wider meat so who am I to say they're wrong? Fat tires do have certain advantages, not the least of which is more traction during acceleration and braking. There is no disputing the "look" either. A fat tire almost always enhances the appearance of the bike, particularly if the bike is from the Softail line.

In some cases, the installation of a wide rear tire can get pretty sticky. The big headache is the width of the standard belt, which precludes fitting a really wide tire. If you have your heart set on installing some rubber that looks like it came off a top fuel dragster you'll need to do some serious engineering work to make it fit. How serious? Let's

TIRES, WHEELS, AND BRAKES

The first part to swap out is the rear splash guard. A 7/16-inch wrench will do the job on the two bolts that hold it in.

After you coat the axle with some lube, start on the right side of the bike and slip it through the axle adjuster, brake caliper bracket, right spacer and then partway into the rear wheel.

Swapping out the rear caliper is just a matter of using a 12-point 3/8-inch wrench to remove the brake line banjo fitting. Replace the caliper with the one from the kit and use the two supplied new washers to reinstall the banjo onto the new caliper.

On the left side, slip the new wheel spacer between the hub and frame. Then send the axle the rest of the way through the wheel and into the spacer and axle adjuster.

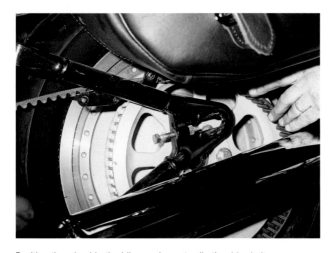

Position the wheel in the bike as shown to slip the drive belt over the pulley and the brake caliper, which is on its swingarm bracket, over the disc.

Then install the outer spacer, lock washer, and nut.

Adjust the rear belt to the spec called out in the manual. Don't forget the tighten down the lock nuts. Then tighten the nut to spec, and install the locking clip.

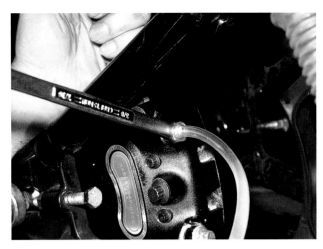

The new caliper needs to be bled so use a piece of clear plastic tubing. . .

Reinstall the lower belt guard. Remember, there's a bolt up front, hidden inside the swingarm by lower frame section, as well as one on the lower and upper swingarm tubes by the pulley.

. . . and an old ketchup bottle to prevent brake fluid from spraying all over the place.

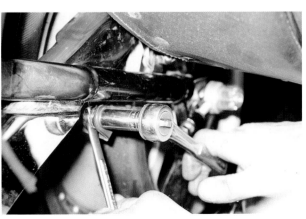

The top guard is held on with two bolts.

Checking and Replacing Wheel Bearings

TIRES, WHEELS, AND BRAKES

🕐 **Time:** 30 minutes

🔧 **Tools:** Lift or jack, factory bearing removal tool or equivalent (optional) punches, hammer. Tools needed to remove wheel

👤👤 **Talent:** Minimal to check; moderate to replace

🐷 **Cost:** $0 (inspection); about $50 if bearings are required

💡 **Tip:** Check the wheel bearings any time the wheels are off the ground.

❗ **PERFORMANCE GAIN:** Finding a bad bearing in the garage means you won't be finding it out on the road

COMPLEMENTARY MODIFICATION: Check belt tension, tire pressure, etc.

Once upon a time, Harley-Davidsons came with wheel bearings that required a fair amount of service. They had to be periodically removed from the wheel, cleaned, inspected, and packed full of fresh grease. Twin Cam owners have it much easier. The new bearings are sealed and require no shimming. They are basically a set-and-forget type. Meaning they are either good and require no attention, or bad and need to be replaced.

The easiest way to check a wheel bearing is to raise the bike a few inches off the ground so that the wheel spins freely without hitching or binding, and the bearings shouldn't make any obvious noise. If the wheel binds, the bearings feel rough or make noise, it's time to replace them. Next position yourself at right angles to the wheel and grasp it at the 6:00 and 9:00 o'clock positions. Try to rock the wheel; if play is felt the bearings need to be replaced, if no play is felt the bearings are fine and need no further attention. By the way *always* replace the wheel bearings as a pair.

To Replace the Bearings

H-D has a very nice bearing removal and installation tool available, as do several of the aftermarket companies.

Although the tools are expensive, they prevent damage to the wheel hubs and make the removal and installation a breeze. Whether it's worthwhile to purchase them, or perhaps to get a few friends together and purchase them communally is up to you.

Here's the alternative method. Insert a punch into the inner sleeve and tap or pry the sleeve to one side; this will allow you to slide the largest punch that will fit through the sleeve until it contacts the inner race of the wheel bearing. Drive the bearing out of the hub by striking it on the inner race. This will destroy the bearing, but you're not going to be reusing it. You can walk the sleeve from side to side, which should allow you to strike the bearing fairly evenly, and prevent it from cocking in the hub. Once the bearing is out, remove the spacer and then drive out the opposite bearing.

If possible, allow the new bearings to sit in the freezer for a few hours before installing them. This will allow them to contract slightly making installation a bit easier. The bearings can be installed with the factory tool or by using a long piece of heavy rod that's been threaded; the shop manual will give you the details. I find it just as easy to drive the bearings into place. Use a bearing driver, socket, or piece of pipe that contacts *only* the outer race of the bearing. Drive the first bearing in. Flip the wheel and install the spacer, then drive the second bearing in. Pretty simple isn't it? Of course if your driver hits anything the outer race the bearing will probably be ruined, but if you work carefully, that shouldn't be a problem. Reinstall the wheel, and don't forget to apply a bit of anti-seize or white grease to the axle.

After everything is nice and tight give the wheel a spin to make sure nothing is binding or pinched. And please, don't forget to pump the brakes a few times before you road test your handiwork.

Use your finger to rotate the bearing. If it feels rough or binds, it's shot and due for replacement.

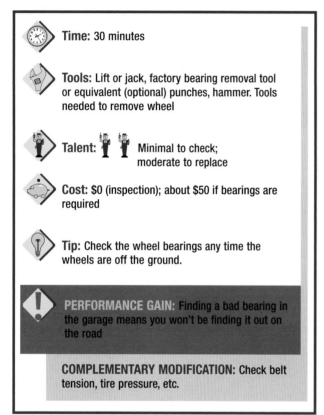

SECTION SIX

The Engine

Breaking in a New Engine

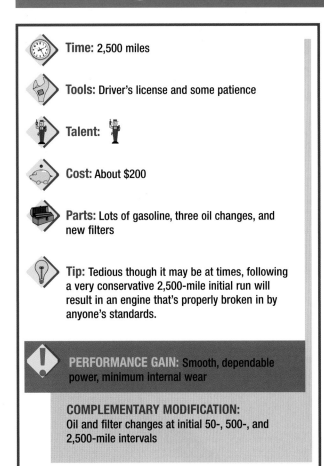

Time: 2,500 miles

Tools: Driver's license and some patience

Talent:

Cost: About $200

Parts: Lots of gasoline, three oil changes, and new filters

Tip: Tedious though it may be at times, following a very conservative 2,500-mile initial run will result in an engine that's properly broken in by anyone's standards.

PERFORMANCE GAIN: Smooth, dependable power, minimum internal wear

COMPLEMENTARY MODIFICATION: Oil and filter changes at initial 50-, 500-, and 2,500-mile intervals

How—or even if—you should break in an engine depends on whom you ask. If you've been riding for a number of years, you've probably heard just about every possible opinion concerning this important subject. And make no mistake, what happens during these first miles does determine how well your engine's parts will fit and work together, as well as how long the motor's useful service life will be before a rebuild is needed. That being the case, I suggest using a safe and conservative break-in procedure. After all, the worst that can happen by taking it easy for the first 2,500 miles is that you've had to control your urge to flog the beast for a few rides. In our opinion, that's a small price to pay for the ability to have fun for the next 70,000 miles.

How an engine is treated during the first couple of hours of its life is especially critical. The first time you start an engine, do it according to its normal procedure. Once the motor fires, let it idle until the rocker boxes get warm. While it's doing that, check for fuel or oil leaks,

smoke, noises that shouldn't be there, or anything else that would indicate a problem. You know, all the things you're hoping you won't find. Then either shut the motor down or take the bike for a ride.

A common mistake an owner makes at this stage of an engine's life is spending a lot of time admiring the new addition—while it overheats. A brand-new engine is when it is most prone to overheating. Here's why: The mating surface of new parts is actually rough, relatively speaking, which causes a lot of internal friction, resulting in excessive heat buildup. The main purpose of breaking in an engine is to give the moving parts time to wear in, smooth each other out. How much time they need depends on how "tight" the engine has been built.

A tight engine has the clearances between its moving parts toward the tighter end of their tolerance ranges, so it needs to be given more time to wear in. (For example, if a part has a fit tolerance of 0.001–0.010 inch, the tight clearance would be 0.001–0.003 inch.) A tight engine is also more susceptible to damage from overheating, a heavy throttle hand, or poor lubrication issues, such as insufficient or dirty oil. As the engine's components wear in (or "seat"), the level of friction drops, which also reduces the heat that the engine generates. Overheating an engine, especially a new one, can result in piston, cylinder, and other internal component, damage. And piston damage is the most common reason why an engine is torn down for rebuilding.

Since a Twin Cam is an air-cooled engine, which means it needs air passing around it to maintain its proper operating temperature, you should not let it idle at a standstill longer than necessary. If you have to make fuel, ignition, or any other adjustments before getting on the road, have a large fan blowing air onto the engine to keep it cool while you're spinning wrenches.

While breaking in a new motor, there are a few things you should avoid, all of which have to do with heat and rpm. Extended periods with the engine idling, riding in stop-and-go traffic, or pulling a heavy load, like towing a trailer or a sidecar, can cause engine damage due to excessive heat buildup.

And while we'll get to what the rpm limits are for different stages of the break-in period in a minute, lugging a motor should also be avoided. Lugging an engine, which is letting its revs drop too low when under a load, can also cause severe engine damage. The touring guys are the biggest offenders here. Looking to keep their revs down to get as many miles as possible from a gallon of gas, they make their motor struggle to pull a full bagger, usually loaded down with a ton of gear, as well as two riders. Damage to the pistons and rings, as well as from ping/engine knock, is possible, especially in hot weather. Keeping the revs between 2,500-3,000 rpm (except during the first 50 miles when it should not go above 2,500) when on the throttle, as well as always running 91-octane or higher fuel, will help prevent ping/knock. However, if it does occur, downshift to bring the engine's revs up. Never try to power your way with more throttle through a ping/knock condition.

That said, I suggest following the advice of noted high-performance engine giant S&S Cycle when it comes to rpm limits during the different stages of break-in. According to S&S' recommended break-in procedure, for the first 50 miles avoid conditions that can cause over-heating. Do not exceed 2,500 rpm, or, if you don't have a tach, stay under 50-55 mph during this time. Also, don't keep the engine turning at a steady speed; vary its rpm and don't lug it. Be sure to take it easy with the throttle and keep the load that the engine has to pull to a minimum, which means definitely no trailers or sidecars. After the first 50 miles, change the oil and filter. Also keep the engine clean, so you can quickly see if there are any fuel, oil, or exhaust leaks.

During the next 500 miles, you can bring the revs up to 3,500 rpm (about 65 mph) for short periods of time. Continue to vary the engine's rpm, while avoiding over-heating or lugging. Once these 500 miles are done, change the oil and filter again.

Now that you've got 550 miles on the motor, you can be a little more aggressive with the throttle during the next 2,000 miles, but don't exceed 3,500 rpm. However, that doesn't mean you can whack the throttle wide open or go drag racing; nor should you haul any heavy loads. Continue to vary the engine's rpm, while avoiding over-heating or lugging the motor. Definitely do some around town riding, which gives you plenty of opportunities to go through the gears, bringing the engine up and down its rpm range.

Once you've got over 2,500 miles on it, you can finally have some fun; the engine is now fully broken-in. If you want to load the beast up, pull a trailer, or rip through the gears, have at it. However, overheating, lugging, and engine ping/knock are still to be avoided. That is, unless you want to trash the engine and start all over again.

Which brings me to one last point, though it's foolish to have to say it: Engines don't heal. If you beat the hell out of your motor on Saturday night, taking it easy for the next week or so doesn't make it all better. The engine will only be corrected, if repairs are done to the damaged or broken parts.

This piston is from an engine that was broken in correctly. Though there are slight marks in the piston's black Teflon-coated skirt, there are few signs of wear and no indications of damage.

This piston, however, came from an engine that was badly overheated when the engine only had less than 50 miles on it. Note the severe gauling on the piston's skirt. Not only is this piston trashed, but the cylinder must be bored out as well.

Dyno Tuning an Engine

 Time: 1–6 hours

 Tools: Access to a dynamometer, eye and ear protection, motorcycle straps, flat-bladed screwdriver, and whatever other tools are needed to change the jets in your carb or adjust the EFI system

 Talent:

 Cost: Anywhere from $50 per hour to $90 per half hour, depending on who is doing the runs, you or a pro

 Parts: An assortment of your carb's main and intermediate jets, smaller and larger than the ones presently in the carb

 Tip: Take the bike out for a 20–30 minute ride, so the engine is up to operating temperature before doing any dyno runs.

 PERFORMANCE GAIN: Could be anywhere from 1 to 10 horsepower, depending on how the bike is already tuned

COMPLEMENTARY MODIFICATION: At the minimum, you should have a freer-flowing air cleaner on the engine, or there's no sense in spending the time or money

The inertia (chassis) dynamometer, or dyno as it is widely called, is an excellent tool for dialing in the adjustable settings on your engine. It is especially useful for adjusting the ignition timing (Project 84 and 85) and fuel settings, be it a carburetor (Project 15 and 16) or EFI system (Project 20 and 21). This is the type of dyno now found in performance shops around the world.

An inertia dyno measures an engine's ability to accelerate an 875-pound roller, which simulates an engine load equal to the bike going down a level road with no wind resistance. Horsepower on this type of dyno is computed by number-crunching the mass, speed, and acceleration of the roller. Multiplying the horsepower reading by the

constant 5,252, and then dividing the answer by the corresponding amount of rpm determines the engine's torque. In contrast, the formula most people use to compute horsepower is to multiply the engine's torque (in foot-pounds) by the rpm and then divide that answer by the constant 5,252, which gives you the horsepower produced at that specific rpm.

If you've decided that a session on the dyno is just what your bike needs, there are a few basic maintenance items that should be checked before you fork over hard cash for a spin on the machine. These components are also power robbers if they're not properly adjusted and will reduce what your engine can actually put to the rear wheel, whether it's on a dyno or out on the street.

For starters, make sure both tires are at the proper pressure. Though the rear tire is the only one spinning the machine's drum, the front one is being squashed into a wheel stop, so you want it to be up to the task. Next up on the freebie checklist is primary chain and rear belt/chain adjustments. Make sure they're on the money and lubricated/clean, as the case may be. Finally, have the clutch properly adjusted. It's a waste of effort to gain a few extra ponies and then lose half of them to a slipping clutch.

As for safety checks, make sure the oil levels in the engine, transmission, and primary system are where they should be. Once on the dyno, make sure the bike is properly strapped down and there are no loose items lying around near you, the bike, or the dyno's drum. Loose wires, tools, spark plugs, carb jets, and anything else that comes in contact with the bike's rear chain/belt, spinning rear wheel, or the dyno's drum (which can be spinning at up to 200 mph) will become a high-speed missile looking for something to make a hole through. Always wear eye and ear protection.

Now for a few dyno don'ts and dos: Predetermine the rpm stop point for your tests, which should be just before the ignition's rev limiter setting. Don't over-rev your engine. In fact, the horsepower curve is usually dropping before the engine's rpm gets to redline (rev limiter setting) on most engines anyway (at least, it should be), so revving past this point is not doing your engine or you any good. Also, if you're doing dyno runs and the horsepower readings keep getting lower and lower, you're overheating the engine. This shouldn't happen, however, if the dyno is equipped with an adequate cooling blower.

Be sure to make notes on the dyno chart before you make a run, so you know what jets are in the carb for that test. No matter how good your memory is you'll soon forget what graph was run with what jet combination. Do at least three runs of the same test and check them against each other. If you have two graphs that are similar, you have a valid reading of the engine's power. Once the runs are over, downshift through the gears just as you would on the street, and let the engine and the dyno's drum slow down together. Don't just pull in the clutch and let the drum freewheel and never, ever, use the rear brake to stop the drum. You'll only trash the rear tire, brake pads, and disc, as well as scare the crap out of yourself.

I asked Dr. Dyno, who does most of Chris' dyno runs, for a few tests that a beginner can easily do to determine how his engine's air/fuel mixture is set. What he suggested is the following four tests: The first is the most common one done on a dyno: the Roll-On Run, which should be done in fourth gear with the graph showing both horsepower and rpm. This test will tell you the maximum horsepower and torque output of the engine, and what's happening in the top third of the carb jetting (when compared to the other tests), as well as how the carb's midrange is set. (Those with EFI systems should check with their system's instructions to see how to make leaner/richer adjustments.)

Once you've got the bike in fourth gear, bring the rpm to 2,000 and then crack the throttle wide open. Hold it there until the rpm reach your predetermined stop point, then stop the test and shut the throttle. Do three pulls and select one of the two similar graphs for comparison with the next test, the All-Gear Run.

The All-Gear Run is started with the tranny in second gear and the rpm scale changed to show mph (speed). Bring the engine to 2,000 rpm, then whack the throttle wide open and shift up through all the gears all the way to fifth. Bring the revs to redline or very close to it in every gear. (No power shifting, as this will give you false high readings in the form of spikes.) Once you have done at least three runs and have two that are alike, pick one of the two similar ones and have the computer put it up on the screen with the roll-on run you selected. Comparing the roll-on graph and the top of the fourth-gear curve on the all-gear run will give you a good indication of how the engine is running, whether too rich or too lean. If the two graphs match, the main jet is usually correct. If the roll-on curve is below the all-gear one, the jetting is probably too rich, while above means it's probably too lean.

The next series of tests, called the More Air/Less Air runs, will tell you for sure whether the jetting is on the money, or too rich or lean. For this series of tests, change

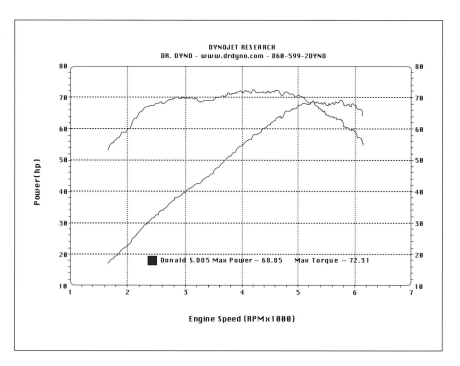

The Roll-On run is the one you usually get from a dyno shop and, if used correctly, is very effective for tuning an engine.

the mph scale back to read rpm. To do the first set, partially cover about a quarter or a third of the air cleaner's intake openings and then do a couple of Roll-On runs. Then remove the blockage, as well as the element from the air cleaner, and make another two Roll-On runs.

If the engine's power increases with the air cleaner partially blocked, the jetting is too lean. However, if you get more power with the air cleaner element removed, the main jet is too rich. Change the jetting accordingly by two jets and then do another two roll-on runs. If the power stays the same or increases, go another two jets in the same direction. Once the power output drops, go back one jet. The main jet is now dialed in.

As for the intermediate jet, or the middle third of the jetting, check the slope of the horsepower curve on the Roll-On run graph that has the main jet properly set. Is it choppy or basically smooth? If it's choppy, it could be due to a too-lean intermediate jet, or the rear chain/belt is not adjusted correctly. If the rear chain/belt checks out okay, go a jet richer on the intermediate and then do another Roll-On run. Did this smooth out the slope? Keep going one jet richer and running another test until the horsepower curve is somewhat smooth. Once changing the jet does not make the slope any smoother, go back one jet leaner. However, if the horsepower curve's slope is smooth on the onset, drop the intermediate jet one jet leaner and do a Roll-On run. Keep doing this until the slope gets choppy, and then go back one jet richer.

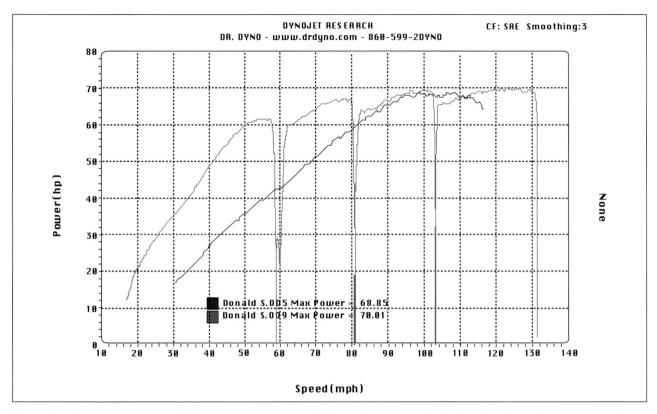

The top of the fourth gear curve on the All-Gear run is compared to the Roll-On graph to get a good indication of how the engine is running, whether too rich or too lean. This one is too rich.

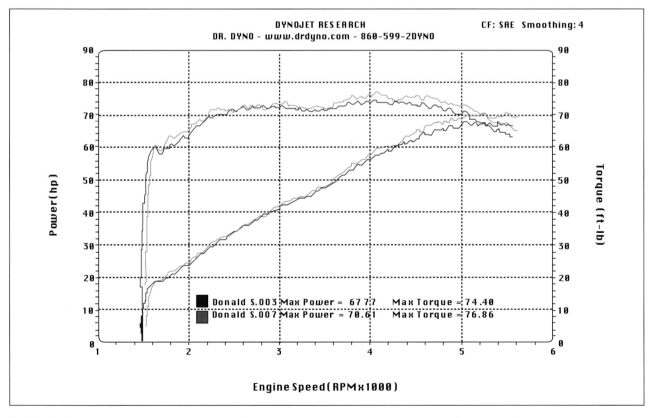

The More Air/Less Air run is another way to determine if the engine's fuel settings are too rich or too lean. On this one, the bike ran better with more air, which confirms that the jetting is too rich.

Installing Adjustable Pushrods

Time: 1–2 hours

Tools: Bolt cutter, flat-bladed screwdriver, 7/16-inch and 1/2-inch open-end wrenches, 3/16-inch Allen wrench

Talent:

Cost: $100–200

Parts: Adjustable pushrod kit, lifter cover gaskets (unless supplied with pushrod kit), and pushrod tube, rocker box, and lifter cover O-rings

Tip: Make sure the adjustable pushrods you plan to install do not require removal of the rocker boxes, as this defeats the main purpose of the installation.

PERFORMANCE GAIN: Makes it a lot easier to change the cams or lifters

COMPLEMENTARY MODIFICATION: This should be done when installing new camshafts

Start the job by removing the spring cap retainers (clips). Do this by levering the spring cap down with a flat-bladed screwdriver.

The easiest way to remove the old pushrods without disturbing the rocker boxes is to cut them in half with a set of bolt cutters. But before you cut, rotate the engine so the lifters are at their lowest point.

THE ENGINE

For the record, the stock non-adjustable pushrods are fully capable of doing their appointed task. In fact, they will do their job for a very long time without any servicing. However, if you want (need) to change the O-rings in the pushrods tubes, install a bolt-in performance camshaft (Project 56 or 57), or remove the camshafts for any reason (like changing the rear cam bearing as shown in Project 54), you should swap out the stock pushrods for a set of adjustable ones at that time. Here's why: To remove the cams or pushrod tubes, you have to remove the pushrods from the engine. However, to do that you have to remove the rocker boxes and rocker arms. That is, unless you can shorten (adjust) the pushrod length enough to slip them in and out over the top of the lifter. And while this is not a necessary upgrade, a set of adjustable pushrods does make the job easier, because you don't have to touch the rocker boxes or rocker arm assemblies. In fact, you don't have to do anything to the heads—as long as the cams you're

installing do not need a set of performance valve springs (Project 46)—other than slipping in a new top O-ring for each pushrod tube.

Start the job by removing the spring cap retainers (clips). Do this by levering the spring cap down with a flat-bladed screwdriver. Then telescope the pushrod tubes (covers) down as far as they will go and put a clothespin onto each pushrod to hold the cover up and out of the way.

Now that you can see the lifters and pushrods, rotate the engine so the lifters for the cylinder you plan to work on first are at their lowest point. Because the whole point of this installation is to not disturb the rocker boxes, we're

119

going to cut the old pushrods out with a set of bolt cutters. Some mechanics may choose to use a cutting wheel on the pushrods, but you must be very careful not to get metal fragments in the engine, or hit the cylinders with the cutting wheel. I recommend using bolt cutters.

After you've removed the pushrod-tube assemblies from the engine and thrown out the old pushrods, replace the O-rings in the rocker boxes, one per pushrod. If you're going to reuse the stock pushrods tubes, slide off the lower pushrod cover and replace the O-ring on the bottom of the upper pushrod cover. Then reinstall the lower cover. Do this for both assemblies. We're going to install a set of new S&S pushrod covers. If you plan on using these or a different manufacturer's parts, don't forget to put a new O-ring in each one.

The adjustable pushrods we're going to install are also from S&S. To do this, you also have to remove the lifter covers, which is why S&S supplies new lifter cover gaskets with its pushrod kit. Remove the lifter covers using a 3/16-inch Allen wrench. After you clean off the old gasket from the cover and engine case, position the new cover gasket onto the engine case, but for now leave the cover off.

S&S adjustable pushrods come in two lengths: The long-bodied ones are for the exhaust valves, while the short-bodied ones are for the intakes. (The intake valves are the ones closest to the air cleaner, while the exhaust valves are closest to the exhaust pipes.) Select the new intake pushrod and fully compress it to make it as short as possible. Do this by loosening the locknut on the pushrod extension and screwing the extension all the way into the pushrod's body. Then slip the now-shortened pushrod into its tube assembly. Do the same for the exhaust pushrod.

With new O-rings in the lifter cover and rocker box, slip the lifter cover (properly orientated) over the bottom end of both pushrods. Now put the pushrod assemblies into position under the rocker box with the top of each pushrod engaging the pocket made for it in its rocker arm, which is inside the rocker box. Then position the bottom end of each pushrod over its lifter. Let the lifter cover drop into position on the engine case. Using your fingers, screw out both pushrod extensions, so that each pushrod can sit in the top of its lifter without the top of the pushrod coming out of its pocket in the rocker arm. Once this is done, put a little blue Loctite on the threads of the stock lifter cover Allen bolts and reinstall the cover. Be sure to torque the bolts to 90–120 inch-pounds.

You can now adjust both pushrods as per your kit's instructions with the appropriate open-end wrenches. Once the adjustments are finished, tighten down the pushrod's locknut to keep the setting from changing. Then wait about 10 to 15 minutes for the hydraulic lifters to bleed down, or you'll bend the new pushrods when you rotate the engine to do this install on the other cylinder. The lifters have bled down when you can spin both pushrods with your fingers. You can now do the same procedure on the other cylinder.

Once all the pushrods are adjusted and the lifters have all had a chance to bleed down, fully extend all the pushrod tubes and ensure that they fully seat to the rocker boxes and lifter covers. You can then pop in the spring cap retainers (clips) with a flat-bladed screwdriver.

Arrange the lifter cover, pushrod tubes, and pushrods which are fully compressed, so they are ready to be installed as a unit onto the engine.

With a new lifter cover in place and a little blue Loctite on the threads, you can now reinstall the stock lifter cover bolts and torque them to 90–120 in-lbs using a 3/16-inch Allen.

Then adjust the pushrods as per the kit's instructions. Be sure to allow the lifters time to bleed down before rotating the engine to do the other cylinder. Once all the pushrods are adjusted and locked down, you can pop in the retaining clips. Make sure the tubes are fully seated to the head and lifter block.

Installing Custom Lifter Covers

 Time: 30 minutes

 Tools: 3/16-inch Allen wrench, inch-pounds torque wrench, gasket scraper

 Talent:

 Cost: $225

 Parts: Two new lifter cover gaskets, two new lifter covers, new pushrod gaskets

 Tip: Make sure the covers you get will compliment whatever custom cam cover you're going to install.

PERFORMANCE GAIN: A slicker-looking engine

COMPLEMENTARY MODIFICATION: Do this cover swap when installing adjustable pushrods, because you have to remove the pushrods to install the lifter covers

Though I wouldn't disassemble an engine just to bolt up a set of custom lifter covers, it's a great upgrade to do if you have to remove them for any reason, like when swapping out the stock pushrods for adjustable ones, or when changing the camshafts. This is especially true if you've installed a custom cam cover (Project 52) and matching tranny side cover (Project 77). Hopefully, the manufacturer who made the cam and tranny covers you've chosen also offers a set of matching lifter covers, like the chrome billet aluminum ones you are going to install from Pro-One. The accompanying photos show you how to install them, as well as how to install a set of lifters. I wanted to show you how to do the lifters in this project, since it is not covered in any other part of the book.

On Evos and earlier Big Twins, the lifters (also called tappets) operated in lifter blocks, which are removable and, therefore, replaceable if they are damaged in any way. This is not the case on the Twin Cams. A TC's lifters are positioned in holes (bores) in the right crankcase, one

right over each cam lobe, which means a catastrophic failure of a lifter in its bore—if it badly scores the bore—requires right crankcase replacement. Thankfully, as of yet, I have never heard of this happening on any Twin Cam engine.

The Twin Cam's lifters are very dependable automotive hydraulic units. Each lifter has a wheel on its bottom end that rolls on the cam lobe below it. As the engine and therefore the cams, rotate, each lifter wheel rolls up and down on its cam lobe. On the other end of each lifter, there's a cup that holds the bottom end of the pushrod it controls. As the lifters roll up and down the cam lobes, it makes the pushrods go up and down, actuating the rocker arms they control in the rocker boxes.

To install the lifters and covers, start by lubricating the lifter bores in the right crankcase with some assembly lube. After putting some lube onto the bearings of each lifter wheel, drop each lifter into its bore. Make sure the flat side, which is on one side of the top of the lifter, is toward the raised section of case that's under the lifter cover and right next to the lifter bores. (Note: If you're reinstalling the stock lifters, they should go back into the same bore as before. Do not put a used lifter into a different lifter bore.)

This flat section on each lifter mates with a locking pin, which keeps each lifter properly aligned with its cam lobe. The pin just sits alongside each set of lifters between the lifters and the section of case right next to the lifter bores.

After lubricating each lifter's bore and wheel, drop the lifters into their bores with the flat side towards the raised section of case that's right next to the lifter bores.

THE ENGINE

121

You can then assemble the pushrod tubes as per Project 43. Then slip the correct pushrods—a long pushrod for the exhaust valve and a short one for the intake—into their tubes. Assemble the two pushrod assemblies you'll need for one cylinder. Then slip a new O-ring into each of the two pushrod tube holes in the lower rocker box.

Put a new lifter cover gasket onto the right case and a new O-ring into both pushrod holes in the new lifter cover. The lifter cover for each cylinder must be installed onto the engine as an assembly with the required pushrods and tubes. Be sure you have the lifters for the cylinder you're working on at their lowest point, or you won't get the pushrods in over them. (Note: Even with the lifter positioned as such, the exhaust pushrod will be a pain to get in place over the lifter with a high lift cam.)

Once the lifter cover, pushrods, and pushrod tubes are properly positioned over the lifters and right case, bolt the cover into place using the supplied Pro-One hardware, with a little blue Loctite on the bolt threads. Use a 3/16-inch Allen to torque the bolts to 90–100 in-lb. Then adjust the pushrods as per the manufacturer's instructions and complete the pushrod installation as per Project 43. After the lifters bleed down, which usually takes about 10 to 15 minutes, you can do the same for the other cylinder.

After putting a new lifter cover gasket onto the right case and a new O-rings into the rocker box and lifter cover, position the pushrods, pushrod tubes, and lifter cover onto the right case.

The flat section of each lifter is there to mate with a locking pin. This pin sits alongside each set of lifters between the lifters and the section of case right next to the lifter bores.

Bolt the cover into place using the supplied Pro-One hardware, with a little blue Loctite on the bolt threads, using a 3/16-inch Allen. Torque the bolts to 90–100 in-lbs.

Installing Roller Rocker Arms

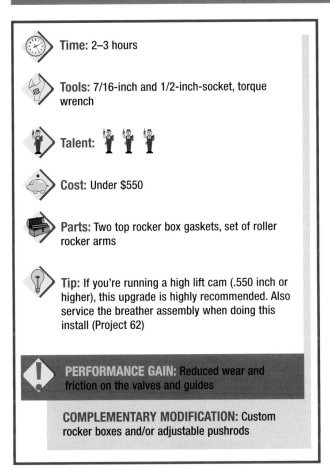

Time: 2–3 hours

Tools: 7/16-inch and 1/2-inch-socket, torque wrench

Talent: 👨 👨 👨

Cost: Under $550

Parts: Two top rocker box gaskets, set of roller rocker arms

Tip: If you're running a high lift cam (.550 inch or higher), this upgrade is highly recommended. Also service the breather assembly when doing this install (Project 62)

PERFORMANCE GAIN: Reduced wear and friction on the valves and guides

COMPLEMENTARY MODIFICATION: Custom rocker boxes and/or adjustable pushrods

Ever wonder why knowledgeable mechanics insist on installing a set of roller-equipped rocker arms whenever they build a high performance engine? It's because they understand at a deeper level what a rocker arm does and how its job gets harder when high–lift performance cams are installed in an engine. But before I get into that, I'll first briefly go over how your engine's valve train works.

Though all previous OHV (overhead valve) H-D Big Twin engines have a single, four-lobe camshaft in them to operate all four valves, your Twin Cam engine has two camshafts, hence its name. That means each cylinder has its own camshaft and each cam has two lobes on it, one for the intake valve and one for the exhaust. These lobes control when the head's valves open and close to let in a fresh fuel/air charge for burning (intake); or let out the burnt gases of combustion (exhaust), as the case may be.

Positioned in holes (lifter bores) in the right crankcase over each cam lobe is a hydraulic lifter, also known as a tappet. As the engine rotates, the cams rotate and their lobes make the lifters go up and down in their

bores at different times. On the top end of each lifter there's a cup that holds the bottom end of the pushrod it controls. When a lifter rises in its bore, it lifts its pushrod up. The other end of the pushrod—which is connected to a rocker arm located in the rocker box atop the cylinder head—then pushes up on the right arm of its rocker. The rocker arm—there's two rockers in each box, one per pushrod—rotates on a shaft like a seesaw. When one arm of the rocker pushes up, the other arm, which is positioned right over the end of the valve it controls, pushes down. The downward motion of the rocker arm pushes the valve down through its guide, which is a metal tube in the head that keeps the valve aligned with its seat. This lifts the valve's head off its seat in the cylinder head, opening the valve. When the cam's lobe drops the lifter down in its bore, this allows the valve's springs to pull the valve back onto its seat (closing it), which forces the rocker arm and pushrod to follow the descending lifter.

Now that you have a working idea of how the valve train does its job, let's take a closer look at the task of the rocker arms. As stated, each rocker has two arms: One has a cup to engage the top of the pushrod, while the other is just a curved machined surface (pad) that presses on the end of the valve's stem. The arm we're interested in is the one with the machined pad.

Here's the problem: When the rocker arm is pushing down on the valve, its pad is actually rubbing back and forth across the end of the valve stem. This makes the stem push against two sides of the valve guide, which results in excessive wear and egg-shaping of the guide. It also causes excessive wear on all sides of the valve's stem because the valve rotates in the guide during normal engine operation.

Here are the main components of the rocker arm assembly: the rocker support plate, two roller rocker arms, and two rocker arm shafts. Not shown are the four support plate mounting bolts.

On a stock engine this isn't really a problem but, on an engine with a high lift cam, instead of pushing, the rocker arm tends to thrust against the end of the valve stem, which increases enough wear and friction losses to make it a problem. To keep these losses in check, roller rocker arms are a good idea when running a cam with more than a .510-inch lift. (Stock is .495 inch.) However, with lifts of .550 inch or more, roller rockers are highly recommended.

Tom Pirone of TP Engineering, which makes roller rocker arms, explains the benefit of a roller opening a valve this way, instead of a pad: Put the palm of your hand flat on a table and apply some pressure. Then quickly move your hand back and forth across the table about 20 times. You'll find that it takes a lot of effort to do this and your hand gets real hot. It also rocks the table back and forth, which is what happens to a valve in its guide with a stock rocker. Now place a round pen under your palm and do the same test. With the pen (roller) under your hand, it moves over the table easily with no heat buildup (friction) and no rocking table. That's the difference between a rocker arm with a roller tip and one with a machined pad.

Here's how to install a set of Crane roller rocker arms in your Twin Cam, be it an 88 or 88B. Do one rocker box at a time. Remove the top rocker cover using a 7/16-inch socket, followed by the gasket. Rotate the engine so both

the pushrods for the cylinder you're working on are at their lowest position. (This way there's no tension on the rocker arms from the valve springs.) Then remove the complete rocker arm assembly from the lower rocker box using a 1/2-inch socket. There's no need to remove the lower rocker box or the pushrods and tubes.

With the rocker assembly on the workbench, slip out the rocker arm shaft (noting which end has the notch) and stock rocker arm. After inspecting the stock rocker arm shaft for damage, if you are reusing it, position a new roller rocker arm—there are two versions, so be sure to use the one that'll position a roller over the valve stem—in the support plate the same as was the old one. With lots of oil on the rocker arm and shaft, insert the shaft through the support plate and into the new rocker, with the shaft's notch properly positioned to align with the bolt hole in the support plate. Do the same for the other rocker arm. (You may want to also service the breather assembly at this time. If so, check out Project 62.)

The rocker arm assembly can now get positioned in the lower rocker box. If you are installing adjustable pushrods, remove the stock pushrods and their tubes from the engine and follow the steps in Project 43. If you are reusing the stock pushrods and tubes, leave them as they are, but position the pushrods so they contact the arm of their respective rockers correctly. Then install and torque all four support plate bolts, in the sequence shown in the service manual, to 18–22 foot-pounds. Once a new top gasket is in place, you can reinstall the top rocker box. Torque the bolts, with a little blue Loctite on the threads, as per the sequence in the H-D service manual, to 15–18 foot-pounds. Then do the other rocker assembly in the same way.

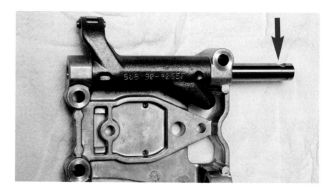

After lubing the shaft and inside of the rocker arm, install the rocker and shaft into the support. The shaft goes in with the notch positioned to align with the bolthole in the support plate.

Here's how the finished rocker assembly looks. Note which side of the support plate gets the roller-tipped arms.

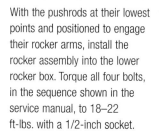

With the pushrods at their lowest points and positioned to engage their rocker arms, install the rocker assembly into the lower rocker box. Torque all four bolts, in the sequence shown in the service manual, to 18–22 ft-lbs. with a 1/2-inch socket.

Once a new top gasket and the breather assembly are in place, install the top rocker box. Torque the bolts, in the sequence shown in the service manual, to 15–18 ft-lbs. using a 7/16-inch socket.

Installing High-Performance Valve Springs

 Time: 2 hours

 Tools: Inside caliper (divider), dial indicator (caliper), valve spring compressor, Andrews or Trock valve spring checker, 1/2-inch wrench, 1/4-inch Allen

 Talent:

 Cost: $100–150

 Parts: Performance valve spring kit

 Tip: If you're installing a set of high-compression forged pistons (to match long-duration cams), be sure to get a set with deep valve pockets, so the valves don't hit the piston.

 PERFORMANCE GAIN: Allows you to use high-performance cams

COMPLEMENTARY MODIFICATION: Port the heads for better airflow

With both collars installed on the valve, measure the distance between the inside faces at the point where the valve springs contact the collars. Use an inside caliper to do this.

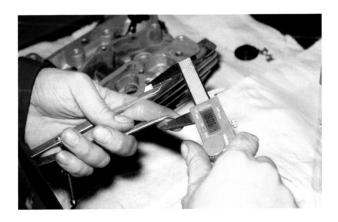

Then measure what that distance is using a dial indicator to get the installed height of the spring. If you need more installed height, you must sink the valves deeper into their seats in the head.

THE ENGINE

Before I dive into the whys and how-tos of a high-performance valve kit, let's first discuss how valves of a Twin Cam compare with and differ from those of an Evo. For starters, the angles of the valves in the head (the valve angles) of a Twin Cam are the same as these of an Evo. A Twin Cam also uses the same size intake valve. The TC's exhaust valve, however, has a head that's a little thicker and about .030 inch smaller in diameter than its Evo cousin. (The exhaust port is also smaller than that of an Evo, as is the TC intake port.) To help a mechanic identify them, TC exhaust valves are marked with an indent in the center of their face. With the intake valves being the same and the exhaust valves just a tad smaller, it stands to reason that the Twin Cam's valve springs and keepers are the same as these of an Evo, which they are.

This, of course, means the high-performance valve spring kits made for Evo Big Twins will also probably fit a Twin Cam. However, most of the manufacturers of valve

spring kits for Twin Cams have specific kits for them, so be sure to choose one of these when selecting a kit. This also means that using Evo high-performance valves is the way to go when working over a Twin Cam head. When installing bigger valves—which really should be done after the intake and exhaust tracts have been ported a bit and blended to the valve seats—you can use the same oversized intake and exhaust valves that have been used for years in high-performance Evos. (The actual diameter of the valves depends on the engine's performance specifications.)

The need for high-performance valve springs depends on what cams you're going to use in the engine. A true bolt-in cam set is called that because no other changes have to be made to the engine to install and use the cams. You can just bolt it into the engine with no modifications to the heads, valve spring packs, or any other part of the engine.

A set of cams with higher-than-stock valve lifts and longer durations usually requires a performance valve–spring kit, which uses higher pressure springs. High-performance springs help the valves follow a more aggressive cam lobe profile and eliminate valve float and valve bounce. Valve float is when the valve stays off its seat even though the cam would allow it to close. Valve bounce is when the valve hits its seat and then bounces back off of it. Both of these conditions occur because the valve springs are not strong enough to make the valve closely follow the lobe of the cam that controls it. In both cases, the valve is off its seat—protruding into the combustion chamber where the piston or the other valve could hit and bend it—when it should be closed.

While I'm on the subject of valve float, a couple of things should be mentioned. First, performance valve–spring kits usually include lightweight spring retainers. Lighter-than-stock retainers reduce the inertia of the moving parts, which also reduces the chance of valve float. This is also why some builders use lightweight (lighter-than-stock) pushrods. However, the pushrods must be strong enough to resist flexing under the pressure of the valve springs, which will cause a different set of problems, including a loss of power.

Cams with a lift higher than stock and/or more duration may also require modifications to the pistons, heads, and valve guides. Here's why: Once you increase how long and when the valves open and close, as well as how far they open, you have to make sure there's adequate clearance between the valves and piston; the coils of the valve springs; the valve spring retainers and valve guides; and the two valves themselves. If there's not enough clearance, parts will hit other parts, making a mess inside your engine.

In fact, you cannot install a set of very high lift cams in a Twin Cam and still use the stock chain-drive system. This is because the lobes on each cam pass so close to each other at one point of their rotation—chain-driven cams rotate in the same direction—that they will hit each other if too high a lift (cam lobe) is used. Gear-driven cams, like those available from Andrews and S&S, rotate in different directions, which means the lobes in the gear-driven version can't hit, no matter how tall the lobes are.

When installing higher lift cams you should check to make sure there's adequate clearance between the valves and piston, especially if you're also popping in a set of high-compression forged pistons (to match long-duration cams). And though these pistons usually come with deep valve pockets, since most are installed along with hot cams, you should still check the clearance. Project 50: Claying High-Compression Pistons shows you how to do this simple procedure. Definitely check the clearance if you're going to use the stock cast pistons.

As for the other four clearances you should check—installed height of the spring, clearance between the valve spring retainers and valve guides, clearance between the coils of the valve springs, and clearance between the two valves themselves—I went to a local guru of the valve train, Fred of Fred's Auto Machine. Guys like Fred are scattered all across America and they are the local go-to guys for performance-valve work.

Here's how and why Fred checks these four important clearances: With the top collar, which is held in place with the two valve keys, and lower collar on the valve, measure the distance between the inside face of both collars where the valve springs sit on the collars, using an inside caliper. Then measure what that distance is by measuring the distance between the two arms of the inside caliper using a dial indicator. This measurement is the installed height of the spring. The required height is listed in the cam's specification sheet by the camshaft manufacturer. If you need to increase the measured height, so it matches the manufacturer's specified height, you must sink the valves deeper into their seats in the head.

Though modern high-performance spring kits come with retainers that will usually not hit the valve guide, you should still check the clearance between the retainers and guides. This is a concern because when you increase the lift of the cam and, therefore, the distance the valve will lift off its seat in the head, you also increase how far down the valve spring and its top retainer will be compressed/pushed down toward the valve guide and its seal. Here's how to check this: With the valve seal on the valve guide, use a dial indicator to measure the distance from the top of the seal to the inside face of the lowest part of the top collar, which is the part closest to the valve stem. You must have a minimum of 0.060 inch more than what the lift of the cam is, as specified in the cam's specification sheet. For example, if the cam's lift is .540 inch, you'll need a minimum of 0.600 inch (0.540 + 0.060 inches) between the collar and the seal. If you don't have enough room,

With the valve seal on the guide, use a dial indicator to measure the distance from the top of the seal to the inside face of the top collar. You need a minimum of 0.060 inches more than what the lift of the cam is.

machine away some of the top of the valve guide (shorten it) to increase the clearance between the guide and seal, and the inside face of the top collar. Or, if you're installing new guides, shorten them 0.200 inch from the port (bowl) side and then drive the guides 0.100 inch deeper into the head (on the spring side) when installing them.

When you increase the distance the valve will lift off its seat in the head, you also increase how much the valve spring will be compressed. If the spring is compressed too far, the coils of the spring will bind against each other, jamming and possibly breaking valvetrain components. To check this measurement, install the valve springs into their normal places over the valves using a valve spring compressor. Then install the keepers (keys) into the outer face of the top collar to hold it all together. (Make sure the keys are fully seated before removing the valve spring compressor.)

Install an Andrews or Trock valve spring checker on the head using the supplied bolts. Then compress the valve spring using a 1/4-inch Allen on the tool's compressing screw. Using the dial indicator on the tool, measure how far the spring can be compressed before its coils touch each other, which is called *coil bind*. (Slip a piece of paper between the coils to see when they touch.) This measurement must be at least the sum of the lift of the cam plus another 0.100 inch. For example, if the cam's lift is .540 inch, you'll need a minimum of 0.640 inch (0.540 + 0.100 inches) between the collar and the guide.

Double check this measurement by zeroing out the dial indicators. Then, with the tool's arms lying on top of the top collar, compress the valve spring the sum of the lift of the cam plus another 0.100 inch. The coils of the springs should not bind (use the paper trick). If they do, you must change out the spring kit; it is not the correct one for this cam.

The last clearance to check is the distance between the two valves when they are open. Do this by using the Andrews or Trock valve spring checker. Compress both valves the distance that the cam would open them, which is listed in the cam's spec sheet as the lift at TDC (it's usually around .200 inch or so), using the tool. Then measure the gap between the heads of the two valves. There should be at least 0.060 inch between the closest edges of the valves. If there is not enough clearance, there are two ways to increase valve-to-valve clearance and correct the problem. One is to machine the edges of the valves to reduce the outside diameters. Another is to sink the valves deeper into their seats, which is also what you do to increase the installed height of the spring. However, this may reduce airflow through the valve seat. Thankfully, valve-to-valve clearances are usually fine, as is.

There's one more thing you should also check: Some performance springs are larger in diameter or taller than the OEM parts, so be sure to check for adequate clearance and modify the cylinder head and/or rocker boxes as needed, so you have at least 0.060 inch between the spring packs and the sides of the head and rocker boxes.

Install the valve springs into their places over the valves using a valve spring compressor, complete with collars and keepers (keys). Make sure the keys are seated before removing the valve spring compressor.

With a spring checker on the head, measure how far the springs can be compressed before its coils touch each other. The coils must not bind at the total valve lift spec plus 0.100".

Installing TP Pro-Vent Rocker Boxes

THE ENGINE

Time: 2–3 hours

Tools: A foot-pound torque wrench, an inch-pound torque wrench, blue Loctite, 7/16- inch and 1/2-inch sockets, flat-bladed screwdriver, 3/16-inch Allen

Talent:

Cost: $900

Parts: TP Pro-Vent rocker box kit

Tip: Now's the time to swap out to a set of adjustable pushrods.

PERFORMANCE GAIN: A slick set of boxes that'll stop oil blowby, as well as dress up your engine

COMPLEMENTARY MODIFICATION: This is the best time to install a set of roller rocker arms

Whether your stock rocker boxes are chrome or silver, a custom set of billet beauties really sets off an engine. And if you install them when you've already got the engine apart for some performance modifications, the only additional expense you'll incur are what the actual parts cost. After all, it takes the same amount of time and effort to install a custom set as it does to install stock.

As for TP Engineering's Pro-Vent rocker boxes, these components are more than just another pretty face. These chrome billet offerings will not only jazz up your engine, they also have a specially designed air/oil separating system that prevents oil from passing out of the heads (oil blowby) and into the air cleaner—with the next stop being all over the right side of the engine. And though most people think this is only a problem on Evos, it does happen on Twin Cams that have had some major performance modifications made, like a 95-inch or larger displacement increase. (It can also occur if there's a problem in the engine, like a faulty oil pump.)

As for the actual installation, start by lubricating the TP rocker shafts and the bore of the rocker arms for one rocker box assembly. (Do only one box at a time.) Then position a TP rocker shaft into the lower rocker box. Be sure the notch in the shaft will align with the hole for the rocker carrier bolt on the pushrod side of the rocker box. Then position a rocker in the box—be sure you have the rocker positioned so the arm that presses on the valve is over the oval hole in the rocker box—and send the shaft through. Do the same for the other rocker.

After putting a little blue Loctite onto their threads, put all the bolts and washers into their places in the lower box: The two long Allen bolts go on the left side of the engine and the four short hex bolts go in the middle and on the right side. The four large carrier bolts go into the four holes at the ends of the rocker arms.

Install the pushrod tubes with all new O-rings, onto the engine. Then, if installing the stock pushrods, slip them into their tubes; black for exhaust and silver for intake. Rotate the engine so both lifters for this head are at their lowest position. (If you are installing adjustable pushrods, see Project 43.)

To position one of the special lower box gaskets supplied with the TP kit onto the cylinder head, make sure the gasket is properly orientated to the head, bolt- and channel-wise.

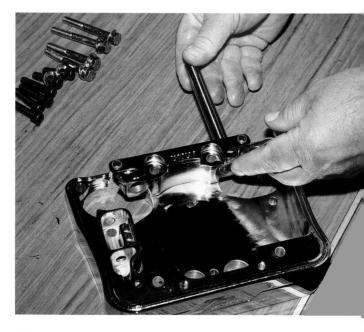
After lubing the rocker shafts and arms, position a shaft in the lower box. Be sure the notch in the shaft will align with the hole for the carrier bolt on the pushrod side of the box.

Place the lower box/rocker assembly onto the head, taking care to mate the pushrods to their respective rockers. Thread in all the bolts, leaving them a little loose until you get them all threaded, then tighten the lower box bolts, as per the sequence in the service manual, to 120–168 inch-pounds using a 3/16-inch Allen and a 7/16-inch socket. You can then torque the four rocker arm bolts, as per the sequence in the service manual, to 18–22 foot-pounds using a 1/2-inch socket. After putting the TP O-ring into its groove in the lower box, install the top box using the supplied chrome Allen bolts and washers. Put a little blue Loctite on the threads and torque the bolts to 90–100 inch-pounds with a 3/16- inch Allen.

Be sure to let the lifters bleed down for 10 minutes or so (until you can spin the pushrods with your fingers) before rotating the engine to do the other rocker box. Then fully extend all the pushrod tubes and ensure that they fully seat to the rocker boxes and lifter covers; pop in the spring cap retainers (clips) with a flat-bladed screwdriver.

Put a rocker in the box, with the arm over the oval hole in the rocker box, and send the shaft through. Do both rockers this way. Then put all the bolts and washers into the lower box.

Place the lower box/rocker assembly onto the head, and thread in all the bolts. Then tighten the bolts, as per the sequence in the H-D service manual, to the proper torque.

Positioning one of the special lower box gaskets supplied with the TP kit onto the cylinder head. Then install the pushrod and tubes, with both lifters at their lowest position.

After putting the TP O-ring into its groove in the lower box, install the cover using the supplied chrome Allen bolts and washers. Torque the bolts to 90–100 in-lbs with a 3/16-inch Allen.

Installing High-Performance Heads

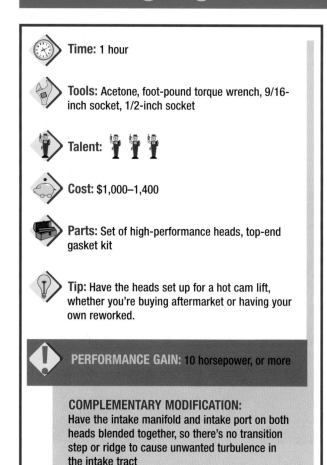

Time: 1 hour

Tools: Acetone, foot-pound torque wrench, 9/16-inch socket, 1/2-inch socket

Talent: ★ ★ ★

Cost: $1,000–1,400

Parts: Set of high-performance heads, top-end gasket kit

Tip: Have the heads set up for a hot cam lift, whether you're buying aftermarket or having your own reworked.

PERFORMANCE GAIN: 10 horsepower, or more

COMPLEMENTARY MODIFICATION:
Have the intake manifold and intake port on both heads blended together, so there's no transition step or ridge to cause unwanted turbulence in the intake tract

THE ENGINE

As great as the Twin Cam engine is compared to the Motor Company's previous Big Twin engines, the stock heads are a mixed bag. On one hand, the combustion chamber is far superior to that of the Evo, and light years better than the hemispherical (hemi) design found on Knuckleheads, Pans, and Shovels. Evos have a rounded chamber, which is cut off on one side like a D. This cutoff section is flat and even with the surrounding gasket surface. When the air/fuel mixture is compressed into the combustion chamber by the piston, the flat section of the head "squishes" the mixture into the rounded section of the head, creating turbulence. This turbulence helps to thoroughly mix the fuel and air in the combustion chamber, resulting in a more efficient burn. This is one of the reasons why an Evo runs leaner and produces more power than the hemi engines, which do not have as good a squish band and, therefore, produce less power for a given amount of air/fuel mixture.

Twin Cam heads, however, have a bathtub chamber, which is a rounded, rectangular shape. This is a better design because it provides a flat squish band all around the combustion chamber, not just on one side like that of an Evo's D. This allows the fuel/air mixture to be compressed into the combustion chamber with more turbulence, which results in a better mixing of fuel and air, and a more efficient burn.

Although a Twin Cam's combustion chamber is better than that of an Evo, the head's ports are not. In fact, a Twin Cam head does not flow air as well, even though TC 88s have a larger displacement—8 inches larger to be exact. The intake port design is okay, being similar to that of an Evo. However, the exhaust port has a diameter that's slightly smaller than the intake. The H-D engineers state that this was done to get higher exhaust gas velocities and, therefore, a more effective evacuation of the cylinder. There's also an anti-reversion step at the exit point of the exhaust port to keep exhaust gases that are already in the exhaust pipe from reentering the combustion chamber.

As for the valves, the Twin Cam uses the same-size intake valve as an Evo, which makes sense seeing the port is basically the same size. In fact, even the valve angles are the same as that of an Evo. However, the exhaust valve is a little thicker and about 0.030 inch smaller in diameter to match the smaller exhaust port. (There's an indent in the center of the valve's face to identify it as a TC-88 exhaust valve and not an Evo unit.)

So what does all this mean to you? Well, the stock heads will do the job if you stay with the stock displacement. However, if you punch the engine out to 95 cubic inches, the smaller exhaust valve, combined with the smaller exhaust port, as well as an intake valve and port that's good for an 80-inch engine, will restrict flow and limit high rpm horsepower. To get the most from a 95-inch or larger displacement engine, you must either replace the stock units with a set of aftermarket performance versions (Delkron, Harley-Davidson, S&S, and STD all offer excellent products) or have the stockers reworked by a professional, like Zipper's or R&R Cycle.

If you choose to have the heads reworked by a pro, you want more than just some porting work. You also want oversized valves and seats, with the seats blended to the port and combustion chamber, and the chamber itself should be reworked. Also discuss with the pro where you're looking for the bulk of the power to be made, down low for a cruiser or up top for a stoplight-to-stoplight screamer. And here's a tip: Forget about the guy down the block with the Dremel. Anyone who works on heads, grinder a-blazing, without a flow bench on hand and years of experience doing heads under his belt, is going to ruin your heads. And once someone has messed with a head, none of the pros are going to touch it.

To give you an idea of the difference that a set of properly flowing heads can make, if you do a full performance upgrade using a balanced combination of components—10:1 pistons, hot cams, and performance ignition, air

Twin Cam heads have a bathtub combustion chamber, which is a better design than what all previous Big Twins had because it provides a flat squish band all around the chamber. Note the indent in the face of the exhaust valve.

cleaner, carb/manifold, and exhaust—and do not change the heads/valves, other than adding the needed spring kit for the cams, you can expect to only get about 84 horsepower and 95 or so foot-pounds of torque out of a 95-incher.

Though that sounds impressive, you should be getting at least a pony per cubic inch and the same in torque, which means you're short about 10 horsepower. The benchmark you should be aiming for is 95 horsepower and 95 foot-pounds of torque. That is, unless you go with a cam that's cut to make more torque than horsepower, as you would want for a Touring model. If that's the case, you'll end up with a few less ponies, but more torque: 90–93 horsepower and around 100 or so foot-pounds.

As for the installation, it's usually the same whether you're installing a set of new aftermarket heads, or the stock set after they've been reworked, as you are going to do. However, an aftermarket head manufacturer may specify special steps. Also, if you are also installing high (pop-up) dome/high compression pistons, you should check piston-to-head and piston-to-valve clearances, as per Project 50.

Start by cleaning the gasket surface of the cylinders and heads with some acetone. Then install a new O-ring on each cylinder dowel. Each head can now get a new gasket and a little 1104 gasket sealer—a very thin skin coat. (However, follow the head manufacturer's instructions on gasket use and preparation if it is different.) Install a head onto its cylinder, followed by its bolts, long on the right and short on the left. (The threads of the bolts should be

After cleaning the gasket surfaces and installing a new O-ring and head gasket onto the cylinder, bolt on a head; long bolts on the right and short on the left. Torque them as per the sequence and values in the manual.

cleaned and lightly lubricated with a little 20W-50 engine oil.) Then torque the head bolts as per the sequence and values in the service manual. Do one head and then the other before moving on to the rocker boxes.

If installing the stock rocker boxes, place a new, lower rocker-box gasket onto each head. Be sure it is facing the correct way, or it'll leak oil like crazy on start-up. As usual, the gasket must align with the bolt holes. However, also make sure that the gasket covers the breather channel that's formed in the head. The lower rocker box can then go on; do one complete box at a time. Bolt it to the head using two long bolts with washers on the left and four shorts bolts with washers on the middle and right, with a little Loctite on the threads. Leave them slightly loose until you install the rocker arm assembly. Now install a new O-ring into each lower box for the breather baffle hole. At this point, follow the instructions for installing pushrods, as per Project 43, and the rocker arm assembly, as per Project 45. Project 47 shows how to install custom boxes, which you can follow to finish the installation, or go through the procedure outlined in the H-D service manual.

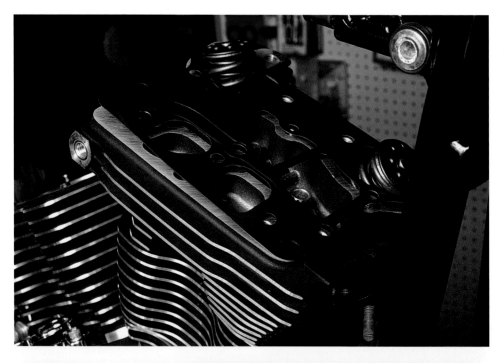

Place a new lower rocker box gasket onto the head. Be sure it is facing the correct way, or it'll leak oil like crazy on start-up. The gasket must align with the bolts holes, as well as cover the head's breather channel.

The lower rocker box goes on next with the two long bolts with washers on the left and the four shorts bolts with washers on the middle and right. Leave them loose until you bolt up the rocker assembly.

Checking Combustion Chamber Size

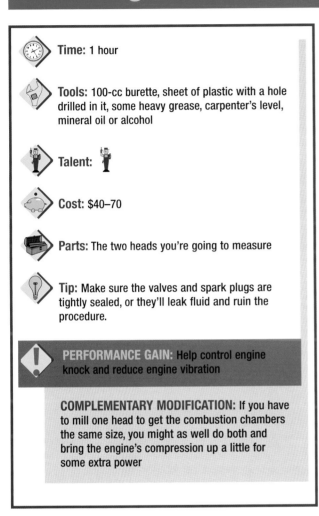

Time: 1 hour

Tools: 100-cc burette, sheet of plastic with a hole drilled in it, some heavy grease, carpenter's level, mineral oil or alcohol

Talent:

Cost: $40–70

Parts: The two heads you're going to measure

Tip: Make sure the valves and spark plugs are tightly sealed, or they'll leak fluid and ruin the procedure.

PERFORMANCE GAIN: Help control engine knock and reduce engine vibration

COMPLEMENTARY MODIFICATION: If you have to mill one head to get the combustion chambers the same size, you might as well do both and bring the engine's compression up a little for some extra power

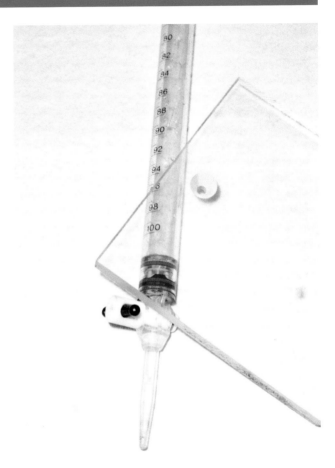

You'll need a 100-cc burette and a perfectly flat piece of plastic that has a single hole drilled in it. Countersink the hole, so it funnels the mineral oil into the combustion chamber.

THE ENGINE

For most people, having both of their engine's combustion chambers the same size is not a concern. However, to the conscientious engine builder, especially one who plans on boosting his engine's compression ratio by using high compression pistons or milling the heads, combustion chamber size is very important.

Combustion chamber volume is critical to a performance builder because it determines the cylinder's compression ratio. And a difference of 10 cc between the engine's two chambers is enough to cause the bane of performance engine builders everywhere: engine knock. It'll also noticeably increase engine vibration because the combustion pressures in the engine's cylinders will not be equal.

You can measure your engine's combustion chamber two ways, and both require the heads to be removed from the engine. The first will give you the true volume of the entire combustion chamber—this encompasses the head's

combustion chamber, as well as the area above the piston's rings—for both cylinders, while the second, which is the one we'll show you how to do, will allow you to make sure both compression chambers—the ones in the heads—are the same size.

To do the first method, bring the piston in the front cylinder to the top of its compression stroke, which is also called the Top Dead Center (TDC) position. Then seal the piston rings to the cylinder with some light grease; be sure to seal the piston all the way around the cylinder. Install the head gasket and head onto the engine; make sure the head is fully assembled, with the spark plug removed, and the valves are seating tightly to their seats, so there are no leaks. Now tilt the engine, so the spark plug hole is the highest point of the combustion chamber. Then fill the chamber

133

After positioning the head on a set of blocks, so it's perfectly level (use a carpenter's level), coat the entire gasket surface with heavy grease.

with alcohol measured from a 100 cc burette to find its exact volume. Once the chamber is filled right up to the spark plug hole, write down the number and do the same on the other cylinder.

The actual compression ratio of the cylinder can be found by adding the cylinder's volume (check out the Cylinder Volume sidebar to find out how to calculate this) and the chamber's volume together and then dividing this total by the chamber's volume. For example, if an engine has an 800 cc cylinder and an 80 cc combustion chamber, the first part of the equation would be: 800 + 80 = 880. This is then divided by the chamber volume (80), which results in 11. This is expressed as an 11 to 1 compression ratio, or 11:1. That means the total volume of both the cylinder (800) and the combustion chamber (80) gets compressed into the chamber at the ratio of 11:1.

To measure just a chamber's volume to see if it's the same as its mate, the valves must be installed in the head and sealed with grease, and the spark plug must be installed. Then, a plastic plate has a small hole drilled into it—countersinking the hole makes the job of filling the chamber easier. After the head gasket surface is cleaned, a thin coat of heavy grease is put onto this gasket surface. The plate is then pressed onto the head and sealed to it. The combustion chamber is then filled with alcohol or mineral oil, which is carefully measured from a 100-cc burette. Be sure to check inside both ports during the test to make sure fluid is not leaking past the valves; also check around the spark plug. The amount of fluid used is read off the burette and written down. Then the other chamber is measured.

If the chamber volumes of the front and rear heads are different, no matter which method you use, the builder can decrease the volume of the larger chamber by removing material from the head gasket surface (also called *decking the head*). If he decides to enlarge the smaller chamber, he can machine the valve seats to sink the valves farther into the head, remove material from inside the chamber, or do both. The important thing is that the combustion chambers are the same size.

Press the plastic plate onto the head with your fingers. You'll know the seal is complete if the grease all around the head is squished down under the plastic sheet.

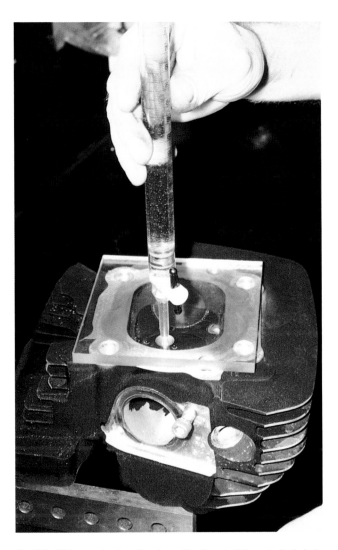

Cylinder Volume

The displacement of a piston-engine's cylinder is the total volume, actually the swept volume, of that cylinder. A cylinder's swept volume is the area that the piston travels (sweeps) over as it moves up and down the cylinder, which is called its stroke. And, just as in high-school math class, the area of a cylinder depends on its diameter and length.

When figuring a cylinder's volume, the diameter is the bore of the cylinder, the length is the piston's stroke. The length of the piston's stroke is measured from the lowest point of its travel in the cylinder, also called its Bottom Dead Center position (BDC), to its highest point in the cylinder, or its Top Dead Center position (TDC). To calculate a cylinder's volume you plug these two measurements into the formula: Bore x Bore x .7854 x Stroke. (By the way, the number .7854 is a constant value, which is needed to make it all work out correctly. This number never changes, no matter what the other measurements are.)

Now, if you wanted to find the actual displacement of an engine, you multiply the swept volume of the cylinder by the amount of cylinders that the engine has, which in the case of all V-twins is two. This gets you the total cubic-inch displacement of the engine. For example, if you use the bore and stroke measurements for a Twin Cam 88, you'll get (3.75 x 3.75 x .7854 x 4.00 inches) x 2 for a total of 88.3575 inches, which gets rounded off to 88 inches.

THE ENGINE

Carefully fill the combustion chamber with mineral oil through the hole in the plastic plate. Check in the ports to make sure no oil is leaking past the valves; also check the spark plug.

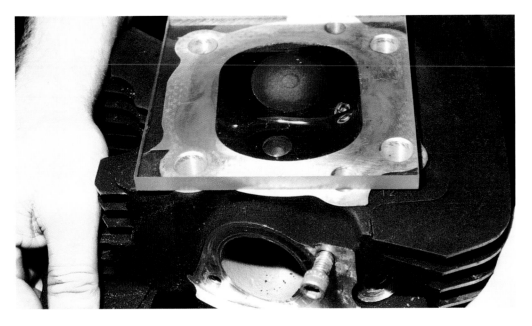

You'll have to tilt the head as you add oil to get rid of the air bubble under the plate. Once done, read the burette to see how much oil it took to completely fill the chamber with mineral oil.

Claying High-Compression Pistons

 Time: 2–3 hours

 Tools: Modeling clay, micrometer, and whatever else you'll need to assemble the top end of the engine

 Talent:

 Cost: $250–400

 Parts: High-compression piston set, top-end gasket/O-ring kit

 Tip: Install a fully adjustable ignition module, so you can adjust the initial timing and the advance curve for maximum power, while controlling engine knock.

 PERFORMANCE GAIN: Impressive throttle response, better fuel mileage, as well as a horsepower and torque increase

COMPLEMENTARY MODIFICATION: Now you can install longer-duration, higher-lift cams, which is where you'll really reap the power gains

THE ENGINE

Have you ever been in a pack of bikes and heard one that had an exhaust note that crackled with power when the rider whacked the throttle? That, my friend, is the sound of a high-compression engine! And though some try to imitate it with real short drag pipes or holes in their mufflers, nothing has the crisp bite of a high-compression mill, in sound or throttle response.

Boosting an engine's compression ratio is a time-honored and effective method of enabling an engine to produce more power while also increasing its efficiency (fuel mileage). Increasing the compression will also significantly improve throttle response. However, the big plus of high compression is that you can then run longer-duration camshafts, and that's where you'll really start to rack up the ponies. That is, provided you have the other systems, like the intake, exhaust, ignition, and heads (modified correctly), to make the engine a balanced package. But, like everything in the world, every modification has its pluses and minuses. So, before you head down to the service department with a fistful of dollars, you should understand what a compression ratio is, why it produces more power, and what the possible drawbacks are.

As you've seen in countless tech stories and bike features, an engine's compression ratio is usually written as 10:1. What this means is that the volume of the area above the piston, which is mostly the combustion chamber, and the volume of the cylinder when the piston is at the lowest point of its stroke—called its Bottom Dead Center (BDC) position—will be reduced to one-tenth of that size when the piston is at the highest point of its stroke, or its Top Dead Center position (TDC). The notation 10:1 simply states that the fuel/air mixture will be compressed into the cylinder head's combustion chamber until it occupies a space one-tenth as large as the volume of the cylinder and combustion chamber combined.

Clean the top of the piston with a solvent such as brake cleaner.

The reason increasing the engine's compression enables it to put out more power, is that the piston is driven down in its cylinder by the pressure produced in the combustion chamber by the rapidly burning fuel and air mixture. How hard this pressure pushes down on the piston determines how much power the engine produces. So, if the pressure that the fuel/air mixture is under is increased before it is ignited (the engine's compression ratio is raised), the burning gases will exert even more pressure onto the piston, producing more power. Think of it like a spring: The more you compress it, the harder it pushes back.

That brings us to the question of what compression to use. To feel any real change in power, you need to go up at least half a point (.5) in compression. If you're going to raise the compression to a value below 10:1, you can get away with using the stock cast pistons. However, for ratios of 10:1 and above, using forged pistons, which are stronger than cast ones and more able to handle the increased power, is highly recommended.

It's a generally accepted rule of thumb that you'll gain about 4 to 5 percent more power the first time you bump the compression up one point, such as boosting a stock Twin Cam from 8.9:1 to 10:1. However, the power gained going up another point, from 10:1 to 11:1, is about half of that, or 2 to 2 1/2 percent.

Twin Cam 88s or 88Bs usually respond well to a 10:1 to 10:5.1 ratio. However, an adjustable performance ignition module should also be used. It's also a generally accepted fact that 10:1–10.5:1 is considered a good compression for the street, with ratios above 10.5:1 and up to 11:1 being the practical maximum for a street bike that has to run on pump gas.

Another thing that must be considered when picking a compression ratio is that a light bike, like a Softail Deuce or Dyna Super Glide, can run more compression than a heavy bike, like a Road King or one of the other touring models, especially if it's loaded up. That's because of a couple of problems called detonation and preignition.

Detonation and pre-ignition are notorious for destroying pistons and other parts within the combustion chamber. During normal combustion, the spark plug fires and starts a flame that moves across the combustion chamber as it burns the fuel/air mixture in a controlled manner. Detonation, on the other hand, is the spontaneous and explosive ignition of the fuel/air mixture before the flame caused by the spark plug reaches it. Detonation occurs when temperatures and pressures in the combustion chamber exceed the fuel's critical limit.

Preignition is when the air/fuel mixture is ignited by a hot spot in the combustion chamber before the spark plug fires. Hot spots are usually due to excessive carbon or other deposits in the combustion chamber that, for one reason or another, have become much hotter than normal. However, some engineers consider detonation and preignition so

intertwined they refer to them both as simply engine knock. This dangerous condition is present if you hear a rattling or pinging sound coming from your engine when you open the throttle.

Octane is added to gasoline to raise its critical limit and prevent engine knock. Octane also controls the rate at which the fuel/air mixture burns, so when the spark plug should fire (also known as the ignition timing) can be accurately set to reap the optimum amount of power from each combustion event. The higher the engine's compression ratio, the higher the octane rating required. H-D's service manuals state that its engines require a minimum pump octane rating of 87, which is usually okay for a 9:1 ratio. However, once the compression is raised, 92-octane fuel should always be used.

Moderately boosting the compression, like going from 9:1 to 10:1 or 10.25:1 shouldn't run you afoul of the Big K, knocking, in a big way. However, even stock H-D engines have bouts with knock, due to the very lean fuel/air mixture needed to meet EPA regulations. Thankfully, there are ways to prevent engine knock and two easy ones are to run a richer fuel/air mixture and don't let the engine overheat. In case you haven't noticed, a lean-running engine will rattle and ping more often on a hot day, especially in heavy traffic. The combination of a lean mixture and high engine–operating temperatures aggravates the situation and gives engine knock an open invitation to trash your engine.

Because the Motor Company can't run a richer mix, the method it uses in its 2000 and later Softails, and 2001 and later rubber-mounts models, is to mess with the ignition timing. All Delphi EFI control modules have a ping sensor, which detects whenever the Big K makes an appearance via a process called ion sensing. If the control module detects engine knock, it retards the ignition timing (moves it to a less aggressive setting) until the knocking stops. In fact, if the engine is not set up correctly for a high compression ratio, this system will retard the timing to the point of major engine power loss, which, of course, defeats the purpose of having a high compression engine in the first place. The fix for this is to have the module remapped for high compression pistons, which gives you different ignition and fuel settings. However, if you still have a knock problem, there are a number of aftermarket fuel-system modules around that allow you to fatten up the fuel/air mixture a bit more than will the remapping (see Project 21).

Those with carburetor-equipped bikes can re-jet for a richer mix and install a fully adjustable ignition. This allows you to dial in the initial ignition timing and advance curve that'll keep the combustion boogieman away. The object of the exercise is to use the most aggressive advance curve possible, while still avoiding engine knock. Once correctly dialed in, you'll get the most power from your engine, while also protecting it from damage.

Another way to eliminate knock is to use longer-duration cams, which allows some of the engine's compression

Place a thin layer of modeling clay onto the top of the piston in both valve pockets. Then assemble the engine, so you can gently rotate the engine two or more full rotations by hand. Then remove the heads.

There should be an indent in some, if not all, of the clay from the valves. Carefully cut each clay section in half with a blunt razor. Then measure the depth of the indent in the clay with a micrometer to get the clearance.

to bleed off at low rpm, where engine knock always occurs. (Actually, longer-duration cams are recommended after boosting the compression ratio.)

You can also dual-plug the heads, but that's usually needed when you're running 11:1 and higher ratios. Running two spark plugs in each head also allows an engine to run a higher compression ratio, all things being equal, before problems occur. With a spark plug being fired on each side of the combustion chamber, there are two flame fronts burning the air/fuel mixture instead of one, which reduces the chance for knock to occur.

However, keeping the compression to about 10:1 also helps to steer you clear of the other drawback of raising the ratio: reduced engine component life. This problem is due to the greater loads put upon the engine parts, namely the pistons, connecting rod components, and lower-end bearings, by the higher pressures in the combustion chamber. In fact, ratios in the 11.5:1 range, which is very high for a street bike, can reduce component life by more than 50 percent in an Evo. The bottom line is that you still need to upgrade to forged pistons, no matter what engine design you have, if you go to 10:1 or higher.

There are two ways to boost your compression: milling material off the heads and/or cylinders, or using higher compression pistons. Those interested in the milling option can check out the accompanying table to see how much has to come off to get the compression increase they want. Many people, however, prefer to go with the piston method, as they have to upgrade to forged pistons anyway due to the increased stresses associated with higher compression ratios. This is also the method Harley-Davidson uses with its high compression piston kit.

High compression (pop-up) pistons have a dome that protrudes up into the combustion chamber, instead of the flat top that the stock pistons have. The drawback of a domed piston is that the dome can get in the way of the flame of combustion as it burns its way across the combustion chamber. However, many performance builders feel that with a moderate increase, like 10:1, this should not pose a problem. In fact, some piston manufacturers shape the dome so it will assist combustion by increasing the amount of turbulence in the cylinder, which provides a better mixing of the fuel and air, and, therefore, a better burn.

No matter which method you choose, the end result is that you're moving the piston closer to the valves and head. If there's not enough clearance between these parts, they will collide, resulting in a damaged engine and wallet. So, unless you're using pistons that are specifically matched to the engine's heads, be they stock or aftermarket, you should always check valve-to-piston and piston-to-head clearances with modeling clay to ensure that parts will not touch each other during operation.

Here's how to do it: First, clean the top of the piston with a solvent like brake clean. Then place a thin layer of modeling clay onto the top of the piston in both valve pockets. After you put a very thin film of oil onto the valves, install the heads, without the head gaskets, onto the face of the cylinders. Do not torque down the head bolts (you don't want to stretch the cylinder studs). Just bring the bolts down until they're snug. Install the complete valvetrain, but leave out the O-rings and gaskets, and just snug up the bolts. Do not torque anything. Adjust the pushrods as if you were going to start the engine; if you don't, this test is worthless. Don't forget to give the lifters time to bleed down. (The best way to do this check is with solid lifters, so the hydraulic unit doesn't affect the test.) Leave the spark plugs out.

With the engine set up in this manner, gently rotate the engine two or more full rotations by hand. If you feel a hesitation, *stop*! However, you shouldn't, unless you've done something wrong. Then remove the heads, so you can see the top of the pistons.

If you have done everything correctly, there should be an indent in some, and sometimes all, of the mounds of clay from the valves. (Hopefully, there are no places where the piston touched the head.) Carefully cut each clay section in half with a blunt razor. (Be careful not to mark the top of the piston with the razor.) First check that each valve pocket cut into the piston is wide enough for its valve. Do this by checking where the valve cut into the clay in relation to the valve pocket. If there's not at least 0.050 inch of clearance between the outer edge of the valve and the inner face of the piston's pocket, have the dome of the piston machined.

Now measure the depth of the indent in the clay with a micrometer. On the 10.5:1 Wiseco pistons I installed here, the indent in the clay on the intake pockets stopped 1/8 inch (0.125 inch) from the top of the piston. There were no marks at all in the exhaust pockets. If you use stock-thickness head gaskets, which are 0.059 inch thick, they will compress to 0.030-inch when the head is torqued into place. Adding the 0.125 inch of clearance between the bottom of the clay indent and top of the piston to the .030 inch clearance of the head gasket gives us a piston-to-valve clearance of 0.155 inch. Though Wiseco does not call out a spec in its instructions, a minimum of 0.060 inch is the industry norm, which means we've got plenty of room with this piston, camshaft, and valve setup.

MILLING/RATIO CHART

Amount to Mill	Compression Ratio
0.000 inch	8.9:1 (stock)
0.010 inch	9.17:1
0.020 inch	9.33:1
0.030 inch	9.50:1
0.040 inch	9.69:1
0.050 inch	9.89:1
0.060 inch	10.09:1
0.070 inch	10.30:1
0.080 inch	10.52:1
0.090 inch	10.76:1
0.100 inch	11.00:1

Installing a 95-Cubic-Inch Kit

 Time: 1–2 hours

 Tools: JIMS #1236 piston-ring compressor, piston-ring gapping tool, flat feeler gauge, needle-nose pliers, JIMS #1235 piston-ring expander tool, brass drift, and deburring tool

 Talent:

 Cost: $150–300 pistons only/$450–600 cylinders and pistons

 Parts: Set of big bore cylinders and/or pistons, top-end gasket kit, 5 feet of 1/2-inch ID rubber hose (optional), two clean rags

 Tip: Instead of buying new cylinders, it may be cheaper to bore your stock ones out.

 PERFORMANCE GAIN: Figure almost one horsepower per cubic inch; more if other performance parts also are installed

COMPLEMENTARY MODIFICATION: Go with high compression pistons (10:1), which will also allow you to run a hotter (longer duration) cam

THE ENGINE

Want more power? Get a bigger engine; it's as simple as that. And though increasing your engine's size, also known as its displacement, isn't the only way to get more horsepower and torque out of it, it's a very effective one. Since an engine's displacement is the result of two factors—the bore of its cylinders and the stroke of its pistons—increasing either one (or both of them) will make your engine larger and more powerful. (Of course, adding more cylinders would also do the trick, but that's a helluva lot more work.)

The purpose of a big bore kit is to dramatically increase the diameter of an engine's cylinder bores. The most common Twin Cam upgrade is a 95-inch kit, such as what H-D's Screamin' Eagle offers. These TC 88 kits consist of cylinders that are 1/8 inch larger in diameter (3 7/8 inch) than the stock 3 3/4 inch ones. This increase in bore brings the engine's displacement up to 95 inches.

The best part is that Twin Cams are designed with these displacement increases in mind, so punching out the engine in this way will not shorten engine life. Even if you go with larger bore cylinders, which require the size of the cylinder holes in the crankcases (called the cylinder spigots) to be increased, there are no problems associated with increasing an engine's bore, other than the additional stress and strain that the increased power will put on all the engine and powertrain components. However, the size of the cylinder spigots in the crankcase limits how large you can increase the cylinder bores (you can only go so big before you run out of case), which is why builders who want very large displacement engines must also increase the engine's stroke (see Project 61).

But buying a set of big bore cylinders and pistons is not the only way to make your engine a 95-incher. The stock TC 88 cylinders have walls so thick they can be bored out to the same diameter as the big bore kit cylinders and still have a wall as thick as the new cylinders. In fact, some people prefer to bore out their stock cylinders and have the pistons of their choice fitted instead of getting the SE kits, which come with SE pistons matched to the cylinders by H-D.

Before I get into the actual steps needed to install a set of 95-inch pistons, I should mention that changing the bore of an engine to increase its displacement should not be confused with an overbore, which is a procedure that's done during an engine rebuild to remove imperfections in the cylinder's walls. While an overbore does change the bore size slightly, it's a very small amount—0.005 inch or 0.010 inch usually, depending on the amount of damage to the cylinder walls. Back in the days of Panheads, Shovels, and Ironhead Sportsters, boring out the cylinders to increase displacement was a popular speed trick, seeing big bore cylinders were not easily available. However, today this technique is not very practical. The power gains are minor and it makes the cylinder walls too thin for another overbore, which is required for a proper rebuild.

For our 95-inch upgrade, I ordered up a set of Wiseco 10.5:1 high compression pistons. In fact, I sent our cylinders to Wiseco and the crew there bored them to fit the new Wiseco pistons perfectly. Once you get the pistons matched to the cylinders, no matter if they are new cylinders or bored-out stock, the installation process is the same.

Remove the rocker boxes, heads, pushrods, and intake and exhaust system as per the H-D service manual. Then pull the cylinders off of their pistons, and put a clean rag into the openings into the lower end of the engine. You are now ready to remove the pistons and cylinder studs.

Pull the wrist pin circlip out of the old piston with a needlenose pliers. Then use a deburring tool to clean the circlip's groove, so the wrist pin will come out with minimum pressure.

Now use a brass drift to push the wrist pin out of the piston. You may have to tap the drift with the palm of your hand to start it moving, but there should be no need to use a hammer.

Pull the wrist pin circlip out of the old piston with a needle-nose pliers. Then use a deburring tool to clean the circlip's groove, so that the wrist pin comes out with minimum pressure. You can now use a brass drift to push the wrist pin out of the piston. You may have to tap the drift with the palm of your hand to start it moving, but that should be it. No need to use a hammer. Do the same for the other piston.

Remove all the cylinder studs and replace them with new SE studs, which already have a thread-locking compound on the threads. Don't reuse the old studs that were stretched when torqued during assembly. Always use new studs whenever you pull the cylinders and heads. And be sure to install them to the height specified in their instructions.

After the cylinders are bored and honed to fit your new pistons, do not confuse which piston goes with what cylinder, as they are now matched sets. The end gap of the piston rings must now be checked in their respective cylinders with a flat feeler gauge. Do this by inserting a ring into the cylinder and then pushing it down into the cylinder with the piston until the ring is about 2 inches from the top. This makes the ring even in the cylinder's bore for an accurate reading. Check the ring's end gap with a flat feeler gauge; Wiseco piston rings require a 0.015-inch gap for the two compression rings, but the two oil rings are fine, as is. If you don't have the required clearances, you must open up the gaps with a ring gap tool.

Once the gaps are correct, you can now install the rings onto the new pistons with a ring expander tool, as per their instructions. Make sure the gaps are staggered as per the instructions included with the rings. Then install one wrist-pin circlip into the piston. At this point, some mechanics prefer to put hose over the cylinder studs so they do not scratch the new pistons. Slip the wrist pin partway into the piston, but not far enough to start covering the opening in the piston for the connecting rod. Position the piston onto the connecting rod as per the pis-

ton's instructions—there's usually an orientation mark on the top of the piston—and send the wrist pin through the rest of the way. You can now install the other wrist-pin circlip into the piston.

Put new O-rings on the base of the cylinders and oil dowels. Install a good ring compressor onto the piston, which should have plenty of oil on its rings and sides. Slip the cylinder down over the piston and cylinder studs, and gently work the cylinder down over the piston. Once the rings are all inside the cylinder, remove the ring compressor from the piston and gently push the cylinder down onto the crankcases.

If you are installing high compression pistons, as I am, read Project 50 to see how to check for proper valve-to-piston clearance. You can then reinstall the rocker boxes, heads, pushrods, and intake and exhaust systems as per the H-D manual, or the other projects in this book that cover those procedures.

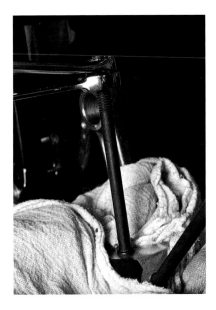

Remove the old cylinder studs by locking two nuts together, and then unscrewing the stud using the lower nut. Then replace them with new SE studs, which have a thread-locking compound on the threads.

Piston ring end gap is checked by putting a ring into the cylinder and pushing it down with its piston, so the ring is even in the cylinder's bore. Then check the end gap with the flat feeler gauge.

Once the gaps are correct, you can now install the rings onto the new pistons with a ring expander tool. Make sure the gaps are staggered as per the instructions included with the rings. Also install one wrist pin circlip.

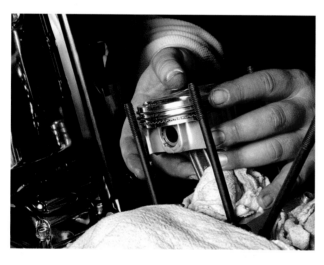

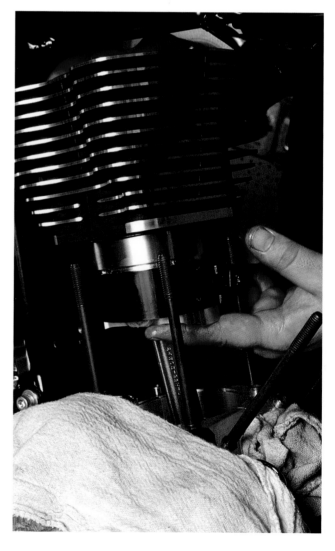

After slipping the wrist pin partway in, position the piston onto the connecting rod, as per the piston's instructions, and send the wrist pin all the way through. Then install the other wrist pin circlip.

Put new O-rings on the base of the cylinders and oil dowels. After installing a good ring compressor onto the piston, slip the cylinder down over the piston and gently work the cylinder down and onto the cases.

Installing a Custom Cam Cover

 Time: 30 minutes

 Tools: 3/16-inch Allen wrench, inch-pounds torque wrench, gasket scraper

 Talent:

 Cost: $375–475

 Parts: New cam cover gasket, new cam cover

 Tip: With the cover off, check the chain tensioner shoe for excessive wear. If the shoe on the tensioner you can see is worn, you know the one inside the cam support plate is also worn, so change them both.

 PERFORMANCE GAIN: A bit more "bling" is a good thing

COMPLEMENTARY MODIFICATION:
Don't just spiff-up the cam cover. Project 77 shows you how to also swap out the transmission's end and top covers

Twin Cam owners have got it a lot easier than Evo riders when it comes to swapping out the stock cam cover for a prettier aftermarket item. That's because the cam cover on TC 88s and 88Bs is just that, only a cover.

On an Evo, the cam cover is a structural part of the engine, and it supports the pinion shaft, which is the right shaft of the flywheel assembly (the heart of the engine) and the outboard end of the camshaft. The cam cover also routes oil through the engine, to a degree, so if you put on a cover from the wrong year, or even just screw up with the gasket, you'll have oiling problems that'll make you bald. Better yet, put a cheap cover on, one that doesn't have its bushings aligned with the camshaft or pinion shaft, for example, and you'll have a very short, yet expensive, first ride after the installation.

When the Twin Cams were designed, a major change was incorporated into the design of the entire engine. On all Twin Cams, the cam cover, rocker covers, lifter blocks, and primary covers were no longer load-bearing components.

These covers are simply that; covers to hold in oil and keep out dirt and grit. Other components were designed to support the load these parts used to handle. In the case of the cam cover, there's now a cam support plate, while the rocker arms are now in a rocker-arm support plate. This was done to get a much quieter engine, which is the same reason why the cams in a Twin Cam are chain-driven and not gear-driven as they are in every other OHV, air-cooled H-D Big Twin.

Now that you know why there are different cam covers, it's time to explain how you make a swap by installing a Pro-One chrome cam cover.

Using a 3/16-inch Allen wrench, start by unbolting the old cover, which is held on by 10 Allen bolts that are all the same length. Then clean the old gasket off of the case. Be careful not to scratch or gouge the gasket surface. Also clean out the cam-cover bolt holes in the right case. Trying to install a bolt into a hole filled with oil and/or dirt will cause the case around the bolt to crack, which will ruin your day for the next month.

Now position a new cam cover gasket onto the right case, taking care to make sure all the holes line up cleanly. Then bolt up the Pro-One cam cover using Pro-One's chrome Allen bolts, with a little blue Loctite on the threads. Alternately tightening the bolts to 125 inch-pounds with a 3/16-inch Allen wrench, as per the pattern in the H-D manual, finishes this installation.

After removing the old cam cover and cleaning off the old gasket, position a new gasket onto the right case. Check that all the bolt and oil holes line up cleanly.

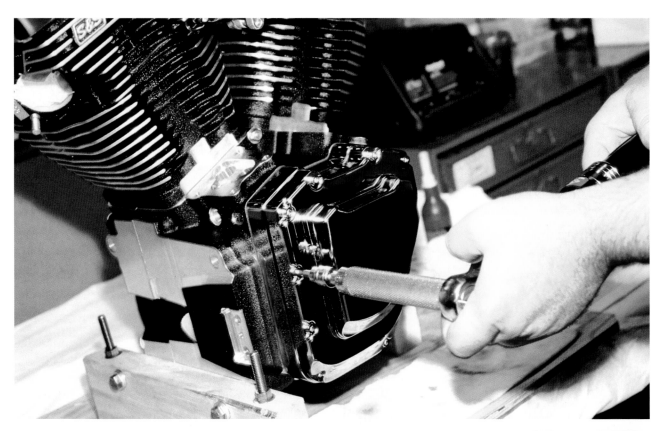

Bolt up the Pro-One cam cover using Pro-One's chrome Allen bolts, with a little blue Loctite on the threads. Tighten the bolts to 125 in-lbs with a 3/16-inch Allen wrench, as per the pattern in the H-D manual.

Here's how the finished job looks. Beats the hell out of the stock cover!

144

Installing an Andrews Camshaft Sprocket

 Time: 1 hour

  Tools: 1/4-inch Allen wrench, 1/2-inch socket, 9/16-inch socket, inch-pounds and foot-pounds torque wrenches, JIMS #1283 tensioner tool kit (comes with two retention pins), #1285-1 sprocket lock, blue Loctite

 Talent: 👷👷

 Cost: Under $100

 Parts: Cam cover gasket, Andrews sprocket kit #288010

Tip: You also should upgrade the rear camshaft's ball bearing to a roller bearing, as the rear cam's stock ball bearing is known to fail (see Project 54).

PERFORMANCE GAIN: The rear camshaft sprocket stays firmly connected to the camshaft

COMPLEMENTARY MODIFICATION: Now's a good time to install a custom cam cover and check the shoe on the cam chain tensioner

This is the Andrews upgrade kit for 1999 Twin Cam 88s. This kit comes with a new sprocket, 3/16-inch drive key, three shims (0.005-inch, 0.010-inch, and 0.020-inch), retaining washer, and bolt.

Note that the drive key is cast as part of the stock sprocket (right). The Andrews sprocket (left) has a more pronounced keyway and a beefier, separate drive key.

THE ENGINE

Back in 1999, soon after the Twin Cam 88 was put into service, a problem arose with the rear camshaft bolt and primary chain sprocket on engines built before September 29, 1998. These early engines use a tapered and keyed cam and sprocket instead of the splined camshaft and sprocket found on all 2000 and later engines. H-D made a design change on both engine versions when it introduced the TC 88B, which completely eliminated the keyed cam and sprocket problem on following engines.

On the keyed camshaft/sprocket setup, the sprocket and drive key are formed as one piece. The key's job is to simply position the sprocket correctly on the camshaft, which is why it's a bit on the wimpy side. A properly torqued bolt and washer was supposed to keep the sprocket and camshaft tightly joined together to eliminate any movement between the two, which would cause the small key to shear. Unfortunately, the bolt was not keeping

things as tight as the engineers planned, so the sprocket moved on its camshaft. Once this occurred, it didn't take long for the head of the bolt to pop off, which, of course, released all load on the sprocket and allowed it to shear its key, shutting down the engine.

After much analysis, the engineers found the cause, which turned out to be three small mistakes that joined forces to become the big one just mentioned. The first mistake was that the wrong type of thread locker was used on the cam bolt's threads during assembly, which resulted in the bolt not getting tightened to the right torque.

The second mistake was that the washer used with the cam bolt was stamped out of a sheet of steel, which resulted in a not-quite-flat washer. That, like the wrong thread locker, resulted in an inconsistent torque load on the bolt when the engine was assembled. Without the bolt being torqued to the correct amount, whether it was due to one or both of these mistakes, the cam bolt wasn't able to hold the sprocket tightly to its cam. The excessive play between the two parts eventually sheared the head off the cam bolt, which brings us to the third mistake.

The head of the cam bolt sheared off easily because the bolt was threaded right up to the head. Normally, this is not a problem, but the threaded portion of a bolt is weaker than a portion without threads, so when the sprocket started wiggling on its camshaft, it worked on the weak bolt until its head sheared off. With the sprocket now wobbling on the camshaft, the sprocket's key quickly sheared, which allowed the sprocket to turn without moving the camshaft, stopping the engine.

Once the H-D engineers figured out what was wrong, the fixes were easy. The assembly line was stopped and an upgrade was implemented. A service bulletin also went out to the dealerships, so all TC 88 engines could be upgraded. Here's H-D upgrade: The thread lock compound was changed to one that would not affect the bolt's torque load during assembly. H-D also started using a bolt that was not threaded right up to the head. The last change was to the washer, which was no longer stamped out. The new one was ground perfectly flat to remove any chance of inconsistent torque. This upgrade lasted until the 2000 production year engines, when H-D completely eliminated the problem by changing the keyed rear camshaft and drive sprocket to the splined one found on all current TC 88 and 88B engines. The camshaft sprocket's bolt and washer were also changed to parts that are much stronger than the originals.

However, while all this was still going on, Andrews Products came out with its own fix. Andrews offers a sprocket with a separate drive key (P/N #288010), which is much beefier than the cast-in key on the H-D sprocket, as the accompanying text and photos show. However, in light of the problem with the rear camshaft ball bearing on some mid-2000 and earlier engines, I recommend that you also consider changing the rear camshaft's outer bearing from a ball bearing to a roller bearing (see Project 54).

To install the Andrews kit, disassemble the engine as per the procedure outlined in Project 65, Aligning a Twin-Cam Oil Pump. Once you have the stock sprockets off, you'll see that there's a shim on the rear cam. Remove it, as you will not need it with the new Andrews sprocket.

To check sprocket alignment, install the Andrews primary cam sprocket (with its key), and the (pinion) crank sprocket, with their bolts and washers, but without

the primary cam chain, onto their respective shafts. The drive key should be a snug fit in both the cam and sprocket's keyway. However, do not force the drive key in. If needed, file or stone the key for a snug fit. You may also have to file it for proper length, as the key should not interfere with the retaining washer, which must be flat and tight to the face of the sprocket.

Then put a straight edge across the face of both sprockets, following the sprocket alignment procedure outlined in Project 56. If needed, install the appropriate Andrews shim under the Andrews sprocket. Once the sprocket alignment is correct, reassemble the engine as per the procedure in Project 65.

The stock sprocket (right) uses a separate thick shim, while the Andrews sprocket (left) is machined to eliminate this shim and uses only a thin shim to get proper sprocket alignment.

Replacing the Rear Camshaft Ball Bearing

 Time: 3–4 hours

 Tools: Basic mechanic's tools, access to a hydraulic press, foot-pounds torque wrench, JIMS #1283 tensioner tool kit (which comes with two retention pins), JIMS #1285-1 sprocket lock, JIMS #1277-2 cam-bearing removing tool and cam installing tool, JIMS #1277-1 cam support–plate press tool, JIMS #1277-3 cam bearing tool, and two JIMS #33443-84 Evo lifter-base alignment tools

 Talent:

 Cost: Under $150

 Parts: Cam cover gasket, lifter cover gaskets, pushrod tube O-rings, rear roller bearing (H-D #8983), rear cam shim kit (H-D #25938-00), front cam retaining (snap) ring (H-D #11494-SUB1), front cam ball bearing (H-D #8990A), blue Loctite, and new rocker box gaskets (unless you're installing new adjustable pushrods)

 Tip: Swap out the stock non-adjustable pushrods for a set of adjustable ones, as shown in Project 43.

 PERFORMANCE GAIN: Your engine will stay together longer

COMPLEMENTARY MODIFICATION: Swap the stock camshafts for a set of performance cams (Project 56 or 57), since you'll have them out anyway

Wen problems with the rear camshaft's outer bearing first surfaced, the engineers at H-D thought the fault lay with the camshaft support plate. Changes were made in an effort to correct the problem, which is why there have been a few versions of the plate since it was first introduced. However, the rear outer bearing itself was the main culprit, with the fix being changing out the stock ball bearing for a roller bearing, which is what H-D did on all engines assembled after mid-2000. As for the front camshaft's outer bearing, it is also a ball bearing, but it is not subjected to the same loads as the rear bearing and, to date, no problems with it have been reported.

When and if the rear ball bearing goes bad, it doesn't let go all of a sudden. It first starts to get noisy under the gearcase cover. If the bike is brought to an experienced H-D mechanic, he should be able to tell that the bearing is going bad before it lets go completely. In the event of a failure, the damage is usually confined to the components in the gearcase and return oil system, but not always. If this does occur, and the engine has never been altered or worked on in any way that will void the H-D warranty, the Motor Company will replace all damaged parts and cover all labor charges under the owner's warranty, at no charge. In fact, because this became a major concern of owners, Harley-Davidson sent those with affected engines a letter, dated January 22, 2001, which extended the warranty on the cam bearing to five years or 50,000 miles. This warranty is also valid for future owners of the bike. However, Harley-Davidson will not pay for the repair before the bearing fails, or on any engine that has been altered in any way that voids the H-D warranty.

If you own one of the affected engines, you can either keep a close ear to the gearcase on your engine or have the rear outer ball bearing swapped out for the H-D replacement roller bearing, even though it is at your own expense. I suggest that when you do the bearing swap, you also put in a set of adjustable pushrods, as this will greatly reduce the amount of time it will take to do the job. I also suggest that if you are considering installing performance camshafts, this is the time to do it, as the labor is almost the same.

Two last points before I get to the actual job: If you're thinking of also changing the front cam's outer ball bearing to a roller bearing, forget it. While the rear bearing's end play can be set to the proper spec with shims, the front cam's end play is preset to the ball bearing with a snap ring. No roller bearing available at the time of this writing will exactly replace the front bearing.

Also, if you have an early-style tapered-shaft rear cam (see Project 53), it's another good reason to consider replacing the stock cams with a later-style splined version. There are some good bolt-in ones offered by a number of companies that will give your engine a little more get-up-and-go without compromising reliability or requiring headwork. Or you could go for a higher-performance cam, depending on what other modifications are made to the engine.

Start the job by putting an oil catch pan under the right side of the engine. Then remove the cam cover using a 1/4-inch Allen wrench. Once the cover is off, clean the old gasket from the cover and engine case as the oil drains into the pan. Seeing you have to remove the cams from the engine to change the bearing, you have to first remove the pushrods to release the pressure from the valve springs in the heads. If you wish to reuse the stock, non-adjustable pushrods, you must remove the rocker boxes, as shown in Project 47. Or, you can cut the old pushrods out and install new adjustable ones, as shown in Project 43.

Once you have the pushrods out of the way, follow the instructions given in Project 65 for removing the primary cam chain and sprockets from the cam support plate. Some mechanics prefer not to mess with the lifters and covers, and simply use the wire from a metal binder clip to keep the lifters out of the way during the job. However, if you prefer to remove the lifters and covers, remove the bolts using a 3/16-inch Allen wrench. Then slide the lifters out of their bores in the right crankcase. Be sure to mark them so you can put each one back into the same bore, in the original orientation (same side facing out). Then clean the old gaskets off the covers and case.

Back at the cam support plate, remove the shim from the rear cam and set it aside for later use. Also remove the black chain guide shoe from the cam support plate. After using a 3/16-inch Allen to remove the camshaft support plate and oil pump mounting bolts, pull the whole support plate assembly from the engine, cams and all. Do not remove or disturb the oil pump, unless you plan on upgrading it as per Project 66. You should, however, install a new O-ring on the face of the pump and, if it's a TC 88B engine, on the counterbalancing system's tensioner oil feed hole on the lower left corner of the gearcase. (Also clean the 88B's tensioner screen when you change its O-ring.)

Just as you did for the primary cam chain tensioner, use the JIMS #1283-1 tool to turn the secondary cam chain tensioner to release its tension on the secondary cam

chain. Then insert a retention pin to keep the tensioner away from the chain. (Check the face of the tensioner's shoe. If worn, replace it.) After you remove the bearing retainer plate from the back of the support plate (four Torx T20 screws hold it on) and the snap ring from the outer end of the front cam, use a JIMS #1277-2 tool and a hydraulic press to press the cams and their bearings out of the support plate. Once the cams are out, remove the (inner) secondary cam chain from the sprockets on the cams, noting the dark link, which should be facing the same way (out toward you or in toward the plate) when you reinstall the chain. You can then press the old ball bearings off both cams using a JIMS #1277-2 cam-bearing removal tool. (Note: If you are going to install new cams, don't bother with the old bearings.) You must also remove and replace the front cam bearing because you have to remove both cams to change the rear bearing while the cams are chained together, and the bearings are damaged when you remove them from the cam support plate.

To install the new bearings, a roller (with its inner race removed) for the rear cam and a ball in the front, align the two bearings onto the cam support plate, with the lettered side facing up toward the press. With the cam plate properly supported with the JIMS #1277-1 cam support–plate press tool, press each bearing into the plate with a JIMS #1277-3 cam bearing tool, taking care to only press against the bearing's outer race. (If you press against the ball bearing's inner race, you'll ruin the bearing.) The new roller rear cam bearing came with a shim, an inner race, and a small O-ring, which should be installed onto the cam at this time, in that order. Then position both cams in the secondary cam chain (noting the dark link) and turn them so the two dots stamped into their outer ends face each other.

With the retention pin still holding the tensioner out of the way, press both cams (the much longer one is the rear cam) into their bearings in the support plate, at the

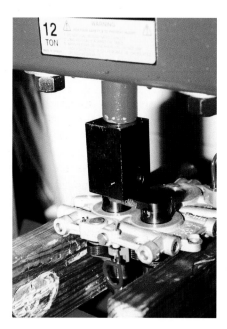

After you remove the holding clip from the back of the plate (four Torx T20 screws hold it on) and the snap ring from the front cam, use a JIMS #1277-2 tool to press the cams and their bearings out of the plate.

Once the cams are out, remove the secondary cam chain from the sprockets on the cams. Then press the old ball bearings off both cams using a JIMS #1277-2 cam bearing removal tool. (If you're installing new cams, skip this step.)

same time, using a JIMS #1277-1 tool. (Note: The journal of the front cam is slightly longer than the one on the rear cam, due to the snap ring groove, so you have to start it into its bearing first.) You can then reinstall the bearing retainer plate onto the back of the support plate, verifying that the hole in the retainer aligns with the oiler hole in the support plate, using the four Torx T20 screws with a little blue Loctite on their threads. Torque the screws to 20-30 inch-pounds in a crosswise pattern. Then remove the retention pin from the secondary cam chain tensioner on the back of the support plate and reinstall it into the same tensioner, but from the front of the support plate, so it'll still keep the secondary tensioner off the secondary chain. Install a new retainer (snap) ring into the groove on the outer end of the front camshaft.

With the bearings installed and the support plate so prepared, follow the cam installation procedure laid out in Project 56, as well as the procedure in Project 65.

The new roller rear cam bearing came with a shim, an inner race, and a small O-ring, which should be installed onto the rear cam (the much longer one) at this time, in that order.

Then align the two new bearings onto the cam plate, with the lettered side facing up towards the press. Be sure you have the roller bearing (with its inner race removed) on the rear cam hole and the ball bearing on the front.

With the cam plate properly supported with the JIMS #1277-1 cam support plate press tool, press each bearing into the plate with a JIMS #1277-3 cam bearing tool, taking care to only press against the bearing's outer race.

Then position both cams, so the two dots stamped into their outer ends face each other. Then put them into the secondary cam chain (noting the dark link). Keep the dots aligned.

You can then reinstall the bearing retainer plate onto the support plate using the four Torx T20 screws with a little blue Loctite on their threads. Torque the screws to 20–30 in-lbs. in a crosswise pattern.

With the retention pin still holding the tensioner out of the way, press both cams into their bearings in the support plate, at the same time, using a JIMS #1277-1 tool. Then install a new retainer (snap) ring onto the front camshaft.

Replacing the Inner Camshaft Bearings

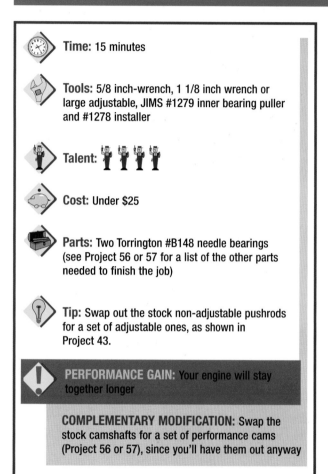

Time: 15 minutes

Tools: 5/8 inch-wrench, 1 1/8 inch wrench or large adjustable, JIMS #1279 inner bearing puller and #1278 installer

Talent: 👤👤👤👤

Cost: Under $25

Parts: Two Torrington #B148 needle bearings (see Project 56 or 57 for a list of the other parts needed to finish the job)

Tip: Swap out the stock non-adjustable pushrods for a set of adjustable ones, as shown in Project 43.

PERFORMANCE GAIN: Your engine will stay together longer

COMPLEMENTARY MODIFICATION: Swap the stock camshafts for a set of performance cams (Project 56 or 57), since you'll have them out anyway

There is usually no need to do this upgrade if you're not installing high-performance camshafts and/or valve springs. The stock inner cam bearings will usually be okay with the stock cams and springs. However, the additional stress placed on the inner bearings by either of these engine upgrades has been known to cause bearing failure, which is why I recommend replacing the stock inner cam bearings with Torrington units when installing new camshafts. In fact, if you have to go into the engine this deep for any reason, even if you're not installing performance parts, the smart move would be to replace the stock INA bearings.

Following the steps outlined in Project 56 or 57 will get you to this stage of the installation, which is when the gear case cavity is stripped down and ready for the cam installation. (The oil pump can be left in place.) Start the job by disassembling the #1278 puller tool until the remover (puller) part of tool, which is the piece with the four grooves in it, is separate from the rest.

Insert the puller's grooved end through the old cam bearing. You'll probably have to tap it in with a soft hammer to get it completely through the bearing. Then install the puller's body with puller bore facing toward bearing. After putting a little oil on the face of the washer and the nut's threads, tighten the nut. Then put a little oil onto the tool's pin and slip the pin through the center of the puller until the pin is even with the end of the puller. You can now use a 1 1/8-inch wrench to turn the puller's nut clockwise until the old bearing is out of its hole in the engine case. (This tool will also keep the bearing's rollers from falling into the engine.) You'll probably have to hold the puller with a 5/8-inch wrench to keep it from turning as you remove the bearing. Remove both bearings in the same way.

After lubing the JIMS #1278 installation tool's threads, you can assemble the tool. Start by threading the tool's screw into the plate. Then thread the cam bearing driver onto the end of the screw. Now push the cam bearing installer tool onto the end of the cam bearing driver. Then position a new cam bearing, letter/number against the tool, onto the end of the cam bearing installer. After putting a little press lube on the outer case of the bearing, position the tool onto the engine case with the two large holes in the plate over the engine case's bearing bores. Install the JIMS tool—and new bearing—onto the case using the tool's four Allen thumbscrews. (Put a little lube on the threads.) You now can carefully turn the screw in until the cam bearing starts in its bore. Then screw the installer in until the tool contacts the engine case, which correctly positions the new bearing below the case's surface. Simply repeat the process for the other bearing.

To remove an old bearing, insert the puller's grooved end through the old cam bearing. Chances are you'll have to tap it in with a soft hammer to get it to go completely through the bearing.

THE ENGINE

Put a little oil onto the tool's pin and then slip the pin through the center of the puller until the outer end of the pin is even with the outer end of the puller.

Then slip the puller body over the puller, with the bore in the puller body facing towards the bearing. After putting a little oil on the washer, install the nut and washer onto the puller and snug up the nut.

Now use a 5/8-inch wrench to keep the puller from turning as you use a 1-1/8-inch wrench, or large adjustable, to turn the puller's nut clockwise. Turn the nut until the old bearing is removed. Then do the other bearing.

To install a new bearing, assemble the JIMS installation tool by threading the tool's screw into the plate. Then thread the cam bearing driver onto the end of the screw.

After you push the cam bearing installer tool onto the end of cam bearing driver, slip a new bearing, letter/number side facing out away from the engine, onto the end of tool.

With the tool positioned so the two large holes in tool's plate are over the engine case's bearing bores, install the JIMS tool onto case using the tool's four Allen thumb screws.

Then carefully turn the screw in until cam bearing starts in its bore. You can now screw the installer in until the tool contacts the engine case, which correctly positions the new bearing in the case. Then remove the tool and do the same for the other bearing.

Installing High-Performance Cams

Time: 3–4 hours

Tools: Basic mechanic's tools, T20 Torx drive, access to a hydraulic press, foot-pound torque wrench, JIMS #1283 tensioner tool kit (which comes with two retention pins), JIMS #1285-1 sprocket lock, JIMS #1277-2 cam-bearing removing tool and cam installing tool, JIMS #1277-1 cam support–plate press tool, JIMS #1277-3 cam bearing tool, and two JIMS #33443-84 Evo lifter base alignment tools. If replacing the stock inner cam bearings, a JIMS #1279 puller and #1278 installation tool

Talent:

Cost: $325–425

Parts: New cam cover gasket, lifter cover gaskets (optional), rear roller bearing (H-D #8983), rear cam shim kit (H-D #25938-00), front cam retaining (snap) ring (H-D #11494-SUB1), front cam ball bearing (H-D #8990A), two inner cam bearings (Torrington #B148, recommended), blue Loctite, new pushrod tube O-rings, and new rocker box gaskets (unless you're installing new adjustable pushrods)

Tip: Swap out the stock non-adjustable pushrods for a set of adjustable ones, as shown in Project 43. Also upgrade the rear cam bearing to a roller style, as per Project 54, if equipped with a rear cam ball bearing.

PERFORMANCE GAIN: Installing the correct camshafts for your engine's performance modifications will allow the engine to develop 10–20 percent more power, depending on engine components and cam installed

COMPLEMENTARY MODIFICATION: A freer-flowing air cleaner and exhaust system should be installed before or with a high-performance cam. If installing camshafts with a lift higher than the stock .495-inch cams, you must install a higher-performance valve spring kit (Project 46) that matches the camshaft's lift

While changing out the air cleaner, exhaust pipes, ignition, and even changing or modifying the carburetor, are the most common types of performance modifications that owners make, a growing number are realizing that they can reap significant power increases by following these modifications with the right performance camshafts. In fact, the power gains can be quite dramatic, if the correct cams are combined with a balanced combination of performance modifications. That's because the Motor Company, due to strict EPA exhaust-emission regulations, must build its engines with camshafts that have a decent lift, but very short durations, which drastically limits the amount of power the engine can produce, especially at high rpm.

Before I discuss some tips for picking a specific camshaft and show what it takes to install a set into a Twin Cam 88 or 88B, I should go over what the terms *lift* and *duration* mean. A cam's lift is how high the lobe of the cam lifts the valve it controls off its seat in the cylinder head. This measurement is expressed in inches, as a decimal value. For instance, if a cam is said to have a .500-inch lift, it means the valve rises .500 inch, or 1/2 inch, off its seat in the head at its highest point.

As for a cam's duration, this is the amount of time that the valve is lifted off its seat (how long it is held open) between two specific reference points, as measured in degrees of flywheel rotation (I'll get to this in a minute). For example, if an intake valve's duration is listed at the top of the duration column on the cam's data sheet as 252 with the number .053 inch, this means that the cam will open the intake valve for 252 degrees of flywheel rotation, measured from the time the tappet (lifter) has been lifted .053 inch from its lowest point by the cam's lobe to when the lifter has dropped back down to .053 inch above its lowest point.

Because the position of the flywheels determines where the pistons are in their cylinders, all measurements for camshaft position (as well as ignition timing) are based on flywheel position. Seeing one full rotation of the flywheel assembly is a circle, one full rotation of the flywheel is 360 degrees. This means each stroke is 180 degrees. Using the degrees of a circle to mark various flywheel positions enables engineers and mechanics to have reference points for things like when the spark plug fires or when the lobe on a camshaft opens and closes a valve. Again using an intake valve duration of 252 degrees as an example, the intake is open for 52 degrees at the end of the exhaust stroke, the 180 degrees of the intake stroke, and the first 20 degrees of the compression stroke, which gives it a duration of 252 degrees (52 + 180 + 20 = 252).

This is not what the classic model of the four strokes (intake, compression, power, and exhaust) of a four-cycle engine shows, which is the intake and exhaust valves open for only a single stroke of the flywheels, or 180 degrees. A cam's durations cannot be that short if you want the engine to make a reasonable amount of power. Unfortunately, the cam found in all stock TC 88s has a short duration, which is one of the reasons why your 88-cubic-inch engine only makes about 62 horsepower and runs out of juice at high rpm. If you want your engine to produce more power, it needs a performance cam to work with freer-flowing intake and exhaust systems.

That brings us to the question, "What cam do I install?" The answer depends on what modifications have been made to the engine, the engine's displacement, use of the bike (heavy touring, racing, light cruising), and where in the rpm range does the owner want the bulk of the power to be produced. Racers want the power in the high rpm range, or top end. Cruising bikes are better off with more low- to midrange power, because those engines rarely go above 5,000, though they don't need to. However, touring bikes need lots of torque in the lower rpm (low-end) range for pulling power around town and uphill when heavily loaded, with good power in the midrange.

To make the selection process a little easier for you, here are a few camshaft tips:

Don't make the common mistake of ordering the hottest cam in the catalog just because it costs the same as a milder one. Radical cams are for radical engines.

While bolt-in cams require no engine modifications, hence the name, cams with high lifts and/or long durations require head work, and possibly some other machine work (see Project 46).

Radical cams require a performance exhaust, ignition, carburetor/EFI system, and valve kit, as well as high compression and high-flow cylinder heads to perform correctly.

Big displacement engines can handle hotter cams than a stock motor, so a 95-inch will perform better than an 88-inch with the same hot camshaft because the larger engine can handle the hotter cam's higher airflow.

A set of mild cams offers moderate power increases throughout the rpm range; as such, they are great for heavy touring bikes.

An engine's compression ratio is a major consideration when choosing a cam. A high-compression engine will tolerate more duration than will a low-compression engine.

In most cases, a great cam for a low-compression engine has plenty of lift with conservative duration numbers.

While increasing duration reaps hefty increases in high-rpm power, low-rpm performance suffers and the engine's power band is narrower.

Every increase in duration moves the engine's power band higher on the rpm range. Generally speaking, every 10-degree increase in duration moves the power band up about 500 rpm.

One last tip for those of you who also plan on increasing your engine's compression ratio, but are worried about engine knock and starter woes: Installing a cam with a longer intake duration will reduce the engine's tendency to ping at lower rpm, which is where it always occurs, while also increasing power at the mid- and high-rpm range.

If in doubt about what to buy, call one of the excellent camshaft manufacturers presently offering cams for TC 88s, such as Andrews Products, Crane, S&S Cycle, and, of course, Harley-Davidson, just to name a few, and ask their technician for recommendations. In fact, we recommend checking your selection with a technician before you shell out any of the green stuff.

For this installation, we used a set of Crane cams that required a high-performance valve spring kit because the lift was higher than the stock cams. Project 46 explains why this must be done. Also, we recommend removing the stock inner cam bearings and replacing them with Torrington bearings when installing any performance cams (Project 55).

Start the job by putting an oil catch pan under the right side of the engine. Then remove the cam cover using a 1/4-inch Allen wrench. With the cover off, clean the old gasket from the cover and engine case as the oil drains into the pan. Because you are going to remove the cams, you have to first remove the pushrods to release the pressure from the valve springs in the heads. If you wish to reuse the stock non-adjustable pushrods, you must remove the rocker boxes, as shown in Project 47. Or, you can cut the old pushrods out and install new adjustable ones, as shown in Project 43.

When you have the pushrods out of the way, follow the instructions given in Project 65 for removing the primary cam chain and sprockets from the cam support plate. Some mechanics prefer not to mess with the lifters and covers, and simply use the wire from a metal binder clip to keep the lifters out of the way during the job. However, if

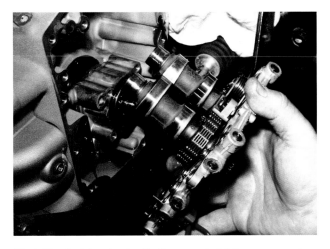

After lubing the inboard ends of both cams, reinstall the cam support plate assembly into the gearcase. (Note: The two dots on the outer ends of the cams should still be facing each other.)

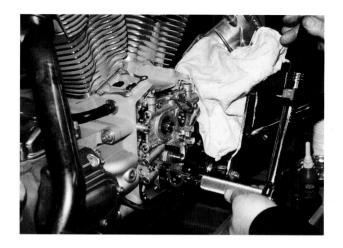

Bolt the support plate to the engine, following the procedure and torque values in the H-D manual, with a little blue Loctite on the bolt threads. Do the same for the oil pump, as per the procedure in Project 65.

With the original shim on the rear cam, and the primary sprocket and (pinion) crank sprocket reinstalled onto their respective shafts, put a straight edge across both sprockets and measure the gap.

you prefer to remove the lifters and covers, remove the bolts using a 3/16-inch Allen wrench. Then slide the lifters out of their bores in the right crankcase. Be sure to mark them so you can put each one back into the same bore, in the original orientation (same side facing out). Clean the old gaskets off the covers and case.

With the primary camshaft chain and sprockets removed from the cam support plate, follow the procedure in Project 54: Replacing the Rear Camshaft Bearing. The only difference in the procedure is that instead of reinstalling the old stock cams, you'll install the new performance cams with the new bearings. (I also suggest you replace the two stock H-D #9198 [INA #SCE148] inner cam bearings as per Project 55.) We'll pick up the installation here with the bearings installed and the support plate prepared for reinstallation into the engine's gearcase cavity.

After lubing the inboard ends of both cams, reinstall the cam support plate assembly into the gearcase. (Note: The two dots on the outer ends of the cams should still be facing each other.) Bolt the support plate to the engine, following the procedure and torque values in the H-D service manual, with a little blue Loctite on the bolt threads. Then align and bolt the oil pump, which is held by the four bolts around the pinion shaft bushing, to the support plate, following the procedure in Project 65. However, do not yet reinstall any other parts as per Project 65. When the pump is aligned and bolted up, come back to this section.

With the support plate fully installed, it's time to shim the rear camshaft's primary cam sprocket. Start by putting the shim you originally took out of the engine back onto the end of the rear cam. Then reinstall the primary cam sprocket and (pinion) crank sprocket, with their bolts and washers, but without the primary cam chain, onto their respective shafts. These sprockets will only go on one way, seeing the crank sprocket has a flat side and the primary cam sprocket has one spline that's thicker than the others.

Then put a straightedge across the face of both sprockets. (Note: It may be easier to do this with a smaller than normal washer on the crank sprocket.) Does the straightedge lie flat against the face of both sprockets? If there's room to put a flat feeler gauge larger than 0.005 inch between the straightedge and the face of either sprocket, you need to change the cam shim as per the procedure in the H-D service manual.

Once the correct shim is in place, remove both sprockets and reinstall the chain guide into its spot on the support plate. Check the dots on the ends of both cams with a straightedge. Are they still aligned? Keeping the two cam dots so aligned, position both sprockets into the primary cam chain (noting the dark link), so the alignment dots on the face of the sprockets are aligned to each other. Then reinstall the sprockets and finish the job as per Project 65.

Change the rear cam shim to get the needed gap. Once the correct shim is in place, check the dots on the ends of both cams with a straight edge. Are they still aligned?

Keeping the two cam dots aligned, position both sprockets in the primary cam chain (noting the dark link), so the dots on the face of the sprockets aligned to each other, and slip the sprockets onto their shafts.

Then, with the JIMS #1285-1 tool between the sprockets to keep them from turning, install the stock sprocket bolts and washers and torque them to spec.

Then remove the JIMS lock tool and retention pin. Now recheck the sprockets' alignment dots; are they still aligned sprocket-to-sprocket?

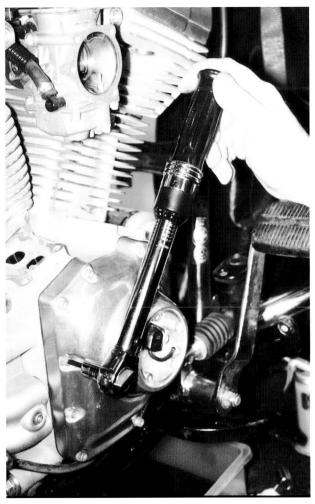

You can now reinstall the cam cover, with a new gasket, and torque the bolts to 90–120 in-lbs. using a 1/4-inch Allen wrench.

Installing S&S Gear-Driven Cams

 Time: 3–4 hours

 Tools: Basic mechanic's tools, access to a hydraulic press, foot-pound torque wrench, JIMS #1283 tensioner tool kit (which comes with two retention pins), JIMS #1285-1 sprocket lock, JIMS #1277-2 cam-bearing removing tool and cam installing tool, JIMS #1277-1 cam support–plate press tool, JIMS #1277-3 cam bearing tool, JIMS #1279 puller and #1278 installation tool, and two JIMS #33443-84 Evo lifter-base alignment tools

 Talent:

 Cost: Around $500

 Parts: S&S or Andrews gear-driven camshaft kit, lifter cover gaskets, pushrod tube seals, front cam retaining (snap) ring, blue and red Loctite, modeling clay

 Tip: Swap out the stock non-adjustable pushrods for a set of adjustable ones, as shown in Project 43. This will greatly reduce the amount of time it takes to do the job.

 PERFORMANCE GAIN: Installing the correct camshafts for your engine's performance modifications will allow the engine to develop 10–20 percent more power, depending on engine components and cam installed

COMPLEMENTARY MODIFICATION: A freer-flowing air cleaner and exhaust system should be installed before or with a high performance cam. If installing camshafts with a lift higher than the stock .495-inch cams, you must install a performance valve spring kit (Project 46) that matches or exceeds the camshaft's lift

Cams that have higher-than-stock valve lifts and longer durations require performance valve spring kits, which use higher pressure springs, to help the valves follow these more radical cam lobe profiles and eliminate valve float and valve bounce. Valve float is when the valve stays off its seat even though the cam would allow it to close.

Valve bounce is when the valve hits its seat and then bounces back off of it. Both these conditions occur because the valve springs are not strong enough to make the valve closely follow the lobe of the cam. In both cases, the valve is off its seat—protruding into the combustion chamber where the piston could hit and bend it—when it should be closed.

Many engine builders feel that the stock, Twin Cam chain-drive system, with its two chains and two chain tensioners, is not strong enough to handle the higher pressures put on the system by the performance valve springs needed for high-lift, long-duration cams. That's why they recommend changing to a gear-driven camshaft setup when using more radical cam profiles.

There are a number of advantages to running a gear-driven system, like the one used on Evos, Shovelheads, and all other Big Twin Harleys, instead of the chain-driven one found on Twin Cams. First off, there's less maintenance, since gears do not wear out like chain guides or tensioner shoes. Gear-driven cams also don't have any chain lash or slack to deal with, so cam timing is dead-on accurate—a very important point when trying to increase engine performance.

Another performance consideration has to do with the amount of lift a cam can have. Gear-driven cams rotate in different directions; stock chain-driven cams rotate in the same direction. Unfortunately for the chain arrangement, the lobes on each cam pass so close to each other at one point of their rotation that they will hit if too high a lift is used, which limits cam lift height. The lobes in the gear-driven version can't hit, no matter how tall the lobes are.

Another benefit to the gear drive is ease of assembly: Exact sprocket alignment and the tedious shimming required for the chain system is not needed with gears. There are also a lot fewer parts to install with the gear version.

Gears also reduce the loads placed on the cam bearings because there are no spring-loaded chain tensioners to deal with, which is why S&S supplies two new, quality ball bearings for the cam support plate with its kit instead of a ball bearing for the front cam and a roller bearing for the rear.

The main drawback to the gear-driven system is the reason why H-D had to go to a chain system in the first place: noise! Chains are quieter than gears and it was only EPA restrictions that forced the Motor Company to abandon the system that had served it well for so many years and go to chains.

As for the actual installation, start the job by putting an oil catch pan under the right side of the engine. Then remove the cam cover using a 1/4-inch Allen wrench. Once

THE ENGINE

the cover is off, clean the old gasket from the cover and engine case as the oil drains into the pan. Because you have to first remove the pushrods to release the pressure from the valve springs in the heads, you must either cut them out and replace them, as per Project 43, or remove the rocker boxes, as shown in Project 47.

Once you have the pushrods out of the way, rotate the engine so that the alignment dot on the face of the primary cam sprocket is aligned with the dot on the face of the (pinion) crank sprocket. Remove the lifter covers using a 3/16-inch Allen wrench and then slide the lifters out of their bores in the right crankcase. Be sure to mark them so you can put each one back into the same bore and have the same side of the lifter facing out away from the engine. Then clean off the old gaskets from the covers and case. (Note: Some mechanics prefer not to mess with the lifters and covers, and simply use the wire from a metal binder clip to keep the lifters out of the way during the job.)

Use a JIMS #1283-1 tool to turn the primary cam chain tensioner to release its tension on the (outer) primary cam chain. Then insert one of the retention pins that come with the kit to keep the tensioner away from the chain. Insert a JIMS #1285-1 tool to lock the sprockets and use a 9/16-inch socket on the top bolt and a 1/2-inch on

With new S&S-supplied ball bearings in the cam support plate and the dots on the cams align, press both new S&S cams into the plate with a JIMS #1277-2 tool.

the pinion bolt. Remove the primary cam sprocket and (pinion) crank sprocket and primary cam chain as an assembly. Then remove the shim from the rear cam and set all these parts aside and remove the black chain guide shoe from the cam support plate. Then pull out a retention pin from the chain tensioner while controlling it with the JIMS tool. (Never just pull out the pin if the chain is not installed or damage will result to the tensioner due to the tensioner's 35–40 pounds of spring pressure.) Remove the tensioner from the cam support plate. Use a 3/16-inch Allen to remove the camshaft support plate and oil pump mounting bolts and then pull the whole support plate assembly from the engine.

Do not remove or disturb the oil pump, unless you plan on installing an S&S baffle plate as per Project 64 or plan on swapping it out as per Project 66. You should, however, install new O-rings on the face of the pump and, if it's a TC 88B engine, the counterbalancing system's tensioner oil feed hole on the lower left corner of the gearcase. (Also clean the tensioner screen when you change the O-ring).

Just as you did for the primary cam chain tensioner, use the JIMS #1283-1 tool to turn the secondary cam chain tensioner to release its tension on the secondary cam chain. Then insert a retention pin to keep the tensioner away from the chain. After you remove the bearing retainer plate from the back of the support plate (four Torx T20 screws hold it on) and the snap ring from the outer end of the front cam, use a JIMS #1277-2 tool and a hydraulic press to press the cams and their bearings out of the support plate and set them aside. Then remove the black chain guide shoe from the cam support plate and pull out a retention pin from the chain tensioner while controlling it with the JIMS tool. Remove the tensioner from the cam support plate.

After you install the new S&S-supplied ball bearings as per Project 54, as well as the inner cam bearings with the new ones from S&S as per Project 55, it's time to install the bearing retainer plate onto the back of the support plate. After verifying that the hole in the retainer aligns with the oiler hole in the support plate, use the four Torx T20 screws with a little blue Loctite on their threads. Torque the screws to 20–30 inch-pounds in a crosswise pattern.

After ensuring that the timing marks on the cam gears are aligned, press the S&S cams into their bearings into the support plate using a JIMS #1277-1 tool and hydraulic press. (Note: The journal of the front cam is slightly longer than the one on the rear cam, due to the snap ring groove, so you have to start it into its bearing first.) Once the cams are fully installed, put a new retaining ring onto the end of the front camshaft.

After lubing the ends of the cams, align the camshafts with the bearings in the crankcase and gently slide the support plate over its dowels. Do not force it! Install the plate bolts and torque them to 90 inch-pounds. Then align the oil pump and install the pump bolts as per Project 65.

As for the drive gears, first install the crankshaft gear, timing mark out, onto the crankshaft and torque the bolt (with a little red Loctite) to 25 ft-lb. With the drive gear key in place, install the rear-cam drive gear (mark out). Rotate until timing marks align. Using the supplied thick washer, torque the bolt (with a little red Loctite) to 34 ft-lbs.

Finally, check the inside of the cam cover for cam-drive gear interference, as per the S&S instructions. Do this by putting a little putty on the inside of the cam cover; then bolt the cover to the engine. Spin the engine over, so the gears will turn under the cam cover, then pull the cover, and measure how deep the gear cut into the putty. Ensure there is 0.030-inch clearance between the gear and cover. (Measuring from the cover to the bottom of the mark left by the gear.) Relieve the cover, if needed.

Install the drive gear and drive key onto the rear cam with the timing dot facing out and aligned with the dot on the pinion shaft gear. Install the S&S cam bolt (with some red Loctite) and washer and torque to 34 ft-lb.

Install the cams and support plate into the engine. Use Loctite 243 (blue) on all the plate and oil pump bolts and torque them to 95 in-lb, as per the service manual's procedure.

Here's what the finished installation looks like: no chains, shoes, or tensioners in sight.

Install the S&S pinion shaft gear with the timing dot on the tooth facing you. Install the S&S pinion shaft bolt (with some red Loctite) and stock washer. Torque the bolt to 25 ft-lb.

Put some clay on the inside on the cam cover to check the clearance between the cover and rear cam gear. Install the cover and check for the minimum of 0.030-inch clearance, as per the S&S instructions.

Installing a Delkron Camshaft Support Plate

Time: 3 hours

Tools: Basic mechanic's tools, access to a hydraulic press, inch-pounds and foot-pounds torque wrenches, JIMS #1283 tensioner tool kit (which comes with two retention pins), JIMS #1285-1 sprocket lock, JIMS #1277-2 cam bearing removing tool and cam installing tool, JIMS #1277-1 cam support plate press tool, JIMS #1277-3 cam bearing tool, and two JIMS #33443-84 Evo lifter base alignment tools, T20 Torx drive, retaining ring tool

Talent: 👤👤👤

Cost: $400

Parts: Delkron support plate, rear roller bearing (H-D #8983), rear cam shim kit (H-D #25938-00), front cam retaining (snap) ring (H-D #11494-SUB1), front cam ball bearing (H-D #8990A), blue Loctite, new cam support–plate O-rings, new pushrod tube O-rings, new cam cover gasket, lifter cover gaskets (optional), and new rocker box gaskets (unless you're installing new adjustable pushrods)

Tip: Swap out the stock non-adjustable pushrods for a set of adjustable ones, as shown in Project 43, to greatly reduce job time

PERFORMANCE GAIN: No flexing or warping, even when used with high lift cams and strong valve springs

COMPLEMENTARY MODIFICATION: This is the perfect time to install a set of performance camshafts

In keeping with its plan to have all covers simply be covers, and no longer load-bearing engine components to cut down on engine noise, H-D's engineers ditched the cone-style cam cover that had dominated the Big Twin landscape for almost three decades and came up with the camshaft support plate. And just as its name implies, it supports the engine's two camshafts, the outboard end of the camshafts,

to be exact, as well as the outer end of the pinion (crank) shaft of the right flywheel. The support plate bolts directly to the right crankcase, as does the new cam cover, which is now simply a cover to keep dirt out and oil in.

The cam support plate is also a major part of the engine's oil distribution network. Oil comes from the oil pump, which is mounted to the inside face of the support plate, and is sent through the plate, into the right case, to the oil filter for cleaning. Once filtered, oil is returned to the support plate, where it is then distributed throughout the engine via the various passageways drilled into the plate.

Mounted on the outer face of the cam plate are the sprockets, chains, and other components that are used to drive the cams. The pinion shaft, which is the only gearcase component that still has a bushing, protrudes through the plate and has a sprocket on it that drives the primary chain. The primary chain connects to a larger sprocket that's mounted onto the end of the rear cylinder's cam, which protrudes through its bearing in the support plate. Behind the plate is another chain, the secondary chain, which connects the two cams via sprockets on the cams. Both chains have spring-loaded tensioners for consistent adjustment and are oiled via tiny holes in the cam plate.

Now that you know what the cam support plate does, it's time to discuss what can go wrong with the stock unit. For starters, the stock unit has gone through a couple of revisions since its introduction in 1999. The first was to make common the cam support plate for the 2000 engines, so that the same plate could be used on both the TC 88 and TC 88B. On the 88B, an oil passage on the support plate aligns with a passageway in the right crankcase, which supplies oil to the balance shaft assembly's chain tensioners. On the TC 88, a blind boss on the case covers the plate's oil passage. (To use a 2000 and later support plate on a 1999 engine, use a screw to plug the passageway that the 2000 TC 88's boss would cover.)

The next change was due to problems with the rear camshaft bearing (see Project 54) with the newest version being #25267-99B. If yours is an earlier plate with a different dash number (-99 or -99A), which should be stamped right on it, it's a good idea to upgrade to the new version, or better yet, a Delkron unit, which is the reason for this project.

No matter what version it is, the stock cam support plate is made of die-cast aluminum. This plate has warped in some engines, which necessitates replacement (maximum allowed is 0.010 inch), as it will throw out the clearances on other parts in the gearcase, such as making it impossible for the oil pump's O-ring to seal, causing oiling and blowby problems. The die-cast plate may also flex under the load of high-performance valve springs and high-lift cams.

In contrast, the Delkron plate, which will not flex under any load it should encounter in the engine, is machined out of solid billet 6061-T6 aluminum to precise tolerances to tighten up the alignment of the cams and pinion shaft bore. High tolerance dowel locators are used for a precise cam bore-to-cam bore location. The plate's oil passages have also been improved to increase the efficiency of the engine's oiling system. The Delkron cam support plate comes complete with pressure regulator valve, pinion shaft bushing, Viton O-rings, and mounting hardware.

To do this installation, disassemble the engine as described in Project 56, Installing High Performance Cams. Then, after lubing the outside of two new bearings, press them into the Delkron cam support plate using a JIMS #1277 tool set. Install an H-D bearing retainer using four stock H-D T-20 Torx bolts, with a little red Loctite on their threads. Torque the bolts to 20–30 in-lb. After pressing in a set of cams into the support plate, as per Project 56 or 57, an H-D retaining ring is installed onto the outer end of the front camshaft using the proper tool. The Delkron plate can then be bolted to the engine using the Delkron-supplied bolts, with a little blue Loctite on the threads. These bolts get torqued to 95 inch-pounds with a 3/16-inch Allen, as per the sequence in the H-D service manual. You can then align the oil pump and secure it to the cam support plate, as per Project 65.

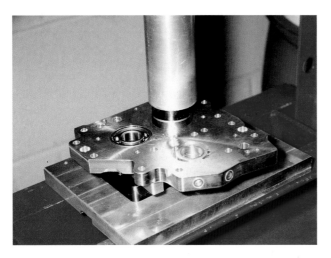

After lubing the outside of two new bearings, press them into the Delkron cam support plate using a JIMS #1277 tool set.

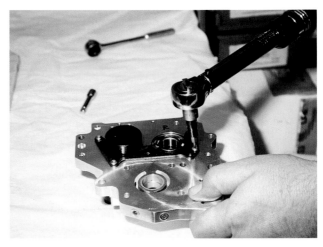

An H-D bearing retainer can now get bolted into place using four stock H-D T-20 Torx bolts, with a little red Loctite on their threads. Torque the bolts to 20–30 in-lbs.

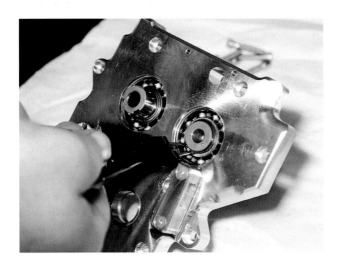

After pressing in a set of cams into the support plate, as per Project 56 or 57, an H-D retaining ring is installed onto the outer end of the front camshaft using the proper tool.

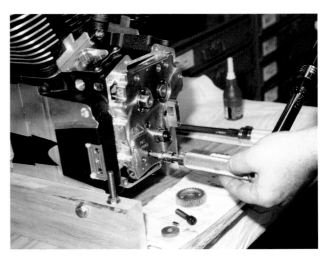

The Delkron plate is bolted to the engine using the Delkron-supplied bolts, with a little blue Loctite on the threads. These bolts get torqued to 95 in-lbs. with a 3/16-inch Allen, as per the sequence in the H-D service manual.

Blueprinting the Engine

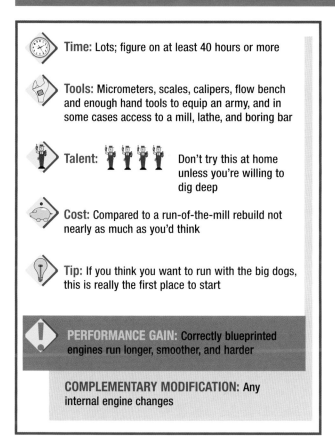

Time: Lots; figure on at least 40 hours or more

Tools: Micrometers, scales, calipers, flow bench and enough hand tools to equip an army, and in some cases access to a mill, lathe, and boring bar

Talent: Don't try this at home unless you're willing to dig deep

Cost: Compared to a run-of-the-mill rebuild not nearly as much as you'd think

Tip: If you think you want to run with the big dogs, this is really the first place to start

PERFORMANCE GAIN: Correctly blueprinted engines run longer, smoother, and harder

COMPLEMENTARY MODIFICATION: Any internal engine changes

You may have heard the urban legend that the best bikes are built on Tuesday, Wednesday, or Thursday and the worst ones are built on a Monday or Friday. The logic behind the story, and it applies to anything built on an assembly line, is that the workers are busy planning their weekend on Friday, and recovering from it on Monday. This means that the build quality of the motorcycles tends to suffer on those two days because they don't take the time to match the parts or assemble the bikes as carefully as they might have. The end result being engines and motorcycles that have sloppy fitting pieces, and as such tend to be under-performers. You're welcome to draw your own conclusions as to the validity of the weekday theory, but it does try to explain why identical bikes built on the same assembly line may have significant differences in the way they perform.

As with most urban legends there is a grain of truth to the weekday theory but it's a bit more matter-of-fact than you'd think.

Consider this: Every component of every engine has a built-in degree of misfit. This unfortunate circumstance arose because engines are built of mass-produced parts on an assembly line where time and environment are constrained. The guy who assembles the crankshaft assembly is undoubtedly very skilled at his particular job, but that doesn't necessarily mean he is very skilled at assembling the entire engine. For example, the allowable runout of the Twin Cam–series flywheels at their rim is between 0.000 and 0.010 of an inch. The closer you get to the first measurement, the smoother the engine will run, the more power it'll make and the longer it'll last. But the second measurement is commercially acceptable.

When the engines are assembled on the production line the vast majority of them will of course have the runout somewhere in the middle. But a few will have the runout set at 0.000, or zero, while some will have the runout at 0.010 or ten thousandths. Ten thousandths of an inch may not seem like much but consider that the addition of one more thousandth of an inch, to 0.011, would push the run out over the edge into the unacceptable. Which flywheel assembly would you rather have in your bike?

The thing is that every component in your engine is in the same predicament. Now as luck has it, certain engines that come off the assembly line will have components that are as precisely matched as the system allows. Others will have components that fall at the opposite end of the spectrum. This is one reason why your bike smokes your buddy's identical model every time you roll 'em on.

By definition, blueprinted engines are ones that have been carefully hand assembled so that every single piece fits as precisely as the designer intended it to.

On the surface, that may seem a daunting enough task, and it is. But the reality is that a good tuner goes even deeper. Any good mechanic should be able to assemble an engine correctly. In fact, a well-assembled engine, built by a competent wrench can be a very good engine indeed. But blueprinting takes engine assembly to another level.

For example, maybe the factory-recommended oil pump clearances aren't the best for making horsepower. Perhaps a gentle hand lapping of the gears and setting up the pump with an extra thousandth of clearance can free up a horsepower or two. Guys that blueprint engines for a living, at least the ones that are good at it, know what to tweak, and how much to tweak it. As an aside, most of them know this because they've been doing it forever, and have tweaked a fair amount of motors onto the junk pile while they searched for what worked, and what made expensive noises.

My first inclination was to tell you that blueprinting is a job best left to the experts, and quite frankly, in many cases it is.

Spending the hours needed to hand fit a wrist pin to a piston and its rod assembly until it's a perfect match takes a special dedication that most guys, no matter how dedicated they are, just don't have.

But the fact of the matter is that the dedicated enthusiast, particularly those of you with a penchant for perfection and a need for speed, can indeed blueprint your own motors.

In reality it doesn't really take that much more work than building a motor the normal way. What it will take is the patience to scrutinize every detail, compare it to factory specification, and cajole the part into the correct fit. For example, if the acceptable ring end gap is listed as between .010 and .020 and your rings come in at .015, you'll have to correct the fit until you get exactly what you want. This may mean wading through several sets of rings until you stumble upon ones with the correct end gap. Or it may mean buying a ring gapper and filing an oversize set down until the gap is perfect. Likewise, the cylinder heads; you'll want to CC them, and correct any inequities before bolting them on. I'm sure you get the picture.

Look at it this way, if the engine has to come apart anyway, what's the sense in simply reassembling it? Anyone can do that; in the end blueprinting is all about paying attention to detail, and who better than you to do that on your bike?

Blueprint Caveats

Normally, blueprinting won't produce huge power gains in a stock engine. However, if the engine is assembled with lots of aftermarket goodies, chances are good that a thorough blueprinting will set free a whole bunch of hidden horsepower.

By the same token, blueprinting works on more than just the mill. Reliability, handling characteristics, and even comfort can all be improved by fine-tuning the entire motorcycle. Pay careful attention to things like belt alignment, tire pressures, steering head bearing adjustment, and so forth. The end result will be a much sharper-feeling bike that won't let you down on the road.

THE ENGINE

The serious engine builder's tool box contains as many measuring devices as it does wrenches. If you're seriously thinking of blueprinting your own mill, you'll need all of these and more.

Balancing the Engine

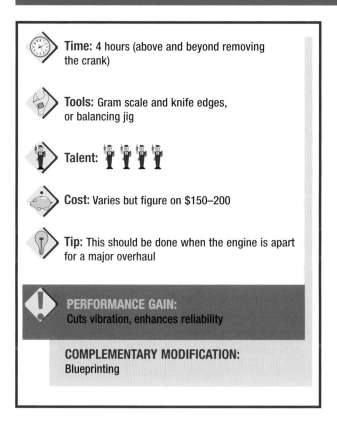

Time: 4 hours (above and beyond removing the crank)

Tools: Gram scale and knife edges, or balancing jig

Talent: ★★★★

Cost: Varies but figure on $150–200

Tip: This should be done when the engine is apart for a major overhaul

PERFORMANCE GAIN:
Cuts vibration, enhances reliability

COMPLEMENTARY MODIFICATION:
Blueprinting

By nature, all Harley-Davidson engines shake to one degree or another. Fortunately, the Twin Cam motors are far better than what preceded them, and as anyone who's ridden a Twin Cam can attest, the B motors with their counterbalancers are particularly good.

However, there are instances when balancing a motor can pay big dividends in smoothing things out. Bear in mind that balancing can only be performed by disassembling the entire motor. It's generally something to consider when the motor is apart for another reason, as opposed to something done as a stand-alone project.

When I discuss balancing an engine, I'm really talking about balancing the crankshaft. All crankshafts must be balanced to some degree. If they weren't, the engine would shake itself to bits in short order; still, achieving a perfect level of balance is impossible. The object of balance is to simply move the level of objectionable vibration beyond the rpm range where it will damage the engine and annoy the rider. In that respect, the factory does a credible job; however, their intent is to build a crankshaft that's balanced to a degree suitable for use as a mildly tuned street bike using stock components or factory-approved options. When the engine is substantially modified or non-factory

components are installed—particularly big bore pistons—the factory balance factor may no longer be suitable.

Balancing a crankshaft isn't a job that can be taken lightly; in fact, it might be considered one of the "black arts" of tuning. This is one job that is really best left to the pros; the consequence of getting it wrong is disastrous. Here is how to balance a crankshaft, with some theory rather than the actual mechanics of the job.

If balancing the crankshaft by itself were our only concern, the job would be as easy as balancing any other rotating part, such as a wheel, for example.

The problem is that the crankshaft is joined to the connecting rods and pistons, which are reciprocating parts. Reciprocating parts cannot be balanced. However, they can be counterweighted to offset the weight of their parts. By counterweighting them we can reduce vibration, which extends engine life and makes the bike more comfortable to ride. The amount of counterweight that's used varies, but it is always a percentage of the combined weights of the big and small ends of the connecting rod, plus everything attached to it, including the pistons, rings, wrist pin, and wrist pin clips (which must be identical if balance is to be achieved). It is always expressed as a percentage, and referred to as the Balance Factor. In a Harley-Davidson engine the counterweights are cast into the flywheel assembly.

Balance factors are the subject of much debate. In general, they range from 35 to 85 percent of total weight of the reciprocating parts, depending on the engine's state of tune, and its intended use. Most builders agree that a balance factor of 60 to 65 percent is about right for a hot-rod street motor. As a rule of thumb, the lower the state of tune, the lower the balance factor; a mildly tuned touring bike engine (think FLHTC here) will work perfectly well with a balance factor that hovers in the 35 to 40 percent range. However, a Top Fuel motor, capable of spinning to 10,000, may need to be balanced at 85 percent just to prevent it from ripping itself to shreds.

The balance factor like most things is always somewhat of a compromise. A particular balance factor may make the engine smooth as glass at 4,500 rpm, yet allow it to shake like a dog passing a peach pit at all other speeds. Conversely, the same engine using a second balance factor may have a tolerable vibration at any speed above idle, with a sweet spot at say 2,800–3,000 rpm. If the bike is intended for use as a general street ride, I know which one I'd select.

A balance factor that works just fine may no longer be the hot tip if the engine is used in a different frame; frames resonate at different frequencies. An engine that worked fine in a heavy touring frame may vibrate like a jackhammer when placed into an aftermarket custom frame. In a worst-case scenario it could even cause the frame to crack.

It should also be pointed out that altering the balance factor can work both ways; in one case a vibration may cease to exist, in another case it may create a new one.

There are so many factors to consider when choosing a balance factor and coming up with any hard-and-fast rules as to what constitutes the ideal balance factor is for all practical purposes impossible. Although as stated above there are certain numbers that generally work best for Harley engines.

It also should be pointed out that while balance factors are somewhat controversial, at least in the sense that every engine builder has his favorites, most of the guys doing it for a living know what factor works best with which combination of parts.

In theory, balancing a crankshaft is fairly simple; in *theory*. First, each end of the connecting rod is weighed along its attendant hardware. In the case of the bottom end, that includes the big end bearings of the rod. The rods need to be hung horizontally with no friction while they are being weighed to get an accurate measurement. Next, the pistons and their hardware, rings, pins, and clips are weighed. Add the total weight of the small end of each rod and both piston assemblies together (in this case we combine the total weight of both assemblies because both rods and pistons run on a common journal). Multiply the sum by whatever balance factor you've chosen. Add that number to the total weight of the big end of the rod. Install the appropriate "dummy" weight onto the crankpin. Position

the crank on the knife-edges, find the heavy spot, and remove the correct amount of metal, symmetrically from both flywheels, until the crankshaft is in balance. (Metal can be removed or added to balance the crank, but it is most commonly removed.) Sounds easy, doesn't it? For the guy with the tools, know-how, and experience, it's not difficult, but trust me, it's never easy.

100 Percent

You might wonder why an engine is never balanced using 100 percent as the balance factor. Good question. As mentioned, the balance factor is always a compromise; we want the least amount of intrusive vibration over the greatest rpm range. If we were to use 100 percent as the balance factor, in theory, we would achieve perfect balance when the piston was at Top Dead Center and Bottom Dead Center. Unfortunately, anytime the crankpin was at 90 degrees there would be nothing opposing the counterweight. Consequently, the vibration would be horrific plus it would be at right angles to the cylinder axis, rather than in line with it. Assuming that the engine didn't shake itself apart it would be like riding a paint shaker. In the real world we choose a balance factor that allows for the least amount of vibration, in the rpm range that we use most often.

The balancing holes are drilled symmetrically in the heaviest portion of the flywheel.

Installing a Stroker Kit

 Time: 2 hours

 Tools: Hydraulic press, JIMS flywheel assembly removal tool #1047-TP (use with #1048 hard cap), JIMS Timken bearing-race removal tool #94547-80A and installation tool #2246, JIMS sprocket shaft–bearing installation tool #97225-55 (must use with JIMS tool #97225-55), JIMS engine sprocket–seal installation tool #39361-69 (used with tool #97225-55), JIMS pinion-bearing installation/removal tool #1146, a micrometer, and a dial indicator

 Talent:

 Cost: $1,300 (without cylinder kit), under $2,400 (with cylinder kit)

 Parts: Stroker flywheel assembly, new Timken bearing set or left main bearing (depends on year of engine), new pinion bearing, new pinion-bearing retaining clip, crankcase sealant, two crankcase dowel-pin O-rings, new sprocket shaft seal, blue Loctite

 Tip: 2003 and later engines do not use a Timken bearing set on the sprocket shaft. We recommend installing a Zipper's upgrade kit when stroking these engines

 PERFORMANCE GAIN: With a properly built engine, you should easily get double-digit horsepower and torque gains. How much more power depends on how much larger you make the engine and the engine's other performance parts

COMPLEMENTARY MODIFICATION: Select a set of cams, and intake, ignition, and exhaust systems that will work well with the engine's new larger displacement

Strokers! Back in the day, these engines ruled the open road and Main Streets all across America. Making an engine a stroker was a drastic modification that involved using the flywheels from a different model engine to increase your motor's displacement in a big way. As stated in Project 51, boring out the cylinders to gain a few extra cubic centimeters (cc) was a common way to get a little more power way back when. But, you gained cubic inches and lots of power by stroking it!

The flywheels in a Harley-Davidson engine change the up-and-down movement (stroke) of the pistons into the rotating motion needed to turn the engine sprocket, and eventually, the bike's rear wheel. The pistons are connected to the flywheels by the connecting rods. The top end of the rod is attached to the piston, via the wrist pin, while the other end is attached to the flywheels, via the crankpin. The location of the crankpin in the flywheels is what determines the engine's stroke. By moving the crankpin closer to the outer edge of the flywheels, you increase the engine's stroke, which increases the engine's displacement.

When you increase an engine's displacement all you're doing is increasing the area over the pistons, so more air/fuel mixture can be compressed and burned. The more mixture you can efficiently burn, the more power the

Start the build by installing the new Timken races into the left case using a JIMS Timken race installation tool #2246. Then reinstall the Timken race snap ring, taking care not to damage the case.

THE ENGINE

engine will produce. The displacement of a piston engine is the total volume, actually the swept volume, of all the engine's cylinders. A cylinder's swept volume is the area that the piston travels (sweeps) over as it moves up and down the cylinder, which is called its stroke. And, just as in high-school math class, the area of a cylinder depends on its diameter and length.

When figuring an engine's displacement, the diameter is the bore of the cylinder, while the length is the piston's stroke. The length of the piston's stroke is measured from the lowest point of its travels in the cylinder, also called its Bottom Dead Center position, to its highest point in the cylinder, or its Top Dead Center position. To compute an engine's displacement you plug these two measurements into the formula: bore x bore x .7854 x stroke.

Once you have the swept volume of one of the cylinders, and multiply that number by the amount of cylinders that the engine has—which in the case of all V-twins is two—to get the total cubic inch (or cubic centimeter) displacement of the engine. For example, if you use the bore and stroke measurements for a Twin Cam 88, you'll get (3.75 x 3.75 x .7854 x 4.00 inches) x2 for a total of 88.3575 inches, which gets rounded off to 88 inches.

To increase the stroke, and thus increase the engine's displacement, the stock flywheels are swapped out for a set that has the crankpin located farther out from the flywheel's center. Back in the 1940s, 1950s, and early 1960s, the most common way to stroke your Knucklehead or Panhead was to use the flywheels from an 80-inch H-D flathead. An 80-inch flathead (also called a Big Flatty) has 4 1/4-inch stroke flywheels. The 74-inch versions of the Knuckle and Pan have 3 31/32-inch-stroke flywheels, so this modification made the pistons travel 9/32 inch farther in their cylinders due to the crankpin being located more

than 1/8 inch closer to the flywheels' outer edge. (Actually, the pistons move 9/64 inch, which is just a tad more than 1/8 inch, farther up and down the cylinders, for a total of 9/32 inch more swept volume.) This boosts the cubic inch displacement from the engine's original 74 inches to the Flatty's 80 inches, seeing the bore of the cylinders is the same (3 7/16 inches) in all three engines. (By the way, a lesser-known stroke upgrade of the time was to shove Indian flywheels into a H-D 45-inch flathead.)

In late 1978, The Motor Company jumped onto the 4 1/4 inch bandwagon and started offering an 80-inch Shovelhead alongside its 74-inch models. The more powerful and smoother-running 80-inch (4 1/4-inch-stroke) engines proved to be as dependable as the 74-inch (3 31/32-inch-stroke) versions, so the 80 inch quickly became the favorite of H-D owners, and the 74-inch versions were soon discontinued. When the 80-inch Evo Big Twin was introduced in 1984, it was equipped with the popular 4 1/4-inch stroke.

Fast forwarding to the Twin Cams, both stock TC engine versions have a stroke of 4 inches, which is just 1/32 inch (0.031 inch) longer than the 3 31/32-inch stroke that most 74-inch Knuckleheads, Pans, and early Shovels have. When the H-D engineers designed the Twin Cams, they did so knowing these engines needed to be strong enough to easily handle the Screamin' Eagle big bore and stroke kits that were to soon follow.

As it is with all things mechanical, getting a bit more in one area means losing a little somewhere else. The trick is to know the benefits and drawbacks of each modification, know what you want the engine/bike to do, and build it to do that job well.

When you move the crankpin closer to the flywheels' outer edge (stroke it), you increase the amount of leverage the pistons have to turn the flywheels. This is why a stroked engine has more torque at lower rpm than a stock one, aside from what power the additional cubic inches produce. In a heavy bike, like a Touring model, this increase in

Then install a new Timken bearing onto the JIMS 4-5/8-inch flywheel assembly's sprocket shaft using a JIMS or S&S Cycle (shown) bearing installation tool and a lot of assembly lube.

Place the left case onto the flywheel assembly. After using a micrometer to measure the spacer supplied with the Timken bearing set, slip the spacer over the shaft, followed by the other Timken bearing.

lower-end torque will give you plenty of grunt at low rpm, as well as great pulling power for passing on the highway or climbing hills. In a light bike, like a Softail, you can go to much taller gearing for highway cruising and still have plenty of power for off-the-line performance.

One drawback of a longer stroke is that the engine takes longer to rev up (build rpm), which affects how fast the engine/bike will accelerate. Thankfully, the performance loss resulting from the stroke increase we're talking about will be more than compensated for by the increase in power, so acceleration should be much better, not worse.

Another possible drawback of a longer stroke is shorter piston life due to increased piston speeds and side loads. Piston speed is how fast a piston travels in its cylinder at different engine rpm. When an engine's stroke is increased, the distance the piston must travel in its cylinder also increases, as I've already mentioned. However, the *time* the piston has to travel this greater distance has not increased. For example, if the stroke has been increased from 4 to 4 3/8 inches, the piston must now travel 3/8 inch farther in the same amount of time, so it must move faster. After all, 3,000 rpm means 3,000 revolutions per minute, no matter how far the piston has to go for each revolution.

Piston side load is how hard the piston rubs against the cylinder's bore. Though the piston moves in a straight line, the connecting rod attached to it moves in an arcing motion as it follows the rotating flywheels. This arcing motion causes the piston to press hard against the rear face of the cylinder bore when the piston is pushing down on the rod during the power (down) stroke. The arcing connecting rod also presses the piston against the front side of the bore on the compression and exhaust (up) strokes. The farther the crankpin is from the center of the flywheels (or the longer the stroke), the more severe the connecting rod's angle (arcing motion)

To install the bearing fully onto the shaft, while also pulling the flywheel assembly into the left case, use the JIMS or S&S tool again. Be sure to put a lot of assembly lube onto the parts you are pulling together.

to the vertical-moving piston, which increases the piston's side loads. However, the small stroke increases we've been discussing should not get you afoul of these drawbacks of long stroke engines, but it will still give you lots of power!

Now that you've got a good foundation of stroke information, it's time to install a set of stroker wheels into a Twin Cam 88. There are a number of stroker kits available from a number of manufacturers, such as Harley-Davidson, JIMS, and S&S Cycles. There are also a few almost completely assembled stroker/big bore Twin Cam engines on the market, such as the S&S 124 inches and the JIMS/Harley-Davidson 120 inches. The stroker kit we'll be installing is from JIMS and it's a 4 5/8-inch-stroke flywheel assembly from a JIMS 116-inch stroker/big bore cylinder kit. And though you need to bore out the stock H-D Twin Cam cases to install the kit's big bore cylinders, we're only going to cover installing the flywheel assembly in this project. Project 51 covers a big bore cylinder install.

Start this installation by pressing the stock flywheel assembly out of the left crankcase and splitting the cases (after first removing all nine case bolts, right?) using a JIMS #1047-TP tool with a JIMS #1048 hard cap. Then remove the Timken race snap ring, taking care not to damage the case. Now press out the old Timken bearing races from the left case using a JIMS Timken bearing-race removal tool #94547-80A. Also remove the outer retaining ring and pinion bearing from the right crankcase using a JIMS pinion bearing installation/removal tool #1146. (Tip: You should also tap out both inner cam bearings from the right case at this time; it will be a lot easier than doing it later on with the special tool, as shown in Project 55.) Then give both crankcases a thorough washing and check them for cracks or any other case damage.

The sprocket side of the flywheel assembly on 1999–2002 Twin Cams is supported by the two tapered Timken bearings, which are positioned in the left case with their tapered ends facing each other. These bearings also set the flywheel assembly's end play. Start the build by installing the new Timken races into the left case using the JIMS Timken race installation tool #2246. Reinstall the Timken race snap ring, taking care not to damage the case. Then install a new Timken bearing onto the JIMS 4 5/8-inch flywheel assembly sprocket shaft using a JIMS sprocket shaft-bearing installation tool #97225-55, which must be used with JIMS #97225-55 tool, and a lot of assembly lube. This flywheel assembly comes fully assembled, trued, balanced, and ready to install.

Use a micrometer to measure the thickness of the spacer supplied with the bearing set. Then place the left case onto the flywheel assembly. After you slip the Timken bearing set's spacer over the shaft, do the same with the outer Timken bearing; however, the bearing will not go all the way over the sprocket shaft. To install the bearing fully onto the shaft, while also pulling the flywheel assembly into the left case, use the JIMS #97225-55 tool. Again, put a lot of assembly lube onto the parts you are pulling together.

Once the flywheel assembly is fully pulled into the left case, complete with outer Timken bearing, measure how much the assembly can move in and out (in the same direction you pulled it in) of the case. Measure the amount of movement using a dial indicator. The allowable range is 0.003–0.010 inch. If your end play is not within spec, remove the flywheel assembly from the case and change the Timken bearing spacer to a thicker or narrower one to get it where it needs to be. H-D offers 15 different spacers, so be sure to take the time to get the end play correct. (Note: 2003 and later engines use a pinion bearing on both sides of the flywheel assembly, so install this bearing, as per the service manual procedure and not like the Timken setup.)

Moving to the right case, install the new pinion bearing using a JIMS #1146 tool. Once the bearing is fully seated, install a new retaining ring. (Tip: Some mechanics prefer to also heat the right case in an oven to 350 degrees F before trying to install the bearing. This expands the case and makes it easier to get the bearing in.)

The JIMS 116-inches flywheel kit also comes with JIMS piston oiler jets, which must be used with this kit. Be sure to check to see if the kit/brand you're installing has these or some other special requirements. The JIMS piston oiler jets are installed using a 3/32-inch Allen, with a little purple (222) Loctite on the supplied bolts.

It's now time to seal up the lower end: After coating the mating surfaces of the crankcases with a thin skin of sealant, install two new O-rings onto the crankcase dowel pins. You can then put the two case halves together, taking care not to knock out any of the pinion bearing rollers, which are only loosely held in place by the soft inner roller support, as you slip the right case over the pinion shaft. (Using a JIMS #1288 tool to spread the pinion bearing's rollers will make the job easier.) Be sure to first lube up the pinion bearing and shaft with lots of assembly lube before bringing them together.

You can now install the nine case bolts, which all get torqued to 10 foot-pounds and then to 15–19 foot-pounds, as per the sequence in the H-D service manual for your engine. Finish this part of your build by installing a new sprocket shaft seal using a JIMS engine sprocket seal installation tool #39361-69, which is used with tool #97225-55.

Next, install the new pinion bearing into the right case using a JIMS #1146 tool. Once the bearing is fully seated, install a new retaining ring. (Tip: Some mechanics prefer to heat the case before installing the bearing.)

The JIMS 116-inch flywheel kit we're installing also comes with JIMS piston oiler jets, which are installed using a 3/32-inch Allen, with a little purple (222) Loctite on the supplied bolts.

It's now time to seal up the lower end. After coating the mating surfaces of the crankcases with a thin skin of sealant, install two new O-rings onto the crankcase dowel pins.

Put the two case halves together (don't lose any pinion bearing rollers) and install the nine case bolts, as per the torques and sequence in the service manual. Finish by installing the new sprocket shaft seal.

Servicing the Breather Assembly

⏱ **Time:** 1 hour

🔧 **Tools:** 3/8-inch socket/wrench, inch-pound torque wrench

Talent: ※

Cost: Under $25

Parts: New umbrella valve, foam element, breather O-ring, and bottom and cover gaskets

💡 **Tip:** Do this whenever you have the top rocker box covers off to help keep oil out of the air cleaner

❗ PERFORMANCE GAIN: A cleaner right side of your bike

COMPLEMENTARY MODIFICATION: Do this when installing roller rocker arms (Project 45) or custom rocker boxes (Project 47)

For years, the bane of 1992 and later Evos has been oil puking out of the air cleaner and all over the right side of the bike. Before this, H-D's crankcase venting system was simply an open-ended hose that allowed pressurized air from the engine to vent to the atmosphere. Then the EPA stepped in and said that the Motor Company had to clean up its act. H-D's answer to the problem of oily mist from the engine polluting the environment was to have the engine vent into the air cleaner through a passageway in each cylinder head. The plan was to make the pressurized oily air from the crankcases travel up into the rocker boxes, so the oil would drop out of the air as it rose. Once in the rocker boxes, the pressurized air, and whatever small amount of oil that was still with it, would pass through a one-way umbrella valve that only allows the air to leave the engine (not come back in) and go into the air cleaner. Once in the air cleaner, this pressurized air is sucked back into the intake system, to be burned in the combustion chamber.

At least, that was the plan. Unfortunately, as Evo owners know, this system doesn't work well and more than just oily mist would find its way into the air cleaner. So Harleys

continued their tradition of spitting out oil, only now it ended up all over the side of the bike instead of on the ground under the engine. Using gravity to separate oil from the pressurized air, and a simple umbrella valve to keep liquid oil from escaping from the rocker boxes, just wasn't enough to do the job.

When designing the Twin Cam 88, the engineers knew this and so they devised a whole new way of handling return oil, as well as changing the entire breathing system to combat this very annoying problem. The new oiling system is covered in Project 66, as is installation of a Feuling high-flow oil pump; I'll cover just the Twin Cam breather system here and only touch lightly on the oil return system.

This new breather system is possible because of the Twin Cam's dual-scavenging pump, which keeps a lot less oil in the crankcase area of the engine. The crankcase is where air inside the engine gets saturated with oil, due to the thrashing flywheel assembly, and pressurized due to the descending pistons. That means there's less oil in the pressurized air that goes to the rocker boxes.

But that's not the only change. There are now three stages to H-D's oil scrubbing plan once the pressurized air gets to the rocker boxes via the Evo's first line of defense: Gravity. Gravity still assists in separating oil from the rising

The parts of the breather assembly are the two cover bolts (not shown), filter element (white), umbrella valve (black), breather housing, bottom gasket, top cover, and top cover gasket. Also shown is the rocker arm support plate to which all of this bolts.

After you've cleaned the old oil off the components, the bottom gasket can go onto the support plate. (Note: Though we've removed the support plate, you can do this with the plate in its rocker box.)

The round, white foam filter element is then pressed into the breather housing.

air as it makes its way up the pushrod tubes to the rocker boxes.

In the rocker boxes, the oily air, in its quest to escape the engine and vent to the atmosphere, passes under the rocker support plate and into the new breather assembly through a hole in the support plate. Once inside, it goes through the first stage of the new oil scrubbing plan: A tortuous path, which is a channel that gases find easy to follow, but liquids do not, that causes the larger oil droplets to separate from the air. This path leads the pressurized air over a wall into another compartment, where it then has to rise up and pass through the second stage, a foam filter element that's about 1 inch in diameter, which scrubs any remaining oil from the pressurized air. This oil falls to the bottom of the breather assembly and drains out through two tiny holes in the rocker arm support plate, into the bottom rocker box, where it is then returned to the gearcase and, eventually, the oil tank/reservoir.

The now less-oily air then passes through the third and final stage, which is the same one used on the Evo: A rubber, one-way umbrella valve that only allows air to pass out of the engine, and not back in. However, just as it does on Evos, if overwhelmed with oil, which will happen if there's too much oil in the breather assembly for the two tiny holes to deal with, this umbrella valve will let oil leak into the air cleaner along with the air.

On a stock or mildly modified engine, the new breather system is able to keep oil out of the air cleaner and off the side of your bike. Heavily modified and/or larger displacement engines, however, sometimes do have this problem, which is why two aftermarket companies have come out with two different solutions: S&S offers a reed valve for TC

88s only (Project 64), while TP Engineering has special rocker boxes for both TC 88s and 88Bs (Project 47).

As for the oil-removing stages, all three are contained in the breather assemblies (one per rocker box), the parts of which are the filter element, umbrella valve, breather housing, bottom gasket, top cover, top cover gasket, and two cover bolts. (The rocker arm support plate forms the bottom of the breather assembly.)

To service the breather assembly, take it apart and wash all the old oil off the components. The gaskets, umbrella valve, and foam filter element should be replaced. If you have removed the rocker arm support plate from the engine for some other modification or repair, also replace the breather assembly O-ring located in the lower rocker box under the support plate. However, the breather assembly can be serviced while the rocker arm assembly is still in the lower rocker box.

Assembly starts with the bottom gasket going onto the rocker arm support plate. The round foam element is then pressed into the breather housing. The breather housing is then flipped over and placed onto the support plate, and a new umbrella valve is secured into its hole in the breather housing. The top cover, complete with new cover gasket, can then be placed onto the breather assembly. With the rocker arm support plate bolted into the lower rocker box, the breather assembly can be bolted to the rocker support plate via the two breather bolts, which are torqued to 90–120 in-lb using a 3/8-inch wrench/socket. With a new rocker box gasket in place, install the top rocker box. Torque the bolts, with a little blue Loctite on the threads, as per the sequence in the service manual, to 15–18 ft-lb.

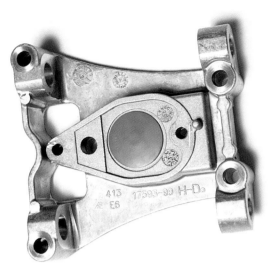

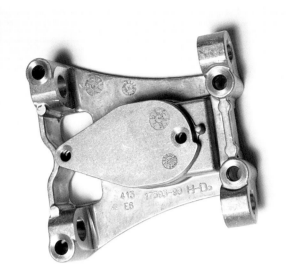

After the breather housing is flipped over and positioned onto the support plate, install a new umbrella valve by pressing its stem into the hole in the breather housing.

After the cover gasket is on the housing, the top cover can be positioned on the breather assembly.

Once the rocker arm support plate is bolted to the lower rocker box, the breather assembly can be bolted into place using a 3/8-inch wrench/socket. Torque both bolts to 90–120 in-lbs.

SECTION SEVEN

The Engine Oil System

PROJECT 63
Installing an Oil Cooler

 Time: 1/2 to 1 hour

 Tools: Flat-blade screwdriver, Allen wrench

 Talent: ▮

 Cost: $200–$300

 Parts: Oil cooler, new oil filter, a few quarts of recycled dinosaur

 Tip: Put down lots of old newspaper; this can get messy!

 PERFORMANCE GAIN: An oil cooler will help dissipate the heat produced during the combustion process and picked up by the oil that's squirted onto the underside of the pistons by the piston jets in the lower end. This will help the oil protect your engine, increasing its life span.

COMPLEMENTARY MODIFICATION: Installation of an oil temperature gauge, and cylinder head temperature gauge

When it comes to bang for the buck an oil cooler is practically a nuclear explosion of value, especially if the engine has been modified in any way. At the risk of rehashing the obvious, an internal combustion engine is nothing more than a hot air pump. Engines make power by heating up air, which then expands and drives the piston downward. Everything else is just a detail. The problem is that when we produce the heat needed to make the engine run, we create a lot of excess heat. That heat needs to be shed and part of the engine oil's job is to help dissipate that heat.

Under normal circumstances, that is, a stock engine, seeing moderate use, our Harleys work just fine; the oil does its thing, one of which is getting rid of some of the excess heat created during normal running. But when things change, the stock lubrication system may not be up to the task. What causes things to change? Good question; how about getting stuck in traffic on a hot summer day, serious engine modification, or packing a passenger and

full saddlebags on an extended trip. If any of the above circumstances sound like a situation you may or do often encounter, an oil cooler will prolong your engine's life, no doubt about it.

When shopping for an oil cooler, first, look for one made by a reputable manufacturer. Lockhart, Jagg, and H-D all make good ones as do several other companies. Next, make certain that the cooler includes a thermostat. Like the thermostat in a water-cooled engine, the thermostat in an oil cooler regulates the oil temperature. Oil that's too cool does a poor job of lubricating and in a worst case scenario will do more harm than good. The thermostat lets the oil warm up quickly and helps maintain it at the correct operating temperature. Overall an oil cooler will prolong engine life, even that of a stock engine, and it's a very simple installation.

Start by draining the old oil, something this Softail rider apparently hasn't done in awhile.

Next remove the oil filter.

The Jagg cooler adapter comes in two halves. Bolt the base half on using the existing oil filter stud. (The base is the part without the hole line fittings.)

Position the cooler where it fits best. This went on the left downtube.

Line up the cutouts on the rubber gasket with the machined passages on the outer half of the adapter (the one with the oil line fittings) and bolt the halves together with the supplied Allen screws. The halves are bolted from both sides.

Run the lines from the filter housing to the cooler in a gentle arc to avoid kinking them. The hose clamps should be tight, yet not so tight that they cut through the hose.

The oil lines (supplied along with the clamps) go on next. Tighten the clamps securely but don't trim the hose yet.

Install a new filter and fill the bike with fresh oil.

Installing an S&S Crankcase Breather Valve

 Time: 3–4 hours

 Tools: Basic mechanic's hand tools, inch-pounds and foot-pounds torque wrenches, blue Loctite, JIMS #1283 tensioner tool kit (which comes with two retention pins), JIMS #1285-1 sprocket lock, and two JIMS #33443-84 Evo-lifter base alignment tools

 Talent:

 Cost: $125

 Parts: S&S reed valve, gearcase O-rings, cam cover gasket, new pushrod tube O-rings, lifter block gaskets, and new rocker box gaskets (unless you're installing new adjustable pushrods)

 Tip: Cutting out the stock non-adjustable pushrods and replacing them with adjustable ones will make this job a lot easier

 PERFORMANCE GAIN: 1–2 horsepower in the midrange

COMPLEMENTARY MODIFICATION: Do a performance camshaft install at the same time

Your Twin Cam engine has to be vented to the atmosphere to relieve the pressure built up in the crankcase caused by the downward motion of the pistons on their power and intake strokes. As the piston descends in its cylinder, the air in the crankcase, where the flywheel assembly lives, is pressurized because the pistons make the airspace in the crankcase smaller when they descend. This pressure must be relieved, or it will force oil past the piston rings and into the combustion chamber, as well as push oil past O-rings and seals in the engine. On the Twin Cams this pressurized air is allowed to pass through the air spaces between the rollers and the inner and outer races of the pinion bearing and go into the engine's gearcase section. Once in the gearcase, it travels up the pushrod tubes and into the rocker boxes, where the Twin Cam's breather

assembly (see Project 62) is supposed to vent it safely, and oil-free, into the air cleaner. The engine can then draw this air back into the engine's combustion chamber for burning.

So much air passes through the pinion bearing and into the gearcase that it caused a noise-only problem (there was no operational problem) on the first-year Twin Cams, the 1999 models. The axial play tolerance allowed between the bearings and races on these engines was 0.006–0.022 inch. However, when the axial play was 0.014 inch or more, the bearings rattled in the airstream like castanets. H-D's fix was to reduce the tolerance to 0.002–0.008 inch on all bearings installed after September 27, 1998.

Earlier on, I stated that the Twin Cam's breather assembly job is to clean up the pressurized, oily air from the crankcase and safely vent it oil-free into the air cleaner. Unfortunately, some owners of 95-inch and larger engines are having problems with oil carryover, which is when oil is blown out of the crankcase breathers in the heads and into the air cleaner. This is especially true on bikes that are run at high speed for long periods of time.

S&S, well known for its large displacement engines, encountered the same problem on its 124-inch Twin Cam-style engine. However, years earlier, it had solved the same problem on its big-inch Evo-style engines by using a Digital Signal Processing (DSP) dyno, which is an engine dyno that allows technicians to run an engine with electronic sensors inside critical areas, so the S&S techs could know what's happening inside the engine. What S&S found when it tested its own 124-inch Twin Cam, as well as H-D

Start by putting some assembly lube onto the breather valve's O-ring. (Note the four steel reed valve along the outer edge of the valve.)

Twin Cam engines that had been modified with S&S stroker and big-bore kits, on the DSP dyno was that the pressure in the crankcase, gearcase, and rocker boxes was constantly increasing and decreasing.

The problem was that though the pressurized, oily air from the crankcase was blowing past the pinion bearing, into the gearcase area, and up the pushrod tubes as it's supposed to, it was also going up the cylinder-head oil drain passages that allow oil to return to the gearcase after lubricating the top end. In fact, air was being blown into the rocker boxes and then sucked back out every time the pistons went up and down their cylinders. This prevented the oil in the rocker boxes from fully draining into the gearcase, so it could be removed from the engine and returned to the oil tank/reservoir. After a while, enough oil accumulates in the rocker boxes to overwhelm the breather assemblies and overflow into the air cleaner.

S&S' fix was to develop a crankcase breather valve that controls the airflow between the crankcase and gearcase on Twin Cam 88s. (Sorry, this valve will not fit on Twin Cam 88Bs because its counterbalancer–system drive sprocket is where the breather valve must go.) S&S' breather valve uses old two-stroke engine technology: Reed valves. The breather valve has a machined, billet aluminum body fitted with four steel reed valves, which let air flow in only one direction. This breather valve slides over the pinion shaft and fits between the pinion bearing's outer retaining ring and the oil pump. These four reed valves allow air to pass through the pinion bearing and into the crankcase when the pistons descend in their cylinders, but do not let the air return into the crankcase when the pistons rise back up.

This stops the air from moving up and down the cylinder-head oil drain passages, so oil can drain out of the rocker boxes and into the gearcase, as per the engine's design.

Installation of the breather valve is very easy. Unfortunately, you have to first empty the gearcase of all its components, including the oil pump. Once the pinion bearing is exposed, put some assembly lube onto the breather valve's O-ring. Then just slide the body of the breather valve over the pinion shaft until it sits in the crankcase's pocket for the pinion bearing. (Do not disturb the pinion bearing's retaining ring.) After putting a little light grease onto the valve's wave washer to hold it in place, slide the washer over the pinion shaft until it sits inside the cavity of the reed valve. You can then reinstall the oil pump and the rest of the gearcase components.

Other Causes

Of course, there are also other causes for oil carryover that are easier to check and fix, such as an overfilled oil tank/reservoir or a clogged/kinked oil return line. Also, if an engine was not properly reassembled after some performance work, like a misaligned oil pump, or missing, poorly installed, or incorrect O-rings in the gearcase, there will be oil circulation and venting problems, which can result in oil carryover into the air cleaner. Ditto for a warped oil pump or cam support plate.

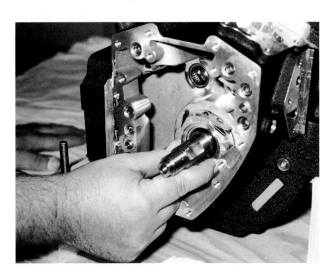

After putting some lube on its O-ring, the first part to install is the breather valve, which just slides over the pinion shaft and sits in the pocket for the pinion bearing.

Next in is the breather valve's wave washer, which just slides over the pinion shaft and sits inside the cavity of the reed valve. (You may want to put a little light grease onto the washer to hold it in place.)

Aligning a Twin Cam Oil Pump

Time: 1 hour

Tools: 1/4-inch Allen wrench, 1/2-inch socket, 9/16-inch socket, inch-pounds and foot-pounds torque wrenches, JIMS #1283 tensioner tool kit (comes with two retention pins), #1285-1 sprocket lock, blue Loctite, and two #33443-84 Evo-lifter base alignment tools, nylon or plastic pry tool

 Talent:

Cost: Under $10

Parts: Cam cover gasket

Tip: We suggest you torque the oil pump bolts to only 90 inch-pounds

PERFORMANCE GAIN: It will help keep the engine oil consumption where it should be and hopefully stop oil blowby into the air cleaner

COMPLEMENTARY MODIFICATION: Now's a good time to install a custom cam cover and check the shoe on the cam chain tensioner

Got a problem with excessive oil loss and oil blowby into the air cleaner? As it turns out, these annoying traits may be due to a misalignment of the oil pump to the pinion shaft. (Though installing an S&S pinion bearing baffle plate, Project 64, or a set of TP Engineering's air/oil separating rocker boxes (Project 47) may be the only way to fix the problem.) The Motor Company is aware that sometimes there's an alignment problem with the gerotor-type oil pump in both the Twin Cam 88 and Twin Cam 88B engines. In response, it issued a service letter to all its dealerships called Tech Tip 54, which describes the correct procedure for establishing the proper alignment of the oil pump.

The old procedure involved tightening the six cam support–plate bolts to spec, as per the sequence in the service manual. The four oil pump bolts were then screwed in

until they just touched the cam support plate, and then backed out a 1/4 turn. As the engine was rotated, which was done to make sure the pump was running true on the pinion shaft, the oil pump bolts were tightened until snug. They were then torqued to 90–120 inch-pounds.

The new procedure, as outlined in Tech Tip 54, requires the mechanic to use two alignment tools, which are the same ones used to align an Evo Big Twin's lifter blocks. That full process follows. Personally, I prefer the new method to the old, as it's much more precise and easier to do.

Start the job by putting an oil catch pan under the right side of the engine. Then remove the cam cover using a 1/4-inch Allen wrench. Once the cover is off, clean the old gasket from the cover and engine case as the oil drains into the pan. Then rotate the engine so that the alignment dot on the face of the primary cam sprocket is aligned with the dot on the face of the (pinion) crank sprocket.

Use the JIMS #1283-1 tool, which comes in the JIMS tensioner tool kit, to turn the primary cam chain tensioner so it releases its tension on the (outer) primary cam chain. Then insert a retention pin (#1283-2), which is also supplied in the kit, through the tensioner and into the cam support plate to keep the tensioner away from the chain. (Note: Check the face of the tensioner's shoe. If it's worn, replace it, as well as the one on the other side of the cam support plate. Also, never just pull out a retention pin from a chain tensioner if the chain is not installed, or damage will result to the tensioner due to its 35–40 pounds of spring pressure. Always use the tensioner tool to control the tensioner.)

Insert a JIMS #1285-1 tool to lock the sprockets, so you can remove the sprocket bolts. Use a 9/16-inch socket on the top sprocket bolt and a 1/2-inch on the bottom sprocket bolt. Noting that the chain has a dark link that faces either out towards you or in toward the engine when the chain is installed on the sprockets, remove the primary cam sprocket and (pinion) crank sprocket and primary cam chain as an assembly. (You may have to gently pry the sprockets off their shafts using a nylon or plastic pry tool.) If your chain doesn't have a dark link (some early models don't), make a mark so you'll know what side of the chain faces out. The chain must go back on facing in the same direction as before. There should be a thick shim on the end of the rear camshaft, under the cam sprocket. Leave it there.

Remove all four oil pump bolts, which are the ones that circle the crank sprocket. Then install the two Evo Big Twin–lifter block alignment tools into oil pump bolt holes

#3 and #4 (they are numbered as such on the cam support plate) and tighten the tools to 90 inch-pounds. After cleaning the oil off the threads of all the pump bolts, put a little blue Loctite on the threads of two bolts and install them into oil pump bolt holes #1 and #2, in that order. Torque the bolts to 90–120 in-lb. You can then remove the two alignment tools and install the two remaining oil pump bolts, just like the first two, into positions #3 and #4, in that order. Torque the bolts to 90–120 in-lb. The pump is now properly aligned to the pinion shaft.

You can now start the reassembly by checking that the dots on the ends of both cams are aligned side by side. Keeping the two cam dots aligned, position both sprockets into the primary cam chain (noting the dark link), so the alignment dots on the face of the sprockets are aligned to each other. Then slip the sprockets onto their shafts (they should go on without having to turn the engine, if you took the time to do this step in the beginning) and install the OEM bolts and washers. Be sure you do not turn the cams; those alignment dots must stay in the proper position while installing the sprockets and chain. The only shaft you are allowed to turn to get the sprockets to go on is the crank (pinion) shaft, which is moved by turning the engine. (An easy way to do this is to put the tranny in fifth gear and move the rear wheel.)

With the JIMS #1285-1 tool between the sprockets to keep them from turning, torque the (top) primary sprocket bolt to 34 ft-lb using a 9/16-inch socket and the (bottom) crank sprocket bolt to 24 ft-lb with a 1/2-inch socket. Then remove the JIMS lock tool and retention pin. Now recheck the sprockets' alignment dots; are they still aligned sprocket-to-sprocket?

After you remove the sprockets and chain, use two JIMS #33443-84 Evo lifter base alignment tools to align the pump, as per the instructions in this project.

Here's a close-up of the oil pump bolts and alignments tools. Note the numbers on the support plate, which are used for proper order of assembly.

After aligning the two dots on the sprockets, use a JIMS #1283-1 tool to release the tension on the chain. Then insert a tensioner retention pin to hold the shoe off the chain.

Reinstall the sprockets—with the alignment dots matched up—and chain (don't forget the dark link) onto the shafts. With the JIMS tool between the sprockets, install the stock hardware, torquing the bolts to spec.

PROJECT 66

Installing a Feuling Oil Pump

 Time: 3–4 hours

 Tools: Basic mechanic's tools, inch-pounds and foot-pounds torque wrenches, blue Loctite, JIMS #1283 tensioner tool kit (which comes with two retention pins), JIMS #1285-1 sprocket lock, and two JIMS #33443-84 Evo-lifter base alignment tools

 Talent:

 Cost: $500

 Parts: Feuling Super Pump, gearcase O-rings, cam cover gasket, new pushrod tube O-rings, lifter block gaskets, and new rocker box gaskets (unless you're installing new adjustable pushrods)

 Tip: Cutting out the stock non-adjustable pushrods will make this job a lot easier

 PERFORMANCE GAIN:
Improve oil flow and pressure

COMPLEMENTARY MODIFICATION: While you're in here, swap out the cams, as well as the inner cam bearings, for some high-performance versions

Your starting point has the old pump removed and the case clean and ready for the new pump.

There are only two reasons why an owner would want to change out his Twin Cam oil pump, with the first being because the stock one was destroyed. This occurs because either the rear cam bearing went bad and took out everything in the gearcase section of the engine, or the engine's flywheels are out of true.

The cam bearing problem, which is isolated to engines assembled in 1999 and early 2000 (see Project 54), is the usual cause of oil pump failure, if it happens at all. However, when the flywheels are out of true, it causes the pinion (crank) shaft to spin off-center in the oil pump. And since the pump is crank-mounted and -driven (I'll get into this more in a moment), the shaft's excess movement trashes the inside of the pump, usually within the first 6,000 miles or so of the engine's life.

Once the pump is destroyed, there are presently only two choices for pump replacement: a new stock unit or a

Feuling Super Pump, which brings us to the second reason for oil pump replacement: Higher performance. Once an owner has substantially beefed up the engine, performance-wise, he may want to have more oil, at a higher pressure, pumping through his more muscular mill.

The Feuling Super Pump is a bolt-in replacement billet aluminum pump. Feuling states that the pump provides 40 percent more supply volume and 60 percent more scavenge volume than the stock TC 88 oil pump. The Super Pump features larger diameter gerotors, aerospace materials, and closer tolerances than the stock die-cast H-D pump. Since the photos cover how this pump is installed, once the gearcase has been emptied of all components, let's go over what type of pump a Twin Cam uses, whether it's the stock unit or the Feuling version.

All Twin Cams, either 88s or 88Bs, use a dry sump, twin gerotor, dual scavenge, crank-mounted and -driven, internal oil pump. And though that's a mouthful, it's really

179

Before you install Feuling's Super Pump into the gearcase, the pump's aluminum sub seal must be slipped into the pump's ported plate. This seal goes into the back of the plate with some lube on its O-ring.

The ported plate can now be slid over the pinion shaft, with the sub seal fitting into the scavenge port in the crankcase.

just a long list of adjectives that describe the style of pump that it is. For example, the term *dry pump* simply means this type of pump has a return section, as well as a feed section. This is because, unlike the oil pump in your car's engine, which is a wet sump type, a Harley's oil supply is kept in an oil tank or reservoir and not in the engine's crankcases. The feed section of a Twin Cam pump brings oil to the pump and then sends it throughout the engine, while the return section picks up oil from the engine's cases after it has done its job of lubing the moving parts and sends it back to the oil holding tank/reservoir. As for a wet sump pump, it doesn't need a return section since it sits in a pool of oil in the engine's crankcase.

As for the term *twin gerotor*, twin means there's a feed and return section to the pump, which is needed in a dry sump system and a *gerotor* refers to the fact that this pump uses rotors instead of gears to produce oil flow and pressure. In fact, a gerotor pump is a superior design and produces high volume and high pressure, as compared to all previous Big Twin oil pumps, which are gear pumps that put out only moderate oil volume and moderate pressures, relatively speaking.

The Twin Cam pump has four gerotors: two for the feed and two for the return section. The thicker rotors are for the return side, which returns oil from the engine to the oil tank/reservoir. (You want the pump to have a greater capacity for getting oil out of than putting it into the engine. If it's the other way around, you'll soon have too much oil and it will start coming out the engine's breather, seals, gaskets, and exhaust pipes.) The thinner rotors are for the feed section, which sends the oil throughout the engine. Each set of gerotors has an inner gerotor, which sits inside an outer rotor. As the inner rotor

After putting some assembly lube onto all the pump's gerotors, slip the Super Pump's body, which comes assembled, onto the pinion shaft, followed by the outer O-ring.

is turned by the pinion shaft it squeezes oil between the two—they have centers that are slightly offset to one another—to produce oil pressure and flow.

As for the rest of the terms, *dual scavenge* means that the return oil is picked up from two places: the gearcase and the crankcase. (All earlier Big Twin pumps only get it from the gearcase.) *Crank-mounted and -driven* means the oil pump is mounted on the pinion (crank) shaft and that shaft drives its gerotors. The last one, *internal*, refers to the fact that the pump is inside the engine, under the cam cover, and not behind it on the outside of the engine like all other H-D Big Twin engines.

SECTION EIGHT

The Drivetrain

PROJECT 67

Installing a Hydraulic Clutch Actuator

 Time: 1–2 hours

 Tools: 5/8- and 11/16-inch sockets, ratchet, 6-inch extension, 3/16-, 3/8-, and 7/32-inch Allen wrenches, 1/2-, 9/16-, and 11/16-inch wrench, T-27 Torx driver, snap ring pliers, and drain oil pan

 Talent:

 Cost: $425–725

 Parts: Hydraulic actuator cover, new transmission side cover gasket, transmission oil, hydraulic line, DOT 5 brake fluid, left-side (clutch) master cylinder, four new crush washers

 Tip: Make sure the hydraulic cover you plan on installing will work with the clutch and transmission you have. For example, H-D's offering will not work with an aftermarket clutch or wider-than-stock transmission trapdoor.

 PERFORMANCE GAIN: A happier left hand due to a smooth, even, easy clutch lever pull

COMPLEMENTARY MODIFICATION: Don't just run a fancy tranny side cover; do the cam cover, too. Project 52 shows you how

There are two reasons to install a hydraulic clutch actuator on a Twin Cam. The first is because you have a beast of a motor sitting between the frame rails and the clutch, you need to send its power to the tranny, and it's giving you a left forearm like Popeye's. The other is simply because it's a trick-and-slick way to get the job done. No matter what the reason, the job is the same, and an easy one at that.

To show you how it's done, I'm going to bolt up a Pro-One hydraulic actuator side cover, which will be powered using an H-D black left-side (clutch) master cylinder. Pro-One's hydraulic clutch actuators are machined from 6061-T6 billet aluminum and then chromed. This unit installs using the stock hardware and comes with a 10-mm banjo

bolt, two banjo-bolt crush washers, and a bleeder screw. This cover fits all 1987–Present Big Twins equipped with either a five- or a six-speed transmission and must be used with a 9/16-inch-bore master cylinder.

A number of other companies also make hydraulic clutch actuators, as well as various master cylinders. Some come as complete hydraulic clutch kits, or you can mix and match components, as we have. Just keep in mind that not all kits will fit all clutches and transmission options. For example, H-D's offering will not work with an aftermarket clutch or a wider-than-stock transmission trapdoor, as you will find on a six-speed tranny.

Start the installation by draining the oil from the transmission, as per Project 5. While it drains, move the clutch cable boot out of the way and loosen the cable adjuster with a 1/2- and 9/16-inch wrench, so the cable has plenty of slack in it. Then remove the retaining (snap) ring from the clutch lever's pivot pin and pull the pin, so the cable is free from the clutch lever bracket. Unbolt the clutch lever bracket from the handlebars by removing its two bolts using a T-27 Torx drive. Set the lever and bracket, and all parts aside, except for the two bracket bolts and the mirror (if so equipped), as you will not need them for this installation.

Once all the oil is drained from the tranny, reinstall the drain plug and torque it to 14–21 ft-lb with a 5/8-inch socket. Then remove the transmission side cover using a 3/16-inch Allen. (You may have to remove the rear exhaust

Our starting point has the oil drained from the tranny and the side cover, as well as the stock clutch handlebar control and cable, removed from the bike. The clutch release pushrod and throw-out bearing are still in the mainshaft.

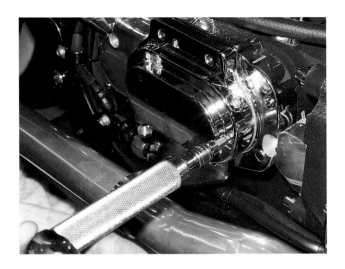

With a new gasket on the case, bolt up the new side cover with the stock hardware, with some blue Loctite on the threads, using a 3/16-inch Allen.

After bolting a new left-side (clutch) master cylinder to the handlebars, use a 12-point box wrench, as well as two new crush washers, to bolt the hydraulic line to it. Then route the line to the tranny side cover.

pipe, depending on model.) Use a 9/16-inch wrench to remove the clutch cable from the cover. Set the cover and cable aside, as you will not need them any longer. (Depending on the hydraulic cover you bought, you may need the oil filler plug. A 3/8-inch Allen will do the trick here.)

Move to the left side of the motorcycle and, with the bike upright (as in standing level, so it will not tip to either side), use a T27 Torx driver to remove the derby cover. Set the cover, hardware, and quad seal aside for later reinstallation. Using an 11/16-inch wrench or socket, loosen the clutch adjuster screw's locknut and screw the clutch adjuster screw out (counterclockwise) a few turns with a 7/32-inch Allen wrench.

Back on the right side of the bike, wipe the now-exposed tranny trapdoor with a clean rag. Leave the clutch release pushrod and throw-out bearing (also called the pushrod end or oil sling) in the transmission's main shaft. Our Pro-One hydraulic cover comes completely assembled and ready for installation, as most do. So, with a new gasket on the case, bolt up the new side cover with the stock Allen bolts, with some blue Loctite on their threads, using a 3/16-inch Allen.

Moving to the handlebars, bolt a new left-side (clutch) master cylinder to the handlebars using the stock, or supplied, hardware and a T-27 Torx drive. We're using a black H-D one to match the stock controls. (However, chrome H-D versions and custom master cylinders are also available.) If so equipped, reinstall the mirror.

Hopefully, your side cover kit came with a new stainless-steel braided hydraulic line. If it didn't, you'll have to have one made up. Goodrich offers hydraulic/brake line assembler kits. (Project 37 also covers installing braided lines.) Using a 12-point box wrench, bolt the new line up to the new clutch master cylinder. Be sure to use two new

Bolt the hydraulic line to the tranny cover, with two new crush washers, using a 9/16-inch wrench. Then bleed the brakes as per Project 36, adjust the clutch as per Project 11, and add new tranny oil as per Project 35.

crush washers. Then route the line to the tranny side cover and clamp it as needed. Be sure not to route it where it may get pinched when the front end is turned, or burned by the hot engine or exhaust pipes. (Following the route the clutch cable took is probably a good choice, but not always.) Bolt the new hydraulic line to the tranny cover, with two new crush washers, using a 9/16-inch wrench.

After pouring in some DOT 5 brake fluid, or whatever is required for your kit, bleed the hydraulic system the same way you would bleed brakes, as per Project 35. (Yes, the new cover has a bleeder valve on it somewhere.) Once the system is bled, adjust the clutch as per Project 11 and close up the derby cover. (You may want to check the primary fluid level before you do.) After checking that the new hydraulic actuator is working correctly, add new transmission oil as per Project 5.

PROJECT 68

Installing a Rivera Pro Clutch

 Time: 1–2 hours

 Tools: Arbor press, assorted press plugs, primary-drive locking tool (#HD-41214), foot-pounds torque wrench, snap ring pliers, assorted hand tools, 1 1/2-inch socket, 30-mm socket

 Talent:

 Cost: $500–650

 Parts: New performance clutch assembly, clutch shell bearing, primary cover gasket, primary oil

 Tip: If the primary chain is iffy, replace it now, as well as the primary chain adjusting shoe. Always replace the clutch shell bearing whenever you remove the clutch hub.

 PERFORMANCE GAIN: No loss of engine power due to a slipping clutch

COMPLEMENTARY MODIFICATION: If vibration is an issue, install a Balance Masters kit, as per Project 71

After removing the retaining ring, press the old clutch hub out of the stock clutch shell using an arbor press and a press plug that has the same outer diameter as the clutch hub.

If you've done some of the engine performance upgrades outlined in this book, your Twin Cam should be putting out the power you always knew it could. Unfortunately, the stock clutch may now be slipping like there's grease between the plates, no matter how you adjust it. That's because the problem is not the adjustment; you need more clutch surface area to handle all the extra ponies the engine is now pumping out.

An axiom in performance work is that once you make the engine put out considerably more juice, you also have to upgrade some of the drivetrain components so they can handle the extra power. After all, the Motor Company gave you a clutch that'll handle the output of the stock engine (around 60–65 horsepower), plus a good bit more. However, when the engine is putting out a lot more power you need a performance clutch to handle it. H-D's

Screamin' Eagle line offers a good one, as does BDL and Barnett (Project 69). Rivera also offers a good one, its Pro Clutch, which is the one I've installed. The Pro Clutch gives you lots more surface area than the stocker, as well as smooth engagement and an even pull when you yank on the clutch lever, and you don't need massive forearms to operate it.

We'll pick up the installation with all the primary drive components removed, except for the rotor, primary chain adjuster assembly, and starter drive. (The primary chain adjuster is opened to accept the chain and is at the bottom of its range of travel.)

Remove the Rivera clutch plates from the new Rivera hub and soak them in new primary oil. Make sure you keep the plates in order. Then remove all the old clutch plates from the stock clutch shell. Press the old clutch hub out of the stock clutch shell by first turning the clutch hub so the sprocket side is facing up. Then remove the retaining ring from its groove in the clutch hub with a snap ring pliers. Position the clutch assembly on an arbor press, sprocket side up, and, using a press plug that is the same outer diameter as the clutch hub, press the hub from the bearing in the clutch shell.

Now turn the shell over and remove the retaining ring from its groove in the shell with snap ring pliers. Turn the shell back over and press the bearing from the shell using a press plug that contacts the outer edge of the bearing. Turn the shell over once again and install the new bearing using

Once you have replaced the clutch shell bearing, you can now press the new Rivera clutch hub into the stock clutch shell using the appropriate press plug until it fully seats in the shell.

the same press plug (the one that contacts the outer edge of the bearing, so the bearing doesn't get damaged) until the bearing contacts the shoulder of the clutch hub bore. Reinstall the bearing's retaining ring.

You can now press the new Rivera clutch hub into the stock clutch shell using the appropriate press plug until it fully seats in the shell. Install the Rivera-supplied retaining ring onto the clutch hub stem.

Slip the stock clutch shell with the Rivera hub, engine sprocket, and primary chain onto the engine and tranny shafts as one assembly. Then assemble the components of the engine-compensating sprocket onto the engine sprocket shaft in this order: sliding cam, sprocket cover, and, with a little blue Loctite on the engine-sprocket shaft thread, sprocket nut. After you put some blue Loctite on the tranny's main shaft threads, the clutch hub main shaft nut can go onto the transmission main shaft. (Note: The clutch hub main shaft nut is a reverse, as in left-hand, threaded nut on the transmission main shaft.) Using a primary drive locking tool between the teeth on the sprocket and the primary chain to stop it from turning, torque the sprocket nut to 150165 ft-lb using a 1 1/2-inch socket and torque wrench. Then move the tool to the clutch hub and torque the hub nut to 7080 ft-lb using a 30-mm socket and torque wrench.

Install the Rivera plates, starting with a steel plate, followed by a fiber plate, followed by a steel plate, etc., until you run out of plates. These plates must be installed in the same order that you removed them from the Rivera hub. The Rivera pressure plate goes in next, positioned with the side stamped "out" facing out. Insert the diaphragm spring. Rivera offers these springs in three versions: black for stock or near-stock engines, silver (the one I used) for street performance up to 110 horsepower, and gold for competition use only.

Next on is the spring retainer and screw pack, with two locking rings. Tighten the four nuts down until they bottom out with 30 inch-pounds of torque. Then bend over the locking tabs with a pliers. After reinstalling the stock clutch adjuster, adjust the clutch, as shown in Project 11; adjust the primary chain as shown in Project 9.

After you have cleaned all of the old gasket off the inner and outer primary covers, install a new gasket onto the dowels in the cover. Then install the primary cover and tighten the cover bolts to 79 ft-lb, in the sequence shown in the service manual. Note: There are long and short screws for the outer cover, which must go in specific locations, as per the manual. Add the required amount of primary oil, as shown in Project 5.

Slip the stock clutch shell with the Rivera hub, engine sprocket, and primary chain onto the engine and tranny shafts as one assembly.

Install the engine compensating sprocket components onto the sprocket shaft in this order: sliding cam (left), sprocket cover (center), and, with a little blue Loctite, sprocket nut (right).

After installing the reverse-threaded clutch hub nut, use a locking tool to keep the primary from turning as you torque the sprocket nut to 150–165 ft-lbs. and the clutch hub nut to 70–80 ft-lb.

The diaphragm spring, which Rivera offers in three versions (black for stock or near stock engines, silver for street performance up to 110 horsepower, and gold for competition use), can then go in.

Install the Rivera plates. Start with a steel one and follow it with a fiber plate, until all the plates are in the clutch shell, just as they were before you took them out to soak them in new primary oil.

Next on is the spring retainer and screw pack, with two locking rings. Tighten the four nuts down until they bottom out with 30 in-lb of torque. Then bend over the locking tabs with a pliers.

The Rivera pressure plate goes in next, positioned with the side stamped OUT facing out.

PROJECT 69

Installing a Barnett Scorpion Clutch Spring Conversion Kit

 Time: 1 hour

 Tools: 3/16- and 7/32-inch Allen, 10-mm socket, 11/16-inch wrench

 Talent:

 Cost: $200

 Parts: Barnett Scorpion clutch-spring conversion kit, primary gasket, primary oil

 Tip: Be sure to check the condition of the primary chain and adjusting shoe, since the cover is off and these parts are accessible

 PERFORMANCE GAIN: Control clutch pressure and lever pull

COMPLEMENTARY MODIFICATION: You should also upgrade the clutch's fiber and steel plates when doing this install. This is especially true if the steels have a blue tint to them, which indicates the clutch has overheated, due to slippage or another malfunction

As mentioned in Project 68, once you've turned your mild-mannered Twin Cam mill into a fire-breather, you'll need to beef up the clutch, so it can handle all the additional power your high-performance engine is putting out. However, a clutch using a single-diaphragm spring-style pressure plate and spring arrangement—which is what's used in a stock H-D clutch—or the high-performance clutch we install in Project 68, is not the only option out there.

The crew at Barnett Tool & Engineering feel that more is better, which is why they offer their Scorpion-billet clutch-spring conversion kit. The Scorpion features six coil springs instead of a single diaphragm spring. Barnett states that its clutch spring arrangement gives the rider the ability to fine-tune the spring pressure of their clutch, which results in positive engagement and release, and linear clutch action. The Scorpion also comes with a

billet-aluminum pressure plate that has been hard anodized to MIL-spec.

The Scorpion comes with two different-pressure spring sets, which gives the mechanic three different pressure settings. Using all six (gold) light-pressure springs will result in the lightest clutch pull (about 24 pounds) and spring pressure load (320 pounds), while using all six high-pressure springs results in the heaviest pull (42 pounds) and spring pressure load (390 pounds). However, using three of each gives the rider a medium lever pull (33 pounds) and spring pressure (350 pounds), which will be what's needed in almost every case where the light spring set is not adequate. (By the way, the stock springs have a lever pull of about 18 pounds and a spring pressure load of 248 pounds.) Most applications will not need to run all six heavy-pressure springs, which is usually only for full race engines.

An added bonus is that once the kit's installed you can change out the springs without pulling off the outer primary cover. All you have to do is remove the derby cover. This way, you can install all six light-pressure springs and see if that does the job. If you find you need more spring pressure to hold your beast in check, just swap out three of the light springs for the heavier pressure ones right through the derby cover. There's no need to mess with dropping the primary oil or changing out the cover gasket.

This pressure plate setup can be used with the stock clutch basket, so there's no need to completely disassemble the entire clutch unless you also want to install performance

With the primary cover off, remove the six pressure plate bolts using a 10-mm socket. Then remove the plate that the bolts held on.

You can then pull the diaphragm spring from the clutch shell. It'll just come right out.

Use an 11/16-inch wrench to loosen the clutch adjuster screw locknut. Then use a 7/32-inch Allen to remove the adjuster from the pressure plate.

clutch plates. In fact, many engines can get away with just swapping out the pressure plate parts and retaining the stock clutch pack.

I'll pick up this installation with the primary cover removed and the oil drained. As you remove your cover, be sure to note where the 3/16-inch Allen long and short cover bolts are located. I suggest you throw out the old primary gasket and use a new one when reinstalling the cover.

Remove the six pressure plate bolts using a 10-mm socket and remove the plate. Then remove the diaphragm spring from the clutch assembly; it'll just come right out. Use an 11/16-inch wrench to loosen the clutch adjuster-screw locknut and use a 7/32-inch Allen to remove the adjuster from the pressure plate. The pressure plate can then be removed from the clutch shell.

Inspect or change the clutch plates, as needed. The plates can be pulled from the shell, but be sure to put them back in the same order. Slip the Barnett Scorpion pressure plate in the same spot as the stock pressure plate in the clutch shell.

Slip a Barnett-supplied bolt and washer into a Barnett spring, or whatever pressure spring you're going to use. Then screw the spring packs into the clutch hub using a 3/16-inch Allen. They already have Loctite on their threads, so there's no need to add more. These Allen bolts must get torqued to 5.8 ft-lb (70 in-lb). There's no need to measure how far the bolts go down because the torque setting gives them the proper height.

You can now loosen the clutch cable and adjust the clutch, as per the service manual or Project 11. Once you've got the clutch adjustment correct, lock down the stock adjuster using the locknut. Then reinstall the primary cover, with a new gasket, and fill with the correct grade and quantity of oil.

The pressure plate can be removed from the clutch shell. You can now inspect or change the clutch plates, as needed, since the plates can just be pulled from the shell. Just be sure to put them back in the same order.

Once the plates have been reinstalled/replaced, slip the Barnett Scorpion pressure plate into the spot where the stock pressure plate was in the clutch shell.

Then screw the spring packs into the clutch hub using a 3/16-inch Allen. They already have Loctite on their threads, so there's no need to add more. These Allen bolts must get torqued to 5.8 ft-lb (70 in-lb).

Slip a Barnett supplied bolt and washer into a Barnett spring, whatever pressure springs you've decided to use. (We suggest going with the light springs, and then upgrading if needed.)

You can now loosen the clutch cable and adjust the clutch, as per the service manual or Project 11. Once you've got the clutch adjustment correct, lock down the stock adjuster using the locknut.

PROJECT 70
Installing a Primary Chain Tensioner

 Time: 1 hour

 Tools: T-40 Torx drive, grinder or file, red and blue Loctite, micrometer or ruler, 9/16-inch socket, foot-pound torque wrench, 3/16-inch Allen

 Talent:

 Cost: $100

 Parts: Primary chain tensioner kit, primary gasket, primary oil

 Tip: Make sure your primary chain is in good shape. If it's shot, replace it when installing the tensioner.

 PERFORMANCE GAIN: Smoother shifts and less vibration from the drivetrain

COMPLEMENTARY MODIFICATION: Lose some more bad vibes by installing a Balance Masters kit, Project 71

Reinstall the stock serrated backing plate, with the Hayden adjuster bolt and C Guideplate, using the stock countersunk bolts. Put a little red Loctite on the threads and use a T40 Torx drive.

It's amazing how poorly a loose primary chain can make a bike perform. The bike will feel sloppy during deceleration, even bucking in extreme cases. The primary chain slapping against the covers can also sound like there's something horribly wrong inside the engine. The transmission will shift poorly and engine vibration will be more pronounced. All traits nobody wants their bike to have, and yet the culprit is just a loose primary chain.

Unfortunately, most owners don't even realize that things are slowly getting worse as the chain gets looser. Many live with the problems for months, not noticing the slow deterioration of their bike's performance. And when they do, many times they think it's something big and wait for weeks until the shop can fit them in for some major work, only to find out that the fix took about 15 minutes. That is, unless the chain is now stretched beyond proper adjustment, requiring an expensive replacement.

A longer-term fix is to get a primary chain tensioner, like the Hayden M6 I'm going to install. The M6 automatically keeps the proper tension on the primary chain at all times, during acceleration or deceleration, and at all points of the chain, not just on the tightest part, which is where the tension has to be adjusted when doing it manually. The M6, through the use of two springs, always has the proper tension on the chain no matter what, which will also extend its useful service life.

Our starting point for this installation has the stock adjuster removed from the inner primary cover, including the serrated backing plate. Start the job by reinstalling the stock serrated backing plate with the longer Hayden adjuster bolt in it—instead of the short stock one—and the Hayden C guideplate on the bolt. Reinstall the stock countersunk mounting bolts, with a little red Loctite on the threads, using a T-40 Torx drive.

The next step is to fit the thinnest Hayden H shim in the kit to the Hayden C guideplate. Because Twin Cam–inner primary covers have a raised area around the chain adjuster location, you may have to remove a little material from the H shim's two inner ears using a file or grinder, so the shim can easily slide up and down the C guideplate as needed.

Slip the smaller-diameter spring supplied with the kit inside the larger one, and put both into the hole made for them in the bottom of the Hayden adjusting shoe. With the thinnest H shim positioned on the C guideplate, as well as the two Hayden springs and adjusting shoe under the primary chain, measure the gap between the bottom face of the shoe and the top of the H shim with a micrometer or ruler. This gap should be 5/8 inch (0.625 inch) for a stock displacement engine, or 1/2 inch (0.500 inch) for a stroker motor.

If needed, install one of the other supplied H shims, after you clearance its two inner tabs, so the shim can move freely on the C guideplate. (Keep all the unused H shims to re-shim the shoe if needed as the primary chain stretches over time. However, if you find you have to install more than three shims to get the proper gap, the primary chain is shot and must be replaced.) Then install the correct H shim, adjusting shoe, and both springs into the adjuster, under the primary chain. After putting a little blue Loctite on the threads, install the Hayden I guideplate (bevel facing in), as well as the supplied washer and nut

onto the bolt using a 9/16-inch socket. Torque the nut to 33 foot-pounds.

To check that there's clearance between the Hayden M6 and the outer primary cover, place the outer cover onto the inner cover without the gasket and check the gap between them through the inspection hole. You want at least 1/16 inch. (Ours had plenty of clearance.) You can then reinstall the outer cover, with a new gasket, on to the inner primary. You'll need to use a 3/16-inch Allen on the bolts, which should have a little blue Loctite on their threads. Then add the proper grade and amount of primary oil, as per the service manual for your year and model bike. The M6 should be checked for wear every 20,000 miles.

Slip the smaller diameter spring supplied with the kit inside the larger one, and put both into the hole made for them in the bottom of the Hayden adjusting shoe.

Measure the gap between the bottom face of the shoe and the top of the H-shim with a micrometer or ruler. This gap should be 5/8 inch (0.625 inch) for a stock displacement engine.

With the thinnest H-shim positioned on the C Guideplate, install the two Hayden springs and adjusting shoe under the primary chain.

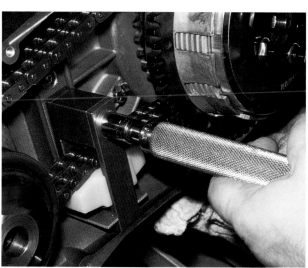

Install the correct H-shim and adjusting shoe with springs into the adjuster, followed by the I Guideplate (bevel facing in). Install the washer and nut using a 9/16-inch socket and torque the nut to 33 ft-lbs.

PROJECT 71
Installing a Balance Masters Kit

 Time: 1 hour

 Tools: 3/16-inch Allen, 1 1/2-inch socket, an impact wrench, 250 ft-lb torque wrench

 Talent:

 Cost: $130

 Parts: Balance Masters compensator kit, primary gasket, primary oil

 Tip: Be sure to check the condition of the primary chain and adjusting shoe, since the cover is off and these parts are accessible.

 PERFORMANCE GAIN: Reduce engine vibration in rubber-mounted Twin Cam engines

COMPLEMENTARY MODIFICATION: Balance the bike's front and rear wheels

THE DRIVETRAIN

Though the Twin Cam 88B has very little engine vibration, due to its counterbalanced lower end, that's not the case with the first generation of Twin Cam mills. The TC 88s have a Harley's normal amount of vibration, but the rider doesn't feel a lot of it due to the engine's rubber mounting system. However, wouldn't it be nice to reduce the level of vibration that the engine puts out, which would smooth things out even more, especially at idle?

To accomplish this worthy goal, I'm going to show you how to install a Balance Masters (BM) compensator kit for Twin Cam 88s, which is manufactured by Sun-Tech Innovations. This kit is easy to install; however, it does require the use of an impact wrench and a torque wrench capable of reinstalling the compensator nut/bolt to 250 foot-pounds.

The Balance Masters compensator plate uses active-engine balancing technology to reduce engine vibration. The BM unit mounts onto the engine sprocket's compensator, between the cover assembly and nut. This is the easiest BM

kit to install, and does help to reduce engine vibration in rubber-mounted Twin Cam engines. Balance Masters also offers balancers for clutch assemblies, and they machine a balancer into the flywheels when an engine is being rebuilt. Balance Masters also states that its balancer unit adjusts for piston ring wear, state of tune, and other factors.

Start by removing the primary cover using a 3/16-inch Allen and draining the oil out of the primary cases. Note where the long and short cover bolts are located as you remove the cover. (We suggest you throw out the old gasket and use a new one during reassembly.)

Then use a 1 1/2-inch socket and an impact wrench to loosen the compensator nut. You can then remove the nut, washer, and compensator cover assembly but do not remove any other parts from the engine compensator sprocket assembly. Then slip the Balance Masters over the top of the cover assembly, followed by the nut and washer. Then reinstall the compensator cover assembly back onto the engine using a 1 1/2-inch socket. Torque the nut to 250 ft-lb.

You can now reinstall the primary cover, without the gasket, to check if the Balance Masters part hits the inside of the outer primary cover anywhere. Ours did not require any cover alterations. (By clearing the cover without a gasket, you've given yourself a little extra room between the cover and the moving parts.) You can then reinstall the primary cover, with a new gasket, using the stock hardware and a 3/16-inch Allen. Then add the proper grade and amount of primary oil, as per the service manual, for your year and model bike.

Start by removing the primary cover using a 3/16-inch Allen and draining the oil out of the primary cases. Note where the long and short cover bolts are located as you remove the cover. Throw out the old gasket.

Then use a 1-1/2-inch socket and an impact wrench to loosen the compensator nut. You can then remove the nut, washer, and compensator cover assembly. Do not remove any other parts from the engine.

Then reinstall the compensator cover assembly, complete with Balance Masters part, back onto the engine using a 1 1/2-inch socket and impact wrench. Then torque the nut to 250 ft-lb.

Reinstall the cover, without a gasket, to check if the BM part hits the inside of the outer primary cover anywhere. If all's well, reinstall the cover, with a new gasket, using the stock hardware. Then add primary oil.

Then slip the Balance Masters part over the top of the cover assembly, followed by the nut and washer.

Installing a Primary Belt Drive

 Time: 2–3 hours

 Tools: Pliers, foot-pound torque wrench, 30-mm, 5/8-inch, and 1 1/2-inch sockets, blue Loctite, straightedge, black marker, flat punch, hammer, 3/16- and 17-mm Allen, 11/16-inch wrench, 1/2-, and 9/16-inch open end wrenches

 Talent:

 Cost: $400–2,500

 Parts: Belt-drive system, dry clutch kit, primary cover gasket, slotted derby cover

 Tip: Though you can grease and seal the inner primary cover bearing, we recommend changing the bearing to one that is sealed.

 PERFORMANCE GAIN: Smoother, quieter primary system, no primary oil to maintain, no primary chain to adjust

COMPLEMENTARY MODIFICATION:
You must change to a dry clutch when running a belt-drive system

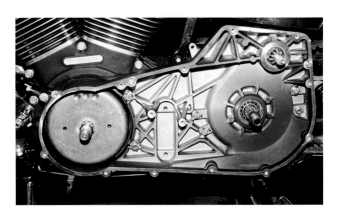

Our starting point has the entire primary drive system removed, down to the inner primary cover, with the jackshaft in place. Don't loosen or remove the inner primary cover.

A s dependable as the stock primary chain and sprocket system is, a primary-belt drive is a quieter, more efficient, and lower maintenance way of transferring the engine's power to the clutch and transmission. After all, isn't that why the Motor Company uses a belt to connect the transmission to the rear wheel?

Primary belt systems come in many sizes. Some, like the one from Rivera, fit inside the stock primary covers. Others are much wider—up to 5 inches—and must be run open, or with just a cover over the outer face. Which one you use is entirely up to your needs and wants. However, all require the use of a dry clutch package. (The stock clutch in all Twin Cams is a wet setup.)

Dry clutches work just as well as the wet variety, but are a bit noisy when you pull the clutch lever in (disengaged). You'll also need to run a slotted derby cover if you

are going to go the route of a closed primary cover, so be sure to order one when you get your belt system. A slotted, or otherwise vented, cover will provide the cooling needs for a belt system for proper operation and longer component life.

The starting point for this installation has the entire primary-drive system removed, down to the inner primary cover, which should not be removed or loosened. Also remove the primary chain–adjuster serrated mounting bar, but be sure to leave the starter jackshaft in place. The first step is to modify the inner primary cover. Pack the cover's transmission mainshaft bearing with the grease supplied by Rivera. Then install the supplied seal (flat side facing out) over the bearing by tapping it into the cover. (You can also replace the bearing with a sealed unit, which is offered by Rivera, but you will have to remove the inner primary cover to do that.)

Moving to the engine, slip the supplied shim onto the engine's sprocket shaft. To make it easier to get the pulley onto the shaft when you have the belt around it and the clutch basket, fit the pulley onto the engine shaft now. You'll need to rotate the pulley until you find a position where the pulley slips easily onto the engine shaft. Then put an alignment mark onto the primary cover and pulley, so later on you can easily find it. Install the pulley nut and snug it down.

Now install the clutch shell/hub assembly onto the transmission shaft and snug the hub's nut down. Do not put the belt around the pulley and clutch shell at this time. Then check for proper pulley alignment by laying a straightedge between the pulley and clutch shell. If align-

THE DRIVETRAIN

ment is satisfactory, the straightedge will be flush with the inner surface of the clutch shell ring gear and line up with the outer edge of the front pulley. If the straightedge is not flush (meaning it's angled), re-shim the front pulley as needed. If the straightedge runs beyond the engine pulley, the shim under the engine pulley has to be bigger. If the belt runs too far to the inside of the pulley, toward the engine, the shim has to be smaller.

Spin the clutch shell and make sure it does not contact the inner primary cover. (It should at all points have at least 0.060-inch clearance between it and the cover.) Then remove the clutch shell and pulley from their shafts. Apply a little of the Rivera-supplied grease to the splines of the transmission mainshaft to prevent corrosion.

Put the belt onto the clutch shell and pulley. Then install the pulley/belt/clutch shell assembly onto the tranny and engine shafts, aligning the mark on the pulley with the one you made on the inner primary. Now slip the supplied ring onto the front pulley. After putting a little blue Loctite onto the engine shaft's threads, install the supplied washer and 1 1/2-inch engine nut and torque nut to 150–165 foot-pounds.

After putting some blue Loctite onto the threads of the mainshaft, install the Rivera clutch sealed hub nut. This sealed nut, which is a reverse-threaded nut like the stock tranny one, prevents transmission oil from leaking out of the mainshaft. Torque this nut to 70–80 ft-lb using a 30-mm socket. Then check the belt's tension, which should be 3/4 to 1 inch total up-and-down movement when the primary system is cold.

With the clutch plates already in the clutch assembly (if they are not, install them as per Project 68), install the pressure plate (with the "out" side facing, you guessed it, out), followed by the Rivera diaphragm spring. The spring retainer (beveled side in, out side out), two lock rings, and four shoulder nuts go on next. Snug the four nuts down with a 5/8-inch socket until they bottom out, then bend over the tabs on the lock rings with a pliers. Install the clutch adjusting screw and locknut. Adjust the clutch as

per the H-D service manual using a 17-mm Allen and then tighten the locknut with an 11/16-inch wrench. Then adjust the clutch cable, as per the H-D service manual, with 1/2- and 9/16-inch open end wrenches.

You now can install the primary cover to check clearance between the bottom of the primary cover and starter ring on the Rivera clutch basket. If needed, grind away some material, but don't get carried away. Just remove enough to get 0.060-inch clearance. You can then install the primary cover with a new gasket, using a 3/16-inch Allen. Remember that you no longer add oil to the primary.

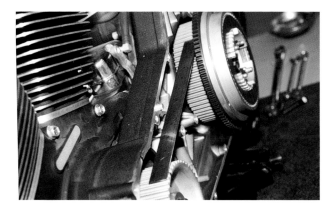

With the clutch shell on the tranny shaft—minus the belt—and the shell's nut snugged down, check pulley alignment by laying a straightedge between the pulley and clutch shell.

Reinstall the belt, clutch shell, and pulley as a unit, aligning the mark on the pulley with the one you made on the inner primary.

After modifying the primary bearing and slipping a shim onto the sprocket shaft, make a mark on the primary cover and pulley. Then install the pulley nut and snug it down.

Then slip the supplied ring onto the front pulley.

After putting a little blue Loctite onto the engine shaft's threads, install the supplied washer and 1 1/2-inch engine nut and torque nut to 150–165 ft-lb.

The diaphragm spring goes on next.

After putting some blue Loctite onto the mainshaft's threads, install the Rivera sealed clutch hub nut. This reverse threaded nut gets torqued to 70–80 ft-lb using a 30-mm socket.

The spring retainer (beveled side in), two lock rings, and four shoulder nuts can then go on. Snug the four nuts down until they bottom out, then bend over all the lock ring tabs.

Seeing the clutch plates are already in the clutch assembly (if they are not, install them as per Project 68), install the pressure plate with the side marked OUT facing out.

Install the clutch adjusting screw and locknut. Then adjust the clutch as per the manual using a 17-mm Allen and tighten the locknut with an 11/16-inch wrench.

PROJECT 73
Installing a Transmission Pulley

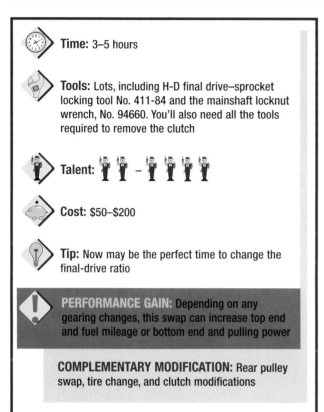

Time: 3–5 hours

Tools: Lots, including H-D final drive–sprocket locking tool No. 411-84 and the mainshaft locknut wrench, No. 94660. You'll also need all the tools required to remove the clutch

Talent:

Cost: $50–$200

Tip: Now may be the perfect time to change the final-drive ratio

PERFORMANCE GAIN: Depending on any gearing changes, this swap can increase top end and fuel mileage or bottom end and pulling power

COMPLEMENTARY MODIFICATION: Rear pulley swap, tire change, and clutch modifications

Replacing the transmission pulley is one of those "dirty dishes" jobs. It ain't fun, and it ain't interesting. But it has to be done once in a while for one reason or another.

There are only two reasons to replace the front pulley or, more technically, the transmission sprocket. The first would of course be for maintenance.

Once upon a time Harley front pulleys had a less than sterling reputation. The factory responded by upgrading them and the problem, as it was, was history. That doesn't mean they don't wear out, they do, although not at the previous rate. So how do you know if the transmission sprocket is worn out? Especially since you can't see the darn thing without pulling the primary case off the bike? Good question. The first rule of thumb is that if the rear pulley is shot, the front one ain't far behind. The second is that anytime the transmission sprocket is exposed for any reason, be it for belt replacement, a clutch overhaul, or whatever, take a good long look at the pulley. Check the teeth for cracks and examine the tooth profile. If anything looks less than prefect, replace the pulley. If you're in doubt as to what constitutes a worn pulley, the factory service manual has a nice little chart that details both belt and pulley problems.

The second reason to replace the front pulley would be to change the gearing. (As of this writing alternate front pulleys were only available aftermarket.) Now, for some strange reason, replacing the front pulley because you want to, as opposed to replacing the front pulley because it's worn out and you have to, seems to make the job more palatable. It's still a pain-in-the-butt job, but somehow it does seem to be more fun.

Gearing Theory 101
A one-tooth change at the front pulley is approximately the same as changing three teeth at the rear pulley. That's a decent-sized change, and one that may alter the final drive ratio more than you'd like. Carefully think this change through before making any decisions. By dropping a tooth on the front pulley, the bike will accelerate harder; however, the top speed will normally be lowered, and the engine will turn more rpm for a given gear. Conversely, if we add a tooth, acceleration will become more leisurely; however, top speed will increase, and the engine will turn fewer rpm for a given speed. What would you rather do, tour or race?

Removing the Guesswork
Because changing the front sprocket is such a headache, I figured you'd like to know an easy way to calculate any changes beforehand. This method works for any sprocket change, front or rear, by the way. Let's suppose you'd like a bit more acceleration and are willing to sacrifice a bit of top speed to get it. We'll further assume, just to make things convenient, that you're riding an FLHT, Electra Glide Standard, and that the top speed is 100 miles per hour. The stock sprocket for the FLT range is 32 teeth. You think that dropping a tooth might provide you with what you need, but you don't want to kill the top end entirely.

What we first need to know is the difference between the two sprockets expressed as proportion. The formula 31 divided by 32 equals .96875, and because there are other factors involved, wind resistance and how much weight the bike is carrying to name just two that affect top speed, we don't need to work to nth decimal point so we can round the number to .9687. Multiply that number times the current top speed: .9687 x 100 = 96.87 miles per hour. With the gearing change, your new top speed is going to be roughly 97 miles per hour, which is fast enough for any Dresser in most people's book.

Now let's pretend we want to raise the top end, and sacrifice a bit of acceleration by going the other way with our gearing. This time the math is 32 divided by 31 equals

1.0322; 1.0322 x 96.87 = 99.98, or just about 100 miles per hour, in my book.

Gearing in the Real World, Some Rules That Work

Gearing isn't the exact science you'd suppose it to be because there are just too many variables, so what we try to do is find a compromise that works the best over a wide range of situations.

While lowering the gearing generally cuts top speed and increases acceleration there are times when a lower gear will increase top speed. For example: there are instances when the overall gearing is so high that the engine simply falls off the torque curve long before it reaches the rev limiter or even the redline. In those cases you're simply droning along in top gear, with the throttle pined wide open while the bike speed remains unchanged or may even start to drop! In those cases, you may be better off to lower the gearing slightly by either dropping a tooth off the transmission pulley or by adding a few teeth to the rear pulley. This will allow the engine to rev a bit higher, and pull a bit stronger. If it can now pull redline in top gear the speed may actually increase slightly compared to the previous taller gearing.

The Nuts and Bolts of It

As I've mentioned several times changing the tranny sprocket is time consuming and something I'd only do if I had to remove the primary cover's contents for some other reason. Here's what you face should you decide or be forced to replace the pulley. The first item of business is to remove the primary and everything in it, including the clutch, the compensating sprocket.

Once that stuff is out of the way you can lock the sprocket using the factory locking tool H-D No. 41184 or the aftermarket equivalent. I'd also strongly recommend using the factory socket wrench and its pilot (H-D No. 94660-37B) to remove and reinstall the sprocket nut. Replace the sprocket and its hardware according to the manual. After the nut has been torqued to a setting of 50 foot-pounds, scribe a mark on the nut that continues onto the sprocket itself. Then rotate the nut an additional 30 to 40 degrees. Here's a tip: each spline on the shaft is approximately 11 degrees apart, so three splines, equals 33 degrees. Complete reassembly per your manual; realistically, this job is going to take the better part of a day, and it's going to require the use of some special tools.

It takes a lot of wrenching just to get to the pulley.

You'll need the factory tool or its equivalent to remove the nut. (JIMS shown here).

Don't forget to reinstall the lock tab. A dab of Loctite on the securing bolts won't hurt either!

Replacing the Drive Belt

 Time: Allow yourself a full day

 Tools: Common hand tools, plus tools required to remove and install the primary drive (see Project 73 for a complete list)

 Talent:

 Cost: Price of a belt averages about $210

 Tip: Now is the time to consider any driveline repairs or upgrades

 PERFORMANCE GAIN: This is generally a maintenance issue. Obviously, a worn or damaged belt is both unsafe and unreliable

COMPLEMENTARY MODIFICATION:
Gearing change

Replacing a worn or damaged drive belt is another one of those dirty dishes chores. There is no way to sugarcoat it. Replacing the final drive belt is a big pain in the butt. You'll need to remove the primary drive, as well as several of the frame parts on the left side of the motorcycle before you can remove the old belt. The manual goes into great detail as far as replacing the belt, therefore, I'll only discuss in general the belt replacement process.

Obviously, the number one reason you'll be replacing the belt is because it's either worn out or damaged. If so, take a very good look at the sprockets. It's even money that if the belt is worn out so are the sprockets. By the same token a stone or other foreign object that may damage the belt can tear up the pulleys just as easily.

Actually, given the magnitude of the job, I'd be tempted to bite the bullet and replace the pulleys and belt as a unit, rather than do the job twice.

Belt Inspection

Start by checking the edge of the belt for cuts, tears, or odd wear patterns. Pay attention to the outer edge of the belt; typically you'll find some beveling there. In and of itself, this isn't a serious problem although it does indicate some sprocket misalignment. Inspect the outside of the belt for stone punctures. These can be difficult to spot so look carefully. Take a good look at the inside of the belt. When the belt is new, a layer of nylon facing and polyethylene covers the tensile or structural cords. Once the facing wears away the only thing holding the belt together are the tensile cords. If the tensile cords are visible, the belt is worn out, and chances are excellent that the pulleys also are kaput. At this point the belt is in serious danger of wearing through. When the belts are new, the thin polyethylene coating is very obvious; however, it can quickly wear off as it is burnished into the belt. This is a normal situation and alone does not indicate belt wear.

Lastly check the belt teeth for damage, particularly for cracks at the base of teeth. The H-D service manual incorporates a very good chart that details belt problems and their solutions as well as common sprocket problems. Use it as a guide before rushing out to buy a new belt.

A picture is worth a thousand words, and in a word this belt is shot.

THE DRIVETRAIN

Swapping to a Custom Sprocket (Pulley)

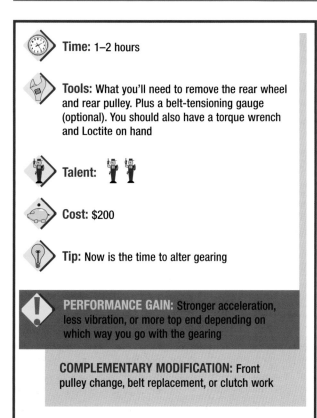

Time: 1–2 hours

Tools: What you'll need to remove the rear wheel and rear pulley. Plus a belt-tensioning gauge (optional). You should also have a torque wrench and Loctite on hand

Talent: 👷👷

Cost: $200

Tip: Now is the time to alter gearing

PERFORMANCE GAIN: Stronger acceleration, less vibration, or more top end depending on which way you go with the gearing

COMPLEMENTARY MODIFICATION: Front pulley change, belt replacement, or clutch work

As detailed in Project 73, gearing changes can be accomplished by changing both the front and rear pulleys but only the front or only the rear. When changing the rear sprocket, increasing the number of teeth will increase acceleration, but decrease top speed and fuel mileage. Decreasing the number of teeth will increase top speed and fuel mileage but decrease acceleration.

The nuts and bolts of swapping out the rear pulley are as straightforward as it gets, particularly if you decide that the only change you want to make is cosmetic. Unfortunately if you decide to alter the gearing by changing only the rear pulley you're going to be relatively limited in your choice of sprockets unless you decide that a belt change isn't going to be a problem. Depending on the model you may be able to fit a smaller rear pulley, and keep the stock belt by pulling the wheel all the way rearward with the adjusters. Of course this may complicate the fitting of the belt guards but that can be dealt with at the time.

If you opt to fit a larger pulley, then you may or may not be able to use the same belt depending on how many

teeth the new pulley has. I'd say as a rule of thumb, a two-tooth increase will work with the stock belt; any more than that and you'll be looking for a longer belt.

This brings us, in a roundabout way, back to square one. If you're going to be installing a new belt anyway, you may as well install a new tranny pulley, etc. I trust you see where I'm going with this, right? Unless you plan on making only a relatively minor gearing change, either up or down, the smart money is to pick a gear ratio that you think will work, and install the appropriate parts and belt as required. This will allow you to seek a balance between the two sprocket sizes and the correct belt length that won't leave the belt adjustment at either extreme (too far forward or rearward).

As a final note, be advised that swapping to a different-sized rear sprocket and belt may well mean that you'll need to swap belt guards and fasteners. Make certain you double and triple check all clearances before and after the guards are installed. It's infinitely better to find out that you have a clearance problem while the bike is still on the bench, than it is to shred the belt before you're out of the driveway.

If you're going to swap the rear pulley, you might as well go all out and opt for a bit of shine as well.

PROJECT 76
Installing a Rear Drive Chain

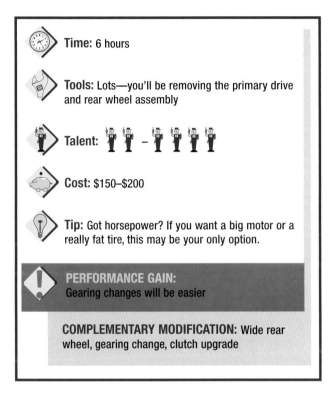

Time: 6 hours

Tools: Lots—you'll be removing the primary drive and rear wheel assembly

Talent: ▮▮ – ▮▮▮

Cost: $150–$200

Tip: Got horsepower? If you want a big motor or a really fat tire, this may be your only option.

PERFORMANCE GAIN:
Gearing changes will be easier

COMPLEMENTARY MODIFICATION: Wide rear wheel, gearing change, clutch upgrade

This is actually more of a Why would I want to do this? than a how to.

Belt final drives have a lot going for them. They are quiet, require little maintenance, and are clean. All good things for relatively mildly tuned cruisers or touring bikes and as Buell fans will be quick to note, belts aren't an altogether bad thing for a sport-bike either.

But there are two flies in the ointment so to speak. First and foremost if you're running a big, high-horsepower street monster of a mill the stock belt may not be able to adequately handle all of the juice your hot rod is pumping out. In that case a super-duty chain may be the only way to get the ponies to the pavement. In conjunction is another performance issue—belt drives make gearing changes somewhat problematic. As pointed out in previous sections the fixed length of the belt means you only have so much leeway when it comes to pulley changes. Change anything more than a few teeth and chances are good that you'll be changing the belt as well. To add fuel to the fire, changing the belt is a pretty involved project, and at best will take you 3 to 4 hours to accomplish.

The other problem is that the width of the belt may preclude fitting a really wide rear tire, if you are so inclined, without making some serious driveline adjustments or installing a thinner belt kit.

There is a solution, of course (isn't there always?).

Why not take a retrograde step and install a good old-fashioned chain drive? For some riders chain drives make a lot of sense. Properly sized chains and sprockets are capable of transmitting huge amounts of horsepower; furthermore, gearing changes become considerably simpler because they can be made by swapping only the rear sprocket, if needed, one tooth at a time. If you get to the point where the range of adjustment no longer covers the chain length, it's a simple matter to thread a new, shorter or longer chain over the sprockets and just like that you're back in business.

Last but by no means least, a chain final drive is a whole lot narrower than a belt, which gives you lots of room to fit that oversized rear wheel and 200 series tire you've been daydreaming about.

On the downside, chains do demand a lot more attention than a belt. Even the best O- or X-ring sealed chains need some periodic lubrication. Even if it's nothing more than a shot or two of WD-40 to prevent the O-rings from drying out. How periodic? Good question but, depending on riding conditions, that could be as often as every 600 miles; if you're a real hard-core touring junkie that could mean a spray every third gas stop! Chains also have a tendency to throw off some lube while they're running. Modern chain waxes are much cleaner and adhere to the links much better than in the bad old days. But some excess will find its way to the rear wheel and chain guards. If this is going to be a problem you may want to rethink your plans. Finally chains tend to make a bit more noise than a belt and of course they require much more frequent adjustment. Bottom line—if transferring big horsepower to the tarmac, rapid gearing changes, and/or a big fat rear weenie are more important to you than an increased maintenance schedule, you might want to consider replacing that rubber band with a strip of steel.

The Nitty and Gritty

Once you've decided that a chain and sprocket set up is the way to go, the rest is fairly easy. Many of the aftermarket companies offer conversion kits. Offset tranny sprockets are available from Baker, CCI, Bikers Choice, and others. These conversions replace the stock tranny pulley and give the chain the correct offset and clearance. The rear pulley is replaced with a sprocket from a 1973 through 1985 four-speed model. The sprockets are installed as you would any pulley; your shop manual will, as always, provide the details. The tricky part for most will be in adjusting the chain so that it runs true and has the proper slack.

THE DRIVETRAIN

201

With the weight of the rider on the bike, the chain should be adjusted to provide from 3/4 to 1 1/2 inches of slack at the midpoint of its run. If you primarily ride two up, have your passenger sit on the bike or allow a bit of extra slack. With the final adjustment made, spin the rear wheel a time or three; if the chain is running true the rollers will appear to be centered on the sprocket teeth. If the chain is offset to one side of the sprocket use the adjuster(s) to center the chain, and then recheck your slack adjustment. Check the chain tension every 600 to 1,000 miles and adjust whenever the slack is double the initial setting.

PROJECT 77
Installing a Custom Tranny Side Cover

 Time: 30 minutes

 Tools: 9/16-inch wrench, snap ring pliers, 3/16-inch Allen

 Talent:

 Cost: $200–500

 Parts: Transmission side cover, side cover gasket, tranny oil, new retaining ring, some light grease, clutch cable O-ring

 Tip: This is a good time to install a new clutch cable or upgrade to a stainless-steel braided one

 PERFORMANCE GAIN: A sharper-looking right side of the transmission

COMPLEMENTARY MODIFICATION: Don't just spiff up the tranny side cover; do the cam cover, too; Project 52 shows you how

In Project 52, I talk about how Twin Cam owners have an easier job than Evo owners when it comes to swapping out the engine's cam cover. Well, when it comes to doing the transmission clutch release (side) cover, they both have the same amount of work to do. That's because the tranny's side cover is the same for all 1987 to present (2004) Big Twins. Because I installed a Pro-One cam cover for Project 52, I'm going to put its mate, a Pro-One–chrome, billet-aluminum transmission side cover, onto the same Twin Cam bike.

My starting point for this installation has the stock cover off the transmission and the clutch release mechanism removed and ready for installation in the new Pro-One billet cover. Begin by putting the pushrod end into the mainshaft, if it's not already there. (The pushrod should already be inside the hollow bore of the mainshaft.)

After putting a new O-ring onto the clutch cable, attach the cable to the side cover using a 9/16-inch wrench. Then install the outer ramp of the release mechanism into the side cover. Put the release mechanism's three

balls onto the outer ramp. (Use some light grease to hold them in place.) The coupling can then go onto the cable and get attached to the inner ramp of the release mechanism. After you position the inner ramp over the outer ramp, install the retaining ring using the proper ring pliers.

You can now install the side cover onto the tranny using the supplied Allen bolts, a new gasket, and a 3/16-inch Allen. When finished, add the proper grade and amount of tranny oil for your model and year bike, and install the dip stick. As you can see, the side cover looks great, especially when combined with a matching cam cover.

Begin the install by putting the push rod end into the mainshaft, if it's not already there. The push rod itself should already be inside the hollow bore of the mainshaft.

After attaching the clutch cable to the side cover, install the outer ramp of the clutch release into the cover. Put the release's three balls onto the outer ramp. (Use some light grease to hold them in place.)

THE DRIVETRAIN

203

The coupling can then go onto the end of the cable. Then attach the coupling to the inner ramp of the release mechanism.

After positioning the inner ramp over the outer ramp, install the retaining ring using the proper ring pliers.

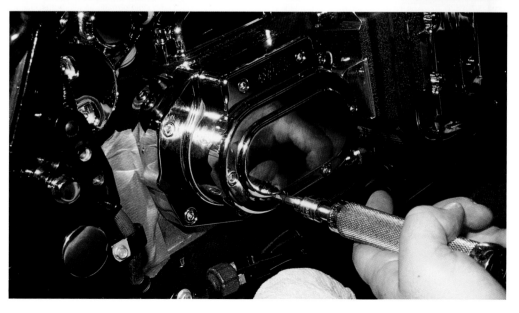

Install the side cover onto the tranny using the supplied Allen bolts, a new gasket, and a 3/16-inch Allen. Then add the proper grade and amount of tranny oil for your model and year bike, and install the dipstick.

PROJECT 78

Installing a BAKER Reverse Shifter Assembly

 Time: 2–3 hours

 Tools: Retaining ring pliers, 7/16-inch socket (Softails do not need this tool), 3/16-inch Allen, 1/4-inch Allen, ratchet, inch-pound torque wrench, flat feeler gauge, blue Loctite

 Talent:

 Cost: $500

 Parts: BAKER reverse-pattern five-speed shift kit (#R171-5), BAKER billet-steel fork kit for five-speeds (#167-5), transmission oil, tranny gasket kit, shifter pawl retaining ring

 Tip: When installing the new shifter drum, do not force it into place. If it doesn't lie flush on top of the case, one (or more) of the shifter fork pins is not aligned with its groove in the drum

 PERFORMANCE GAIN: The reverse shifter pattern will allow you to shift faster when racing, while the BAKER shifter pawl and drum assembly will give you easier, smoother shifts

COMPLEMENTARY MODIFICATION: Since you have to remove the tranny's gear set to change the shifter pawl, you may want to do this upgrade when installing a six-speed gear set. If so, BAKER also offers a reverse shifter for its six-speeds.

If you've ever ridden an Evo, you know how much smoother and easier it is to change gears and find neutral on a Twin Cam. That's due to the biggest difference between an Evo five-speed and a Twin Cam's, besides the configuration of the case: the shifter assembly. The TC's shifter mechanism is a major improvement over the Evo Big Twin version. In fact, present TC 88s and 88Bs require only half the effort needed for gear swapping compared to an Evo.

However, not all Twin Cams have this better system. When H-D was first testing its counterbalanced Twin Cam 88B, which was launched after the rubber-mounted version,

the engineers found that their standard Harley tranny wasn't shifting well. Further investigation identified the cause as the lack of vibration put out by the counterbalanced 88B. It seems the earlier H-D shifter assembly needs the vibration that a standard Harley engine puts out to work properly. The fix, which is incorporated on all TC Softails from Day One (2000 and later) and all 2000 and later FLTs and Dynas, was to redesign the shifter assembly so it would perform better than the old version, even without vibration.

To do that, H-D went to a hollow (low inertia) shifter drum that rotates on ball bearings to significantly reduce friction. This low inertia drum has less mass than the Evo unit, so it doesn't have a tendency to move beyond where the self-centering shift linkage and roller detent mechanism puts it. This drum also has better track profiles than earlier versions due to changes in the grooves in the outer face of the drum, which allow for easier shifting between gears. The biggest track profile modification is wider grooves where the actual gear change takes place. The neutral switch was even changed to get smoother shifts; it no longer rides on the outside of the drum. This modification reduces the friction between the switch and drum.

Another upgrade is the star-shaped cam on the end of the drum, which allows the roller detent spring to complete the second half of the shift. This greatly reduces false neutrals and missed shifts, even if the operator doesn't follow all the way through on a shift. A roller detent follower is also incorporated for easier-to-find neutrals, as well as upshift/downshift stops to control shifter drum over-rotations, which also helps to prevent false neutrals and missed shifts.

Lastly, unlike on the Evo and earlier Big Twin versions, there are hard stops after first and fifth gear. This is due to the Twin Cam shifter drum having five shift pins instead of four. On earlier shifter versions, the ratchet pawl grabs air after it's put into fifth or first gear. However, on a Twin Cam it grabs a pin.

But as good as all these improvements are, you still have to lift up on the shifter lever to run the transmission through the gears (one down, four up). This is not a problem if you just use your bike for cruising. However, if you're into performance, as in ripping through the gears every once in a while, the best and fastest way to shift is by hitting the lever down (one up, four down), especially if you've got forward controls on the bike.

That's why Bert Baker of BAKER Drivetrain has come out with a reverse shifter assembly for Twin Cams. BAKER's reverse-pattern drum kit comes with a low inertia drum for less shift effort and pillow blocks machined out of 6061-T6 aluminum extrusion stock, which results in a significantly stronger block. Also included in the BAKER kit is Bert's torsion spring-loaded roller detent shift system, which gives the rider even smoother and easier gear changes, as well as an easier-to-find neutral. Even the shifter fork pin grooves have been redesigned for smoother shifts.

For this install, I also decided to show you how to install a BAKER shift fork kit, which includes three hard-chrome plated, billet-steel forks that have, among other improvements, a cross-section that's three times thicker than the stockers.

If you are going to install this setup into a bike with a heavily worked engine, you may also want to install a BAKER inner bearing race, which goes onto the main shaft outboard of the pulley, for the inner primary bearing to ride on. This race will stand up to high horsepower and torque better then the stock race will.

Our starting point for this installation has the stock shifter assembly, gear set, and shifter pawl assembly removed from the tranny. You do not, however, have to remove the drive gear from the tranny. The first step is to install the BAKER shifter pawl assembly, which comes fully assembled and just slips right into the stock spot. Using a retaining (snap) ring pliers, install a new retaining ring, which goes on the outside of the case, to hold the pawl in place. You can now reinstall the stock gear set into the case, using a new gasket. You'll need a 7/16-inch socket, and a 3/16- and 1/4-inch Allen (Softails do not need the socket). Torque the 7/16-inch socket and 3/16-inch Allen hardware to 120 inch-pounds and the 1/4-inch Allen to 18 foot-pounds.

The BAKER 2M shifter fork can then go onto the mainshaft's second gear as shown. Ditto for the BAKER 3C fork, which goes onto the countershaft's third gear. The BAKER 1M fork, which is the last one, goes onto the mainshaft's first gear. All the forks should have their pins, which are the studs that engage the shifter drum, facing up and flat. The stock shifter shaft can then go in from the door side of the case, through the door. There's no clip to hold it in place because the end cover takes care of that, as well as a plug on the left side, which we did not have to touch.

With the forks in place, lift the arm of the shifter pawl out of the way and install the shifter drum onto the case. You'll have to get the fork pins to line up with their grooves in the drum to get the drum to sit flush on the case. Finesse it in and do not force it.

Then torque the four stock Allen bolts to 120 inch-pounds using a 3/16-inch Allen. The next step is to measure the gap between the drum's pillow block and washer using a flat feeler gauge. You should have a 0.004–0.008-inch gap. If the gap is not within spec, remove the drum and change the washer to the correct thickness, and then reinstall the drum with blue Loctite on the bolts.

Once this setting—which is the only one you have to do—is correct, finish the job by slipping a new gasket on the case and reinstalling the stock top cover using the stock bolts on which blue Loctite has been added to the threads. These bolts get torqued to 120 inch-pounds using a 3/16-inch Allen. After you do the same for the end cover, add the correct amount of tranny oil.

Our starting point has the stock shifter assembly, gearset, and shifter pawl assembly removed from the tranny. However, you do not have to remove the drive gear from the tranny, which, as you can see, is still installed.

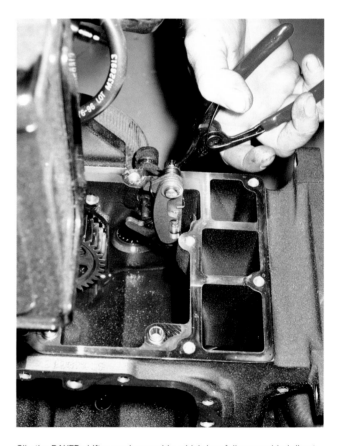

Slip the BAKER shifter pawl assembly, which is a fully assembled direct replacement for the stock unit, into the stock location. Use a new retaining ring, which goes on the outside of the case, to hold the pawl in place.

After you reinstall the stock gearset into the case, using a new gasket, slip the BAKER 2M shifter fork onto the mainshaft's second gear as shown.

Lift the arm of the shifter pawl out of the way and install the shifter drum onto the case. You'll also have to get the fork pins to line up with their grooves in the drum. Torque the drum's bolts to 120 in-lbs.

The BAKER 3C shifter fork can then go onto the countershaft's third gear. Even though the forks are on different shafts, the end of both forks should be even and at the same height.

Using a flat feeler gauge, measure the gap between the drum's pillow block and washer. If you don't have a 0.004–0.008-inch gap, remove the drum, change the washer with one that's the correct thickness, and reinstall the drum.

Once the BAKER 1M fork is on the mainshaft's first gear, check that all the forks have their pins, which engage the shifter drum, facing up and flat as you see here. The stock shifter shaft can then go in from the right.

With a new gasket on the case, reinstall the stock top cover using the stock bolts, with some blue Loctite on the threads, and torque them to 120 in-lb using a 3/16-inch Allen. Then do the same for the end cover.

Installing a Six-Speed Gear Set Kit

 Time: 3–4 hours

 Tools: JIMS main-drive gear puller and installer #353316-80, a grinder, T-50 Torx drive, flat feeler gauge, 1/4- and 3/16-inch Allen, narrow flat-faced tool, and blue Loctite

 Talent:

 Cost: $2,500–3,000

 Parts: Six-speed gear set kit, tranny gasket kit (if not included)

 Tip: Change your bike's gearing, so the lower five give you some serious off-the-line grunt, 'cause you'll still have lots of top end when you shift into the overdrive sixth gear

 PERFORMANCE GAIN:
Lower rpm on the highway

COMPLEMENTARY MODIFICATION: Now's the time to install a custom end/clutch cover, as per Project 77

Tips and Tricks

You must check a few spots on the transmission case for clearance, though a stock case is usually fine as is.

When slipping the gear set into the case you may have to move the countershaft a little so it slips into its case bearing. Put a little blue Loctite on the threads of the BAKER-supplied trapdoor bolts and be sure to sequentially tighten them. Trying to crank one bolt all the way down without walking the trapdoor down by using all the bolts will damage the trapdoor and transmission case. Once the gear set is in the case, spray lots of assembly lube all over the gears and shafts.

Before you close up the top of the transmission, be sure to check that the tranny shifts correctly. Do this by slipping on the shifter arm and spinning the main shaft as you shift up and down through the gears a few times.

Above, left: The first step is to pull the BAKER main drive gear into the case/main bearing using a JIMS#353316-80 main drive gear puller and installer.

Above, right: The next step is to remove and alter the stock shifter pawl, so it will work with our BAKER shifter components. All that's needed is for this tab (arrow) to be removed with a grinder.

If you're the open-highway type, a six-speed tranny may be just the ticket for your Twin Cam. These godsends to high-speed cruising allow you to gear your bike for great around-town riding in the lower five gears, and yet have plenty of low-rpm, top end when you drop the shifter into sixth. That's because a six-speed gearbox has a true over-drive gear for sixth. Bert Baker and his wife Lisa were transmission engineers for General Motors when they set about adding the much desired overdrive sixth gear to an Evo Softail using their aftermarket creation and the rest, as the old saw goes, is history.

There are other manufacturers of six-speed boxes out there now, but I decided to go with the original. I start the install with the stock gear set, trapdoor and all, and shifter assembly removed from the case. The accompanying pho-tos show you the steps needed to make this swap into the stock tranny case. (Note: You'll have to change the shifter assembly regardless of what six-speed gear set you use, because you'll soon have an extra gear to move around.)

After installing a new seal, reinstall the now-altered shifter pawl into the case, followed by the outside washer and retainer clip.

The shift pawl alignment pin then goes in with a little blue Loctite on the threads using a T50 Torx drive.

With a new gasket on the case and a lot of lube on both shafts, slip the gearset into the case and bolt it up using the BAKER-supplied bolts and a 3/16-inch and 1/4-inch Allen wrench. Then make sure both shafts turn easily

Next, install the pillow block with the detent mechanism on it, onto the shifter drum as shown. You'll have to lift up on the detent arm to get it to go onto the drum.

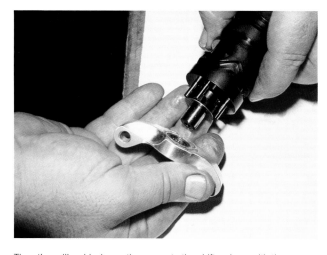

The other pillow block can then go onto the shifter drum with the smallest shim supplied, so you can check the endplay.

The assembled shifter drum assembly can then get bolted onto the case using the BAKER-supplied bolts. You'll have to lift up on the shifter pawl arm to get it to sit in place correctly.

Check the shifter drum endplay with a flat feeler gauge. The desired endplay is 0.005-inch but the range is 0.002–0.010-inch.

Disassemble the shifter drum and install the needed shim—a variety of shims are supplied with the BAKER tranny kit—onto the end of the drum. Then recheck the endplay.

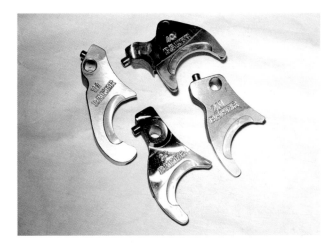

All four shifter forks are different shapes and are clearly marked as to what one they are. Remove the shifter drum again, so you can install the shifter forks onto their gears.

Here are all the shifter forks, properly orientated on their gears. They are the 1 M fork (A), 2 M fork (B), 3 C fork (C), and 4 C fork (D), which is the one for sixth gear.

The shifter fork shaft for forks 1M, 2M, and 3C goes in next. It just pushes in through the trapdoor and is later held in place by the end cover.

After removing the plug in the trapdoor, the shaft for the 4C fork can be pushed into place. Then reinstall the plug, with a little blue Loctite on the threads, using a 1/4-inch Allen.

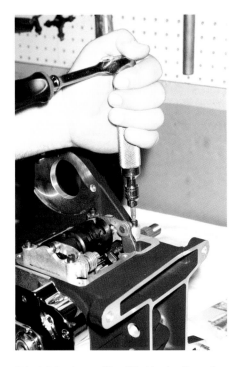

Reinstall the drum, with a little blue Loctite on the bolt threads, using a 3/16-inch Allen. (You'll have to move the forks around, so they'll fit into their grooves in the drum.)

After putting some lube onto the outer and inner edges of the main gear seal, press the seal into the case with your fingers. (No silicone, please!)

The quad seal then goes over the main gear and fits into the gap between the inner race of the bearing and the main gear. Use a narrow flat-faced tool to push it into place.

The pulley spacer then goes over the main gear and into the seal.

BAKER also supplies a new oil filler, which is needed to clear the wider trapdoor. Bolt it up, with the supplied gaskets and spacer block, using a 3/16-inch Allen. Then install the other covers.

SECTION NINE

The Electrical System

PROJECT 80

Installing Aftermarket Digital Gauges

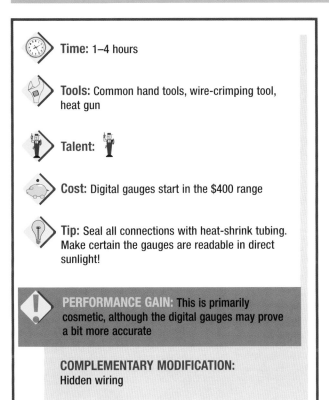

🕐 **Time:** 1–4 hours

🔧 **Tools:** Common hand tools, wire-crimping tool, heat gun

🧍 **Talent:** 🧍

🐭 **Cost:** Digital gauges start in the $400 range

💡 **Tip:** Seal all connections with heat-shrink tubing. Make certain the gauges are readable in direct sunlight!

❗ **PERFORMANCE GAIN:** This is primarily cosmetic, although the digital gauges may prove a bit more accurate

COMPLEMENTARY MODIFICATION:
Hidden wiring

In all honesty, being somewhat of a traditionalist I'm not a big fan of digital gauges. It's not that they don't work, they do; in fact for the most part, they work extremely well. Now that I've made my prejudices known we can move on.

In most cases, digital gauges will be used either to supplement the existing gauges or in a custom situation to replace the stock gauges. You'll need to consider the following criteria when selecting the gauges. Obviously, suitability is the first consideration: make certain that the gauge you select is rated for motorcycle use. Vibration and exposure to the elements will make short work of a gauge not designed to stand up to them. Of course any direct application digital gauge should be more than up to the task, but you might want to think twice before you hang an automotive-style digital gauge on your bike. If there is any doubt as to the gauge's suitability, check with the manufacturer.

Of course styling is a subjective consideration and as such isn't really worthy of comment. If you're building a custom and have determined that a digital speedometer hung from the handlebars is what you want, then by all means, that's what you should have.

A final consideration is the mounting location. Obviously, you don't want the bracket to hit anything as the handlebars turn, but less obvious, perhaps, is the ability to read the guage clearly. If the bracket is too low, too high, or too out of the way, it may be difficult to see the instrument without taking your eyes off the road. An action that may have dire consequences given the right (or wrong) circumstances.

Once you decide which gauge is right for your application the rest is pretty straightforward. Follow the gauge manufacturer's instructions for mounting installation. Once the gauge is in place you'll just have to connect the wires.

Here you'll need the manufacturer's instructions and most likely the factory shop manual. While some gauges may be direct plug-ins, others at some point will need to be spliced into the harness.

Therein lies the tricky part. Make certain that you follow the manufacturer's wiring directions to a "T." Just as important, make absolutely certain that all of the wiring is done in a workmanlike and professional manner. That means no twisted connections wrapped up in a yard of electrical tape and no ground wires that are just stripped and twisted and then stuck under the head of a bolt. It does mean that all joints should be either properly crimped or soldered and that they should be protected with heat-shrink tubing or tape. Ground connections should be properly spliced or a ring terminal properly fastened to the wire and then secured to a known good ground.

The bottom line here is this: being primarily an electrical device, a digital gauge is really only as a good as the wiring that connects it to the rest of the bike.

Remove the speedometer housing and unplug the stock wiring.

Remove the speedometer unit from the housing

Install the new speedometer.

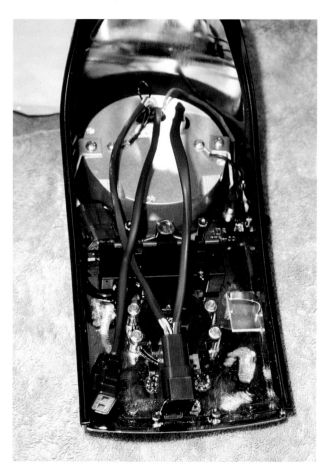

Route the new wiring harness as neatly as possible

Not too shabby. This Dakota Digital gauge also incorporates a tachometer.

Choosing High-Performance Ignition Wires

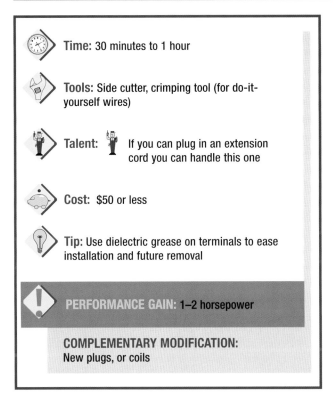

Time: 30 minutes to 1 hour

Tools: Side cutter, crimping tool (for do-it-yourself wires)

Talent: If you can plug in an extension cord you can handle this one

Cost: $50 or less

Tip: Use dielectric grease on terminals to ease installation and future removal

PERFORMANCE GAIN: 1–2 horsepower

COMPLEMENTARY MODIFICATION:
New plugs, or coils

I'll cut right to the chase. The factory-supplied spark plug wires are like every other OEM component on your Harley. When new and in decent condition, they are more than up to their assigned task. However, as with any other component, time and hard use do take their toll. By the same token modifications to the engine very often require modifications to the ignition system. In my book it makes little sense to build yourself a high-compression mill, endow it with a super zapper of an ignition system and then try and fire the thing through a set of wires that are based on 1960 technology.

Bear in mind that simply replacing the stock wires with something from a box labeled "High Performance" won't unleash scads of horsepower. If your stock wires are shot or simply not up to the job, then installing the new wires will either get your horsepower back to where it should be, or at most, provide a very slight increase. By the same token, if your ignition system is lying down on the job in other respects, then replacing the wires probably won't do much to help.

As I've said, new wires in and by themselves won't automatically send the dyno charts off the scale. But here's the thing: the quality of the spark at the plug tip has a direct result on engine power; weak sparks equal soggy motors. The quality of the spark plug wire has a direct

result on the quality of the spark. The less energy it takes to push current through the spark plug wire, the more there is to fire the plug. Ipso facto, good wires equal hot sparks which equal stronger engines, easier starting, and better all-around performance. Choose the right spark plug wires, and it's a win-win combination.

The question is how do you know which ones are the right ones? That's a question that is extremely difficult to answer, in part because in my opinion, the very best wire would be a solid copper cored wire. The only thing wrong with using that type of wire is that it causes radio interference. But the problem is a little deeper than merely screwing up TV or radio reception. Using a non-resistor wire can bollix the ignition-system black box, and in some cases cause some serious problems. So for that reason I'd recommend sticking only with tried and tested aftermarket wires. Without recommending a specific wire, I will say that the most reputable companies are the ones that have been around for a while and are willing to back up their performance claims with hard facts, dyno charts, and solid street credibility. Of course, you can always just choose a wire because it comes in a cool color.

Two simple rules for wire installation and removal:

More wires have been damaged by improper removal techniques than anything else. Do not yank on the wire to remove it from the plug. Grab the plug cap and use a twisting movement to remove it from the spark plug.

Before you install the plug cap smear a little dielectric grease on it. This will make the installation go much easier and make future removal less of a chore. A dab of grease at the coil end isn't a bad idea either.

The choice is almost endless. My advice: Choose a name brand with a proven reputation.

THE ELECTRICAL SYSTEM

Installing a High-Performance Starter

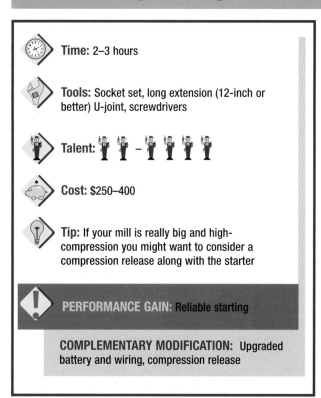

Time: 2–3 hours

Tools: Socket set, long extension (12-inch or better) U-joint, screwdrivers

Talent:

Cost: $250–400

Tip: If your mill is really big and high-compression you might want to consider a compression release along with the starter

PERFORMANCE GAIN: Reliable starting

COMPLEMENTARY MODIFICATION: Upgraded battery and wiring, compression release

Since the introduction of the seminal Electra Glide, the Motor Company has endowed its Big Twins with a variety of starter motors. Some were good, some not so good. In its latest iteration the starter motor is as good as any, as long as the motor is in stock or near-stock condition. The problem is that the starter motor, although perfectly capable of spinning the stock mill over, becomes strained when additional cubes or compression is factored into the equation. When you stir in a few unavoidable circumstances like weak batteries, cold weather, and thick, cold oil, the starter can get downright sulky.

Now obviously, this unpleasant scenario can be caused by anything from a low battery or bad connection to a tired/failing starter motor. If the situation occurs suddenly, and the motor is stock or close to it, my first recommendation would be to avail yourself of the excellent troubleshooting tree of the service manual and ascertain exactly where the problem lies before pulling out the charge card and popping for a new, aftermarket starter.

If everything is bone stock the choice is simple; you can replace the OEM starter with either another OEM or something from the aftermarket. Frankly, you'll have to decide if the price difference between the standard starter and generally higher-quality (and somewhat higher-priced) aftermarket starters is worthwhile to you.

On the other hand, if your stock starter is too lame to spin over the hot rod you've just built you really have very little choice in the matter. Whether you want to or not, you're going to have to thumb through the catalogs until you find a starter motor capable of reliably starting your bike.

Which one to use is up to you. Currently—no pun intended—there are so many good aftermarket starters on the market that picking any one to recommend would be difficult and a bit unfair. Spyke has a great reputation, as do Wags, and Terry Components, to name just three.

With the exception of a direct replacement unit, all of the aftermarket starters will feature more horsepower and torque than the factory starter, in some cases up to double the horsepower and maybe 50 percent more torque. Check the manufacturers' specifications and compare them to each other and the stock starter; remember that all things being equal the more torque the starter generates, the more efficiently it will turn over your engine. Aftermarket starters may also offer some unique features, gold-plated contacts for example, which reduce voltage drop. On the downside, some will require the installation of a larger-capacity battery, or heavier wiring.

Installation of any new starter will involve a trip into the primary cover. The shop manual will document the exact procedure. It isn't a particularly hard job, but it can be time consuming. Essentially you'll be removing the outer cover, and removing the starter jackshaft assembly. Once that's done you can unbolt the starter and replace it.

In the end this isn't a very glamorous project, and you're forgiven if you've just glossed over it. However if you're intent on building a big motor, it is something that you should factor in to the overall plan. Likewise, if your OEM starter has given up the ghost, an aftermarket starter may be a better, and more economical choice.

High torque starters aren't very glamorous, even when they're chromed, but you'll need one if you plan on firing up that big inch motor.

Maintaining Your Charging System

Time: 15–30 minutes

Tools: Voltmeter, T-40 Torx socket

Talent:

Cost: $0

Tip: Perform this check twice a year, or at every major service

PERFORMANCE GAIN: You'll never be stranded with a dead battery

COMPLEMENTARY MODIFICATION: Install a set of trickle charger leads and keep the battery plugged into a smart charger whenever the bike is out of service for any length of time.

Originally this section was to be titled Upgrading Your Charging System; unfortunately for this book, but fortunately for Twin Cam owners, there really isn't anything in the charging system that needs upgrading.

The fact is that the current TC charging system is very, very good indeed. It has to be. Fuel injection systems, electronic ignitions, cruise controls, and all of the other modern conveniences that make our new Harleys so much fun—and arguably so much better than their predecessors—require profoundly reliable charging systems. Without them the little black boxes and microprocessors that tell the components what to do get confused. In fact, get them confused enough and they go "poof" and blow their little electronic minds, which generally results in a long walk home.

As it is endowed with an extremely reliable charging system there isn't much you can or even need to do in the way of routine maintenance. However, that doesn't mean you can ignore it completely. Connections still need checkups, and the battery does require some periodic attention.

Located on the inside of the lower-right front frame rail you'll find the stator/voltage regulator connector. Under normal circumstances this connection needs no

regular service. But as with any exposed connection, dirt, water, and road debris can work some mischief. Inspect the connection whenever you have the opportunity. Make sure the plugs are tight, there are no chaffed wires, and that wire bundle isn't dangling in space where it could become damaged by flying objects. Check the leads on the voltage regulator; there is a possibility that they could be chaffed or cut by the sharp edges on the crankcase. If damage is evident, use electrical tape or "liquid rubber" to repair any damage and make certain the wires themselves have enough clearance to prevent them from rubbing against the case.

Twin Cam models come equipped with a sealed, maintenance-free battery. Outside of checking the battery terminals for corrosion and making certain that the terminal connections are tight, there isn't much you can do with it. If your bike doesn't have a voltmeter, I'd recommend checking the battery voltage occasionally via a handheld voltmeter. The factory recommends checking the voltage and terminals at 2,500-mile intervals. That's not bad advice and should get most of you through a year riding without any undue hassle. By the way, batteries normally lose a percentage of their charge while sitting; hot weather exacerbates this unpleasant situation, so don't panic if you return from a month-long vacation in July and the battery is dead. Although I'd question why you took a month-long vacation in July without your bike!

If you tend to let your bike sit for extended periods of time I'd suggest that your first order of business should be to install a set of auxiliary battery-charger leads to the battery. With those in place you can leave the battery connected to a "smart charger" (H-D sells a very good automatic, on-demand charger No. P/N 99863-93TA; or purchase one from any of several manufacturers such as Deltran or YUASA) whenever the bike is going to be parked for any length of time; the battery will remain fully charged between rides.

Although there are several methods used to check a battery's state of charge, the simplest and most effective method is to use a plain old handheld voltmeter. With the engine and ignition off, apply the probes of the voltmeter to the appropriate terminals. With the meter set to the 20-volts DC scale, the reading should be approximately 12.8 to 13.0 volts. A reading of 12.8 volts indicates that the battery is fully charged. A reading of 12.6 volts or less means that the battery requires some charging. How much charging is the question. Normally you would measure the specific gravity of the battery using a syringe or ball-type hydrometer. If the battery were low you'd then charge it

To access the stator you'll first need to remove the primary cover, the primary drive, the clutch, and the rotor. Fortunately the Twin Cam Stators are very reliable.

until the specific gravity reached 1.27 to 1.28 or all five balls were floating. Because the Twin Cam has a sealed battery this method cannot be used. The shop manual has a nice chart indicating how long the battery should be charged based on the battery voltage and the size of the charger. The factory won't let us reprint that here but suffice it to say that, absent information to the contrary, the rule of thumb is that any battery can be safely charged at one tenth of its rated amp-hour capacity. Since the standard battery has a 28-amp-hour rating that means you can safely charge it at 2.8 amps per hour.

If the battery is low, it might be wise to give the charging system a quick check. With the battery fully charged, and reconnected, start the bike up and hold it at a fast idle. Touch the voltmeter probes to the battery terminals; with all electrical accessories turned off the reading should be approximately 14.0 to 14.5 DC volts. Never try to run the bike with the battery disconnected; doing so will cause a massive electrical meltdown!

If the bike is charging at 15.0 volts or more it's overcharging; at less than 13.0 volts it's undercharging. In either case some detective work will be needed. The factory service manual will lay the procedure out in great detail, although if you're not comfortable working with electricity and meters, charging problems might be something best left to a trained technician.

The only other routine maintenance that the battery needs is the occasional cleaning of the case itself. Dirt and grime on the case can cause the battery to self-discharge. If the battery is particularly dirty use a spray cleaner or better yet a solution of 5 teaspoons of baking soda to a quart of water to rinse down the battery case. Allow the solution to sit on the battery until the bubbling stops, and then rinse the case with cool water.

Battery Inspection Check List

Clean the battery using a mild degreaser or a baking soda and water solution.

Clean the cable connections using a wire brush or sandpaper.

Inspect the battery screws, terminals, and cables for wear, breakage, and corrosion. Make certain the terminals are tight.

Inspect the battery case for swelling, deformation, or cracks. These are indicators that the battery may have been frozen, overheated, or overcharged.

When reinstalling the battery, protect the connections with a thin coat of dielectric grease.

As I've stressed, the TC charging system is far better than what came before it and in reality needs little to keep it that way. With a modicum of easily performed work on your part it should remain so for the life of the bike.

Although this section isn't about a charging system upgrade per se, there is one relatively easy and inexpensive upgrade you can make. Twin-Cam charging systems come in two flavors. Plain vanilla as fitted to the base edition bikes is a 38-amp unit. The high zoot version as fitted to the full boat models is a 45-amp unit. The difference between them is that the high output system uses a laminated rotor with more powerful magnets. Need more amps to float your electric boat? Simply swap your low output rotor for its stronger brother.

Project 84

Installing a Screamin' Eagle Adjustable Map Ignition System

 Time: 1 hour

 Tools: Flat-bladed screwdriver, 9/16-inch open-end wrench, 7/16-, 3/8-, and 5/16-inch sockets, ratchet, long extension

 Talent:

 Cost: $320

 Parts: A Screamin' Eagle adjustable map ignition system

 Tip: Dialing in the ignition timing is best done on a dyno where you can try the different ignition settings to see where the engine develops the most power

 PERFORMANCE GAIN: 1–4 horsepower, depending on engine mods

COMPLEMENTARY MODIFICATION: A properly adjusted ignition is a must on a high-compression engine with hot cams

Many new performance engine builders don't realize how important it is to get the timing of their ignition system properly set. These newbies focus all their attention on pumping in as much fuel/air mixture as possible over the piston. And though this is the way to make more power, properly setting the time when that mixture will be ignited has a lot to do with getting as much power as possible from the combustion event. After all, what's the sense in spending a ton of money getting 10 percent more mixture into the combustion chamber only to lose some of what you would have gained because the spark plugs are firing at the wrong time?

The Ignition Event

As it is with a camshaft, the markers for setting the time when the spark plugs will fire is based on flywheel position and called out in degrees of flywheel rotation. This is

because the position of the flywheels determines where the pistons are in their cylinders, and the position of the piston is one of the factors that determines the best time to start burning the air/fuel mixture in the combustion chamber. Since one full rotation of the flywheel assembly is a circle, one full rotation of the flywheel is 360 degrees. This means that each stroke of the piston up, or down, its cylinder is 180 degrees.

What drives the piston down its cylinder on the power stroke is the pressure created by the burning compressed air/fuel mixture in the sealed combustion chamber. However, if the spark plug ignites the mixture too early, the pressure created starts to push down on the piston while it's still rising on the compression stroke, not on the downward power stroke. Result: The engine is working against itself. If the plug fires too late, the maximum amount of pressure is not exerted onto the piston and horsepower is lost. Firing the spark plug at just the right time allows the pressure from the burning mixture to push its hardest onto the piston during the power stroke. This is why setting the plugs so they fire at the right time is so critical to getting the most power from the fuel and air you get over the piston.

In a perfect world, you'd fire the spark plug when the piston is at the top of its compression stroke (at the 0-degree position), since this is when the compressed air/fuel mixture is at its highest pressure. In the real world, however, the burning mixture would produce a very low amount of horsepower. Here's why: Once the spark plug fires, the combustion event goes through two different stages. During the first one, which is called *combustion lag*, the air/fuel mixture burns very slowly, relatively speaking, because the mixture's molecules must be heated up before

After removing the Dyna's seat and left side panel, this is what you'll see. The ignition module is located behind this electrical box.

they burn. After this occurs, the second stage, called *controlled burn*, takes over and the fuel/air mixture burns at a very consistent rate. Firing the plug at the top of the stroke, the Top Dead Center position, doesn't give the mixture any time to heat up, nor does it allow for it to burn long enough to create heat, and therefore, increase the pressure over the piston. This is why the spark plug must be fired well before the top of the compression stroke. (By the way, on many engines the 0-degree position is when the plugs fire during start-up, since the pistons are moving so slowly and not much power needs to be produced to get the engine idling.)

Moving the time when the plug fires (the ignition timing) to a point away from the TDC (0-degree) position is called *advancing the spark*, while moving it toward TDC is called *retarding the spark*. This phase of ignition timing is called the *initial timing* and it's set automatically by a Twin Cam's ECM based on input from the crank position sensor (CKP). However, though the stock setting is the best for many applications, sometimes an engine will produce a little more power with its initial timing set to a point before or after the stock initial timing setting due to its particular performance parts combination. The Screamin' Eagle adjustable map ignition system allows you to make initial timing adjustments.

Advance Timing

Unfortunately, setting the initial timing is not all there is to it. If it was, there would be no need for a module that gives you different ignition curves. The truth is, though the best time to fire the spark plug is based on piston position, piston speed (engine rpm) also has a lot to do with it.

As the piston moves faster, there's less time for the combustion event to occur, so the plug has to fire earlier (more advanced) than when the piston is moving at a lower rpm (slower). The fix for this is to have the ignition advance itself based on a predetermined curve (rate), which is called an *advance curve*. The faster the engine spins, the more the timing advances. However, different engine specifications, compression ratio, cam duration,

cylinder bore, etc., require the timing to advance at different rates for maximum power output. And that's the point of the SE module's different ignition settings.

The easiest way to know which advance curve is best for your engine is to try different settings and see what happens. The best method is to start with the least aggressive setting (1) and work your way up to the more aggressive settings. Test the setting by riding the bike at full throttle and listen to see if the engine pings, knocks, or rattles. If it doesn't, turn off the ignition and select the next higher advance curve; then run the test again. Once you find the curve that does make the engine ping or knock, turn off the engine and select the next lower setting. This will give you the most aggressive advance curve for your engine's performance components without causing detonation. (Tip: Of all the curves offered with the SE Ignition Module, many feel #4 works best on most 95-inch Twin Cams. If possible, check for best power on a dyno.)

Here are a couple of pointers: If the engine is getting very hot, let it cool down before you continue testing or you'll get engine knock on a setting that would normally work well. Also, always run high-octane fuel in a performance engine, or you, again, will have engine knock sooner than usual. To run the test, have the bike cruising at 2,200 rpm in third gear and going up a slight incline. Then roll the throttle onto wide-open until you hit the rev limiter.

Speaking of rev limiters, put the setting 500 rpm above where the horsepower curve drops off, or below the rpm limit of your valve springs, whichever comes first. After all, why set the rev limiter way above where the engine stops making power? In fact, there's usually no need to go above 6,000 rpm in a street motor, unless you're still making power. As for a Twin Cam B motor, do not go above 6,200, no matter what valve spring kit you put in it.

The Installation

I'm going to show you how to install a Screamin' Eagle adjustable map ignition module onto a Dyna, since they

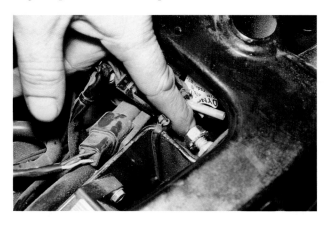

Start by removing the 9/16-inch nut that's under the seat. This holds the top rear corner of the electrical box to the left side of the bike.

Next, remove the two 7/16-inch nuts that are behind the ignition coil (seen here from the right side of the bike), which hold the front of the electrical box.

are the hardest ones to do. On a Softail, the ignition module is located on top of the rear fender, under the seat. Touring models have their module under the right side frame panel.

This system allows you to make timing changes based on engine rpm as well as engine load. It has four selectable ignition maps, rev limits up to 7,500 rpm, and adjustable initial timing. The module mounts in the stock location, as the accompanying photos will show, and there's a hand-held controller that you use to make the changes you want. This unit is for all carbureted Twin Cam engines.

Start the job by removing the seat and left side panel. Then remove the 9/16-inch nut that's under the seat, which holds one corner of the electrical box on the left side of the bike. Next, remove the two 7/16-inch nuts that are behind the ignition coil, which hold the front of the electrical box. The last electrical box bolt to go is a 3/8-inch one that holds the lower rear of the electrical box. You can now get to the two 5/16-inch bolts that hold the ignition module to the frame.

Once the module is loose, squeeze the connector clips, so you can pull the two stock wiring-harness connectors from the ignition module. Now connect the new SE ignition module to the stock harness just like the old module was. Bolt the new module to the frame using the stock bolts. It goes into the exact same spot as the original ECM. Then reinstall the electrical box in the reverse order of how you took it apart.

To adjust the module, plug the Screamin' Eagle Adjustable Ignition Module control panel into the stock wiring harness via the bike's data connector. Then make the settings changes you want, as per the manual, to the new ECM.

Once the module is loose, squeeze the connector clips, so you can pull the two stock wiring harness connectors from the ignition module. Then connect them to the new SE ignition module.

Bolt the new module to the frame using the stock bolts. It goes into the exact same spot as the original ECM. Then reinstall the electrical box in the reverse order of how you took it apart.

The last electrical box bolt to go is a 3/8-inch that holds the lower rear of the electrical box.

You can now get to the two 5/16-inch bolts that hold the ignition module to the frame.

To adjust the module, plug the SE module control panel into the stock wiring harness via the bike's data connector. Then make the settings changes you want, as per the manual, to the new ECM.

Installing an Aftermarket Ignition

 Time: 1 hour

 Tools: 3/16-inch Allen, needle-nose pliers, small flat-bladed screwdriver

 Talent:

 Cost: $280–340

 Parts: Crane HI-4TC or another fully adjustable ignition

 Tip: Dialing in the ignition timing is best done on a dyno

 PERFORMANCE GAIN: 1–4 horsepower, depending on engine mods

COMPLIMENTARY MODIFICATION: A properly adjusted ignition is a must on a high-compression engine with hot cams

Crane's fully adjustable ignition module for carbureted Twin Cams allows a tuner to set the ignition's mode, initial timing, advance slope, rear cylinder offset, and rev limiter by simply turning the proper switch.

THE ELECTRICAL SYSTEM

Since I cover the importance of proper ignition timing and ignition advance curves in Project 84, I'll cover in this project how to install and properly adjust an aftermarket ignition system, such as Crane Cam's HI-4TC fully adjustable ignition module for carbureted Twin Cams. The HI-4TC, which can be used with the original equipment coil, allows a tuner to set the ignition's mode, rev limiter, initial timing, advance slope, and rear cylinder offset. (In case you're wondering where the single- or dual-fire switch is, all Twin Cam engines are single-fire only.) Let's go over each of these adjustments, starting with the mode switch, which is the easiest and first one to set.

The HI-4TC's mode switch simply changes the ignition's advance table and spark mode. The #0 setting is for a single spark and #1 is multi-spark. On the single spark setting, you get one long spark duration and the multi-spark setting gives up to nine short sparks at idle and up to three sparks at 6,000 rpm. As for the #2 and #3 switch settings, these are the same as #0 and #1, respectively, unless the tuner has reprogrammed the EPROM memory. All the advance tables in the HI-4TC are the same when the unit is shipped from Crane. The difference between the two groups is that the #2 and #3 settings can be reprogrammed with Crane's software package, if you choose.

What setting you use is your preference. Normally, an ignition gives a single spark, but some owners like the idea of multiple sparks at start-up to make it easier to fire off the engine. Multiple sparks may also increase the power output of some modified engines.

Next up is the rev limiter, which is adjusted with two switches: the first one sets the 1,000-rpm value, the second sets the 100-rpm setting. That means turning the switches to 6 and 5, respectively, equals a rev limit of 6,500 rpm. By the way, you must set the rpm switches to a value to start the engine. Leaving them on 00 will prevent the ignition from firing.

The rev limiter is there to protect your engine from over-revving, which will damage it. The proper limiter setting depends on your engine's power output and combination of performance parts. The limiter should come in before the valves float and about 500 rpm after the horsepower curve starts to drop off. (In most cases, this is usually before the engine gets to its redline, or mechanical rev limit.) Revving far past the point where the engine stops making more power doesn't do you or your engine any good.

Start with a setting of 62, which will give you a rev limit of 6,200 rpm. This is on the safe side of the stock valve springs' mechanical rev limit. You can then adjust the limiter according to the engine's power curve.

The initial timing is the next adjustment to set. On an Evo, you can change this setting mechanically, by physically setting the ignition's initial timing. However, you can't change the initial timing on a Twin Cam, since it times itself off the flywheel sensor, so Crane allows you to change it electronically.

The initial timing switch has positions numbered from -5 to +4, which move the ignition timing from 4 degrees up from the factory setting to 5 degrees down. For example, if the engine's factory ignition timing is 5 BTDC (Before Top Dead Center) at idle and you select +2, the engine's initial timing is increased (advanced) by two degrees, which makes it 7 degrees BTDC. If the switch is set to -5, the initial timing is reduced (retarded) by five degrees, which puts it at TDC.

We suggest you start the engine with this one set to 0 degrees, so the engine's initial timing is at the stock setting. Then dial in the carb jetting, which must be on the money before you can get an accurate ignition timing adjustment. Once the jetting is right, try retarding the initial timing two degrees (-2) and see if the engine loses power. If it gets stronger, go two more (-4). If the power drops, go back one degree. However, if the engine loses power when you first go two degrees retarded, try going two degrees advanced (+2). If the engine gets stronger, go one more (+3). If the power drops, or starts to ping/knock/detonate, go back one degree to +1. (Tip: Don't do this on an excessively hot day, which will cause the engine to ping sooner than on a more normal day.)

As for the advance switch, this one changes how aggressive the advance curve is. The #0 setting is the slowest/lowest curve, which means the engine will not be fully advanced until about 4,500–5,000 rpm. Of course, that means the #9 setting is the fastest/highest curve. Choosing this one brings in full advanced at 1,500–2,500 rpm and the engine stays at full advance throughout the rest of the rpm range.

A good starting point for this one is position #1. After taking the bike for a test ride, increase the advance curve one notch and take another ride. Continue to make the advance curve more aggressive, one notch at a time, until

the power starts to drop off, or the engine pings/knocks/detonates. Then back off the setting one or two positions, depending on how much power you want to trade for engine safety.

The last adjustment you can make is the rear cylinder offset, which has positions from -5 to +4. This dial allows a tuner to adjust the timing for the rear cylinder separately from the front cylinder. This one allows the pros to get the cylinder temperatures even to get every bit of power out of the engine. We suggest leaving this one at #0 unless you have quite a bit of experience with ignition adjustments and need to alter the rear cylinder's timing.

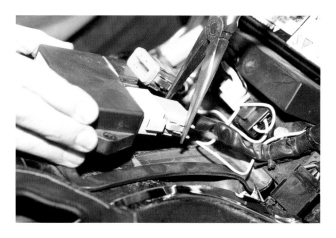
Then unplug both harness connectors from the unit by squeezing the release lever on each side of the connector with a needlenose pliers.

Install the new Crane ignition into the same location as the stock unit using the stock hardware and a 3/16-inch Allen.

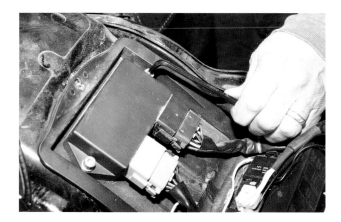
After removing the seat (or the right side cover), unbolt the stock ignition from the bike using a 3/16-inch Allen wrench.

PROJECT 86

Replacing the Thermometer with an Oil Temperature Gauge

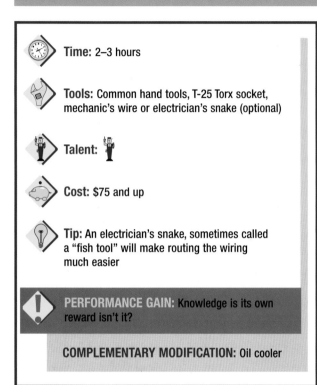

Time: 2–3 hours

Tools: Common hand tools, T-25 Torx socket, mechanic's wire or electrician's snake (optional)

Talent:

Cost: $75 and up

Tip: An electrician's snake, sometimes called a "fish tool" will make routing the wiring much easier

PERFORMANCE GAIN: Knowledge is its own reward isn't it?

COMPLEMENTARY MODIFICATION: Oil cooler

No doubt about it we live in the information age. The problem is that not all information is good information and some of it is superfluous. Case in point the air temperature gauge that comes as standard equipment on the FLHT/C/U and FLTR variants of the Twin Cam lineup. Now I don't know about you, but I'm pretty good at figuring out whether I'm hot or cold. And rarely need a gauge to tell me when to put on warmer clothing. Over the years I've learned that if it's cold when I walk out of the house, it'll be even colder when I get on the bike, so I dress accordingly. For some strange reason the Motor Company figures I need to know what the outside air temperature is while I'm tooling down the road. Quite frankly, Scarlet, not only do I not give a damn, but there are lots of times when I'd really rather not know anyway.

On the other hand there is one temperature that's of great interest to me. Namely the oil temperature. Knowing the oil temperature can warn you of impending oil over-heating, which as we all know can lead to expensive engine noises. Oil temperature gauges are particularly useful when you do a lot of touring, especially on a Dresser in hotter climates. They are available from a wide variety of sources, and come in all shapes and sizes. Ideally what you want is a 2-inch gauge that'll fit in your fairing so you can do away with that semi-useful air temperature gauge.

The most difficult part in installing the gauge in the fairing will of course be removing the outer fairing shell. The manual only devotes ten or so lines to doing the job, so trust me, it's not that big of a deal. Protect the front fender to prevent damage just in case you drop a tool or something. Once the fairing has been removed you can remove the air temperature gauge and install the new oil temperature gauge.

Don't forget that you'll also have to install the oil temperature-sending unit in the appropriate location. Normally, sending units and their associated wiring are included with the gauge kit but not always; check the box before you leave the parts counter. When the sending unit is in place you'll need to wire it to the gauge. Usually the wire can be slipped through the original wiring harness sheath by passing a length of stiff mechanic's wire or an electrician's snake with the wire connected through the sheath; pull the whole works back through. A bit of WD-40 or silicone spray will make the job a lot easier. When the gauge is in place and wired, fire up the engine and make sure it all actually works before reinstalling the fairing and motoring off into the sunset, secure in the knowledge that your engine oil temperature is now being properly monitored.

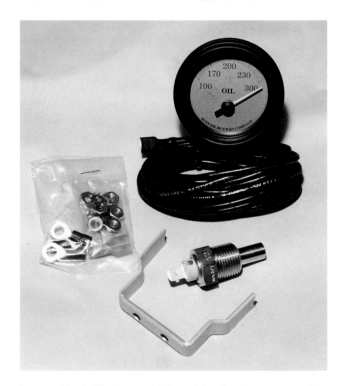

I can usually tell if I'm hot or cold. Determining the oil's temperature is another issue. This oil temperature gauge kit makes it a lot simpler.

THE ELECTRICAL SYSTEM

PROJECT 87

Upgrading the Horn

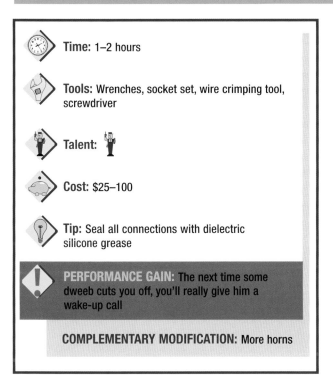

Time: 1–2 hours

Tools: Wrenches, socket set, wire crimping tool, screwdriver

Talent:

Cost: $25–100

Tip: Seal all connections with dielectric silicone grease

PERFORMANCE GAIN: The next time some dweeb cuts you off, you'll really give him a wake-up call

COMPLEMENTARY MODIFICATION: More horns

Traditionally, motorcycle horns have been somewhat lame. In most cases, the horn on a 15-grand motorcycle is little better than the one on a $500 pedal bike.

The situation was bad enough 20 years ago, before the majority of cars had climate control. Nowadays, the average car driver not only has his windows up and the AC on, but is more than likely to be yakking away on a cell phone, applying makeup, or just not paying attention. We've all been there; you're running along minding your own business when all of a sudden someone starts drifting across your bow. You thumb the horn button hoping to get his attention and all that results is a wimpy little bleep. Maybe Captain Volvo notices, maybe he doesn't. What you need is something that will snap him upright like he was hit with a 2x4.

I'd like to be able give you instructions on how to mount a wire-guided missile to the front of your bike but the publisher and the Geneva Convention feel rather strongly about that sort of thing so we'll have to take another tack.

If it's a stock, unobtrusive look you're after you can peruse the many catalogs until you find something you like that will fit your bike. If luck is in your favor, the new one will provide a louder croak than the factory-supplied one; or not. Alternatively, you can mount up a 6-volt horn. Trust me, using a 12-volt system to drive a 6-volt hooter results in a helluva noise. Just remember not to hold it on for more than 2 or 3 minutes at a time.

Of course if you really want to wake up the (brain) dead there is only one solution. Mount an air horn.

Air horns for motorcycle use are driven by either a small compressor or by a can of compressed air. I'd avoid the canned-air version. Mounting a compressor driven air horn can present some interesting challenges. Mainly because the compressor and horn unit do take up a fair amount of space compared to a standard diaphragm-type horn. If you're riding a Dresser, the situation is easy to resolve. If you're not, well then think creatively but remember that the horn itself needs to be positioned where it will do the most good and in such a way as to prevent water from entering. Other than that, all the normal stuff concerning electrical connections applies. The other downside to using an air horn may be the cost. Quality units (such as the Rivco, pictured) are for the most part a little pricey. But like anything else, you do get what you pay for, and the first time you blast some nitwit back into his lane with just the push of a button, it'll seem dirt-cheap!

The Rivco Air Horn kit contains everything you'll need, including lucid instructions.

Not only does it look good, but it's loud enough to wake the (brain) dead.

Troubleshooting the Electrical System

Time: 15 minutes to 4 hours

Tools: Common sense, a volt/ohm meter, test light, and most importantly the factory shop manual

Talent: A basic understanding of electrics

Cost: Troubleshooting takes time, and repairing the problem, i.e., replacing the component, may cost several hundred dollars depending on what went wrong

Tip: Always assume that the simplest thing is at fault—look for a blown fuse, dead battery, or broken wire first

PERFORMANCE GAIN: How about being able to ride home instead of calling for a tow?

COMPLEMENTARY MODIFICATION: Now is the time to check and seal all of the connections, ensure that the grounds are good and that the battery is up to snuff.

THE ELECTRICAL SYSTEM

Most do-it-yourselfers, and even a good number of otherwise competent professional mechanics, have trouble when it comes to electrical problems. Personally, I've always felt this is because we can't actually see electricity.

We have to take it on faith that electrons really are whirring through the wire on their way to doing something useful. We know that when we push a button, something happens: the horn blows, the starter turns, or the lights flash. But most of us really don't know why or how they do it.

When mechanical failures occur, the cause is often obvious. However, when electrical problems come to pass, it's often a mystery.

What if the horn blows weakly or stops blowing? Is the problem in the horn? In the wiring that connects the horn to the switch? In the switch? Maybe the problem's the electrical circuit that feeds current to the switch, or maybe it's the ground.

System overlap makes it even more complicated. Perhaps your bike's getting hard to start. Is it a mechanical or electrical failure in the starter motor or solenoid? Is a weak ignition causing the starter circuit to work overtime? Is it a charging problem that means less current is being provided than is needed to the starter system components? Or is it simply time for a tune-up?

Not knowing how electricity works also can be a problem. If you don't understand the fundamentals, it's hard to do much more than replace a suspect component. That's okay when the problem is a blown turn signal bulb. But it becomes an issue when you may wonder if a bad ignition module worth $500 is causing your headaches. For those of you whose only interaction with electricity is the flicking of a switch, here are a few basics.

The neat thing about electricity is that it behaves in a manner consistent with and governed by well-known, natural physical laws. For instance, electrical current must have a source. This may be a battery, which stores the electricity for later use, or it may be a generator, which creates electricity. This is an important distinction: A battery does not create electricity, only a generator can.

Electricity can be created in two flavors: Alternating Current (AC) and Direct Current (DC). However, only DC can be stored in a battery. Motorcycles that utilize batteries use AC generators to produce electricity. A device called a rectifier then converts the AC to DC, so that it may be stored in the battery.

To accomplish any meaningful work, electricity needs to follow a "path," or "circuit." The circuit includes a source (which for most street bikes means the battery), a conductor (wiring), and a load (whatever work the electricity has to do). The circuit also needs to include a return path for the electricity, called the "ground."

The movement of electricity through a conductor is referred to as "current flow." When a circuit works—that is, current flows from the source to the load and returns back to the source—it's said to be a complete circuit.

Electrical current can only flow when there's an excess of electrons on one side of the load and a deficit on the other. This brings up an interesting point. For years, it was assumed that current flow was from positive to negative. Hence, the power supply of a circuit was marked as positive and the ground (or return side) was marked with a negative symbol.

When it was realized that current flow was actually from negative to positive, it was too late to change the thousands of manuals already in print. Scientists decided to consider current flow as being from positive to negative, while electron flow would be considered to be from negative to positive.

Another consideration is just how lazy electricity can be. Current doesn't want to do anything more than take the path of least resistance. If a circuit is complete, electrons (current) will flow from the source (battery) through the conductor to the load and back to the source. If the path is interrupted, current will either cease to flow (called an "open circuit") or it will try to return to the source via the most direct path (logically enough a "short circuit").

Customarily, when a circuit is open, no real harm will be done. The component just won't work. Open circuits usually result from breaks in conductors, a component failure, or a bad ground that prevents current from returning to the battery and completing the circuit.

On the other hand, short circuits can be problematic. These happen when the conductor-carrying current encounters a direct path to ground. The current then tries to return directly to the source. The problem is that current flow can increase beyond what the wiring can handle, causing the wiring to overheat and melt into a gooey mess or, worst-case scenario, even burst into flames.

Fuses are used to protect against shorts, but they only work if the short is between the fuse and source. If the wiring shorts before the fuse, you've got big problems.

Fortunately, most electrical problems can be prevented with a little preventive maintenance. Check wires for chaffing and worn insulation, particularly where they make sharp bends or are subject to flexing. If accessories are installed make certain that they are wired correctly and fused properly.

Troubleshooting procedures involve tracing current flow via a test light or voltmeter and being able to understand how the component in question is supposed to work. Harley-Davidson factory-supplied service manuals are very good when it comes to electrical troubleshooting. In fact I'd have to say they are among the best in the business. Each sub-section in the electrical category generally provides a brief description of how the component should work, a wiring diagram, detailed instructions on how to troubleshoot the component or circuit, and lots of easy-to-understand diagrams.

What the manual can't provide is some basic rules and common sense. I'll provide a few basic troubleshooting rules; it's up to you to provide the common sense.

Rule number one: Always check the simple things first. A sudden electrical failure generally indicates a blown fuse, so start there. But don't just replace the fuse and hope for the best. Think, before you act; did the fuse blow after you switched on some accessory? Chances are it did; if the fuse blew as you turned on the spotlight for instance, you can be reasonably certain that the problem lies in the spotlight circuit. The solution is simple: either repair the spotlight circuit, or don't use the spots until you can get the bike where it's safe to work on.

Rule number two: An ounce of prevention is worth a pound of cure. When performing normal routine maintenance take time to check the various connections on the bike. Anytime one is apart make certain to coat the terminals with dielectric silicone grease to prevent corrosion.

Rule number three: Electricity needs a source, a path, and a return. When confronting an electrical problem, use your manual as a road map to determine where the current starts, how it gets to the component, and where the return path (ground) lies. After that it's a relatively simple matter to use a voltmeter or test light to determine if you have current, if it's reaching the component and if the component is grounded.

Rule number four: Some electrical problems can be insidious. Particularly those that deal with theft deterrent systems, the EFI, and some charging and ignition scenarios. In these cases some sophisticated equipment and techniques may be required to pinpoint the problem. Troubleshoot the system as far as you can; when you're stymied, call the shop.

Rule number five: When troubleshooting electrical components and wiring use common sense. Poking a hole in the wire with a probe or other sharp object creates a potential water leak. Sure you can seal the hole with tape or silicone but why not trace the wire back to the nearest connector? Unplug the connector and check the current there. If you've current at the connector, but not at the component itself you can reasonably assume that the problem is in the wire itself.

Rule number six: Learn to use your test equipment and trust it. If you use your ohmmeter to test a switch or wire and the meter says the circuit has overly high resistance, believe it.

Finally, remember that electricity may be mysterious, but it really isn't magic. When all else fails bear in mind that electricity must obey the laws of nature, no matter how cantankerous it seems to be. Take some time to learn how those laws are enforced and with a bit of patience, the right tools, and the help of the shop manual, chances are you'll be able to right whatever went wrong.

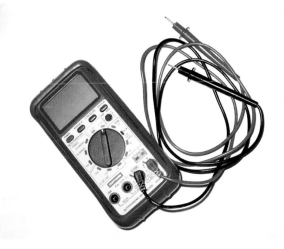

This digital VOM meter is simple and available at any parts store in the land. It retails for less than 40 bucks. With it, the shop manual, and a little common sense you should be able to track down just about any sort of electrical problem you're likely to encounter.

PROJECT 89

Upgrading Your Headlight

 Time: 1/2 to 1 hour

 Tools: Depends on the model in question; Phillips screwdrivers, T-25 Torx driver, straight-bladed screwdriver

 Talent:

 Cost: $15–500

 Tip: Salts found in perspiration can damage quartz bulbs so always handle them by their base. If you inadvertently touch the glass clean it with a rag dipped in rubbing alcohol.

 PERFORMANCE GAIN: Better lights mean safer riding

COMPLEMENTARY MODIFICATION: add-on spotlights, upgraded signals, and taillights

Personally, I'm blind as a bat, especially at night. If I could figure out some practical way to mount anti-aircraft searchlights to my bike I'd do it in heartbeat; that's somewhat impractical I admit but there are I times I wish I could do just that. Fortunately for all of us there are better solutions.

The Twin Cam Harleys come with decent lighting, particularly the FL models, and especially the FLTR. Though that doesn't mean they can't be improved upon.

The Motor Company specifies a 55/60-watt quartz-halogen headlight bulb. Not too long ago this bulb was considered to be cutting edge in the headlight industry. Currently, it's just another headlight bulb. The first upgrade you might consider should be to H-D's optional 55/60-watt xenon bulb. In the last decade, xenon has replaced the halogen gas used in most incandescent bulbs. Xenon provides a whiter light and keeps carbon deposits from forming on the interior of the bulb. In essence, xenon provides you with a light that's 30 percent brighter than a standard halogen bulb and because it's self-cleaning it lasts quite a bit longer. It's also very reasonably priced, fewer than twenty bucks, in fact, and draws the same current as the standard bulb, making this conversion cost-effective.

The next step up is a bulb that's simply more powerful than the standard. Many manufacturers offer more powerful bulbs; in fact some go as high as 130 watts (130/90 watt). The downside to using these bulbs is that under most circumstances they draw way too much current to be practical, that is if your bike has the stock generating equipment. You might be able to get away with something like a 100/55-watt bulb, if you didn't spend much time using the high beam. But unless you're planning on upgrading your charging system I'd recommend you avoid these bulbs, or stock up on a supply of alternators.

If you really want to light up the night the ultimate headlamp is the HID or High Intensity Discharge light. HIDs are a relatively new development. Rather than use a glowing filament, as an incandescent lamp does, the HID uses an arc between an anode and a cathode to produce a brilliant white light. The arc works much like a spark plug and like a spark plug utilizes a coil-type mechanism to step up the motorcycle's 12 volts to the 30,000 needed to fire the light. However, the unit actually draws less current than a standard 55-watt headlight does. The light also uses a clear lens and dichroic reflector, which refracts and focuses the light to recapture some of the light normally lost to the non-visible spectrum. In conjunction with the HID bulb this produces an intense, white light that's approximately 55 percent brighter than an equivalent halogen bulb.

Due to all of the equipment involved, HID lights aren't cheap; a drop-in package for the Road King for example, available from Headwinds, includes the transformer, relay, lens, reflector and bulb, plus all of the associated wiring. It does push the headlight ante into the 500-dollar range. But as they say, you get what you pay for. And if your ultimate goal is to turn night into day, this is the way to do it. Either that or drag around a searchlight, and a tow-behind generator.

That's what I'm talking about! Lots of candlepower and plenty of eye candy.

THE ELECTRICAL SYSTEM

228

PROJECT 90

Hiding Wiring in the Handlebar

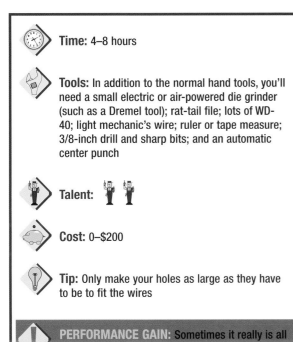

Time: 4–8 hours

Tools: In addition to the normal hand tools, you'll need a small electric or air-powered die grinder (such as a Dremel tool); rat-tail file; lots of WD-40; light mechanic's wire; ruler or tape measure; 3/8-inch drill and sharp bits; and an automatic center punch

Talent:

Cost: 0–$200

Tip: Only make your holes as large as they have to be to fit the wires

PERFORMANCE GAIN: Sometimes it really is all about looks

COMPLIMENTARY MODIFICATION: New switches

Let me be blunt, I'm not a big fan of this modification, although it does look good. Years ago, quite a few motorcycles came with the wiring running through the bars, those bars; had rather generous gussets placed in the area where the wires exited the bars, right in the center of the clamps, and for good reason. The hole created a weak spot; the gusset reinforced that weak spot to make the handlebars much stronger and less likely to break at the hole. That method of drilling the bars worked fine and I have no qualms about it, outside of the fact that replacing the switches and repairing the wiring can be slightly complicated should that ever be needed.

Here's my issue: What this plan suggests is to bore a hole through the handlebar in that same area between the handlebar clamps, only there won't be a gusset to strengthen the area around the hole. Chances are that the bars will be fine afterward but the possibility does exist that the hole will weaken the bars and maybe cause them to snap like a pretzel at an inopportune moment.

My first suggestion, should you desire to hide your wiring in the handlebars, is to source the aftermarket,

including the H-D catalogs, and try to turn up a set of handlebars that are predrilled and reinforced around the critical areas.

Now that I've got that off my chest, let's be realistic. For any number of reasons you may not be able to locate a pair of bars that meet your criteria. Especially if you want to install ape-hangers or some other much-higher-than-standard handlebar. If that's the case you'll need to drill your own.

Let's start with the basics. Clearly, the holes will need to be large enough to allow the wires to pass through them, yet small enough to maintain the structural integrity of the handlebars. Begin by wrapping the area of the handlebars you plan to drill with a few passes of masking tape. The tape will make marking the holes easier, and prevent the center punch and drill from slipping around.

Plan the location of your intended holes carefully and measure accurately, otherwise the wires may end up outside the control pods, which sort of ruins the whole effect. The exit hole should be placed dead center in the knurled area of the bars, so it sits between the area that's clamped. Center punch the hole, and then drill it out with a very sharp 1/4- or 5/16-inch bit.

Next, determine the size of the holes needed. This is best done by trial, rather than error. Use the die grinder and appropriate bit to open up your first hole. Start smaller than the diameter of the bundled wires, and then gradually open it up to the point where the wires will just slide through the hole. My preference is to make the hole an oval, then round it out. The oval should be placed parallel to the tubing, which will lessen the chance that you'll weaken the bars. Cutting the hole in an oval will also make passage of the wires somewhat easier. This is particularly true of the larger center hole where the wires from both sides of the bars will exit. The edges of the hole will need to be chamfered to avoid ripping the wire insulation from the wires as you pull them through.

Chances are that you'll also need to extend the wires somewhat, especially if ape hangers are on the menu, although as an alternative you can buy replacement switches with extended wires. If you decide to splice the wires, stagger the splices so they move easily through the handlebars. Use only solder rated for electrical connections and insulate the splices with heat-shrink tubing. Try to make the splices as small and neat as possible so they don't get hung up in the bars. I'd also recommend you use plenty of lubricant to help ease their passage. WD-40 or silicone spray works well, as does a good coating of dielectric silicone grease. Again, make absolutely certain that the edges

It doesn't get much cleaner looking than this. Hiding the wiring in the bars can be time consuming, and admittedly somewhat tedious, but the uncluttered look is well worth it.

of the holes are well chamfered so they don't inadvertently turn into wire strippers.

To ease the wires through the bars, use a light piece of mechanic's wire or a hunk of stout string (fishing line works well). Pass the wire through the bars, from end hole to center hole. A small nut tied to the end of the string will make it easier to pass it through the bars. Secure your wire harness to the tag line by taping or tying it and, using copious amounts of lubricant, push the harness through the bars while maintaining tension of the line. If you hit a snag, resist the temptation to start yanking away. Back up and try twisting the bundle slightly or

give it another spray of WD-40 and try again. With patience and enough lube it'll go through, as you can guess though; the smaller and neater your splices, the easier it'll make things.

Once all of the wiring has been pulled through you can trial-fit the bars and adjust the controls to your liking. It might not be a bad idea at this point to test each wire with an ohmmeter or continuity light to make sure there are no shorts between the switches and the handlebars. If everything checks out, make all your electrical connections, and of course test them, before buttoning up the rest of the job.

Personal Touches

Detailing Your Bike

 Time: 1–4 hours

 Tools: Water, degreaser, soap, wax, Armor All, soft towels, sponges, plastic buckets, and elbow grease

 Talent:

 Cost: Once you've got the basic supplies, figure about $3 per wash

 Tip: Washing a bike can be a Zen-like experience, relax and enjoy yourself.

 PERFORMANCE GAIN: Clean bikes go much faster; everyone knows that!

COMPLEMENTARY MODIFICATION: Maybe you should clean the garage as well

Does your hog look like a pig? Are all your buddies parking at the far end of the parking lot just so dirt from your ride won't fall off and get their shiny scooters all grungy?

While everyone is certainly entitled to keep his (or her) own bike in his own way, a dirty, filthy bike does say something about its owner's state of mind. Besides, dirty bikes are a pain to work on, and the dirt may hide a minor problem—an oil leak for instance, that could be easily repaired—until it's developed into a major problem. Preventive maintenance plays a huge role in keeping your bike alive and well. Once of the best maintenance routines I can think off is to give your bike a regular bath. Washing and detailing your bike will help you find a lot of little problems before they develop into disasters, a belt out of adjustment, loose or missing bolts, or the aforementioned oil leak.

Motorcycles should always be washed cold, and out of direct sunlight if possible. They should also be washed with a gentle stream of water. Power washers are acceptable, especially if you're on the road somewhere. However, if you do use a power washer, particularly the coin-operated wand-type, be extremely careful. Set the wand on the softest possible setting and avoid directing the stream of water directly into any of the electrics, the wheel bearings, the open exhaust, or air cleaner. You'll also want to avoid blasting the painted parts head on. Those wands often have nozzle pressures approaching 1,000 psi and can do a lot of damage if care isn't exercised.

If the bike is particularly dirty or greasy, spray it down with some sort of degreaser before applying any water. Most motorcycle shops sell some sort of dedicated degreaser/bike wash. S100 has a good reputation as do several other products like Hog Wash or Cycle Care. For my money, good old-fashioned Gunk works just as well, as does Simple Green, and they're a hell of a lot cheaper.

Spray the greasy areas down with the solvent of your choice and allow the stuff a few minutes to do its work. For heavily coated, greasy, grimy areas use a soft-bristle brush or cut-down paintbrush to scrub the area. A few wraps of tape around the steel portion of the brush will prevent any accidental chips or scratches should the brush get away from you.

If the exhaust points upward, seal the opening and any open air filters with a baggie. Use cool water to rinse the entire bike, before scrubbing it down. I generally mix up a bucket of nice soapy water, using dedicated car wash soap. I'm partial to Blue Coral, Turtle wax and Dupont #7 but use whatever floats your boat. Start at the top of the bike and lather it up; soap and water won't hurt a thing. Use a soft clean sponge to wash the bike, rinsing as you go. Another paintbrush can be used around the spokes, or use a spoke brush available at most motorcycle shops to really get in there good.

Rinse the bike completely and repeat the wash cycle if you've missed any areas. At this point you might be tempted to start the bike and whirl her 'round the block to dry it off. While this method has some appeal, a better idea is to blow the bike off with air; a leaf blower, preferably an electric one, can be used, as can any air line. Then towel-dry it with clean, soft towels. This will prevent water spots.

Once the bike is dry you can apply any wax to the painted parts. I like to use a soft, Carnauba paste wax. Carnauba waxes offer excellent protection and can be buffed to high luster. Silicone-based waxes tend to seal any imperfections into the paint, making them difficult to remove down the road. Follow the wax-maker's instructions for application and removal. As a rule of thumb, wax should be applied and removed with a back-and-forth motion to avoid putting swirls into the finish.

Treat the chrome in the same manner; again, I'm partial to Dupont products here, but there are so many good ones out there, a full list would take an entire chapter. The exhaust pipe can be polished and then waxed, though don't expect the wax to last very long. Any heavy deposits, boot stains, and the like can be scraped off with a razor blade, or buffed off with fine steel wool or a balled-up hunk of aluminum foil.

The frame, cables, and all of the rubber bits, except the tires should be treated to a coating of Armor All or other spray protector/polish. While the frame can be detailed with paste wax it's a big pain in the butt, so my recommendation is to make it easy and use a spray here. If you're detailing the tires, be extremely careful not to get anything on the treads themselves. If you do, a bit of brake cleaner will remove it.

Attack the seat with either Armor All or a leather preservative, rub in with a clean rag, and then polish it off with another clean rag. The seat may become slippery so pay attention for the first few miles.

Small brushes and cotton swabs can be used to work the Armor All into the various nooks and crannies to remove excess dirt.

If your bike sports un-coated billet or other bare aluminum, it can be polished with Simichrome, Autosol, or Mother's Aluminum polish until it shines like chrome. If the stuff is clear-coated hit it with a light coat of wax.

Windshields and other plastic pieces can be cleaned with the same soap and water used on the rest of the bike and they can be polished with plastic cleaners, to remove any fine scratches or crazing. Be careful of the windshield; make sure it's perfectly clean before applying any polishing agents, otherwise you'll basically polish the dirt right into the paint.

Finally go over the bike top to bottom and apply a bit of WD-40 or other light lubricant to any of the pivot points on the bike, such as the brake linkages or shift linkage, where lube was washed away during the cleaning.

Before riding the bike in anger take 'er for a short trip around the block to dry out the brakes, and of course to remove any leftover moisture from all of the little hiding places.

Detailing the bike to the nth degree can sometimes be tedious, but the results are always well worth the effort. Make it easy on yourself, enjoy the day, and look forward to all the compliments you'll receive.

Comfort Is the Key

Washing and detailing can be a physically demanding task with lots of stooping and bending. The use of a bike lift or a small stool with wheels can make the whole job a lot simpler. A mechanic's brake stool is perfect for the job; it's low enough and has a small tray to hold your supplies. By the same token a radio or some other aural diversion can make the whole task more palatable. The bottom line is that if cleaning your bike is a pleasant experience, than you'll do it more often. The more often you do it the easier it becomes and so on until you have the cleanest bike in the neighborhood.

With an assortment of OEM detailing products like this on the shelf, you'd think every bike out there would shine like a new penny!

Custom Turn Signals

 Time: 4 hours

 Tools: Common wiring tools, wire crimp/striping tool, heat-shrink gun and tubing, soldering iron, electrical tape, crimp connectors

 Talent:

 Cost: $100–200

 Tip: Bear in mind that turn signals are a safety device as well as an appearance item.

 PERFORMANCE GAIN: Increased visibility

COMPLEMENTARY MODIFICATION:
Any lighting upgrade

The aftermarket bolt-on.

Although I'm old enough to remember when there was some debate over the effectiveness of turn signal lights, those days are long gone. Today it's universally accepted that turn signals do prevent accidents. Besides, like it or not they are required by law, which leads us to our first consideration.

All motorcycle manufacturers, and H-D is no exception, must install turn signals that conform to federal DOT (as in Department of Transportation) law. As such, the size and configuration is more or less fixed. The aftermarket is under no such constraints. They are free to manufacture turn signals in any shape, size, or color they choose. Many of these lights are not DOT approved. They are sold for "show use" or intended to be used in conjunction with the stock, legally approved lights. Now where I live the cops aren't overly particular about the configuration of the signal lights. As long as you have some they seem to figure that you're acting in good faith. The same may not be true where you live. If your plans include a radical revamp of the turn signals, it might be wise to find out just how far you can go before the local gendarmes start handing out equipment violation tickets.

Hand in hand with that particular issue is one of safety. Many aftermarket signals provide light quality that is as good or better than the stock stuff. In fact some of the aftermarket stuff is as visible as a hooker in church, to put it crudely, but just as many aftermarket lights aren't much brighter than a key chain flashlight. Given the choice between something that looks decent and provides me with a fair margin of safety as opposed to something that looks super trick, yet can't be seen from three feet away, I'd probably go for the brighter lights. But that's just me and I have a strong instinct for self-preservation.

Finally, there is the issue of modern self-canceling trickery. Late-model hogs use pretty sophisticated turn-signal circuits and there is always the possibility that an aftermarket signal light, particularly one that uses a bulb of different wattage than the stock setup may confuse the control unit. There are aftermarket fixes available, and in the main they are easy enough to install. But it is something to consider when considering your lighting changes. In all cases a short conversation with the light manufacturer should set you on the right path.

For some of us, upgrading the signals may involve nothing more than a simple swap of lenses. A wide variety of lens styles and trim pieces are readily available to give your bike a custom look. These can be changed in minutes with nothing more than a screwdriver. There are also myriad kits available to relocate the stock signals; these can be an effective way of cleaning up the front end of the bike.

The ever popular and evergreen blue dot.

An H-D Screaming Eagle.

Moving the signals from the handlebars to the fork, for instance, gives the whole bike a much tidier look, and in many cases may actually increase visibility.

At the rear of the bike you're limited only by your imagination, and in some instances the law. Signals can be relocated, they can be installed in the fender rails, and they can be incorporated into the license plate bracket to name just three quick and dramatic changes.

Lastly there are kits available that allow you to transform your signals into running lights; it may not be cutting-edge technology, but it sure helps the rear of the bike stand out on dark rainy nights.

As with anything of this nature, follow the manufacturer's installation instructions to a "T" and use some common sense. If the install involves splicing wires, make sure the joints are properly made and protected with either heat-shrink tubing or high quality electrical tape. All connections should be lubricated with dielectric

silicone grease. Route any new wiring through plastic conduit or the factory harness. Wires should be secured with zip-ties, or tape, not just left to flop around in the breeze. Front signals may foul the tank; trial-fit them and make certain they don't clobber the tank when the forks are turned before you go to the trouble of permanently mounting and wiring them.

The neat thing about this upgrade is that the choices are practically limitless. The downside also is that the choices are practically limitless so my final suggestion here is to check out as many different styles as possible. If you see something you like mounted to someone's ride, ask for a quick demo. To avoid disappointments, as well as a box full of discarded turn signals, try and view as many different lights as you can, preferably in operation, so you get a feel for the light quality as well as the aesthetics of a given light set before you hand the parts guy your hard-earned cash.

Swapping Taillights

 Time: 1–2 hours

 Tools: Common wiring tools, wire crimp/striping tool, heat-shrink gun and tubing, soldering iron, electrical tape, crimp connectors

 Talent:

 Cost: $100

 Tip: The best solution may simply be a chrome cover and accessory lens

 PERFORMANCE GAIN: The taillight may be all that stands between you and some dork with a cell phone!

COMPLEMENTARY MODIFICATION: Upgraded turn signals and taillights, taillight multiplexer

Like the preceding project on turn signals, there are so many taillights out there that I could darn near do a book just on taillights.

To begin with, there are simple dress-up kits available from the factory itself. Chrome surrounds are available as are a variety of chrome accent pieces. These are also available aftermarket. They are simple and inexpensive to install and do a nice job of adding a little eye candy to the rear of the bike. You can take it a step further if you wish and install one of those strobe-type brake-light bulbs.

Next on the list would be a complete taillight replacement. The evergreen tombstone-style taillight fits most of the Twin Cam models, as does the beehive style. These two lamps have been popular for years for good reason. They

look good and they are easy to mount. They also blend in with most fender contours as well as many of the turn signals that are out there. Of course these lights won't fit, or would look out of place on some models; for instance the Dyna Wide Glide might look a little odd with a tombstone light hung from the rear fender but we'll leave that to your sense of style.

By the same token, some of the Dressers also present problems in that area, primarily due to the way the turn signal bar intrudes into the taillight mounting area. It's obviously an issue that can be dealt with, particularly if you're the creative type and handy with body working tools. Filling in all of the bumps and dents that the factory puts into the fender to make the rear-end lighting package fit seems like a lot of trouble simply because you'd like to change the look of the rear light. There are certainly easier, and in my book, more practical solutions. Face it, by the time you're done bumping and grinding, filling and painting, you could have hung an accessory fender in there, with whatever taillight your little heart desired.

Speaking of bodywork, flush-mounting a taillight is something you see more and more of these days, especially on high-end customs. While it's certainly attractive, they are a lot of work to install. Think this one through carefully before you pick up that Dremel.

Most likely, the biggest problem you'll have in adapting a new taillight will be the wiring. Twin Cams, and in fact all bikes built since 1999 with the exception of the

If the stock taillight isn't enough, you may want to consider adding something that will be certain to catch the attention of any tailgaters. These Stay Off My @$$ (SOMA) LED 3-inch lamps from Rivco for instance, or their flashing brake light modulator.

PERSONAL TOUCHES

Softails, use a circuit board with plug-in wiring. These don't present any insurmountable problems but the board will complicate things slightly. The solution here is to identify each wire before performing any open-loom surgery. The shop manual will provide the necessary information as to which wire feeds what bulb.

So far, everything I've discussed has been largely about appearance, which is understandable. But let's not lose sight of the real function of the taillight, which is to let other drivers know that they are approaching another vehicle and to signal them as to your intentions. Without doubt, the more light—or the more noticeable your standard light is—the better you'll be seen. To that end there are several relatively quick-and-easy changes you can make.

Strobe light–type bulbs are available from several sources and are generally a drop-in replacement. When you step on the brake the pulsating bulb is a real attention grabber. Of course your friends may make jokes about disco being dead, but that's the price of safety. Another kit, sold by The Electrical Connection, turns your turn signals into brake lights; these may not be legal in some states so check your local Department of Motor Vehicles regulations before you order one of these kits. Peel-and-stick brake light/taillight kits are also available. Essentially, these are LED strips that can be positioned nearly anywhere on the rear of the bike and plugged into the tail- and brake light circuit. These are a neat addition primarily because they are easy to see from a distance and can be placed anywhere. Several companies offer bolt-on license plate brackets that contain auxiliary lights. One, manufactured by Big Bike Parts, locates an eight-LED light in the top of a bracket that can be wired to provide either brake or running lights; four LEDs on either side of the bracket can be set up as turn or running lights.

Last but by no means least is the BackOFF-light signal module. Many drivers don't even realize that the brake lights of the motorcycle have come on. The BackOFF is designed to pulse the light, a sure way of making certain that the car behind you knows you're on the brakes. When you hit the brakes the module flashes the brake lights in a preset sequence, three short, and one long pulse; it then repeats itself. The module is unobtrusive and easy to install, needing just two connections.

There you have it. It's true that taillights are a safety device. And just as true that they should/need to have some aesthetic value. The best solution in my book is to combine those two attributes; if you opt for a smaller lamp, cover your butt by installing something like the BackOFF light or perhaps a strobe-lamp bulb to make sure you're visible. If you opt to install additional running lights, do it with some style, perhaps by adding a license plate surround with built-in lights or one of the stick-on light strips. After all, there is no reason safety and style need to be mutually exclusive.

The last word in custom taillights has to be this clear prismatic lens and LED light, along with matching turn signals.

Another Rivco product, these chrome tabs mount the SOMA lights to the stock license plate bracket.

Fiberglass Repair

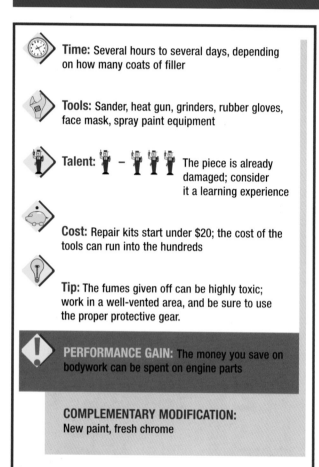

Time: Several hours to several days, depending on how many coats of filler

Tools: Sander, heat gun, grinders, rubber gloves, face mask, spray paint equipment

Talent: The piece is already damaged; consider it a learning experience

Cost: Repair kits start under $20; the cost of the tools can run into the hundreds

Tip: The fumes given off can be highly toxic; work in a well-vented area, and be sure to use the proper protective gear.

PERFORMANCE GAIN: The money you save on bodywork can be spent on engine parts

COMPLEMENTARY MODIFICATION: New paint, fresh chrome

The project heading, Fiberglass Repair, is a misnomer. The fact is, unless you have some aftermarket parts made out of fiberglass stitched onto your bike, your Twin Cam won't have any fiberglass on it. As you might imagine, this would make it difficult to repair. What your bike does have on it are more than a few plastic pieces though, especially if you're riding a Dresser.

Before you start spitting and sputtering about plastic parts on motorcycles, bear in mind that building certain pieces out of plastic offers some serious advantages to the manufacturer, as well as the rider. At the manufacturing level, plastics are inexpensive to work with and complex shapes can be created a lot easier in plastic than they can be in metal. This makes them attractive for things like fairings, side covers, and any non-stressed part. For the rider, the light weight of the plastic offers increased performance and fuel economy, it doesn't rust, and it can be molded in color, which helps hide scratches. From another standpoint plastics are easy to recycle and mostly environmentally friendly. All of that makes them attractive for motorcycle use so I've

no doubt we'll be seeing a lot more of them in the future.

Because the plastic parts or our Harleys are unstressed, chances are that any damage to them has been caused by an accident, as opposed to wear or abuse. Since the plastic pieces are mostly cosmetic, as opposed to structural, the first question is always going to be Should I replace it, repair it, or live with it?

Naturally, the answers are going to be based on individual circumstances and as such, every case will be different. But here are some broad parameters. If the part will cost more to repair than to replace, you're silly to consider repairing it, unless the part is simply unavailable. If the part can be repaired in place, a fairing, for instance, the cost of the new part maybe be offset by the labor required to remove and replace the part. In that case, the repair maybe cheaper over all, than the cost of the new part. In almost every instance the repaired part will need to be refinished, but in some cases the new part will also need painting. In this case it's almost a tossup. Of course some plastic pieces may work just fine with a slight crack or broken tab. If the damage is in a hidden spot, and it doesn't affect the way the bike works you may opt to live with it for awhile. The bottom line is this: If the repair can be done unobtrusively and cheaply, while still looking good, I'd say go for it. If the repair is likely to be expensive, unreliable (hey, it happens to the best) or just really difficult, I'd say go new.

Since I'm not much of a chemist, I'll keep this section brief. Most, if not all of the plastic pieces on your Harley are manufactured from Acrylonitrile Butadiene Styrene or more commonly known as ABS, a form of thermoplastic, meaning that it can be heated and then molded or formed in the desired shape. ABS is generally used for motorcycle fairings, side covers, saddlebags, and things of that nature. Although ABS can be blended with other materials, Polycarbonate, or Nylon, for example, to create hybrids, it's most commonly used in its unadulterated form. What's nice about ABS, outside of the reasons previously mentioned is that it's easy to repair and fillers and paint stick well to it.

Basic repair techniques for use on ABS are as straightforward as with any other material. First I'd recommend you read up on the matter. Since this is one instance where the Motor Company's manual is just about useless, although it will tell you how to remove the broken piece, I'd suggest you pick up a copy of *How To Repair Plastic Body Work* by Kurt Lammon. Kurt's book isn't the most exciting read, but it is informative and will walk you through the repair of all the types of plastics used on Harley-Davidson Motorcycles.

Your first step will be to determine whether or not the repair will be cost effective. Assuming that you've opted to try to repair the damaged piece (what the hell, it's already broken, you may as well give it a shot), you'll need to take the following steps.

First identify the plastic; most plastic pieces, H-D or aftermarket, have some sort of code stamped into them somewhere.

Typically, the piece will simply have a symbol like <ABS> molded into it somewhere. Knowing exactly what the plastic is made of will help you choose the correct repair procedure. Before repairing the piece it must be thoroughly, and I do mean thoroughly, cleaned and degreased. Soap and warm water will work fine for the initial cleaning, or contact your local body shop supply service for dedicated plastic cleaning soap. Plastic cleaning soaps are somewhat gritty which puts a fine scratch finish into the plastic to allow the adhesive to get a good grip. It will also help the prime coat of paint to bite. It's also a good idea to lightly scuff the surface using a red 3M Scotch-Brite pad. If the surface is slimed up with grease, you'll need to clean it more aggressively; your body shop supply can provide you with plastic cleaning solvents; use these with a clean rag to remove any contaminants.

Once it's clean take the time to properly align the edges. In most cases you'll find that the ABS has either cracked or some portion has broken off. A crack won't present any real problem, but a broken off portion will need to be properly aligned before the repair can be done.

The most common way to repair plastic, particularly ABS, is through use of an adhesive. Again, these can be purchased where you picked up your other supplies. Because space here is limited I can't really discuss all of the available options; needless to say, the most common are the two-part adhesives. Typically, these come in tube form. They are mixed and then applied to the broken pieces to rejoin them. If this is your first go-round with plastic, I'd recommend using a common two-part epoxy. These are easy to work with and provide excellent results.

After aligning the parts, rough sand or grind a V-groove into the back of the part; the V-groove provides added strength and makes the repair easier to finish, important when the back side of the repair will be visible. To hold the parts in alignment you can use clamps, duct tape, bailing wire, or anything else that will do the job, including cyanoacrylate glue (such as Super Glue). A piece of aluminum-backed body tape pressed to the front of the crack will help hold everything in alignment and keep the use of body fillers to a minimum.

In some cases, the repair, and/or the material used to make the repair, may call for some reinforcing material, generally fiberglass cloth. The cloth should be cut to overlap the damaged area by at least one inch. Cut the cloth and trial-fit it before you mix up the epoxy.

Follow the manufacturer's instructions and mix up a small batch of epoxy. Start on the back side of the repair;

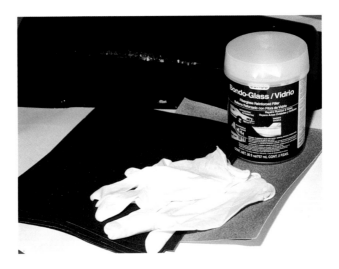

To repair something like this scuffed saddle bag lid, you'll need some filler material, Bondo Pro Glass is an excellent choice, some sand paper in various grits, and a spreading paddle. I'd also recommend rubber gloves.

apply it to the damaged area using a small plastic body spreader. Smooth it over the damaged area and then apply any reinforcing material. Work another coat of glue into the material, while the first is still wet. Allow the back-side repair to harden completely before starting on the front.

Remove any of the holding devices from the front side and grind a V-groove into the crack. The wider the groove, the stronger the repair so don't be afraid to make the groove a good width, maybe 3/4 to 2 inches depending on the thickness of the part and the amount of damage. Open the groove until it meets the filler material applied to the back side. Sand the edges and sides of the groove and round the edges so you get a smooth transition onto the undamaged section of the plastic. Mix up a batch of filler and fill the groove; the filler material should be slightly crowned so it stands a bit proud of the surface. This will make it easier to sand the filler flush. Allow plenty of time for the filler to cure and then start sanding using a 120- to 180-grit paper. Sand the repaired area smooth, featheredging the material onto the original plastic. Low spots will be visible as smooth, shiny areas. Touch them up with sandpaper before adding another dollop of filler to level them off. Once the surface is finished to your liking, prime and paint it using standard painting techniques.

First, rough up the area with a coarse grade of paper, 120 works just fine.

Use a plastic spreader to smoothly apply the filler to the surface. The smoother you get it on now, the less sanding you'll need to do later.

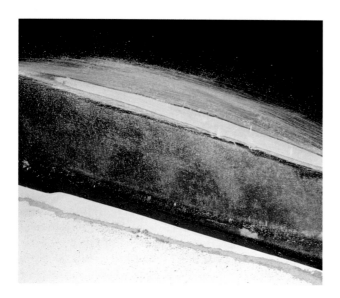

Sand out as many of the scratches as possible, don't worry if a depression forms, we're going to be building the surface up again anyway.

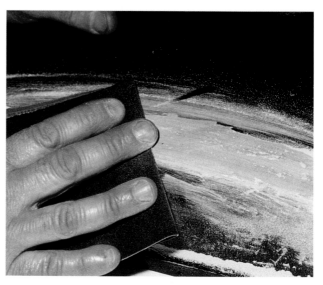

Once the material has set up, begin sanding, working your way towards finer grits as the surface comes down.

If low spots are left, you'll need to mix another small batch of filler and repeat the sanding process. Once the surface is smooth, you can prime and paint it.

A Primer on Paint

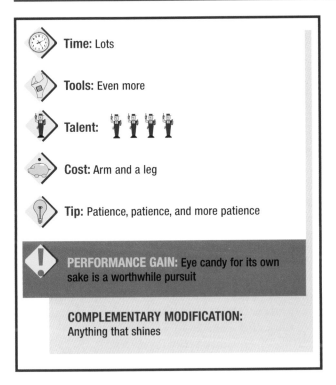

Time: Lots

Tools: Even more

Talent:

Cost: Arm and a leg

Tip: Patience, patience, and more patience

PERFORMANCE GAIN: Eye candy for its own sake is a worthwhile pursuit

COMPLEMENTARY MODIFICATION:
Anything that shines

As they say, "All that glitters isn't gold." In fact all that's red, or black, or purple isn't necessarily red, black, or purple either. Over the years, Harley-Davidson has garnered an enviable reputation for their paint. In fact it's safe to say that their paint jobs are the standard of the industry. They are lustrous, imaginative, perfectly applied, and durable. The fly in the pigment though is describing them.

Obviously there are literally hundreds of shades of the same color, as anyone who's ever gone shopping for house paint or drapes with his better half can attest to. In that respect Harley-Davidson is no different. For example, for red they list literally dozens of distinct shades, everything from Candy Crimson to Signal Red. In fact there are at least a dozen colors alone that may be construed as "red."

How do we tell them apart and how do we describe the exact shade of any color should we need to order up some touch-up paint, or maybe paint our bike in some alternate factory-supplied color scheme?

The answer is simple: Harley assigns a two-letter paint code to every single color. For example, there is Scarlet Red (LZ), Red Voyage (KC), Lazer Red (BT), Midnight Red (BX), and of course Signal Red (GP), plus a host of others. These codes aren't specific to the Twin Cam, in fact the codes are just taken from a list of available H-D paints. But I'm certain you get the point.

Once you know code of the paint you want, which is listed in the parts book, the rest, whether it be buying touch-up paint for your particular model, or buying enough paint to re-do your entire bike, is a straightforward procedure. All you need to know is the model designation, the year, and the color.

With those three facts your favorite parts guy should have no trouble ordering you a tube of touch-up to repair small dings, an aerosol can bigger for projects, or even enough quart cans of paint to color match everything you own to your ride should you so desire. Hell, he can even order up a complete set of bodywork custom painted to any of the available colors.

Perhaps what floats your boat is Purple-Metallic as used in 1987. Well if you waltz on down to the local body shop and tell him you'd like your new Road King painted in Purple-Metallic chances are good that what you'll get won't be the color you had in mind, nor will it be the same color as used by the factory. However if you tell him that the paint you'd like is listed by the factory as code HJ then he can either cross-reference it with his paint supplier or obtain the exact color and the correct base coat and clear coat from the local H-D dealership. And just like that you'll have a brand-new 1987 Twin Cam. Cool isn't it?

The only downside is that not all body shops or paint suppliers may be able to cross-reference the H-D codes to say a PPG or Ditzler color. In that case, you'll have to source the paint through your local dealership; but hell, things could be worse. Can you imagine going into your local house paint store and asking for a quart of Candy Sapphire Sun-glo (VT) to paint your living room walls?

PERSONAL TOUCHES

Paint Repair

 Time: 20 minutes to 1 hour

 Tools: Clean cloths, touch-up paint, polishing compound, wax

 Talent:

 Cost: $20 to over $100

 Tip: Patience is the key to this one

 PERFORMANCE GAIN: Dealing with minor scratches and blemishes now means you won't have cosmetic disaster on your hands down the road

COMPLEMENTARY MODIFICATION: A real good coat of wax will prevent most minor paint damage from occurring

We've all been there and it sucks. In a moment of generosity you let some dink sit on your bike, and he drags his cowboy boots straight across your fender! Or for one brief instant you lose your grip on a wrench and gnash, there goes your gas tank. Whatever it was that caused it, there's now a blemish in your formerly pristine paint job.

Let's face it, no matter how hard you try to keep your bike factory-fresh the odds are always against you. Just riding it down the road will eventually put all sorts of chips in the paint, let alone the previously mentioned unfortunate scenarios. Once you get over the fact that your baby has had her virtue besmirched there are several avenues you can take to rectify the damage, provided of course that the damage is only skin deep.

First calm yourself down; stuff happens and as upset as you may be that the damage was done, raging about it won't get you very far. Of course if a dink did the damage and you choke him within an inch of his life, I think it's justifiable, although most juries probably won't see it that way.

The first thing you'll have to do is assess the damage; is it a minor scuff or blemish in the surface coat that can be polished out? Or is it something that goes deeper than

that? If the paint's been pared through to the primer you'll have to decide whether it can be touched up, or if a call to your favorite painter is in order. My suggestion is to always try to repair the damage; if you can't, or you're just not happy with the way it comes out, then realistically, you're no worse off than you were. Of course if the scrape in the paint includes a dent or dimple in the sheet metal then you're probably going to need professional help, or perhaps learn to live with it.

If the damage is limited to a scrape, scuff, or small scratch you're in luck; well kind of, anyway. As I've already mentioned in the previous project, H-D takes great pride in their paint jobs and they should. Unfortunately, once the bikes leave the factory, stuff does happen. Particularly when the bikes are parked on the showroom floor. Showroom bikes are sat on, fondled, drooled over, and sadly, scratched and scuffed. Since no one wants a brandy-new bike that's been all scuffed up, and neither the factory nor the dealers want to replace any scratched or scuffed bodywork, any damage to the finish of a brand-new, unsold bike, presents a serious problem.

On the bright side, most showroom damage, at least according to my friends down at the local H-D dealership, tends to be relatively minor and is predominately slight scratches and scuffs, the type of thing that most bikes acquire after a year or two of service. Since the Motor Company wants your new bike to look brand spanking new, and presumes that both you and your dealer feel the same way, the factory developed a paint repair kit that can be used to repair most imperfections.

The kit (part No. 39994) ain't cheap; you won't get much change back from a hundred dollar bill. In fact you may have to pony up a few more bucks, but it is comprehensive and it does work. The kit includes several grades of rubbing compound, 1,200-grit paper, buffing pads, cotton clothes, Hook-it pads, a sanding pad, and finishing polishes. It also comes with complete instructions. Of course if you're a little on the chintzy side you can buy the individual components off the shelf, either through H-D or the aftermarket but the final cost will be about the same and the kit includes all of the right stuff in one handy package.

Essentially, the procedure calls for washing the area down with a mixture of alcohol and water to remove any traces of dirt and wax. From there you start polishing and buffing. Depending on the severity of the damage this may involve nothing more than using the finest grade of compound or it may require a bit of sanding followed by polishing and then buffing the area with a drill and Hook-it

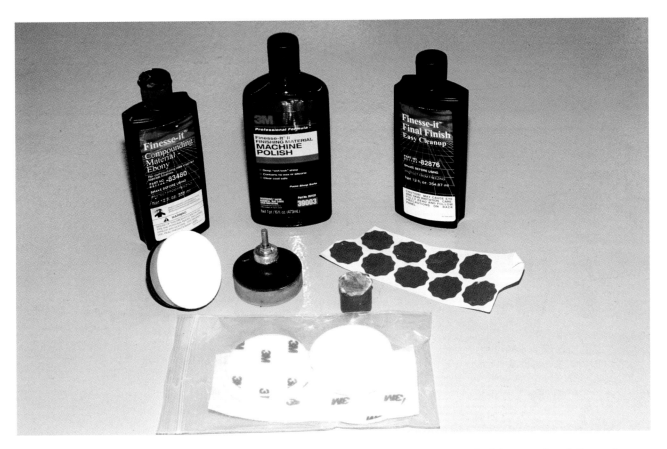

HD dealers use this factory kit to remove showroom blemishes and worse. The kit contains different grades of polish, some extremely fine sandpaper, and polishing pads.

pad. At some point you'll either decide the repair is perfect, it's good enough to live with, or something else needs to be done. At that point you can protect the area with a good coat of Carnauba wax or move on to plan B.

Plan B, ah yes, there is always a Plan B. In this "not-really-the-worst-case scenario," let's imagine that, horror of horrors, somehow your paint has been scraped to bare metal. At this stage you've got three choices. You can attempt a touchup, you can replace the offending part with a factory-painted replacement, or you can have the damaged piece repainted. The last two, we'll consider them Plan C, are decisions only you and your favorite body man can make. Realistically, if the sheet metal or plastic is damaged or dented they are the only choices. But if the bruise is limited to a surface injury, the first, Plan B might just be doable.

Touching up is done all the time; in some instances the repair might not even be noticeable; in others, it will stand out like the proverbial sore thumb, but at this point you really don't have much choice do you?

The first thing you'll need is the correct color touch-up paint. The previous project explained all of that, so for now we'll assume you've got the correct shade in hand. Next pick up a very fine, very high quality, artist's or mod-eler's paintbrush from the local craft or hobby shop. As before, clean the damaged area thoroughly with a 50/50 mix of alcohol and water to remove any trace of wax and dirt. Shake the touch-up paint vigorously to thoroughly mix it. Pick up a drop of paint and dab it onto the scrape; try and let the droplet of paint fall into the damaged area and flow outward; avoid brushing it. Let it dry for a day or two and then remove any overpainting with a very, very fine polishing compound. Clean the area again with the alcohol and water mix. If the spot looks decent you can either build it up with another drop of paint before repeat-ing the process or dab a bit of clear onto it to finish the job. Again let the paint harden for at least 24 hours before attempting any polishing. I've seen good painters/detailers use a toothpick or matchstick as a substitute for the brush but frankly I think the brush is easier to use and does a bet-ter job. This type of work demands a lot of patience so work slowly and methodically and bear in mind that the damage is already done, you can only make it better, and there is always Plan C if you can't.

One last word, a good coat of wax, preferably Carnauba-based will forestall most scratching, as will a bit of common sense; when using a wrench, cover the painted bits with a towel or heavy cloth to prevent accidental dam-age. And the next time the neighborhood dink asks you if he can sit on your bike, politely but firmly tell him "Sure, but only if you're naked."

Installing Chrome Handlebar Control Pods

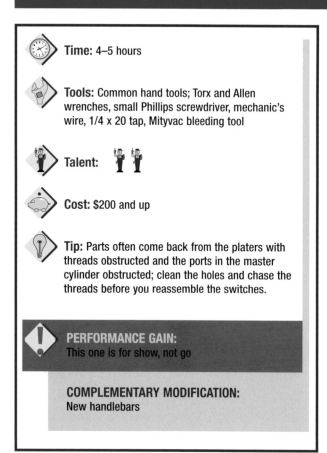

Time: 4–5 hours

Tools: Common hand tools; Torx and Allen wrenches, small Phillips screwdriver, mechanic's wire, 1/4 x 20 tap, Mityvac bleeding tool

Talent: 👤 👤

Cost: $200 and up

Tip: Parts often come back from the platers with threads obstructed and the ports in the master cylinder obstructed; clean the holes and chase the threads before you reassemble the switches.

PERFORMANCE GAIN:
This one is for show, not go

COMPLEMENTARY MODIFICATION:
New handlebars

Eye candy truly is the Harley rider's best friend!

Some of us just want the whole motorcycle to shine like a new penny and there is absolutely nothing wrong with that. You might make the argument that the more chrome, the easier the bike is to keep clean. There are several ways to chrome your handlebar control pods. You can buy them along with the bike by ordering up a CVO, Screamin' Eagle model. (Maybe that's not so practical if you just bought a new Ultra Glide, but it is an avenue to consider.) You can remove all of your hardware, strip the guts and wiring out of it, and ship it off to be chromed. But it will take forever to get the stuff back, or at least it'll seem that way. Then you'll have to chase all the threads and give the master cylinder a good cleaning to make sure that the shiny matter didn't end up where it shouldn't. You can buy aftermarket stuff or do a swap with a shop that offers such a thing but you may end up with an unknown caliber, although some of the aftermarket stuff is of excellent quality. Or you can do what I'd do and that is go directly to that big parts and accessory book and order up the good stuff right from the factory; the bars will fit perfectly, and it's essentially a plug-and-play swap.

So here's the skinny once you decide on one of the above scenarios. The service manual goes into great detail for removing and replacing the switch gear so there is no need to repeat it here. However, the manual doesn't tell you what to look for between removing the OEM black finished pieces and stitching the now-bright shiny jobs back on.

If you're replacing dull OEM stuff with shiny new OEM stuff, there really isn't much to be concerned with. The new factory parts are held to the same high standards as the parts that originally came with your bike. Installing them should be a routine, by-the-numbers job. Bleeding the master cylinder will be the hardest part of the job and even that shouldn't be that difficult. See the sidebar for details.

If you've had your stuff plated, the toughest job will be rebuilding the master cylinder. My advice is to install a factory rebuild kit; no sense fooling around with the old parts, and risking a leak. Hopefully the chrome shop knew their stuff and didn't plate the inside of the cylinder bore. If they did, you might be able to lightly hone out the bore. Or you might need to have the shop reverse the chroming process, strip all the plating, and start fresh. This makes a good case for using an experienced shop doesn't it? It's also

Bleeding the Brakes

The Harley-Davidson–factory service manual has a very easy to follow 10-step method for bleeding your brakes. It's basically the same as everyone else's 10-step method; you fill the reservoir, pump the lever, and open the bleeder screw. If all goes well, the brakes will soon pump up, all the air will be expelled from the system, and you'll have a nice firm lever. The problem is that the bleeding method, just like everyone else's, presupposes that air wants to move downward. It doesn't; air likes to rise through fluid to the highest point of the brake system. When you fill a master cylinder with fluid, the fluid theoretically forces the air through the lines until it reaches the brake caliper where it can be released through the bleed valve.

In reality, the air bubbles become trapped in all of the bends of the brake line and stuck in all of the nooks and crannies. Hence, you often end up pumping the brake lever and opening the bleeder screw until you're blue in the face and with little else but a spongy lever to show for all your hard work.

There are several ways to make bleeding the system much easier. First there are pressure bleeders that force brake fluid into the system from the caliper end under slight pressure. As the fluid enters the system from the bottom, it forces the air toward the master cylinder where it vents into the atmosphere. Pressure bleeders can be air powered (expensive), or manual, basically big syringes, which are cheap. As an alternative, use an old-style, squirt-type oil can, provided it's completely clean. Better yet, use a new one.

To pressure-bleed the system fill the tool with fresh, clean brake fluid, and remember that all H-D's require DOT 5, silicone brake fluid; anything else is unacceptable.

Connect the pump to the caliper and open the bleeder screw. Pump the fluid into the caliper keeping a close eye on the master cylinder. When the fluid reaches the master-cylinder full line, stop pumping and close the bleeder screw. Pump the brake; if everything is well the brake should have a firm feel to it. If not, some residual air may still be trapped somewhere, particularly if the bike has a dual disc brake on it. If that's the case, try some conventional bleeding.

Second on the easy-bleeding top hits list are vacuum pumps like the Mityvac, which can also be used as a pressure pump. In the vacuum mode, the pump is connected to the bleeder screw of the caliper. The master cylinder is filled and the pump activated. While the tool draws a vacuum, the caliper bleeder screw is opened. The vacuum will pull fluid through the system along with any trapped air. Watch the catch cup on the tool; when air bubbles stop forming in the fluid, the brakes should be fully bled.

a great idea to chase all of the threads in the housing using your tap, and run a bit of wire through the master cylinder ports just in case some chrome snuck in where it wasn't supposed to.

Aftermarket direct replacement or exchange parts should first be inspected for overall quality. Make sure the plate job is up to your standards and that the screw holes aren't damaged. Run a bit of wire through the master cylinder ports and inspect the bore for damage. Also make sure that silly things like the master cylinder cover fit properly and that there are no big pit marks or misaligned switch halves. Lastly make sure that the master cylinder bore size is correct for your application. The long and short of it all is that waiting until you bolt the new switch gear onto the bike before you decide it's not good enough is the ultimate waste of energy.

Selecting and Changing Handlebars

 Time: 1–4 hours

 Tools: Basic hands tools, Torx sockets, Allen wrenches, WD-40, long thin screwdriver, old blanket or thick toweling, optional compressed air

 Talent:

 Cost: Figure at least $100; more if peripherals like grips and cables need to be changed

 Tip: Make certain that new bars are what you really want; changing the bars affects more than just comfort; the bike will respond differently to steering inputs.

 PERFORMANCE GAIN: The bend of the bar can really affect the way the bike steers. In my book, low and flat works way better than high, wide, and handsome

COMPLEMENTARY MODIFICATION: Upgraded cables, chrome controls, through-the-bar wiring

The choice of handlebar height, width, and bend is entirely subjective. As such, my recommendation is to always go with the most comfortable choice. There are a few basic rules that if followed will hopefully prevent you from searching through an almost endless selection of tubing in the search for that elusive, perfect handlebar.

Handlebars are described by measurements in several different planes. First is the overall height, which normally is the distance from the lowest point to the highest point, although the highest point may not be where you hold onto the bars. Next is the overall width of the bars measured end to end. Lastly, the bars are measured for sweep, or pull back, which is the distance from the forwardmost portion of the bar to the rearward. Some bars may also be described by the width at the clamping point of the bars. This isn't normally an issue, unless your bike has a nacelle or cover over the handlebars, such as the FL line. In such cases a too-narrow dimension at the clamping point may make the bars difficult or impossible to fit.

For most of us, the handlebar dimensions aren't something that we really consider, even when searching for a new pair. But that's why lots of us end up trying several different pairs until we strike on something that we like, or at least are willing to live with.

If you know the handlebar dimensions you can narrow the search considerably. For example if the bars feel fine as far as the height and width, but just feel like they force you to lean too far forward, a change in sweep may be all you need. If that's the situation, a look through any catalog will point you in the right direction. If the bars feel fine as far as sweep and width go, but just seem a bit low, you can search for the same pattern bar with just a little more rise to it.

But what if you just don't like the bars at all? Well if that's the case then toss 'em and bolt on something you do like, but first let's consider a few simple rules that might make the job easier.

The wider the bar, the more leverage you'll have. If you're swapping bars on a Dresser, or you're already straining to balance your bike at low speeds, it's something to consider. Next, the higher the bars, the less control you'll have over the bike. Ridiculously high "ape hanger" style bars are the worst possible choice of handlebar; they should be considered strictly a styling exercise. If you do go with a super high bar make certain that the clamping area of the bar is well knurled. If it isn't it's liable to slip under hard braking, or at almost any other time, due to the leverage imposed by the long length.

In general, riders that rack up lots of miles or ride at high speeds tend to prefer a lower bar, particularly on unfaired bikes, or ones without windshields. Think of the bars on the FXDX Dyna Super Glide Sport or Dyna Super Glide. Lower bars get you down out of the wind so your body doesn't act like a giant sail. If some sort of wind protection is fitted you can opt for a higher bar. Something to consider if you plan to actually go somewhere on your bike, as opposed to just parking it in front of the local watering hole.

Cable lengths are always a consideration when bar swapping. In general if you're installing bars that mimic the original bend, or aren't terribly different in any dimension, you can probably get away with using the stock cables, although in some instances some creative rerouting may be in order. Bars that are much higher or much shorter will require cables to match.

The mechanics of changing the bars are laid out in the shop manual so I'll just hit a few high points. The thing that presents the most difficulty to the novice mechanic

Choose your handlebars carefully. Few accessories have as much effect on comfort or control.

always seems to be removing that danged left-side grip. There are two easy ways to do it. The first method is to remove the throttle drum, poke an air gun into the open end of the handlebar, use rags to seal the opening, and using shop air, pressurize the bar; it may take a few attempts but the grip should eventually pop free. The second method involves using a long thin bladed screwdriver and some brake or contact cleaner. Work the end of the screwdriver under the grip; spray a bit of cleaner into the gap. Work the screwdriver in a little farther and spritz some more cleaner. At some point the grip should slide free. Of course all of this is moot if you're going to replace the grips. Use a razor blade and cut the bugger off.

Once you've settled on a handlebar, give it a trial fit, make certain it clears the fuel tank, and feels comfortable when you're sitting on the bike. Here's a tip; many times I've seen bars positioned in a way that puts the rider's arms and wrists in an unnatural position. Start by positioning the upright section of the bar inline with the fork tubes. Make any final adjustments from there. Loosely install all of the switches and levers, adjusting them to

their most comfortable position. Don't forget to apply a little light grease on the bar where the throttle tube will ride. Install your cables making sure there is no binding when the forks are swung from lock to lock. Make certain that the brake line is free to compress without catching on anything, and check for any possible chafe or pinch points. If you opted for stainless-steel wrapped cables, make sure they aren't going to saw through any painted parts. Steel cables should always be protected with clear tubing or some sort of insulator, at least when they pass by anything you don't want damaged. Always use a bit of glue grip to secure the grips on both sides and be sure to let it dry for a few minutes before riding the bike.

After everything is comfortably adjusted and tightened down, go through a dry run. Make sure the switches all work, and that the clutch and throttle have the correct free play. Make absolutely certain that the front brake works properly.

Finally, with the engine idling, turn the bars from lock to lock; if the idle speed increases, the throttle-cable free play will need readjusting. Adjust the mirrors, and you're done.

Installing Forward Controls

 Time: 3 hours maximum

 Tools: Common hand tools, anti-seize lubricant, Loctite

 Talent:

 Cost: Depends on what you buy of course, but don't expect much change from a pair of Franklin's

 Tip: Lubricate the pivot points with anti-seize or stiff grease; Loctite everything else

PERFORMANCE GAIN: This one makes the long days in the saddle a lot more bearable

COMPLEMENTARY MODIFICATION:
Bar change, new seat

What's that you say, my friend? You're tired of being folded up like a carpenter's ruler whenever you ride your Dyna or FXR? The solution is simple: Install forward controls.

Forward controls have been around nearly since the inception of the custom motorcycle. If nothing else, they'll provide some degree of comfort particularly on those long straight stretches, and if you're still wearing those 1970s style elephant bell bottoms you can put your feet down without worrying about getting your pants caught on the pegs.

Finding a set of forward controls isn't difficult, everyone from the factory on down offers some type of kit. Due to the proliferation of available kits, picking the exact one you want may be time consuming but, rest assured, you'll find something that floats your boat. My advice here is to proceed slowly. If possible, ride a bike that has the control setup you think you'd like installed on it before plunking down your hard-won shekels. Consider, too, the finish. Chrome? Billet? Chrome-plated billet? Billet-plated chrome? Flat, black sewer pipe? There are lots of kits out there!

Installing the average forward control kit is as easy as falling off a log, not to mention a good deal less painful. In fact this would make one of the better first projects for the budding mechanic.

Depending on the kit and the model you're installing it on, the exhaust may have to come off. You'll also need to remove the OEM brake pedal and shift lever, and of course, the shift lever rod. With some kits, the brake master cylinder may have to be relocated. If so, when deciding on a kit, consider where it will go and if you really want to put it there.

When installing the new kit pay particular attention to the shift rod; make sure that both the transmission lever and the lever on the shifter itself end up as close as possible to perpendicular to each other. If not, the shift action may feel odd, and there is a chance the shifter could bind. Make sure to lubricate the linkage pivot points as well. I've seen more than one instance of a sticking shifter caused by dry pivots.

Once everything is in place, fit yourself to the new pegs, or floorboards if that's the way you've decided to go. Take the time to adjust the angle of the pegs and levers to your liking. Once the rough adjustments are made, use the adjusting turnbuckles in the linkage to fine-tune the shifter and brake pedal height. Make certain that the shift moves freely and that the brake pedal has adequate free play. Once everything is nice-nice, use a drop of blue Loctite to secure the jam nuts. It's not a bad idea to use a drop on all of the securing hardware as well.

All buttoned up? Take 'er for a test ride, in comfort!

These custom floorboards and shifters (left and right) combine eye-candy and comfort.

Selecting and Changing Seats

Time: 1/2 to 1 hour

Tools: Common hand tools

Talent:

Cost: $200 and up

Tip: A good seat is your best riding buddy

PERFORMANCE GAIN: The more comfortable you are, the better you'll ride

COMPLEMENTARY MODIFICATION: How about a nice seat for your passenger as well?

Many moons ago, back in the days when the Shovel Head engine was considered state of the art in H-D engine design, I worked for a guy that had been selling motorcycles since they came with a leather belt drive. Every so often we'd be forced to take in a real bowser as a trade-in. Whenever I questioned his wisdom in accepting some of these motorcycles—and I use the word "motorcycles" in its loosest sense—he'd give me a nod and a wink, and say, "Kid, there's an ass for every seat." He was right.

The seat situation vis-à-vis your Harley is just like that only different. In this case there is literally a seat for every ass. In fact there are so many seats that fit Harleys out there, that attempting to list every one of them or even half of them would be ludicrous, and that's presuming that we stuck to ones that are available just over the counter!

There are seats that are just about style, there are seats that let you rack up the miles, there are seats that are color coordinated and there are seats that can be custom fit to your buns only. You can get seats that are covered with leather, suede, Naugahyde (just what is a Nauga anyway?), Ostrich or snake skin, and just about anything in between. You can have a removable or permanent backrest affixed. You can even get air seats and gel seats. You can get just about any sort of seat you can think of, from an over-the-counter cheapie, to a one-of-a-kind, custom-made,

hand-upholstered model that's lovingly molded to fit only your cheeks and finished with the hide of some exotic beast.

And therein lies the problem. Just how do you choose the correct seat? Good question, but unfortunately one without a hard-and-fast solution. Obviously if you're building an all-out, no-expense-spared custom ride, perhaps one that will only see limited real-world use, you can have someone whip up a seat to complement the rest of the bike. If it's uncomfortable or impractical, who really cares? No one on the show circuit will know that sitting on the thing is like being a guest of the Spanish Inquisition. But what about the rest of us that live and ride in the real world?

Before you rip the stock seat off and start bolting on something else, take a moment to reflect on exactly why you want to replace your current seat. Is it ugly? Or maybe just uncomfortable? My guess is that most H-D seats, at least the ones on Big Twins, get replaced mainly because the owners don't like the way they look, rather than for reasons of comfort. Obviously, selecting a seat solely for its appearance may have some drawbacks.

Use a little common sense. That Corbin Gunfighter looks terrific when you're styling around town (and I'm not picking on Corbin here, the Gunfighter is actually pretty comfortable in most circumstances). But do you really think you and your special friend want to ride from Maine to Sturgis on it? Consider the overall practicality of your choice as well; that yellow anaconda skin with the chipmunk fur inlay will certainly look bitchin'. Until it gets caught in the rain a few times. The lesson here should be obvious. If you're a full-time, all-weather, all-season rider, stay away from the style-at-any-price exotic-type seats. And if you do choose some sort of high-zoot material, at least make sure you get a rain cover with it.

So my first piece of advice is to make sure that the seat you select fits in with your riding style. If you plan on touring on the bike, there are better choices than an old-fashioned bicycle-style seat and matching P-Pad. My second suggestion, after you've decided on a style and brand of seat, is to try and sit on someone's motorcycle that has the seat you think you'd like already bolted on to it. This may take some serious persuading; not many guys like to let total strangers hop on their bikes! But you'll never know if you don't ask, will you? The only real fly in this ointment is that a seat may feel perfectly comfortable when the motorcycle that it's bolted onto is stationary yet turn into an instrument of torture an hour down the road. This isn't always the case of course, and in fact doesn't

Seats, like paint jobs, are a matter of personal taste. This off-the-rack Corbin provides a comfortable, and complimentary finish to this all American custom Softail.

happen all that often; however, it is something to consider. Of course if you're able to persuade someone to actually let you test-ride the seat, with motorcycle attached, then more power to you.

In reality, most of us won't get a posterior trial run, what we'll get is a huge catalog, including H-D's own accessory book, or maybe a dealer's wall full of seats to choose from. In that case it's liable to be a 50/50 shot between numb buns and all-day comfort. So what's the solution?

My first inclination is to suggest you start by looking at the optional seats that the Motor Company offers. Particularly if it's only the appearance of the seat you'd like to change. By using an OEM accessory seat, you know the fit and finish will be up to the same high standards as the original stuff, and that if something odd happens, it'll be covered under warranty. Unfortunately, the factory may not have what you want. If that's the case, my second suggestion would be to hit the aftermarket, where there's a lot of choice. My advice is to always stay with the known manufacturers, or ones that are represented by major distributors. Companies like Corbin, Sargent, Mustang, Le Pera, and Saddleman/Travelcade to name just five, have all been in business a long time and have earned good reputations for a reason. They all make great seats and in some cases, may even offer a custom service that will allow you to modify the stock seat or one of theirs to your liking. They can offer you plenty of input as to which seat will suit you best and if there is some problem, they can generally rectify the situation to everyone's satisfaction.

If you just can't find anything seat-wise that floats your boat you can always turn to the local custom shop. Over the years, I've obtained some excellent results by taking the original seat down to the local upholstery shop and having them stitch up a new cover or cut new foam to my specifications. Custom shops offer the widest available choices in seat cover material and color and most can cut the seat foam to any shape you desire. Unfortunately you'll need to use the stock seat pan, or custom shape your own out of aluminum; few upholstery shops handle that end of the job. If you're not sure where to start should you choose this route, hit the local hot-rod car hangouts and ask around; the four-wheel guys are pretty picky about their interiors and should be able to point you in the right direction. And of course there is always the phone book!

My last piece of advice is simply this: Remember the old proverb, "Act in haste, repent at leisure." If you buy the wrong seat you'll be reminded of it every time you go for a ride. While you can certainly replace your new seat, it's hardly the cost-effective way to go. So take your time, do your research, and reread the first paragraph of this project if you can't find what you want at the first stop.

Applying Coatings

 Time: 1 hour to many months depending on what and how you coat

 Tools: Depends how much of the motorcycle you're taking apart to be refinished

 Talent: ∯ – ∯ ∯ ∯

 Cost: $4.95 up to many thousands of dollars

 Tip: If you plan on coating anything that makes heat or moves, consult an experienced hand before applying anything that isn't stock.

 PERFORMANCE GAIN: Pick the wrong coating and you'll lose performance. Pick the right one, and things may improve

COMPLEMENTARY MODIFICATION: Custom paint, chrome, and polish

Everybody loves to paint, polish, powder-coat, and chrome the various bits and pieces that make up our hogs. But here's the catch: How many of us consider what all that primping and polishing, coating and chroming is doing to the parts we're slapping it on?

Let me explain; there are some parts of our motorcycles that are heat generators. The two most obvious ones are the engine and the brakes. While some heat is a good thing, any excess must be dissipated. If it isn't, the end result is an overheated component. In the case of the engine, overheating results in reduced power, followed shortly by a breakdown of the oil, and if the overheating is allowed to continue, damaged engine components. Overheating the brakes causes them to fade, which usually results in soiled undergarments and, quite possibly, a crashed motorcycle.

Because the Twin Cam engine is air-cooled its cylinders are equipped with fins. The fins act as heat transfer points that allow the heat to radiate outward, and provide more surface area than you'd have otherwise. Heat flows from the combustion chamber into the fins. Air flowing over the fins then removes the heat. A portion of the

engine's heat is also dissipated into surrounding parts, for example the crankcase and outer covers. This is especially true when the bike isn't moving. Of course the oil carries away some of the heat. This heat is released into the airstream when the oil returns to the oil tank, and air flowing across the tank's surface carries it off.

The brake calipers also receive a cooling airflow. They don't get as much air as the cylinders do, but under normal conditions they don't need as much either.

The object of air cooling is to transfer as much heat as possible into the surrounding atmosphere. Some surface treatments, coatings in our case, do this better than others. Coat the surface with the right stuff and cooling is enhanced. Coat it with the wrong stuff and cooling will be retarded, in some cases to the point where overheating and damage can result.

The three most popular coatings used on motorcycles are painting, plating, and powder coating. All three work, and with proper application, work fine. The problem lies in that phrase—"proper application."

The best type of finish for heat transfer is one that is rough cast and unpainted. Rough cast pieces have a lot of little nooks and crannies, which increase surface area making it easier for them to give up some heat This is why older cylinders, heads, and crankcases were left as cast. This is also why they were generally left unpainted. If they were painted they were usually painted flat black.

Black paint, either flat or semigloss, radiates heat well; for that reason it's always been popular as an engine finish, and many brake calipers are also finished in black for the same reason. Lighter colors generally don't work as well. However many factories, the Motor Company included, do use various shades of gray and silver to paint the crankcases. When they are used, these paints are specially formulated to withstand high engine temperatures and to help radiate heat away from the engine. In some instances a clear lacquer coating may also be used to protect a polished finish.

Chrome plating any heat-radiating surface is a bad practice. Plating insulates the surface, which traps heat in. So the first rule is never, ever chrome anything that is a potential source of heat; this includes cylinders, heads, brake calipers, and of course crankcases. I also dislike chrome-plated oil tanks for the same reason, but because the oil tank has so much surface area, plating it can normally be done with no ill affects.

Chrome also produces problems in other areas. Without getting into chemistry 101 it should suffice to say that the chroming process can change the nature of the base metal to which the chrome is applied. If the wrong

PERSONAL TOUCHES

Powdercoated cylinders look great, but they tend to hold heat in, which may lead to overheating problems down the road.

chrome process is used with a part never intended to be chromed, you may (emphasis on *may*), run into something called Hydrogen-embrittlement, which allows the base metal to crack. It might not be a big deal if your light bar cracks after a few months. But if that chrome frame decides to reduce itself to component parts, I guarantee it'll ruin your day. If you really need a frame that shines, have it nickel plated, it'll look better anyway.

Alloy parts can be chrome plated. But in my experience plated aluminum just doesn't hold up very well. If you want some shiny alloy, polish it and then coat it with clear lacquer, which is what the Motor Company and nearly every other manufacturer does. Or do as most of us do and just polish the bejesus out of it anytime it gets dull.

The bottom line on chrome is this: Avoid chroming major engine components, especially those that need to transfer a lot of heat and parts, such as frames, that were never intended to be chromed in the first place. I'd strongly advise against chrome plating brake calipers as well. If you want your stoppers shiny, buy polished billet.

Powder coating is a process that essentially sprays very fine plastic beads onto electrically charged, heated metal.

The metal is generally heated to something close to 600 degrees F and then the beads are blasted on with a spray gun. The piece being painted is grounded and the spray gun charged and polarized with a small bit of current. This gives the part being coated and the coating material opposite charges so they attract each other. This improves adhesion and practically ensures that no portion will go uncoated. When the beads hit the part, they stick, melt, and spread evenly across the surface. When the parts cool they are for all intents plastic coated and as such impervious to most types of damage.

Powder coating isn't without its problems. The high temperatures involved preclude the coating of any soldered part, and many light-gauge pieces. Color choices are limited and while the finish is perfectly acceptable for frames and structural bits, it's sometimes too coarse for cosmetic items, although that's changing on an almost daily basis. Powder coating may also be problematic when very high temperatures are involved such as an exhaust system. If a colored exhaust system is your thing, look into one of the ceramic coatings available, or use tried-and-true hi-temperature paint.

I'd also caution against powder coating some engine parts, particularly the cylinders and heads. Because powder coating essentially plastic-wraps the part, it tends to trap heat so I'd save its use for things like frames and other non-heat-producing parts.

So far, all of our coatings have focused on outside use. As an aside, you should be aware that some internal parts are coated as well. For a number of years now the Motor Company has been coating the piston skirts with an anti-friction compound. The compound reduces break-in time and extends the life of the piston and cylinder. It's good stuff, and shows how seriously the factory takes things like heat transfer.

It's been said that clothes make the man and I suppose that in a sense that's just as true where motorcycles are concerned. Although in this case it's the outer coatings we cover our bikes with that can make, or in some cases break, our bikes.

Coating Common Sense

Be careful when coating heat sources: chrome and in most cases powder-coats hold heat in.

Factory frames should be painted or powder-coated. If you're building a Twin Cam custom using an aftermarket frame, consult the manufacturer before plating it. Fork components can be polished, painted, or powder-coated; chrome is also acceptable, although I'd be leery of chroming the triple clamps.

Chroming the brake calipers is a no-no, and I'm not too fond of chrome rotors either—primarily because plated rotors don't stop very well, especially when they get wet.

In my opinion, sheet metal looks best painted. But there are instances where chrome or powder coating is acceptable, or even desirable, so when it comes to things like fenders, tanks, and trim, let your imagination and good taste be your guide.

When in doubt as to a coating's suitability, consult your plater, painter, or powder-coater. These guys know what works, and just as importantly, what doesn't.

Don't expect any plated or powder-coated piece to be ready to install when you get it back. Always run a tap through the threaded holes and run a short piece of wire through each and every passage.

Powdercoating is sometimes a little coarse for some body parts, although I like the way this matte-finished fender came out.

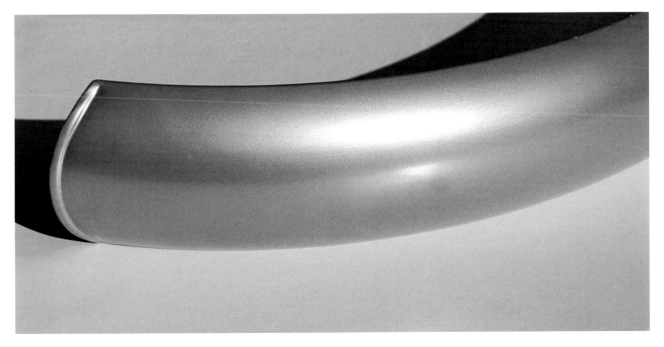

Though not all of the companies listed here were named in the text, they also make excellent products for your bike that can be bolted up like the ones shown. A quick check of their web site or a call will let you know what they offer.

Andrews Performance
431 Kingston Court
Mt. Prospect, IL 60056
847/759-0190
www.AndrewsProducts.com

Back-Off Lights
RIVCO Products Inc.
440 South Pine Street
Burlington, WI 53105
262/763-8222
www.RivcoProducts.com

BAKER Drivetrain
9804 East Saginaw
Haslett, MI 48840
517/339-3835
www.BAKERdrivetrain.com

Balance Masters
PO Box 9154
Canoga Park CA 91309
818/882-8431
www.BalanceMasters.com

Barnett Tool & Engineering
2238 Palma Drive
Ventura, CA 93003
805/642-9435
www.BarnettClutches.com

Bassani Exhaust
North County Customs
1631 North Placentia Ave.
Suite E
Anaheim, CA 92806
714/680-6737
www.NorthCountyCustoms.com

Corbin Seats
2360 Technology Way
Hollister, CA 95023
831/634-1100
www.CorbinSeats.com

Crane Cams
530 Fentress Blvd.
Daytona Beach, FL 32114
904/252-1151
www.CraneCams.com

Custom Chrome
See your local Custom Chrome dealer
www.CustomChrome.com

Delkron Manufacturing
5159 South Prospect St.
Ravenna, OH 44266
330/577-0006
www.Delkron-Mfg.com

Deltran Corp.
801 US Highway 92 East
Deland, FL 32724
386/736-7900
www.BatteryTender.com

Dr. Dyno
860/599-2396
www.DrDyno.com

Dynojet Research
2191 Mendenhall Drive
North Las Vegas, NV 89031
702/639-1159
www.Dynojet.com

EBC Brakes
EBC Buildings
Countess Road
Sylmarnorth, Hampton
England NN57EAV
425/486-1244
www.EBCbrakesUSA.com

Fred's Auto Machine
151 Grassy Plain St. Unit 2C
Bethel, CT 06801
203/744-2950

GMA Engineering
13525 A Street
Omaha, NE 68114
402/330-5105
www.GMAbrakes.com

Harley-Davidson of Danbury
51 Federal Road
Danbury, CT 06810
203/730-2453
www.HDofDanbury.com

Harley-Davidson
Motor Company
3700 West Juneau Ave.
Milwaukee, WI 53201
www.Harley-Davidson.com

Hayden Enterprises
840 East Parkridge Ave.
Suite 106
Corona, CA 92879
800/664-6872
www.HaydensM6.com

Headwinds
221 West Maple Avenue
Monrovia, CA 91016
626/359-8044
www.Headwinds.com

Hemi Design
3147 South Austin Blvd.
Cicero, IL 60565
708/652-1033
www.HemiDesign.com

Jagg Oil Coolers
3958 North S.R. 3
Sunbury, OH 43074
740/965-8837
www.Setrab.com

JIMS USA
555 Dawson Drive
Camarillo, CA 93012
805/482-6913
www.jimsUSA.com

K&N Engineering
1455 Citrus Avenue
Riverside, CA 92507
909/826-4000
www.KNfilters.com

Le Pera
8207 Lankershim Blvd.
N. Hollywood, CA 91605
818/767-7462
www.LePera.com

Mustang Seats
278 Town Hill Road
Terryville, CT 6786
860/582-9633
www.MustangSeats.com

Performance Machine
6892 Marlin Circle
La Palma, CA 90623
714/523-3000
www.PerformanceMachine.com

Pro-One Performance
2700 Melbourne Avenue
Pomona, CA 91767
909/445-0900
www.PRO-ONE.com

Race Tech
1501 Pomona Road
Corona, CA 92880
909/279-6655
www.RaceTech.com

Rivera Engineering
12532 Lambert Road
Whittier, CA 90605
562/907-2600
www.RiveraEngineering.com

S&S Cycle Inc.
14025 County Highway G
Viola, WI 54664
608/627-1497
www.SScycle.com

Spectro Oils
993 Federal Road
Brookfield, CT 6804
203/775-1291
www.GoldenSpectro.com

Spyke
11258 Regentview
Avenue
Downey, CA 90241
562/869-9333
www.SpykeInc.com

STD Development
Company
10055 Canoga Avenue
Chatsworth, CA 91313
818/998-8226
www.STDDevelopment.com

SuperTrapp Industries
4540 West 160th Street
Cleveland, OH 44135
216/265-8400
www.SuperTrapp.com

Trock Cycle Specialties
13N417 French Road
Hampshire, IL 60140
847/683-4010

TP Engineering
5 Francis J. Clarke Circle
Bethel, CT 06801
203/744-4960
www.TPeng.com

White Brothers
24845 Corbit Place
Yorba Linda, CA 92887
888/926-7337
www.WhiteBros.com

Wiseco Pistons
7201 Industrial Park Blvd.
Mentor, OH 44060
440/951-6600
www.Wiseco.com

Works Performance
21045 Osborne Street
Canoga Park, CA 91304
818/701-1010
www.WorksPerformance.com

Zipper's Performance
Products
6655-A Amberton Drive
Elkridge, MD 21075
410/579-2100
www.ZippersPerformance.com

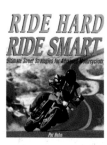

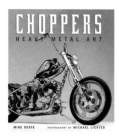
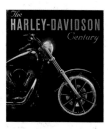
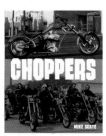
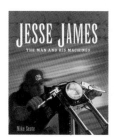
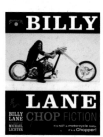